Praise for MY COUNTRY IS THE WORLD

"Staughton Lynd led a truly exemplary life."
—NOAM CHOMSKY, author of *Illegitimate Authority:*
Facing the Challenges of Our Time

"This collection could not come at a more important moment, in the wake of Staughton Lynd's death, documenting his tireless writing and speaking to end the cruel US war of aggression against the Vietnamese people, an important intervention at this time of renewed United States warmongering in the South China Sea."
—ROXANNE DUNBAR-ORTIZ, author of *Not a "Nation of Immigrants":*
Settler Colonialism, White Supremacy, and a History of Erasure and Exclusion

"Over the course of their long and fruitful lives, Staughton and Alice Lynd have modeled what it means to be engaged citizens of a democracy. This rich collection of Staughton's writings and speeches in opposition to the Vietnam War affirms his place in the front rank of the American radical tradition. Trenchant and scathing, they have lost none of their power in the ensuing decades."
—ANDREW BACEVICH, author of *On Shedding an Obsolete Past:*
Bidding Farewell to the American Century

"This treasure trove of rare and previously unpublished letters, speeches, interviews, essays, and manifestos gives depth and life to the most vibrant antiwar movement in US history; and it does so from the perspective of one of its greatest and most brilliant activists, Staughton Lynd. What a fabulous contribution to public memory of a vital, but much forgotten, past."
—CHRISTIAN APPY, author of *American Reckoning:*
The Vietnam War and Our National Identity

"*My Country Is the World* is a brilliant and incisive text, taking us back
to Staughton Lynd's days at the leadership, politically, personally, and
even spiritually, of the anti–Vietnam War movement. Lynd was the voice
of the deep sentiments for peace, beyond the usual left-of-center opposition,
to the very heartland of opposition. He found that heartland before
any others, and his contribution was vast."
—PAUL BUHLE, author of *Marxism in the United States:
Remapping the History of the American Left*

"My husband, David Mitchell, spent two years in jail for challenging the draft
based on the principles established at Nuremberg after World War II. The
Supreme Court ruled against hearing his case, however, Justice Douglas, in a
dissenting opinion, said that his case; raised "sensitive and delicate questions"
that should be heard and addressed. David and I greatly respected and admired
the work of Alice and Staughton Lynd during the Vietnam period and
throughout their lives. Luke Stewart's collection of Staughton Lynd's writing,
speeches, and statements is an important reflection of that tumultuous period
and provides deeper insight into the growth of the antiwar movement.
It is a valuable addition to the literature of the period."
—ELLEN S. MITCHELL

"Stewart has assembled a remarkable collection of speeches, writings,
FBI files, and organizational platforms that not only document Lynd's
legendary opposition to the Vietnam War but also place him in an American
radical tradition. This collection stands out among the growing number of
works on Lynd. It provides the most comprehensive overview of his anti–
Vietnam War years and serves as a resource of primary documents masterfully
placed in historical context. Lynd's principled scholarship and activism, and
Stewart's agile presentation of them, provide inspiration for generations
of yesterday and today. A first-rate, exemplary work."
—CARL MIRRA, author of *The Admirable Radical:
Staughton Lynd and Cold War Dissent, 1945–1970*

MY COUNTRY IS THE WORLD

STAUGHTON LYND'S WRITINGS, SPEECHES, AND STATEMENTS AGAINST THE VIETNAM WAR

Edited by Luke Stewart

Foreword by Staughton and Alice Lynd

Haymarket Books
Chicago, Illinois

Published in 2023 by
Haymarket Books
P.O. Box 180165
Chicago, IL 60618
773-583-7884
www.haymarketbooks.org
info@haymarketbooks.org

ISBN: 978-1-64259-847-6

Distributed to the trade in the US through Consortium Book Sales and
Distribution (www.cbsd.com) and internationally through Ingram Publisher
Services International (www.ingramcontent.com).

This book was published with the generous support of Lannan Foundation and
Wallace Action Fund.

Special discounts are available for bulk purchases by organizations and institutions. Please call 773-583-7884 or email info@haymarketbooks.org for more
information.

Cover design by Eric Kerl. Cover photo of Staughton Lynd, Dave Dellinger, and
Bob Moses and others marching against the Vietnam War, after being splashed
with red paint by anti-communist opponents.

Printed in Canada by union labor.

Library of Congress Cataloging-in-Publication data is available.

10 9 8 7 6 5 4 3 2 1

Staughton Lynd

November 22, 1929–November 17, 2022

May he rest in peace.

CONTENTS

ABBREVIATIONS

ACLU	American Civil Liberties Union
AFSC	American Friends Service Committee
ARVN	Army of the Republic of Vietnam
BRPF	Bertrand Russell Peace Foundation
CADRE	Chicago Area Draft Resisters
CALCAV	Clergy and Laymen Concerned about Vietnam
CCI	National Citizens' Commission of Inquiry on US War Crimes in Vietnam
CCCO	Central Committee for Conscientious Objectors
CIA	Central Intelligence Agency
CNVA	Committee for Non-Violent Action
CO	conscientious objector
CORE	Congress of Racial Equality
CPUSA	Communist Party of the United States
DRV	Democratic Republic of Vietnam
ERAP	Economic Research and Action Project
FBI	Federal Bureau of Investigation
FOR	Fellowship of Reconciliation
HUAC	House Un-American Activities Committee
IWCT	International War Crimes Tribunal
JCS	Joint Chiefs of Staff
M2M	May Second Movement
MAAG	Military Assistance Advisory Group
MFDP	Mississippi Freedom Democratic Party
MOBE	The National Mobilization Committee to End the War in Vietnam
NCCEWV	National Coordinating Committee to End the War in Vietnam
NSA	National Security Agency
NUC	The New University Conference
PAVN	People's Army of Vietnam

POL	petroleum, oil, and lubrication facilities
PLAF	People's Liberation Armed Forces
RVN	Republic of Vietnam
SANE	National Committee for a Sane Nuclear Policy
SDS	Students for a Democratic Society
SFRC	Senate Foreign Relations Committee
SISS	Senate Internal Security Subcommittee
SNCC	Student Nonviolent Coordinating Committee
SSOC	Southern Student Organizing Committee
SUPA	Student Union for Peace Action
SWP	Socialist Workers Party
WRL	War Resisters League
WSP	Women Strike for Peace
VC	Viet Cong
VVAW	Vietnam Veterans against the War
YAF	Young Americans for Freedom
YSA	Young Socialist Alliance

FOREWORD

Staughton and Alice Lynd

taughton and Alice Lynd were most active in opposing the Vietnam War in 1965–1970. Staughton's public speaking and direct action reached their height in the months following his trip to Hanoi with Tom Hayden and Herbert Aptheker in December 1965. Alice began draft counseling in New Haven late in 1965, published the book *We Won't Go: Personal Accounts of War Objectors* (Beacon Press, 1968), and thereafter became coordinator of draft counseling in the Chicago metropolitan area.

STAUGHTON: A curious fact about the very large and hugely successful movement against the Vietnam War is that we who protested were unable to decide what caused the United States invasion.

The most obvious explanation for American intervention was that it was prompted by a desire to exploit Vietnamese economic resources. But which resources? I can recall solemn discussions as to whether tungsten or offshore oil was the motivating substance. Another suggestion was that the United States was motivated by a desire to find a Vietnamese market for Japanese products that would forestall any tendency for Japan—not Vietnam—to fall to an imagined communist empire seeking to expand.

The explanation I have found most persuasive, although far from proved and economic only in the sense that it is based on economic class, is offered by Christian Appy in the last of his persuasive books on the Vietnam War, *American Reckoning* (Viking, 2015). According to Appy, all the men who sent Americans to Vietnam

> felt a deep connection between their own masculinity and national
> power.... They imagined foreign policy as a constant test of individual
> as well as national toughness.... The foreign policy establishment was
> composed overwhelmingly of privileged men. It was an astonishingly

homogeneous group. Their ideas about manhood were forged in a common set of elite, male-only environments—private boarding schools, Ivy
League secret societies and fraternities, military service in World War II,
and metropolitan men's clubs. As historian Robert Dean has demonstrated,
this "imperial brotherhood" viewed themselves as stoic and tough-minded
servants of the state. Intensely driven and competitive, they also regarded
themselves as part of a fraternity of like-minded men whose core commitment was to advance American power. Indeed, any serious challenge to
American power was felt by these men as a blow to their own.[1]

I have two compelling memories of the antiwar movement as I experienced
it. The first memory is that the rationale of a majority of those who refused to
fight in Vietnam was not "religious training and belief" as recognized by the
law governing conscientious objection. David Mitchell, for example, was not a
pacifist. He grounded his refusal to fight on the legal principles relied on by the
United States at Nuremberg to convict Germans who had initiated and taken
leading roles in World War II. Mitchell told the courts that convicted him that
he refused to take part in conduct that the Nuremberg proceedings had condemned as war crimes and acts against humanity.[2]

It seemed to me that the principles on which David Mitchell took his stand
were in a tradition originating in Tom Paine's self-description as a "citizen of the
world." Another memorable statement to the same effect was Thoreau's declaration that Americans purporting to oppose slavery in the United States should be
men first and Americans "at a late and convenient hour." Implicit in these words
of Paine and Thoreau were the principles enunciated in such post–World War II
documents as the Universal Declaration of Human Rights.

These principles—the Nuremberg principles, as they are described by the
editor of this book, Luke Stewart—were also foundational for the Student
Nonviolent Coordinating Committee (SNCC). Both Howard Zinn and I were
present at an improvised memorial service for the three young men murdered on
the first day of the 1964 Mississippi Freedom Summer project. On that occasion
Bob Moses, a much-respected SNCC spokesperson, commented that the United
States was sending soldiers around the world to bring freedom to Vietnam but
refused to provide federal marshals to protect unarmed volunteers seeking to
bring freedom to African Americans in Mississippi.

My second memory of those troubled times may be less familiar. What
Stewart calls a "war crimes movement from below" was more necessary because
organizations or leaders from whom one might have hoped to hear ringing declarations against the war were largely silent. The first big demonstration against
the war was organized by Students for a Democratic Society (SDS) and took

place in Washington, DC, in April 1965. (By "big" I mean that ten thousand people were expected, and an estimated twenty-five thousand came. Later on, crowds of many thousands were commonplace in cities across the country.) That evening there took place a meeting at the office of the Institute for Policy Studies. A representative of SDS caused general consternation when he announced that SDS wished to confront the causes of the war and would not be organizing further events directed against particular wars.

The concern was well founded. As draft calls escalated and the United States invasion of Vietnam intensified in the summer of 1965, apprehension grew that unless some sort of protest took place before students returned to campus in September, when they did so they might find that public opposition to the war would be forbidden. To forestall any such happening, some defiant manifestation of resistance seemed called for.

Thus the Assembly of Unrepresented People was organized and held on the anniversaries of Hiroshima and Nagasaki Days, August 6–9, 1965. Participants sought to assemble on the steps of Congress and declare that there might be someone at war with the people of Vietnam, but we were not. Many persons including myself were arrested. Alice attended a workshop on conscientious objection and learned of the possibility of becoming a draft counselor.

Step by inexorable step, the invasion of Vietnam became ever larger. In early November, a young Quaker named Norman Morrison burned himself to death within sight of Defense Secretary McNamara's office in the Pentagon. A month later, Tom Hayden agreed to go with Herbert Aptheker and myself to Hanoi.

That trip cost me my livelihood and career as a historian. Alice and I later became lawyers and turned to accompaniment of rank-and-file laborers and prisoners.

ALICE: Draft counseling was a way that I could contribute to the antiwar movement compatible with being a wife, mother, and nursery school teacher. I thought of draft counseling as encouraging people to find some way of dealing with the draft consistent with their deepest sense of what life is all about and what they wanted to do with their lives.

There were many ways that a man could resist the draft: apply for recognition as a conscientious objector, refuse to register for the draft, refuse induction if drafted, refuse to go to Vietnam, go to Canada, or consider some other alternative. The irony of draft counseling is that for every guy who got off, someone else would be drafted.

I wanted what people did about the draft also to be envisioning a better kind of society. Methods needed to be consistent with what we were trying to build. Whether one man stayed out of either the military or prison was less significant than whether the experience led him on to more conviction, courage, and direction in ensuing struggles.[3]

Most young men who sought draft counseling faced these questions essentially alone, knowing very little about what others had done, where to turn for information, how to weigh possible consequences, where they wanted to take a stand and on what grounds. As a draft counselor I asked questions, trying to discern, What was this young man trying to resolve? What possible course of action was he considering? What might be the consequences? What conflicts might there be with his loved ones? What might be the implications for his chosen vocation, his long-term future?

As a draft counselor, I discovered that there were two experts in the room. I might be an expert on Selective Service requirements, but the counselee was the expert on his own life. Although we did not have a word for it at that time, draft counseling was a form of accompaniment.

Later, as a lawyer, I again found that the client and I were two experts. When practicing labor law, I could read the contract or the regulations. But I had to ask, What is past practice? How have these words been understood on the shop floor? What do they actually do? And still later with prisoners, the authorities might tell them to use the grievance procedure; but if they did, how could they do so without triggering the response, "You write me up; I write you up!" Once again, what foreseeable consequences were they willing to take? Since it is the counselee, the client, or the prisoner who has to bear the consequences, it better be that person who makes the critical decisions.

As we look back, we again encounter questions without any good answers. The Vietnam War is still with us.[4] Suicides among veterans are disproportionately high. Many participants in the Vietnam War (and since then in the wars in Iraq and Afghanistan) continue to suffer from psychological effects. They rebel against the use of violence in a kind of combat that includes fighting an enemy who cannot be clearly identified, or in which it is hard to tell who is a combatant and who is a civilian, or presents situations in which colleagues are being killed but there is nowhere to return fire, or that requires the soldier to take part in a war that lacks moral clarity, or is perceived to be unjustified and futile.

Being under extreme danger, the main thing soldiers are committed to protecting is their platoon. When some member of the platoon gets killed, it is devastating for all. A survivor feels guilty: "Maybe if I had only done *this* it wouldn't have happened."

It seems that even for those who volunteer for military service, what Quakers call an "inner light" or "that of God in every person," has caused many participants to suffer from "moral injury."

What is "moral injury"? Moral injury is a sense of guilt and remorse as to something irrevocable that a person did, saw, or failed to prevent, that offends a person so deeply that it shakes his or her moral foundation. Questions prey on the conscience: "How could that have happened?" "How could I have done that?" "How could somebody else have done that?" "What can I believe in if these things can happen?"

Dr. Jonathan Shay, a psychiatrist working for the Department of Veterans Affairs, first used the term *moral injury* to describe the reactions of Vietnam veterans to atrocities committed in Vietnam.[5] Shay's books were based on the testimonies of countless Vietnam veterans whom Shay encountered in his clinical practice. He talked with veterans who felt a sense of betrayal of "what's right" by a commander somewhere above the soldier in the chain of command, such as who was assigned to perform the extremely dangerous job of "walking point" at the head of a military unit doing reconnaissance (especially at night); negligence in directing use of existing jungle trails, already known to the enemy, rather than laboriously cutting new but safer trails; and providing troops with rifles, gas masks, and other equipment that did not work.[6]

The result in many instances in Vietnam was what Shay calls a "choking-off of the social and moral world."[7] As frustrations and a sense of betrayal mounted, there was a cutting off of ties to other people, an erosion of a sense of community, a drying up of compassion, a lack of trust, anger and violence against self or others, and an inability to form stable, lasting relationships with other human beings.

Shay offers a crucial piece of evidence. Ninety percent of the patients who complained bitterly were themselves volunteers.[8] One is led to wonder whether volunteers were *more* disillusioned than conscripts because volunteers had higher expectations.

Policy makers in Washington evidently assumed that the military's problems in Vietnam arose from the fact that young men in the United States were drafted to fight there. They therefore substituted a volunteer military for an army recruited by conscription.[9] But the evidence appears to show that this change did not solve the problem of disenchantment and shame among members of the armed forces. The problem for the United States military in Afghanistan and Iraq, just as in Vietnam, was not caused by how American soldiers got to the battlefield but by the predicaments in which they found themselves when they got there.

In recent years, the definition of *moral injury* has focused less on the betrayal of trust by higher military authority and more on acts by oneself or others that violate the person's fundamental sense of right and wrong. They do not forgive themselves, and they expect to be judged and rejected by others. They isolate themselves, feeling helpless and hopeless.

Moral injury tends to develop slowly and deepen over time. People suffering from moral injury and post-traumatic stress disorder experience some of the same things: anger, depression, anxiety, insomnia, nightmares, reckless behavior, and self-medication with alcohol or drugs. They recall and reexperience painful thoughts and images. They may avoid people or situations that trigger memories. Close relationships with family and friends, especially those involving intimacy, suffer and deteriorate when normal emotional responses become numb. Their religious beliefs may seem hollow, or they may come to believe that God is not good. Suicide is the ultimate self-punishment.

Camilo Mejía, who served as a staff sergeant in Iraq from April to September 2003, and who suffered from both post-traumatic stress disorder and moral injury, came to believe "that the transformative power of moral injury cannot be found in the pursuit of our own moral balance as an end goal, but in the journey of repairing the damage we have done onto others." "I no longer view the suffering of others as alien to my own experience. I view hunger, disease, and the brutality of war and occupation as global-scale issues, not as issues of individual nations." And repairing the damage "within ourselves will require a life-long commitment to atone for the wrongs we have committed against others."[10]

STAUGHTON: So what is the message of this book? During at least the past sixty-five years, in Cuba (Bay of Pigs), Libya, Afghanistan, Iraq, and endless elsewheres, the United States has been mindlessly repeating a disastrously misconceived foreign policy. We never learn. In the name of what we pronounce to be the process of development that all other societies should copy, we repeat one disaster after the next.

The essential elements are always the same: a puppet government picked and installed by the United States; ignorance of the language and culture of those whom we presume to instruct; disregard of due process, as for the unindicted prisoners at Guantanamo; savage mistreatment of anyone we decide to feel threatened by.

Meantime, disintegration of the American presence in Afghanistan proceeded in a manner uncannily similar to the end of United States authority in Vietnam. Block letters in a *New York Times* headline that ran across the front page proclaimed on 16 August 2021, "TALIBAN CAPTURE KABUL, STUNNING U.S. AS A 20-YEAR EFFORT UNRAVELS IN DAYS."[11]

As Pete Seeger asked in song, "When will they ever learn?"

The figure in the American past with whom I feel most connected is Tom Paine.

He condemned "summer soldiers and sunshine patriots." Alone among the Founding Fathers, he consistently opposed enslavement of African Americans.

When he was made an honorary member of the revolutionary legislature in France, he spoke out against executing the king and as a result was almost executed himself.

Paine's father was a Quaker, and in his book *The Age of Reason* Paine sought to disentangle the teaching of the Bible about the "least of these" from patent irrationalities. Before his death, he asked the Quaker congregation in New Rochelle whether he might be buried in the Quaker cemetery there. They said no.

I did what I could in the 1960s to oppose the escalation of America's invasion of Vietnam. Had I remained an Ivy League scholar, I would never have come to know rank-and-file working-class spokespersons like John Sargent and Ed Mann or prisoners like George Skatzes.[12] I was spared time in prison but lost my livelihood as an academic historian. I have no regrets.

INTRODUCTION

Luke Stewart

Worlds collided for Staughton Lynd on a sunny Mississippi day in August 1964. It was Friday, 7 August 1964, to be exact.

Lynd was en route to Meridian for the beginning of the Freedom School Convention as part of the Mississippi Freedom Summer, the voter registration project organized by the Student Nonviolent Coordinating Committee (SNCC). That same weekend other Freedom Summer volunteers were going to Jackson to participate in the Mississippi Freedom Democratic Party (MFDP) convention to elect delegates to the Democratic National Convention in Atlantic City. Before the beginning of the respective conventions, an informal memorial service was held for Michael Schwerner, James Chaney, and Andrew Goodman, three civil rights workers who went missing at the beginning of the summer project when they were investigating an arson at Mount Zion Baptist Church in Philadelphia, Mississippi. The church had just agreed to offer space to the Freedom Schools. On August 4, the brutally beaten bodies of the three were found in an earth dam with multiple gunshot wounds. As it turned out, Schwerner, Chaney, and Goodman were murdered by the Ku Klux Klan on June 21, the night they went missing.

Lynd, coordinator of the Freedom Schools, attended the memorial service with other civil rights workers. At the site of the charred remains of Mount Zion Baptist Church, Bob Moses, the tireless civil rights worker and director of Freedom Summer, surprised those in attendance with that week's front-page news: "LBJ Says Shoot to Kill in the Gulf of Tonkin." On the day Schwerner, Chaney, and Goodman's bodies were found, President Lyndon Johnson addressed the nation on television, saying that the communist forces of the Democratic Republic of Vietnam had attacked two US destroyers, the USS *Maddox* and *Turner Joy*, in the Gulf of Tonkin off the coast of North Vietnam. This set off a chain of events that led to reprisal bombings by the United States over North Vietnam on August 5 and power plays in Washington, DC, for the passage on August 7 of the Tonkin Gulf Resolution, which gave President Johnson a blank check "to take all necessary measures to repel any armed attack against the forces of the United States and to prevent further aggression." This, more than any other event in the conflict, set the United States inextricably down the path toward further escalation and full-out war in Southeast Asia. A growing consensus has emerged that these murky events in the Gulf of Tonkin on August 4 never happened.[1]

Under the hot Mississippi summer sun of August 7, Moses connected the struggle for civil rights and the need to oppose the escalating conflict in Vietnam. "This is what we're trying to do away with—the idea that whoever disagrees with us must be killed."[2] This was the first time that Staughton Lynd heard about the escalation of the conflict in Vietnam, busy as he was with the Freedom Schools, and this had a profound effect on him. Just as in the Lynds' foreword to this edited collection, he would continuously refer to this moment throughout the Vietnam War, connecting the struggle for freedom of African Americans at home and the necessity to end the war in Vietnam.

These events marked the beginning of the journey for Staughton Lynd's opposition to the war in Vietnam.

★ ★ ★

This is a collection of Staughton Lynd's writings, speeches, interviews, and statements against the Vietnam War. Between 1965 and 1967, Lynd was perhaps the leading national voice against the war in Vietnam because of his participation in key events of the nascent opposition to the war in 1965. Chief among these was Lynd's late December 1965 fact-finding trip to North Vietnam as unofficial diplomat to explore possibilities and clarify the peace terms of "the other side" in attempts to foster negotiations between the Vietnamese revolutionaries and the United States. By this point, Lynd was regularly featured in the national news and a prominent voice of opposition on the campus of Yale University, where he was an assistant professor of history. A profile in the *New York Times* while he was in Hanoi identified Lynd as a Quaker, a Marxist, and a leader of the New Left (that amorphous term that Lynd identified in the article as a blending of the pacifist and Marxist traditions). One activist quoted by the *Times* referred to Lynd as "the best political spokesman on the left."[3] Lynd later remembered that 1965 "was the year of most intense political activity in my life."[4]

Lynd was involved in many of the key debates about the nature of the war, ways to oppose it by building a mass movement of resistance, and ultimately how to end it. This is where Lynd departed from other public intellectuals of the time who opposed the war. He was simply not content with observing and documenting what he viewed as an illegal, immoral, and unjust war in Vietnam; he was one of the leading proponents and practitioners of nonviolent revolution and war resistance in the United States. Lynd signed seditious statements such as the "Declaration of Conscience against the War in Vietnam" (January 1965), "A Call to Resist Illegitimate Authority" (September 1967) and the "Complicity Statement in Support of the Boston Five" (January 1968). Both Staughton and Alice Lynd pledged in February 1965 that they would refuse to pay that portion of their income taxes going to the Defense Department. Throughout the war the Lynds aided and counseled young men groping for answers as to how to respond to the draft—the process by which the Selective Service System conscripted men between the ages of eighteen and twenty-six into the armed forces (1-A eligible for military service) or offered various classifications such as the student (2-S) deferment, which allowed university students to avoid the draft. The Lynds, especially Alice, specialized in counseling young men on conscientious objector status (1-O or 1-A-O). In June 1966, Staughton Lynd helped establish the Fort Hood Three Defense Committee, which aided and supported David Samas, Dennis Mora, and James Johnson as the first active-duty soldiers to refuse orders to depart for Vietnam. Supporting active-duty military resisters, just like draft resisters, also carried the possibility of heavy fines and imprisonment under US sedition laws. Lynd also argued that the United States should offer massive reparations to the Vietnamese people and in the meantime supported Quakers who attempted to send medical supplies to both sides in the conflict. This advocacy and leadership by word and by deed made Lynd a national and international figure as he crisscrossed the United States, made regular speaking engagements in Canada (Toronto, Ottawa, Montreal, and Vancouver), traveled to North Vietnam in December 1965 to January 1966, spoke against the war in London in February 1966 (where he also was a featured guest on the BBC program *24 Hours*) and in April 1966, attended the World Peace Council in Geneva in June 1966, and was asked to participate in the Bertrand Russell International War Crimes Tribunal (IWCT).

According to the United States government, many of these activities violated the laws of the United States, and Lynd was on the cutting edge of offering arguments justifying both civil disobedience (the breaking of unjust laws in order to change them or alter the course of history) and civil resistance (the upholding of domestic and international law in the face of government violations of, for instance, the war-making powers of the US Constitution, the United Nations Charter, or the Nuremberg principles). This activism also made Lynd a target of the American national security state and a late addition to the Cold War anti-communist blacklist of people who lost their jobs, and in some cases livelihoods, because of their political beliefs and affiliations. It was Lynd's trip to North Vietnam and his address to a gathering of North Vietnamese intellectuals wherein he argued that the war was "immoral, illegal, and antidemocratic," which eventually got him blocked from tenure at Yale and blacklisted from the university altogether. Yale's president, Kingman Brewster, argued that such comments gave "aid and comfort" to the enemy, words taken from the law against treason.[5] For all these reasons, the Central Intelligence Agency, even though it was constitutionality barred from domestic intelligence gathering, identified Lynd throughout this period as "the notorious 'national peace leader,'" whose "appeal among the new left is enormous, and his views and attitudes can be taken as indicative of the new left," and who "has not missed a major cause of the Left for years."[6] Lynd would also be added to the Federal Bureau of Investigation's Security Index on 27 August 1965 as someone whose "background is potentially dangerous; or has been identified as member or participant in communist movement; or has been under active investigation as member of other group or organization inimical to U.S." Moreover, he was singled out as a "subversive" who offers "expression of strong or violent anti-U.S. sentiment."[7] The Security Index allowed the FBI to arrest and indefinitely detain Lynd and others on the list in the event of a national emergency. The Senate Committee on the Judiciary, with the aid of the Senate Internal Security Subcommittee, singled out Lynd as one of the intellectual leaders of the movement in a 236-page report released in October 1965 documenting communist subversion via the antiwar movement. The report quoted from two of the speeches presented in this collection—the 17 April 1965 SDS March on Washington and the 22 May 1965 Berkeley Teach-In—and argued that Lynd was "one of the most active speakers in opposing the present policy of the United States in Vietnam" and indicated his "antagonism for the U.S. Government."[8]

What are the core elements of Staughton Lynd's opposition to the war in Vietnam? In many respects, Lynd's antiwar activism was informed by events as they unfolded and by debates as they emerged in intellectual as well as activist circles. Lynd's antiwar praxis—the merging of theory and practice—can be boiled down to the following fundamental ideas and principles, which are expressed in the speeches, articles, interviews, and statements in this book.

1. Lynd was at the cutting edge of identifying the war as representing a constitutional crisis—an undeclared war that up until February 1966 evaded

any serious public debate in Congress—as well as an illegal war under international law. Therefore, the war was an act of aggression as defined in the Nuremberg judgment of 1945 and the Nuremberg principles of 1950 and was outside the confines of the United Nations Charter of 1945, which allowed for the use of force only in the case of self-defense after an attack occurs until the Security Council can deliberate and intervene in a conflict. In order to confront such an unimaginable catastrophe, what Lynd viewed as a national and international emergency, especially in the nuclear age, the antiwar movement was justified in working outside the traditional boundaries of civic engagement (petitions, marches, and voting) and participating in nonviolent revolution to stop the war. In this regard, Lynd consistently advocated for various forms of resistance and direct action.

2. To build the antiwar movement, activists and intellectuals could not fall into the trap of the Cold War anti-communist consensus and exclude individuals and groups who were from the Communist Party or Trotskyists. Moreover, in order to build the broadest possible coalition, the antiwar movement should not engage in coalition politics with the Democratic Party. This was informed by the humiliation of the Mississippi Freedom Democratic Party trying to seek representation at the Democratic National Convention in Atlantic City in August 1964 and only coming out with two delegates. Moreover, it was the party of Lyndon Johnson, which had just escalated the war in Vietnam to include the bombing of the North and substantial ground forces and combat operations in the South even though the president campaigned as a peace candidate in 1964. For Lynd, it was simply not good enough for activists to give the incumbent president a pass on foreign policy in order to obtain domestic policy victories. It was equally unacceptable to red-bait activists who were trying to build coalitions to oppose the war, as this fed the very symptom they were opposing.[9]

3. Lynd was part of the portion of the antiwar movement that called for an immediate withdrawal from Vietnam of all US troops when it was unpopular to do so. Moreover, he called on President Lyndon Johnson and Secretary of State Dean Rusk to negotiate directly with *both* the North Vietnamese government and the National Liberation Front of South Vietnam. Writing in the pages of the *New York Times Magazine*, Arthur Schlesinger Jr., liberal historian and former member of the John F. Kennedy White House, who publicly debated Lynd in January 1966,

argued for a middle way out of Vietnam between "widening the war or disorderly and humiliating withdrawal." In 1965 Schlesinger defended the Johnson administration's war in Vietnam, but by 1966 he viewed the escalation as a mistake. Therefore, Schlesinger argued for the so-called enclave strategy, wherein enough US forces would remain in Vietnam to convince the Vietnamese communists that they could not win an outright "victory," as the US would not simply withdraw before a negotiated settlement. Schlesinger cautioned peace liberals that "the object of the serious opposition to the Johnson policy is to bring about not an American defeat but a negotiated settlement."[10] To Lynd, this was an American-centric view of the war that did not take seriously the views of the Vietnamese revolutionaries who were fighting a civil war to gain independence after domination first by the French and then the Americans. By traveling to North Vietnam in late December 1965 to early January 1966 to talk with diplomatic representatives of the North Vietnamese and the National Liberation Front, Lynd sought to clarify the Vietnamese revolutionaries' negotiating position and propose a solution toward ending the war based not only on American demands but also on the realities on the ground in Vietnam. For Lynd and others within the radical antiwar movement, it was magical thinking to suppose the United States could simply dictate the terms of Vietnam's surrender, because of the history of Vietnam's resistance to foreign intervention and the recent history of French defeat in 1954. Lynd's on-the-ground experience in North Vietnam and talking to representatives of the Democratic Republic of Vietnam and National Liberation Front led him to better understand that the war was going to be a protracted, long-drawn-out conflict, and in order to save as many lives as possible the United States should withdraw from Vietnam.

4. Because the war (1) was unconstitutional, (2) violated international law, and (3) led to the commission of war crimes and crimes against humanity, Lynd advocated that those being asked to serve in Vietnam should refuse to do so. By invoking not just the war powers found in the US Constitution but also the United Nations Charter, the judgment at Nuremberg in 1945, and the Nuremberg principles of 1950, Lynd was crucially part of a movement advocating a new kind of war resistance during the Vietnam War. While Lynd was a Quaker and a pacifist, he argued that traditional pacifist opposition to war based on one's individual conscience and the statutory form of conscientious objection found within the American tradition were not enough to confront the illegality of the war or easily reconcilable with the new types of war resisters

who emerged in opposition to the draft or military service who were not "opposed to participation in war in any form." Lynd actively supported the draft or military resisters who were opposed to Vietnam in particular and who also might have fought during World War II, for instance. This new war resistance, based not just on pacifistic or individualistic opposition to war or on civil liberties, was grounded in post–World War II legal and political frameworks that sought to abolish wars that were not in self-defense or sanctioned by international law. Between 1965 and 1972, of the roughly 100,000 Selective Service Act offenders—people who burned or returned their draft cards, those who did not sign up for the draft on their eighteenth birthday, or others who failed to report for induction—22,500 were indicted, 8,000 of them were convicted in the courts, and 4,000 subsequently went to prison. A clear majority of those who were indicted, 72 percent, were not pacifists; nor were they members of the historic peace churches.[11] This was unprecedented in US history, and both Staughton and Alice Lynd helped contribute to the broadening of this antiwar resistance beyond traditional pacifist circles.

5. Lynd was no doctrinaire leftist. While he faced criticism from other pacifists such as David McReynolds or Robert Pickus, from democratic socialists such as Michael Harrington or Irving Howe, and from liberals like Arthur Schlesinger and Robert Scalapino, Lynd did not let his opposition to the war cloud his judgment on the best tactics and strategies needed to effectively oppose it.[12] Lynd was able to absorb criticism and often reached out to those he disagreed with in order to build understanding of differences or clarify disagreements. As the war progressed, Lynd not only debated supporters of the war—Democratic liberals and conservatives alike—but he also engaged in very strenuous arguments within the antiwar coalition itself, and for this he found himself on the outside of the radicalized movement by the end of 1967 and into 1968. This tendency toward introspection and commitment to engage in telling the truth as he saw it meant in practice not straying away from taking unpopular positions. For instance, on many occasions Lynd was critical of the Vietnamese revolutionaries for committing what he viewed as war crimes, and he went on to refuse to participate in the Bertrand Russell–sponsored International War Crimes Tribunal because it would not consider the war crimes committed by both sides in the conflict. Lynd's commitment to his principles meant that by the end of 1967, just as the movement transitioned from the fringes of pacifist, student, and liberal peace group opposition to a mass movement of millions of participants, he would move out of the

national spotlight and call for a new kind of grassroots activism building bridges between students and the working class, the campus and the inner city, between African Americans and whites.

6. Lynd connected his opposition to the war in Vietnam to the traditions of American radicalism he contemporaneously wrote about as a professional historian. Lynd's intellectual contributions to the antiwar movement are rooted in finding a tangible American past that he sought to bring to a new generation of radicals to demonstrate that there was a homegrown tradition worthy of embracing. This radical tradition was brilliantly illuminated in two major publications: *Nonviolence in America: A Documentary History* (1966) and Lynd's seminal *Intellectual Origins of American Radicalism* (1968). In reading the following materials, we can gain an intimate portrait of a historian working through his ideas in real time as Lynd embodied the essence of what he viewed as an American radical tradition. In speech after speech and writing after writing against the Vietnam War, Lynd consistently quoted from Thomas Paine, William Lloyd Garrison, Henry David Thoreau, and Eugene Debs to put forth the argument that contemporary radicals needed to reach into the past in an era of stultifying Cold War and possible nuclear Armageddon to pursue an international solidarity that said, as the radicals before them, "My country is the world, my countrymen are all mankind." Lynd took specific aim at identifying the United States as an exceptional country, especially after 1945, and argued throughout the 1960s that "no longer can there be a temptation to identify the promotion of universal human values with the interests of any nation-state" and that there needed to be a "clear and unequivocal assertion that there is an interest of humanity distinct from all national interests."[13] This historicizing the present was also apparent in Lynd's call for nonviolent revolution that linked the pacifist roots of nonviolence with the contemporary adoption of civil disobedience by the civil rights, antinuclear, and antiwar movements.

7. During this period, Lynd was involved in numerous debates about radical history, the university, and the meaning of being an intellectual. Speaking to the graduating class at Morris Brown College, a historically Black liberal arts college in Atlanta, on 12 December 1963, Lynd argued, "Being a scholar is painful; it is joyful; it is also dangerous. . . . But not all scholarship occurs in colleges. Indeed, if we stick to the definition of scholarship as truth-seeking, we will have to recognize that most of the great truths were discovered in the city, not on the campus, and learned

not from books but from life."[14] This orientation is what led Lynd to move beyond simply the responsibility of intellectuals, as famously espoused by Noam Chomsky in February 1967, to articulate the responsibility of *radical* intellectuals in March 1968 at the New University Conference at the University of Chicago. For Lynd, radical intellectuals had to have one foot on campus and the other "foot solidly off campus" and embrace an "experimental attitude with respect to life-styles."[15] Lynd argued for combining theory and practice in one's life and intellectual endeavors, as displayed during Freedom Schools in the summer of 1964 or at the Vietnam teach-ins in 1965–1966. To do this meant that the commitment to university life would necessarily become secondary because of the institution's corrupting influences (competition instead of cooperation between scholars and the "bait of tenure"). Lynd argued,

> It is a very peculiar sort of radicalism which permits one only to be arrested in summertime, or obliges one to hurry home from Hanoi to be on time for a seminar. But that is the kind of radical one has to be so long as one's first commitment is to university life. If it is symbolic, one-shot, moral-gesture radicalism, that may be not so much because of our ideological orientation as because of the academic schedule. The point is that whatever we may think, or think we think, university life requires us to act as if our radicalism were episodic and of secondary importance.[16]

Lynd was a serious scholar who published five academic books before he was blacklisted: *Anti-Federalism in Dutchess County, New York: A Study of Democracy and Class Conflict in the Revolutionary Era* (1962), *Nonviolence in America: A Documentary History* (1966), *Reconstruction* (1967), *Class Conflict, Slavery, and the United States Constitution: Ten Essays* (1967), and *Intellectual Origins of American Radicalism* (1968).[17] Nonetheless, he also believed that in seeking truth one could not fail to act when confronted with injustice.

Therefore, according to Lynd, one's scholarship and "view of the world grows out of . . . his socially-conditioned experience" and for this reason the "truth we discover will be affected by the lives we lead." Moreover: "That portion of the truth to which we are led, the truth which seems to us significant, is not independent of our experience as whole human beings." For the radical intellectual, this type of endeavor would necessarily precipitate a less than full-time and rotating life within the university. This would require the radical to develop an alternative lifestyle, finding alternative sources of income and rotating familial obligations.[18]

8. Lynd was crucially part of the New Left and a regular collaborator and defender of the radical student movement embodied by the emergence of

the Student Nonviolent Coordinating Committee (SNCC) and Students
for a Democratic Society (SDS). Throughout the 1960s, Lynd was a leading theoretician of participatory democracy in the American context,
and he developed an enduring relationship with key figures in the movement. Despite this direct linkage to the New Left and student radicalism,
Lynd also transcends the label, often repeated in the media in the 1960s,
as leader of the New Left. Lynd was many things, and this label, or stereotype, is too limiting to understand the full breadth of Lynd's intellectual and activist trajectory. Lynd's parents' involvement with the so-called
Old Left, the death of Joseph Stalin in 1953, Nikita Khrushchev's speech
condemning Stalinism in 1956, the civil rights movement, the Cold War,
and the nuclear arms race would all influence Lynd's understanding of the
left broadly and of American radicalism in particular. All these influences
helped Lynd to conceptualize a new leftism that was more than the youthful radicalism of SNCC and SDS and would not only challenge militarism and the Cold War but also connect various movements and struggles
together to build a more humane and progressive American society during
the 1960s. This is perhaps best symbolized by Lynd's transition in 1967 and
1968 to taking a step back from the national and international spotlight in
order to build a new American socialism and working-class solidarity at
the local, grassroots scale.

In the introduction to *Nonviolence in America*, Lynd distilled the various traditions of peace activism and nonviolence in US history from the
Quakers, the abolitionists of the 1840s and 1850s, and the anarchist and
progressive movements of the late-nineteenth and early-twentieth centuries to the labor movement of the 1930s, the conscientious objectors from
the world wars, and finally the post-1945 civil rights movement. For
Lynd in *Nonviolence in America* and in other materials contained herein,
the New Left movement of the 1960s was at best an amalgamation of
these traditions, culminating in the push for nonviolent revolution in the
United States. The best way to do this was through direct action, spontaneity, and participatory democracy.[19]

9. The Lynds joined a Quaker meeting in 1963 in Atlanta. They had found
that the values of the Religious Society of Friends meshed with theirs:
a belief in an "inner light" in each person, peace, simplicity, equality,
consensus decision-making, and speaking truth to power, among others. While it is important to highlight Staughton's Quakerism, it is also
important not to overemphasize it as a primary factor in his opposition
to the war. While some pacifists were primarily motivated by their

religious beliefs, Lynd's adherence to Quakerism is perhaps better understood as part of a constellation of influences informed also by Marxism,
anarchism, and nonviolence. Throughout this collection there is an odd
absence of religious language to describe his opposition to the war. At the
same time, for a Marxist, there is an equally odd absence of Marxian ter-
minology to describe American society and foreign policy. "I see myself
as a product of Marxist and pacifist thought, neither of one school nor the
other, but influenced by both," he told the *New York Times*' John Corry
after returning from Hanoi in 1966.[20] Instead, Lynd very much preferred
the language adopted by the civil rights movement and the idea of the
"blessed community," which was first used, as Lynd pointed out in his
book *Intellectual Origins of American Radicalism*, by the Anabaptists. It is
with this book and in *Nonviolence in America* where we can see the blending
of these traditions that clearly influenced not just the New Left but also
Lynd himself. Speaking at the fall retreat of the Methodist Theological
Fellowship at the University of Chicago on 3 November 1967, Lynd situ-
ated "The Vision of the New Radicalism" as "deeply rooted in democratic
and Christian thought": the use of direct action and civil disobedience
based on ethical and moral beliefs, participatory democracy, and the idea
that "the individual owes his allegiance to a universal law higher than the
law of any nation state, and immediately evident in conscience."[21]

While Lynd's talk in November 1967 is not readily available, tucked
away in Lynd's papers at Kent State University, the fusion of the religious
radicalism of the Anabaptists in pre-Revolutionary America, the abolitionists of the nineteenth century, anarchists, progressives, and socialists
with the post–World War II New Left is clearly evident in Lynd's historical writings, especially the introduction to *Nonviolence in America* and the
conclusion to *Intellectual Origins of American Radicalism*. This fusion would
be later described by Lynd and the Yugoslav anarchist Andrej Grubacic
as the Haymarket Synthesis, explored in depth in *Wobblies and Zapatistas:
Conversations on Anarchism, Marxism and Radical History*. During the 1968–
1970 period, when the New Left broke with its founding principles of
participatory democracy, consensus decision-making, and nonviolence,
Lynd would consistently return to these ideas, imploring the youthful
militants to return to the "blessed community" and re-embrace "spontaneity and comradeship."

While there is some danger in singling out any one individual's writings,
speeches, statements, and interviews against the war in Vietnam because of the

sheer scale, breadth, and diversity of the movement, Staughton Lynd is none-theless central for our understanding of how the movement emerged from the fringes of pacifist, intellectual, and student opposition in 1964–1965 to a mass movement by 1967. Lynd certainly did not speak for the movement as a whole, and as this collection demonstrates, he was at the center of some of the most heated debates on the nature of the war and US foreign policy; tactics and strat-egies for movement building; and ways to end the war in Vietnam. Moreover, as we can see in the evolution of the documents presented here, Lynd was also a trenchant critic of the antiwar movement's tactics and strategies. Ironically, at the same time the movement emerged as a powerful force in US political life by the end of 1967–1968, Lynd also found himself increasingly on the outside of the movement he dedicated and sacrificed his livelihood to build as the more mili-tantly radical elements began embracing violence over nonviolence and engaged in sectarian infighting and revolutionary vanguardism. While Lynd never went away, still participating in the antiwar movement and key debates, as the read-ings demonstrate after 1967 he began advocating for a more localized, grassroots form of organizing.

One of the principal benefits of this collection is that we can explore the pro-gression of Lynd's thinking and activism in response to yet one more escalation or yet one more movement tactic and strategy. Much of this thinking is not linear, as Lynd is in a persistent state of reflection and offering new ideas after actions were tried. As this collection demonstrates, Lynd was constantly providing state-ments and suggestions to the movement and, on many occasions he released these in *Liberation*, the radical pacifist journal edited by David Dellinger, A. J. Muste, and others. This was all part of Lynd's belief in participatory democracy and the need for experimentation and spontaneity, as there was no guidebook for how to respond to such an unprecedented war and national emergency. Lynd's position in the movement meant that these suggestions would get a fair hearing. From 1965 to 1967, it was well outside of the mainstream public opinion to take a position against the war and conscription, let alone calling for an immediate withdrawal of US troops from Vietnam. Lynd was at the center of efforts to build this movement, critique the legality of the war under the US Constitution and international law, and offer an alternative to large-scale military interventionism to solve the problems of a revolutionary world. Lynd's activism against the war and his writings, statements, speeches, and interviews offer us a way to under-stand why people opposed the war and how Lynd himself was able to cut across various movements on a local, national, and international level.

Why, after the fall of Saigon in April 1975 and the end of the Vietnam War, do we need to explore Staughton Lynd's arguments opposing the war? While the antiwar movement was the largest and most sustained in the nation's history, its ideas are taken for granted, and stereotypes abound about who was involved, why they opposed the war, and what happened. The image of the youthful, long-haired, rebellious baby boomers flashing peace signs and spitting in the faces of returning Vietnam veterans miraculously endures today. It was, in the words of countercultural antiwar activist Abbie Hoffman, a "revolution for the hell of it." This is despite the fact that much of the scholarship on the antiwar movement has, in one way or another, disabused us of these ideas and illuminated the diversity, breadth, and effectiveness of the movement that spanned class divides, genders, ages, and importantly, included soldiers, veterans, and disillusioned government whistleblowers. Ken Burns and Lynn Novick's critically acclaimed documentary series *The Vietnam War* does little to broaden the public's understanding of the antiwar movement. Of the eighty interviewees, Burns and Novick present the stories of only two avowed members of the movement (while also featuring the voices of veterans and family members impacted by the war who turned against it from personal pain and experience). Even though 10 percent of the American public were active in the movement or sympathized with it, the two activists' appearance is concluded with them apologizing for their actions.[22]

As a young historian, beginning serious study of the antiwar movement during my undergraduate years, I am consistently confronted with questions about the antiwar movement that are stereotypical, assumptive, or derogatory. During one academic job interview, a committee member looked annoyingly at my research statement and asked point blank, "Antiwar, war resistance, what does this all mean?" Many of these stereotypes and assumptions persist. It is easy to make an argument against a stereotype or an image of a movement. It is much more difficult to respond to a nuanced argument about the nature of the war and of US foreign policy after 1945 and the imperative to confront such a war with civil disobedience and mass resistance justified by domestic and international law. It is for this reason that it is important to read the words of those who opposed the war and the arguments they made against it. Oftentimes these arguments were directed at the recent statements and actions of the US government. These arguments are key to our understanding of what the opposition to the war was made of.

On an individual level, there is space to deepen our understanding of Staughton Lynd's contribution to the history of American radicalism, antiwar movements, pacifism, and nonviolence in the twentieth and twenty-first centuries. To date, there is no single volume presenting Lynd's writings, speeches, statements, and interviews against the Vietnam War to a scholarly as well as a general readership. Much of what is presented here is otherwise inaccessible or out of print. Therefore, my intention is to complement what is already available. During the Vietnam War, outside of extensive writings and speeches, Lynd wrote two books about the war: *The Other Side* with Tom Hayden in 1966 about their trip to North Vietnam and *The Resistance* with Michael Ferber in 1971 about the draft resistance movement. Since the end of the Vietnam War, Lynd has been committed to reflecting on his experiences in the various movements he has been engaged in and offering lessons to whoever seeks to pick up the torch or continue carrying it. Much of this later writing documents his personal experiences in the antiwar movement and has been extremely valuable for a young historian of the movement such as myself. Chief among these works are *Living inside Our Hope: A Steadfast Radical's Thoughts on Rebuilding the Movement*, Lynd's wide-ranging conversation with Andrej Grubacic in *Wobblies and Zapatistas: Conversations on Anarchism, Marxism, and Radical History*, and finally with Alice Lynd, *Stepping Stones: Memoir of a Life Together*. There are two biographies of Lynd—Carl Mirra's *The Admirable Radical: Staughton Lynd and Cold War Dissent, 1945–1970* and Mark W. Weber and Stephen H. Paschen's *Side by Side: Alice and Staughton Lynd, the Ohio Years*—and a career-spanning collection of Lynd's writings edited by Grubacic titled *From Here to There: The Staughton Lynd Reader* in which some materials against the Vietnam War are presented.

This is not a comprehensive collection documenting Lynd's opposition to the war, as that would fill multiple volumes: large files exist of correspondence, filling boxes in multiple archives, diaries, and notebooks, papers presented at conferences and other materials cherished by historians writing about the past. Rather, this collection is designed to be representative of Lynd's arguments against the war, for peace negotiations and immediate withdrawal of US forces from Southeast Asia, and statements proposing tactics and strategies for building a mass antiwar movement. Lynd's alternative vision for American society during the height of the Cold War presents a unique opportunity to refocus on and reanalyze the growth and impact of the largest, most disruptive and sustained antiwar movement in US history.

CHAPTER 1

DECLARATIONS OF CONSCIENCE

Introduction

In the fall of 1964, the Lynds were making the transition from Atlanta, where Staughton taught American history at Spelman College, to New Haven, Connecticut, after accepting a position in the Department of History at Yale University. Lynd was fresh off his experience in Mississippi and began his first year of a five-year tenure-track position at the famed Ivy League school. It was also a presidential election year in which President Lyndon Johnson was vying to win the presidency in his own right after inheriting the office from the slain John F. Kennedy in November 1963. His opponent, Senator Barry Goldwater, was advocating for greater US engagement in Southeast Asia. On August 4, 1964, in the aftermath of the Gulf of Tonkin incident, after President Johnson already ordered retaliatory strikes against North Vietnam, he told the nation and the world "we still seek no wider war" and ran as a peace candidate in the 1964 campaign.[1]

As Lynd was settling into his new life at Yale University, the young scholar remained active in the civil rights movement, participating in events and discussions with Yale students and faculty in the fall and winter.[2] Writing in his memoir, Yale chaplain William Sloane Coffin recalled being shocked when Lynd told him in October 1964 that "it wouldn't make any difference whether President Johnson or Senator Goldwater won the November elections" with regard to the war in Vietnam.[3] That November, Lyndon Johnson won the presidency in a landslide victory. A few weeks after the election, Staughton Lynd was a guest speaker at the sixteenth annual *National Guardian* dinner, where he argued that "this whole society is watching calmly, as if from a window, while people are murdered day after day in Vietnam." This was an explicit analogy to the March 1964 murder of Kitty Genovese, which the *New York Times* had erroneously reported had been witnessed by thirty-eight people from their windows who did not even call the police. This gruesome murder led to the coining of the "bystander effect" and produced much commentary throughout the country about whether Americans were losing their sense of social responsibility.[4]

Declaration Of Conscience
AGAINST THE WAR IN VIETNAM

Because the use of the military resources of the United States in Vietnam and elsewhere suppresses the aspirations of the people for political independence and economic freedom;

Because inhuman torture and senseless killing are being carried out by forces armed, uniformed, trained and financed by the United States;

Because we believe that all peoples of the earth, including both Americans and non-Americans, have an inalienable right to life, liberty, and the peaceful pursuit of happiness in their own way; and

Because we think that positive steps must be taken to put an end to the threat of nuclear catastrophe and death by chemical or biological warfare, whether these result from accident or escalation --

We hereby declare our conscientious refusal to cooperate with the United States government in the prosecution of the war in Vietnam.

We encourage those who can conscientiously do so to refuse to serve in the armed forces and to ask for discharge if they are already in.

Those of us who are subject to the draft ourselves declare our own intention to refuse to serve.

We urge others to refuse and refuse ourselves to take part in the manufacture or transportation of military equipment, or to work in the fields of military research and weapons development.

We shall encourage the development of other nonviolent acts, including acts which involve civil disobedience, in order to stop the flow of American soldiers and munitions to Vietnam.

NOTE: *Signing or distributing this Declaration of Conscience might be construed as a violation of the Universal Military Training and Service Act, which prohibits advising persons facing the draft to refuse service. Penalties of up to 5 years imprisonment, and/or a fine of $5,000 are provided. While prosecutions under this provision of the law almost never occur, persons signing or distributing this declaration should face the possibility of serious consequences.*

NAME	ADDRESS

Some of those who have signed this Declaration—

J. Malvern Benjamin, Jr.
The Rev. Lloyd A. Berg
Rev. Dan Berrigan, S.J.
Rev. Philip Berrigan, S.S.J.
Kay Boyle
James Bristol
Emile Capouya
Gordon Christiansen
William C. Davidon
Dorothy Day
David Dellinger
Barbara Deming
Ralph DiGia
Lawrence Ferlinghetti
W. H. Ferry

Maxwell Geismar
Rabbi Everett E. Gendler
Paul Goodman
Robert Brookins Gore
Richard B. Gregg
Ammon Hennacy
Paul Jacobs
Erich Kahler
Roy C. Kepler
Paul Krassner
Irving Laucks
Sidney Lens
John Lewis
Roger Lockard
Staughton Lynd
Bradford Lyttle
Milton Mayer
David McReynolds
Stewart Meacham
Helen Mears
Mary Meigs
Morris R. Mitchell
Mrs. Lucy Montgomery
A. J. Muste
Otto Nathan
Robert B. Nichols
Linus Pauling
Jim Peck
Diane di Prima
A. Philip Randolph
Earle Reynolds
Bayard Rustin
Ira J. Sandperl
Marc Schleifer
Glenn E. Smiley
Monte G. Steadman, M.D.
Harvey Swados
Marjorie Swann
Robert Swann
Ralph T. Templin
Samuel R. Tyson
Denny Wilcher
George Willoughby

Please return signed petitions to one of the sponsoring organizations listed below.

Catholic Worker
175 Chrystie Street
(Att: Tom Cornell)
New York, N. Y. 10002

Committee for Nonviolent Action
325 Lafayette Street
New York, N. Y. 10012

Student Peace Union
5 Beekman Street, Room 1029
New York, N. Y. 10038

War Resisters League
5 Beekman Street, Room 1025
New York, N. Y. 10038

Figure 1.1: The original version of the Declaration of Conscience. Courtesy of Staughton and Alice Lynd.

As 1964 turned into 1965, Lynd remained preoccupied with debates about the civil rights movement and discussions about expanding the Freedom School model he helped create in Mississippi. In February 1965, he was invited to Selma, Alabama, by SNCC workers to begin discussions about organizing a Freedom School there. It was on the plane home that he first read of the attack by the National Liberation Front of South Vietnam (the NLF, or pejoratively, the Viet Cong, meaning Vietnamese Communist) on the US air base at Pleiku, killing eight US soldiers and wounding another 109. Eleven helicopters and aircraft were destroyed.[5] A similar attack by the NLF on the Bien Hoa air base on November 1, 1964, occurred during the presidential election *yet* elicited no major retaliation. This time, with the election over, the Johnson administration wasted no time in launching retaliatory strikes. At the time of the Pleiku attack, McGeorge Bundy, Johnson's national security adviser, was in South Vietnam and would later tell journalist David Halberstam that "Pleikus are like streetcars" because an attack of this nature would come around again. Such a statement proved to be accurate, as NLF fighters attacked the US barracks at Qui Nhon on February 10, killing twenty-three Americans. The Johnson administration launched its first strikes against North Vietnam since August 1964 and publicly asserted that the United States began bombing communist forces in South Vietnam.

In response to the retaliatory bombing campaign over North Vietnam, Yale students and faculty created the Ad Hoc Committee to Protest the War in Viet Nam to organize events and demonstrations. On February 11, the group held its first event at Yale's law school auditorium with over six hundred in attendance and featured Staughton Lynd along with a fifteen-minute video interview with Senator Wayne Morse (D-Oregon). Lynd was quoted the following day in the *Yale Daily News* as saying, "Our government tonight in Southeast Asia is doing something dangerous and wrong" and cautioned against telling "anyone else how to express oneself at this moment." Nonetheless, the history professor argued that "the treason of the intellectuals in the past is not that we failed to believe but failed to act. All too often the credo of the University is 'believe what you will but don't believe it too intensely!' I would like to urge you to believe what you will but act on what you believe."[6] He read the Declaration of Conscience against the War in Vietnam, which committed its signers to refuse to participate with the war (document 1). In one of the Federal Bureau of Investigation's first intelligence reports on Lynd's opposition to the war, the bureau noted, "Inasmuch as the Declaration of Conscience on the war in Viet Nam and the statements made by Staughton Lynd . . . could possibly be in violation of the Sedition Statute, the Bureau may desire to bring this information to the attention of the Department [of Justice]."[7] Following the successful event, on February 13 the committee organized an antiwar rally and march where Lynd also spoke. In document 2, Lynd responds to criticisms in the *Yale Daily News* to both these events.

After the Pleiku raid and the retaliatory air strikes against North Vietnam, the Johnson administration took advantage of the window of opportunity and launched the massive, sustained bombing campaign over North Vietnam known as Operation Rolling Thunder in late February (which was stalled until the beginning of March due to heavy rain) and in early March sent the first round of combat troops into South Vietnam. These acts of war were conducted without congressional debate or sanction and instead were defended on February 27 in the State Department's white paper "Aggression from the North: The Record of North Viet-Nam's Campaign to Conquer South Viet-Nam" and a March 8 "Legal Basis for United States Actions against North Vietnam."[8] The Johnson administration justified these actions by arguing that it was defending South Vietnam, an independent nation-state, from external aggression by the communist North Vietnam and internal aggression by the equally communist National Liberation Front. The Johnson administration was able to make these arguments relying on the pervasive and omnipresent post-1945 anti-communist consensus that gripped members of both the Democratic and Republican Parties as well as the media. Therefore, as the State Department argued in March 1965, the US intervention was legally justified under Article 51 of the United Nations Charter because it was requested by the South Vietnamese government, the Republic of Viet Nam (RVN), to aid in its self-defense against foreign aggression and because the North Vietnamese violated the Geneva Accords of 1954, which brought an end to the First Indochina War between the Viet Minh and the French. Secretary of State Dean Rusk would later add to the list of justifications the United States' responsibility to act in South Vietnam's self-defense under the provisions of the 1955 Southeast Asian Treaty Organization created by the US in the aftermath of the Geneva Accords to protect South Vietnam.[9] To call into question these justifications, as Lynd and others in the antiwar movement did throughout the war, opened them up to charges of being communist dupes, anti-Americans, un-American, and unpatriotic.

As the documents in chapter 1 demonstrate, Staughton Lynd challenged these central justifications of the US war effort in Vietnam. In various speeches and articles throughout 1965, Lynd argued that the conflict in Vietnam was not the result of "aggression from the North," as the State Department argued in its February 1965 white paper. For critical journalists, astute commentators, the antiwar movement, and Vietnamese revolutionaries, the roots of the conflict lay in the unresolved outcome of the 1954 Geneva Accords. For Lynd and others, the conflict was more akin to a civil war that originated in South Vietnam in opposition to the dictatorship of Ngo Dinh Diem after the rejection of the Geneva Accords. The period from May 1954 to 1956 set into motion the major justifications for US intervention in Vietnam, with the minimal objective of creating a viable noncommunist government in South Vietnam once the French were defeated and left. The Eisenhower administration, followed by Presidents John F. Kennedy, Lyndon Johnson, and Richard Nixon, simply viewed international peace negotiations after the French defeat at Dien Bien Phu in May 1954 with hostility and never intended to recognize an agreement that could hand a communist government a victory in Southeast Asia, let alone the power over their own country. The peace agreement consisted of two separate documents: the "Agreement on the Cessation of Hostilities in Viet Nam, 20 July 1954," which brought an end to Franco–Viet Minh conflict, and the Geneva Accords of 1954, which cemented the final agreement in the two-month-long effort to end French dominion over Southeast Asia. Therefore, the Geneva Accords cite the cessation agreement as their main authority.

The main provisions of the Geneva Accords, provided in appendix B, prohibited the introduction of foreign troops, weapons, and munitions (Article 4) and decreed that no foreign military bases be established (Article 5). Moreover, the demilitarized zone created along the seventeenth parallel and the de jure "regrouping zones" in North and South Vietnam enunciated in the "Cessation of the Hostilities" agreement between the French and Viet Minh were recognized from the very beginning as "provisional and should not in any way be interpreted as constituting a political or territorial boundary" (Article 6). Crucially, Article 7 of the accords called for the establishment of national elections in July 1956, which Article 14(a) of the "Cessation of the Hostilities Agreement" recognized "will bring about the unification of Viet-Nam."[10]

In this sense, there were not two distinct nation-states created at Geneva, and in fact the accords expressly forbade such an act. At the time, the United States did not sign the Geneva Accords and instead issued a statement that it would respect its provisions. Even before the accords were signed, the Central Intelligence Agency sent Colonel Edward Lansdale, fresh from his success over the Huk insurgency in the Philippines, to South Vietnam to ensure that a viable government in South Vietnam would be created. In June 1954, Ngo Dinh Diem returned to Vietnam from the United States and assumed power as prime minister of what was being called the "State of Viet Nam," with Emperor Bao Dai still as figurehead leader. Under the provisions of the Geneva Accords, France slowly extricated itself from its former colony, and the United States assured its major international commitment by sending military and economic aid and creating the Army of the Republic of Vietnam under the command of the newly created Military Assistance Advisory Group. Meanwhile Lansdale, under the CIA's Saigon Military Mission, engaged in covert military and psychological warfare operations in both South and North Vietnam, which included commando raids into the North, attempting to subvert North Vietnamese political and economic reforms. Diem consolidated power after surviving coup attempts and insurrections and, following a referendum, became president of the newly created RVN, a brazen attempt to create a nation-state, which was expressly forbidden under the Geneva Accords.

The 1956 consultations between North and South Vietnam and elections were never held, and this led to unresolved grievances that the North Vietnamese maintained lay at the heart of any future diplomatic and political solution to the conflict. When Diem's repression in the South became too intolerable, the National Liberation Front in South Vietnam was created in 1960 to begin an armed struggle against the Diem regime.[11] The United States' policy of shoring up the Saigon government lasted for twenty years and led to President John F. Kennedy committing special forces, advisers, weapons shipments, helicopters, and the spraying of defoliants beginning in 1961. When the US policy failed by 1964–1965 to defeat the southern insurgency, this led directly to President Johnson's major escalation in February 1965.

In response to Johnson's intensification of war, a teach-in movement emerged, first originating at the University of Michigan on 24 March 1965 and then quickly spreading throughout the United States. In this atmosphere of bubbling dissent, Staughton Lynd was invited to chair an Emergency Meeting on Vietnam organized by the University Committee to Protest the War in Vietnam (document 3). Facing growing questions in the media and thanks to the teach-in movement, President Johnson delivered a major address at Johns Hopkins University on April 7, placing the blame for the conflict on the shoulders of the North Vietnamese and their refusal to stop their aggression in South Vietnam. Lynd responded to the speech, writing to the editor of the *New York Times* that the war in Vietnam was a civil war and not, like World War II, a question of foreign aggression needing to be stopped by military intervention (document 4).

During these early days of the war, the decision by the SDS in December 1964 to plan a rally and a march against the Vietnam War for April 1965 landed like a rock in a still pond. Buoyed by the teach-in movement and local organizing across the country, SDS took advantage of the moment and focused its energies on its "March on Washington to End the War in Vietnam" on April

17. In publicizing the event, the Yale SDS chapter held a rally on campus where Lynd spoke and announced that the Lynds would be refusing to pay the portion of their income taxes earmarked for the Pentagon. Noting that they understood the possible financial and legal consequences of taking such an act of civil disobedience, the Lynds wrote in their letter to the Internal Revenue Service,

> Yet, reluctant as we are to take this step of civil disobedience, we find it morally impossible to contribute to the war in Viet Nam.
>
> Americans ask of Nazi Germany: "How could they stand by while Jews were sent to extermination camps?" We feel unable to stand by while napalm explosives, foliage experiments, and poison gas are used by Americans; and interrogation of prisoners by torture is practiced under American direction, in a war that seems to us unnecessary and wrong.
>
> In our small way we hereby say no to that war. In doing so we feel we are in the American tradition of John Woolman (a Quaker who refused to pay war taxes during the French and Indian War) and Henry Thoreau.[12]

Not without controversy, the March on Washington represented the coming together of diverse groups, even including leftists from the Communist Party, the Socialist Workers Party, and other Marxist organizations. SDS, supported by people like Staughton Lynd, argued that the movement had to be "non-exclusionary," and this provoked an attempt on the part of some social democrats, socialists, and pacifists such as Bayard Rustin, A. J. Muste, Norman Thomas, and others to boycott the events. Others, like William Sloane Coffin, did not want to attend out of fear that SDS was becoming too radical and that the rally was only preaching to the choir. After the success of the event, Coffin regretted not going, and Muste distanced himself from a statement he signed warning against the participation of Communists in the protest.[13] The march and rally brought out an estimated twenty to twenty-five thousand people and, as document 5 explains in more detail, featured Staughton Lynd as chair of the rally.

That night after the March on Washington, some leading participants gathered to plan future antiwar actions at the offices of the Institute for Policy Studies located off Dupont Circle. For Lynd and the others present, they were surprised to hear the representative of SDS state that they would not be taking the lead in any future anti–Vietnam War activities. The following day, April 18, SDS held a meeting of its National Council where various proposals were tabled in preparation for its national meeting to be held in June. During this crucial period, the members of SDS believed it was more important to focus on its community organizing project, known as the Economic Research and Action Project, and to avoid getting bogged down in what it perceived as a "single-issue" movement against the war in Vietnam. The student radicals believed that in order to stop "the seventh war from now," as Paul Booth argued, they had to focus on the systemic problems within US society that brought about the war in the first place. Lynd, who agreed with the underlying analysis of SDS, nonetheless viewed the escalating war in Vietnam as a clear and present danger requiring immediate confrontation, and he began in earnest to keep the opposition alive throughout the spring and summer.[14]

After the successful weekend in Washington, when it was clear that SDS was going to withdraw its national efforts against the war, while local chapters continued work on the campuses, Lynd spent the next several months running with the proposal made by Tom Hayden at the April 18 SDS meeting that called for a new Continental Congress to be convened in opposition to the war in Vietnam. While not taken seriously by the students, Lynd found the idea refreshing as a historian of the American revolutionary tradition. During this period, he would attend several meetings in downtown Manhattan with the Committee for Non-Violent Action, the War Resisters League, the Catholic Worker community, and other pacifist groups to brainstorm a series of actions that would develop over the coming months. It is here where Lynd became an organizer against the war and not simply an invited speaker at rallies and teach-ins.

One of the most consequential speeches Lynd gave during this period was at the Berkeley Teach-In on May 21–22, sponsored by the newly created Vietnam Day Committee (document 6). Here Lynd took Hayden's idea of a new Continental Congress and proposed several other ideas for sustaining the antiwar movement when students left campus for the summer. It was this speech, recorded by the University of California Police and carefully documented by special agents of the FBI, that would lead to Lynd's name being added to the FBI's Security Index. In particular, the bureau paid close attention to Lynd's call for the Continental Congress, to his creating a war crimes tribunal, and to his advocacy of nonviolent revolution, which he hoped would force President Johnson and his advisers to resign. The FBI monitored how Lynd's proposals were being picked up by peace groups—such as the Los Angeles Committee to End the War in Vietnam and Women Strike for Peace—and tried to verify the contents of Lynd's speech. Moreover, various memoranda reporting on Lynd's speech at Berkeley, including other events discussed in chapter 2, generated by the FBI that led to Lynd being included on the Security Index were forwarded to the White House, secretary of state, attorney general, CIA, various regional offices of the Secret Service, the Office of Special Investigations at the Department of Justice, the FBI's Domestic Intelligence Division, and the intelligence divisions of all the armed forces, in addition to those of the Army Military District of Washington and the Naval District Washington. By the summer of

1965, Staughton Lynd's antiwar activities accorded him a heightened status in the national security bureaucracy.[15]

The fast pace of these early months of opposition to US escalation in Vietnam would only increase over the summer of 1965. Lynd was now at the forefront of the movement against the war, and his words and proposals were taken seriously throughout the United States, including within the higher echelons of the US government.

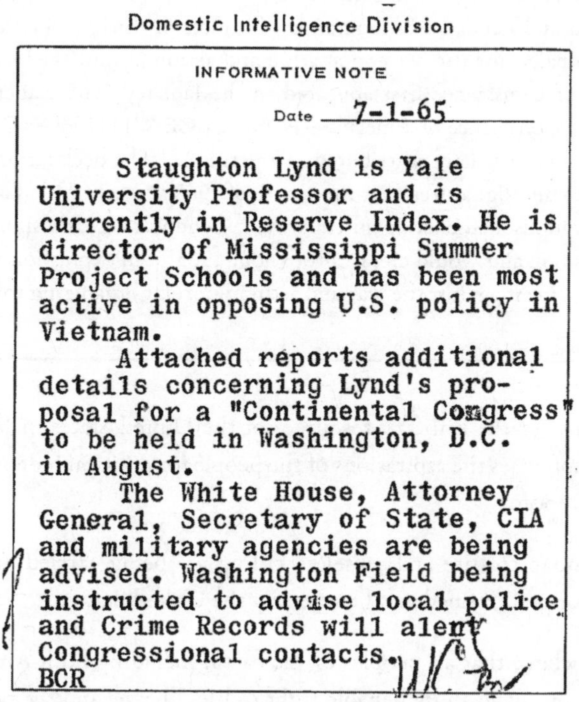

Domestic Intelligence Division

INFORMATIVE NOTE

Date ____7-1-65____

Staughton Lynd is Yale University Professor and is currently in Reserve Index. He is director of Mississippi Summer Project Schools and has been most active in opposing U.S. policy in Vietnam.

Attached reports additional details concerning Lynd's proposal for a "Continental Congress" to be held in Washington, D.C. in August.

The White House, Attorney General, Secretary of State, CIA and military agencies are being advised. Washington Field being instructed to advise local police and Crime Records will alert Congressional contacts.

BCR

Figure 1.2: William C. Sullivan, director of the FBI's Domestic Intelligence Division, signs off on this Informative Note on 1 July 1965, alerting the White House, Department of Justice, Central Intelligence Agency, and military intelligence of Staughton Lynd's proposal for the Assembly of Unrepresented People. Source: Lynd's FBI file.

Document 1

THE DECLARATION OF CONSCIENCE AGAINST THE WAR IN VIETNAM, JANUARY 1965

The Declaration of Conscience was initiated by a coalition of peace groups—the Catholic Worker, the Committee for Nonviolent Action, the Student Peace Union, and the War Resisters League—after a successful day of action against the Vietnam War on December 19, 1964, in which peace activists demonstrated and handed out thousands of leaflets in thirty US cities. As part of a campaign for further cooperation and action against the war, the Declaration of Conscience first appeared in the January 1965 leaflet "An Appeal to the Conscience of America—FOR PEACE WITH HONOR IN VIETNAM" and was later distributed as a petition.[16] The declaration garnered six thousand signatures over the course of 1965 and committed its signatories to civil disobedience against the war.[17] Lynd was an early signatory to the declaration and would cite it throughout 1965 as an expression of the growing movement against the war and as an important organizing tool.

Because the use of the military resources of the United States in Vietnam and elsewhere suppresses the aspirations of the people for political independence and economic freedom;

Because inhuman torture and senseless killing are being carried out by forces armed, uniformed, trained and financed by the United States;

Because we believe that all peoples of the earth, including both Americans and non-Americans, have an inalienable right to life, liberty, and the peaceful pursuit of happiness in their own way; and

Because we think that positive steps must be taken to put an end to the threat of nuclear catastrophe and death by chemical or biological warfare, whether these result from accident or escalation—

We hereby declare our conscientious refusal to cooperate with the United States government in the prosecution of the war in Vietnam.

We encourage those who can conscientiously do so to refuse to serve in the armed forces and to ask for discharge if they are already in.

Those of us who are subject to the draft ourselves declare our own intention to refuse to serve.

We urge others to refuse and refuse ourselves to take part in the manufacture or transportation of military equipment, or to work in the fields of military research and weapons development.

We shall encourage the development of other nonviolent acts, including acts which involve civil disobedience, in order to stop the flow of Americans soldiers and munitions to Vietnam.

NOTE: *Signing or distributing this Declaration of Conscience might be construed as a violation of the Universal Military Training and Service Act, which prohibits advising persons facing the draft to refuse service. Penalties of up to 5 years imprisonment, and/or a fine of $5,000 are provided. While prosecutions under this provision of the law almost never occur, persons signing or distributing this declaration should face the possibility of serious consequences.*

Document 2

LETTER TO THE EDITOR, *YALE DAILY NEWS*, 18 FEBRUARY 1965

In what would become the first of many letters to the editor of the *Yale Daily News* clarifying his comments and views on the Vietnam War, Staughton Lynd responds here specifically to the tone and tenor of the coverage about the February 11 event and the February 13 march from Yale to the New Haven Green.[18] Lynd takes specific issue with the idea that the marchers intended to provoke a confrontation with members of the right-wing Young Americans for Freedom (YAF), who were there as counter-demonstrators in response to the protest. This letter to the editor is perhaps one of the first pieces written by Lynd staking out his position in opposition to the war in Vietnam.

To the Chairman of the *News*:

I would like to thank the *News* for the substantial accuracy of its stories on the protest rallies of last Thursday and Saturday. But I must also deplore the use of terms such as "demagogic," "emotional," "irrational," "hypocritical," in your editorial comment.

As for the alleged "irresponsibility" and "hypocrisy" of the marchers Saturday in passing so close to the YAF rally, were you aware that the march followed the route agreed to in advance with the New Haven police?

Both the speeches Thursday and the statement distributed Saturday made clear the logic of those who oppose the war in Vietnam. I believe most participants in the two rallies would support the following version of an opposition consensus:

1. In Vietnam the United States is fighting, not an external aggressor, but a revolutionary independence movement supported by a majority of the people. (Richard Starns wrote in the *New York World Telegram*, Jan. 4, 1965: "There is not one shred of credible evidence that the bulk of munitions used by the Viet Cong originate in the North." Walter Lippman stated nine months ago: "The truth, which is being obscured from the American people, is that the Saigon government has the allegiance of probably no more than 30 per cent of the people.")

2. The United States has practiced or condoned chemical destruction of crops, the use of jellied-gasoline explosives, and torture in the interrogation of prisoners. (A wire-service dispatch which appeared in the *New Haven Register* and

elsewhere, states: "Chances of surviving field interrogation are often extremely poor. Death can come for prisoners under the tracks of armored vehicles, by decapitation or by bleeding to death after both hands have been chopped off or by a bullet through the head.")

3. American presence in Vietnam, and particularly our recent escalation of the war, drive the Vietnamese into the arms of China. (C. L. Sulzburger wrote in the *New York Times*, Dec. 5, 1964: "Ho [Chi Minh] worries about Washington's ultimate trump—the threat of wholesale escalation. Destructive air raids could upset Ho's wobbly economy and invite intervention by Peking's infantry. The last thing Ho wants is Chinese occupation.")

4. The United States government escalated the war in Vietnam without exhausting the possibilities of negotiation, and without consulting or informing the American people. Such a course of action, understandable if in response to a provocation demanding immediate decision, was not justified by the recent attacks on American installations. These attacks were made with American weapons and no evidence has been forthcoming to demonstrate that they were planned by North Vietnam.

My own concern both on Thursday and Saturday was to kindle a recognition among those to whom I spoke that all of us have some responsibility for anything done in Vietnam by United States armed forces, or by South Vietnamese under our direction. Is this irrational demagogy? Another view might hold that to understand a situation intellectually yet fail to act on that understanding is itself a form of unreason.

I hope that this dialogue can be continued among members of the University community with mutual courtesy and respect.

Staughton Lynd, assistant professor of history

Document 3

REMARKS AT EMERGENCY MEETING ON VIETNAM, CARNEGIE HALL, NEW YORK CITY, 1 APRIL 1965

Given Staughton Lynd's growing stature within the peace movement, he was invited to chair an Emergency Meeting on Vietnam organized by the University Committee to Protest the War in Vietnam on April 1 at Carnegie Hall. It was reported that 2,500 people attended the meeting, and other speakers besides Lynd included Senator Ernest Gruening (D-Alaska); Robert Browne, an African American economist and former officer for the US Agency for International Development in Cambodia (1955–1958) and Vietnam (1958–1961); and Charles Capper of the Students for a Democratic Society (SDS), who spoke about the upcoming March on Washington.

This country is presently waging an undeclared war so evil and so dangerous that the imagination can hardly comprehend it. Last Sunday my six-year-old son said to me: Daddy, if they drop a bomb on our house, I will walk to Academy Street, and then to Green Street, and then to my friend Dante's. He was seeking a way to keep his fear under control, to domesticate war and the rumor of war in the familiar world of his child's imagination.

But we adults dare not domesticate our fears. Until this February the American people regarded the fighting in Vietnam like a Grade B thriller on the late late TV show. They gazed impassively at the murder in Southeast Asia as residents of this city, looking down from their high-rise apartments, have watched as murder took place on the streets below them. Until this February the American people kept Vietnam at a distance, they unconsciously anaesthetized their sensibilities so that the screams, the blood, the smell of burning flesh could not reach them.

It is difficult to comprehend the war in Vietnam. No matter what we have lived through, few of us have been prepared by life to apprehend words like the following:

> One day I came home and there were two security agents waiting for me. I was taken to the town of Faifo and for months on end I was tortured badly. Once I recovered consciousness and found I was stark naked, blood oozing from the wounds all over my body. There were others in the cell. I heard a woman moaning and in the half dark saw the woman in a pool of blood. She had been beaten into having a miscarriage. Then I made out an old man. An eye had been gouged out and he was dying. Alongside him was a

thirteen or fourteen year old boy, also dead; a little further away, another dead youth with his head split open.

How can we respond adequately to this sentence from the morning paper: "Some 70 U.S. Air Force planes poured tons of napalm and phosphorus bombs plus tanks of fuel oil into a 19,000-acre stretch of Communist-infested jungle 25 miles northeast of Saigon in hope of setting the forest on fire"?

Those who direct this war are forever reminding us of Nazi aggression in the 1930's. It is an inappropriate analogy. The Nazis were military invaders, the Vietcong is essentially an internal revolution. But we remember Nazi Germany, too. We remember our question: Why didn't the people do something to stop it? And we are determined that, numbed as we are by events almost too large for the imagination, hopeless as we often feel as to whether our action can be effective, nevertheless, we will not sit by in silence. We intend to act.

An American people disturbed as never before by the military conduct of its own government is groping for adequate actions. Hundreds of university professors, like those sponsoring this meeting, have placed ads in major newspapers. Thousands of students will march on Washington April 17 (and adults are not excluded). Two thousand Americans, including Linus Pauling, Eric Fromm, Paul Goodman and John Lewis, have signed a Declaration of Conscience pledging civil disobedience against the war in Vietnam. Others are for the first time planning to refuse the payment of taxes. Lee Stern, 50 years old, has been fasting since the first week of February to protest the war. A month ago I was privileged to speak against the war in Bridgeport with an eloquent Vietnamese exile, Dr. Vo Tan Minh. He said that in the Buddhist belief each man must choose his path of personal righteousness. Since then Dr. Vo has chosen his: he too is now fasting on behalf of his people and to ask that the war end.

In closing, I should like to underline the fact that Vietnam is not only a foreign policy crisis, it is also a constitutional crisis. The *New York Herald Tribune* said in 1962: "The United States is deeply involved in the biggest secret war in its history. Never have so many United States military men been involved in a combat area without any formal program to inform the public about what is happening." *The Nation* stated in 1963: "The truth is that the United States Army is fighting an undeclared war that has never received the constitutional sanction of the United States Congress." If that was true two and three years ago, what shall we say of the present, when for two months the President has escalated the war without once stopping to explain his policy to Congress or the people?

We need to ask the question: Can Congress by a simple resolution give away its constitutional power over the declaration of war? According to a *San Francisco*

Chronicle poll, 82% of the American people favor negotiation with China and the Soviet Union, 80% believe that Vietnam is not essential to American security, and 54% believe we should pull out our troops. Can Congress sign away its duty to represent the majority of the people? and if Congressmen insist on delinquency, should they not be recalled and replaced?

Another thing. A democracy depends on the inalienable right not to be lied to. Now, we have been lied to before. In the U-2 crisis the State Department presented a "cover story," and Ambassador Stevenson told the United Nations that America had no connection with the Bay of Pigs invasion. But this was emergency prevarication; in the case of Ambassador Stevenson, he had apparently been misinformed; above all, it was temporary prevarication. None of these excuses are available for our government's deliberate mishandling of the truth about Vietnam.

First we were told that the Americans in Vietnam were mere advisers. Then it was denied that we were using napalm. Then it was said that chemicals which, according to Jerome Wiesner, were potentially more dangerous than radioactive fallout, were merely weedkillers. Now it is said that gas which kills only some of the people some of the time is a non-lethal benevolent incapacitator. Considerable ambiguity, to say the least, surrounds the incidents of Tonkin Bay and the Pleikhu barracks. And the State Department has never spoken honestly about the postponement of the 1956 election provided for by the Geneva accords.

Now this is sustained lying, it is, as it were, distance as opposed to mere sprint running. And speaking only for myself, I think the time has come when we should say to the elected officials who make such statements, that there is also a benevolent incapacitator in the United States Constitution known as impeachment.

Friends tell me that I use the word "Fascist" too loosely. Suppose we forget that word and think of the book and movie, *Seven Days in May*.

Will any one deny that the way we make and unmake puppet governments overseas is Seven Days in Mayish? Can there be any argument as to whether the foreign policy mindset which says that we can stop revolution everywhere by blowing it to bits in Vietnam is Seven Days in Maylike? Surely a policy which tortures prisoners, sprays defoliants, drops napalm and phosphorus, and experiments with benevolent incapacitators which kill only the very young and very old, can fairly be termed Seven Days in Mayist?

If so, then this question presents itself: How long can we spend half the Federal budget on Seven Days in May, how long can we permit our foreign policy right hand to play Seven Days in May while the domestic left hand "overcomes"—how long can we do this without creating political generals who will cross the Rubicon separating foreign from domestic policy, make and unmake *our* government, hold back social change in *this* society, kill and experiment on white people as well as dark? If in Vietnam the United States supports a government characterized by what Bernard Fall calls "an all-pervading capricious lawlessness," can any of us really be safe at home?

The point is that war *is* death and dictatorship, and to the extent that we as a society give ourselves up to war and the spirit of war—to hierarchical and secret decision-making, to unexplained policies, to callous disregard for human life, to systematic insensitivity to the gentle and organic arts of peace—to that extent death and dictatorship will prevail throughout our way of life, our way of life will become a way of death, and we shall *be* overcome.

Let us therefore recur to the good words written by Thomas Jefferson to our minister in revolutionary France: "We surely cannot deny to any nation that right whereon our own government is founded—that every one may govern itself according to whatever form it pleases, and change these forms at its own will."

Let us recur to the words of Franklin Roosevelt in 1944: "France has had the country for nearly one hundred years, and the people are worse off than at the beginning. France has milked it for one hundred years. The people of Indochina are entitled to something better than this."

And let each of us seek his personal path of righteousness in the spirit of Henry Thoreau who wrote, Vote your whole self not a strip of paper merely; or as they are saying it down South these days: Let each of us seek the appropriate moment to put his body on the line.

Document 4

"CIVIL WAR, NOT INVASION," *NEW YORK TIMES,* 14 APRIL 1965

Despite the fact that the United States was now bombing North Vietnam and combat troops had landed in South Vietnam, it is important to note that from August 1964 to the emergency meeting of April 1965 at Carnegie Hall, there were no public congressional investigations or hearings on the situation in Vietnam.

On April 7, President Lyndon Johnson addressed the nation at Johns Hopkins University in a speech titled "Peace without Conquest." In Baltimore, the president proclaimed,

> The first reality is that North Viet-Nam has attacked the independent nation of South Viet-Nam. Its object is total conquest.
>
> Of course, some of the people of South Viet-Nam are participating in attack on their own government. But trained men and supplies, orders and arms, flow in a constant stream from north to south.
>
> This support is the heartbeat of the war.

Placing the blame for the war solely on the shoulders of the North Vietnamese, President Johnson announced that the United States was still open for "unconditional discussions" for peace with the Vietnamese communists.[19]

In response to the speech, Staughton Lynd wrote the following letter to the *New York Times.*

To the Editor:

President Johnson's speech leaves unchanged the basic fallacy in American policy toward Vietnam. He continues to assume that the conflict there is essentially a military invasion, like those of Nazi Germany, when in fact it is essentially a civil war. The Vietcong is still regarded as the agent of a foreign power, supported by "some of the people" of South Vietnam.

Proceeding on this mistaken assumption, the President has offered to negotiate unconditionally with all interested parties except our actual antagonist. In effect this is a formula for avoiding negotiation. In approving this formula as "the olive branch that balances the arrow in the eagle's claws," The *Times* endorses the escalation it previously opposed.

The policy of escalation stands or falls with the assumption that opposition to the Saigon Government is directed and supplied primarily from North Vietnam.

If that assumption is false, then the creation of peace in Southeast Asia requires that American bombing in the North stop at once. If we continue bombing, we will make of the basic fallacy in our policy a self-fulfilling prophecy: it will bring North Vietnam, China and the Soviet Union increasingly into the war.

Even when our bombing stops, we shall have to face the fact that American military intervention in Vietnam has been on a scale far surpassing that of any other country, and the fact that democratic election in a unified Vietnam would in all probability bring to power a Communist-led government. The real challenge to American policy in Southeast Asia remains: Do we have the capacity to confront these realities maturely?

This challenge cannot be avoided by the otherwise-commendable desire to share our economic surplus with the poor of the world. So long as the essence of our policy in Southeast Asia is the use of gas, torture and napalm to crush an indigenous social revolution, a Mekong Delta Authority will be a fig leaf to hide barbarism.

The President cannot expect North Vietnam to agree to negotiations while being bombed. Bombing is itself a formidable "condition." To hold out olive leaves while dropping bombs is to suggest not unconditional negotiation but unconditional surrender. Peace in Vietnam requires: (1) a willingness to deal directly with the Vietcong; (2) an end to bombing.

Document 5

EXCERPT OF SPEECH AT FIRST MARCH ON WASHINGTON, 17 APRIL 1965

On 17 April 1965, the first national demonstration and march against the Vietnam War was organized by the Students for a Democratic Society (SDS). Lynd was asked to chair the rally, and other speakers included Paul Potter of SDS, I. F. Stone, Bob Moses, and Senator Ernest Gruening, along with musical performances from Joan Baez, Judy Collins, and Phil Ochs. Estimates vary on the number of participants, but somewhere between 20,000 to 25,000 people gathered at the Lincoln Memorial to hear speeches before marching to the US Capitol to read the Declaration of Conscience against the War in Vietnam. In addition to chairing the March on Washington, Lynd was a featured speaker.[20] Below is an excerpt from Lynd's speech.

Americans often ask: Why didn't the German people do something about it? Only in the last few weeks have I begun to wonder: What exactly did we expect them to do? Their situation was different from ours, but not that different. They too watched helplessly while their government incinerated men, women and children. They too were represented by a legislature which handed over its constitutional authority for war and peace to the executive. They like ourselves were lied to by their government, not once or twice, but over and over again in a sustained course of deception.

Thus, in our case, we have been told by the State Department that an internationally-agreed-to plan for nationwide Vietnamese elections in 1956 was a Communist trap; we have had soldiers called advisers, lethal chemicals called weed-killers, lethal gases termed benevolent incapacitators; we have had an attack by a small guerrilla contingent on a barracks whose guards were absent or sleeping transformed into a Hanoi-masterminded conspiracy demanding aerial retaliation until, a week later, it was explained that bombing North Vietnam was not retaliatory; we have had a belated and utterly inadequate explanation of an escalation policy, which offered to negotiate with everyone except the people we were fighting, which spoke of peace but said not one syllable about ending war ...

What should the Germans have done? Since February 7 countless Americans have been groping for insight as to how to be responsible, seeking to find some adequate means of action even in the jaws of Leviathan. Hundreds of professors, resolved that the treason of intellectuals elsewhere shall not be repeated here, have spoken out through open letters. Students and teachers together have conducted teach-ins across the country, determined that Veritas shall not be locked out of the university. As the French intellectuals resolved that an Algerian war conducted by torture was a war which they were morally obligated to obstruct, so 3,500 Americans, including Linus Pauling, Eric Fromm, Paul Goodman, and SNCC national chairman John Lewis, have signed a Declaration of Conscience pledging civil disobedience against the war in Vietnam. An equal number of priests, ministers and rabbis have cried out to the President: In the name of God, stop it! A few, like my wife and me, are refusing to pay taxes. Others are sitting-in at the State Department and fasting: one refugee from Hitler's Germany has burned herself to death. We are here on behalf of all these, the living and the dead, all who, horror-stricken by this terrible war, have tried to put their voices and bodies in the way.

But we are here on behalf of more than these. We are here to keep the faith with those of all countries and all ages who have sought to beat swords into plowshares and to war no more. We are here on behalf of millions of men and women throughout the world who are crying out, What has happened to the United States? We are here on behalf of Jean-Paul Sartre. And we are also here on behalf of those 8,000 miles from us for whom the Easter and Passover season brings death, not life. We are here on behalf of brave men who have been fighting for their country's independence three times as long as we fought for ours, and with much less foreign assistance. We are here on behalf of the American soldiers who do not understand the reason for the war in which they are dying.

Above all we are here on behalf of the women and children of that land which we have turned into a fiery furnace, whose eyes as they look out at us from the pictures and the posters, ask us, why?

Document 6

REMARKS AT THE BERKELEY TEACH-IN, 22 MAY 1965

The first teach-ins began at the University of Michigan on 24 March 1965, and the idea spread quickly across the country with an estimated one hundred colleges and universities hosting teach-ins in the spring and summer.[21] The teach-ins featured both opponents and proponents of the war (sometimes US government officials were sent to provide the Johnson administration's justification for the war). In this case, one of the nongovernmental speakers, Professor Robert A. Scalapino (political scientist, UC Berkeley) had initially agreed to participate but withdrew just before the event. In a statement published in the *San Francisco Chronicle*, Scalapino blasted the teach-in as "symbolic of the new anti-intellectualism" and "rigged" with antiwar speakers. The professor concluded the gathering's objective was "propaganda, not knowledge" and a "travesty."[22] Lynd begins his speech by addressing Professor Scalapino and other liberal intellectuals like him. Lynd's speech at the teach-in was particularly important because he made several proposals for continued antiwar activity over the summer, as he feared that when the students went home over summer break the momentum would be lost.

Here Lynd speaks in front of an audience of fifteen thousand at UC Berkeley.

I have been asked to read the following statement regarding the Dominican Republic:

The Declaration of Berkeley

May 21, 1965

Whereas the people of the Dominican Republic have suffered too long under the oppressive yoke of brutal and tyrannical governments;

Whereas the Dominican people are presently demonstrating their determination to defend their democratic rights and liberties to the death on the streets of Santo Domingo;

Whereas the provisional constitutional government of Colonel Francisco Caamaño Deño is the duly constituted government of the Dominican Republic, having been established by a quorum of the 1963 congress which was elected by a majority of the Dominican people in free elections;

Whereas the provisional constitutional regime has decreed the holding of free elections in the Dominican Republic within reasonable time;

Therefore be it resolved: We, the undersigned students, faculty, members of the University community and citizens of the United States recognize the provisional government of Colonel Francisco Caamaño Deño to be the true and only duly constituted government of the Dominican Republic.

Those of you who wish to join me in signing this statement may do so at the table near the Student Union.

Now to turn to Vietnam.

First, a word to Professor Scalapino. I too believe in precise and responsible intellectual discourse. But I think it exposes a curious and revealing double standard that a man who finds it possible to support the government of South Vietnam, with its indiscriminate napalm bombing of unprotected villages and its torture of men, women and children, should find it impossible to attend our meeting on the ground that the program is—God save the mark—"unbalanced."

I am employed by Yale University, the institution which produced the architect of the Bay of Pigs, Richard Bissell; the creator of Plan Six for Vietnam, W. W. Rostow; and that unagonized reappraiser, McGeorge Bundy. Hence, while Professor Scalapino considers himself an expert on Vietnamese insurgents, I consider myself something of an expert on American counter-insurgents. I think I know something about the Ivy League training which these unelected experts receive: a training in snobbishness, in a provincial ethnocentrism, in a cynical and manipulative attitude toward human beings. Look at the American Secretaries of State in the twentieth century and I think you will find that almost without exception they were former corporation lawyers. They were what the President of Yale calls "public entrepreneurs," that is, corporation lawyers who spend part of their time in Wall Street defending the interests of their private clients, and part of their time in Washington defending the general interests of their class. I think you need to say to your teachers, as I need to say to my colleagues, that annihilation in a Brooks Brothers suit is still murder.

And I would like to say this to Professor Scalapino. You say that no self-respecting intellectual would attend this meeting. But the educated community of the entire world now remembers those professors who spoke up in Nazi Germany with gratitude. And I predict that the time will come when the entire academic community of the United States will say of those few professors who publicly opposed what we are doing in Vietnam: "They kept the spirit of truth alive."

We have been talking a long time at this teach-in and our thoughts should now be turning to action. But I would like to make two analytical points which bear on the action we must take.

First, this country is not only in a foreign policy crisis, it is in a constitutional crisis. The *New York Times* has stated that a style of executive decision-making hitherto employed only in temporary emergencies has now become almost a way of life. The Johnson Doctrine means not only that we refuse to give people in other countries the opportunity to determine their own destinies, but also that in this country the government will do what it likes, without permitting the creation of an informed public opinion or debate in Congress.

Therefore, those of you have been concerned with the Freedom Democratic Party must realize that it is not only some Negroes in Mississippi and Alabama who are unrepresented, it is—with respect to our present foreign policy—all of us. And those of you involved in the Free Speech movement, and similar groups on other campuses, must turn your attention to the unelected Board of Regents who run this country.

Second, this morning's *San Francisco Chronicle* has made the point for me that we are about to commit tens of thousands of American soldiers to full-scale ground warfare in Vietnam. Professor Scalapino said at last week-end's Washington teach-in that we would only put in a few more troops, who would repulse the Vietcong during their monsoon offensive and bring them to the conference table. As a historian I consider this proposition fantastic. Four hundred thousand French soldiers were unable to defeat the Vietminh. Why should we assume that a handful of American soldiers will convince the Vietcong after one campaign that they cannot conquer Vietnam? Our troops are going to be there a long time. Professor Schlesinger, who sought at Washington to defend the Administration's position with a difference, represents himself as a spokesman for Senator Robert Kennedy. Does he know that, according to Homer Bigart, Robert Kennedy said in February 1962: "The United States is in a war in Vietnam. American troops will stay till we win." This is hardly a formula for negotiation.

Here let me make a digression. I found that quotation in a publication of the W. E. B. DuBois Clubs entitled "The United States' War in Vietnam." There are some who, sincerely opposed to the terrible war in Vietnam, nevertheless feel that certain groups—such as Progressive Labor, the May 2nd Movement, and the W. E. B. DuBois Clubs—should be excluded from the movement because they do not understand honesty and truth. I should like to testify as a historian that this DuBois Club publication seems to me the best analysis of the war's origins produced by any of the anti-war groups.

There will be an escalation of the crisis this summer, produced by the landing of tens of thousands of American troops. As the casualty lists mount there will be a crystallization of public opinion in one direction or the other: either toward increased repression at home and a rallying to the Administration; or a wave of revulsion against the war. We can effect which of these takes place.

What then is to be done?

One strategy which has been suggested is coalition politics within the Democratic Party. The critical flaw in this strategy was suggested by Michael Harrington himself in an article in *Partisan Review*. He wrote: "'escalation' of the Vietnamese ... crisis would not only end talk of the War on Poverty, and of the Great Society, but threaten World War III." That escalation has occurred. Coalitionism now means coalition with the marines.

As an alternative strategy I offer nonviolent revolution.

For the benefit of F.B.I. agents present, let me make clear that I am not advocating violent overthrow of the United States government. I am advocating nonviolent retirement of the present Administration, that is, the creation of civil disobedience so persistent and so massive that the Tuesday lunch club which runs this country—Johnson, Rusk, McNamara, Bundy—will forthwith resign. We do not live in a parliamentary government where a vote of no confidence can compel an administration to resign, as the British compelled their administration to resign in the Suez crisis. Yet we cannot wait until the next Presidential election in 1968. Therefore we must vote with our feet by marching and picketing, if necessary vote with our backsides by sitting in jail.

Is this merely what Bayard Rustin has called a moral gesture? Is there any chance of such a strategy succeeding? I think, Yes.

In the first place: There are two spirits in conflict in this country. One is that of an article in yesterday's *Wall Street Journal* which said, "Battle statistics are showing a dramatic change. Last month's 3,120 Vietcong dead was up from 1,965 in March." Death, too, is thus now listed on the Stock Exchange. The other spirit is that of the 38 Columbia University students who, when 12 others were recognized at an anti-war demonstration and threatened with expulsion, wrote to the University administration and said: We were there also, if you kick the 12 out then kick us out too. I just don't see how in the long run this spirit can be defeated. People may die, people may suffer, but in the long run Stock Exchange morality cannot defeat the ethic of solidarity.

Secondly, I believe in the power of world public opinion. One reason I favor civil disobedience in Washington this summer is that it will have international visibility. To my mind, one of the most important things about the Selma protests was the sit-ins at the White House. Hitherto there has been a kind of mental sound barrier against direct action in Washington. Among suggestions for this summer are:

—That professors organize themselves in a parallel Senate Foreign Relations Committee, hold the hearings in Washington the Senate committee has failed to hold, and continue until Bundy shows up.

—That concerned persons conduct a teach-in on the steps of the Pentagon after leafleting government employees throughout Washington. The Committee for Nonviolent Action has planned this for June 16.

—That there be convened in America a new war crimes tribunal, made up of men whose spiritual authority is unquestionable such as Vinoba Bhave, Danilo Dolci, Paster Niemoeller, Michael Scott, and hopefully Martin Luther King, who would conduct an inquiry into the moral responsibility for the horror in Vietnam.

—That there come together in Washington a new continental congress made up of representatives from community unions, Freedom Parties and campus groups, which would say in effect: This is a desperate situation; our government no longer represents us; let us see what needs to be done. Under its aegis mass civil disobedience could take place on such symbolic dates as Hiroshima Day and Labor Day.

Finally, I believe in the power of nonviolence. In the 1840's Thoreau said that one man ready to die could stop slavery in America. I think all of us here this week-end should search our hearts and souls for the courage and clarity of spirit to go to the White House, to go to the Oakland Army Terminal on June 22, if possible to go to Vietnam and stand in front of the flame-throwers, and say: "If blood must be spilt, let it be mine and stop killing Vietnamese children. If you must search and destroy, let me save you the trouble, here am I. And if you are worried that the natives overseas are restless, we want you to know that the natives at home are restless, too, and perhaps you should make a contingency plan to keep some of the Marines here to deal with us."

CHAPTER 2

WE ARE NOT AT WAR
WITH THE PEOPLE OF VIETNAM

Introduction

Staughton Lynd emerged as a leading critic of the war in Vietnam in early 1965. Now he was at the center of an effort of disparate groups and individuals attempting to build a national movement against the war that included students, pacifists, leftists, and civil rights activists. In the aftermath of his speech at the Berkeley Teach-In, Lynd's proposals for increasing resistance to the war were spreading quickly. "Yale professor Staughton Lynd stirred the 15,000 people at Vietnam Day with his call for immediate action, including civil disobedience," the Vietnam Day Committee (VDC) announced in the first edition of its newsletter. It then printed information Lynd provided in a letter to the VDC: "A schedule of activities for the summer and fall has taken shape, including: the Pentagon Speak-Out June 16; a teach-in and preach-in sponsored by New York area teachers in July; demonstration in Washington on August 6 (Hiroshima Day) of signers of the Declaration of Conscience; in mid-October, an international teach-in in Canada and a rally, including civil disobedience, at Berkeley." Lynd added that he was working with his friend Bob Moses of SNCC (who subsequently changed his name to Robert Parris in late 1964) and George Clark of the British Committee for Nuclear Disarmament to organize an "international war crimes commission," an idea suggested by Lynd at Berkeley that never came to fruition. Nevertheless, the VDC "is working with Professor Lynd and others to develop what the peace movement today lacks, especially on the campus: national organization and national coordination."[1]

UNITED STATES DEPARTMENT OF JUSTICE
FEDERAL BUREAU OF INVESTIGATION

In Reply, Please Refer to
File No.

WASHINGTON, D.C. 20535

JUN 1 7 1965

SPEAK-OUT AT THE PENTAGON
JUNE 16, 1965

Reference memorandum dated June 16, 1965.

On June 16, 1965, [   ] announced at
the Committee For Non-Violent Action (CNVA) "Speak Out",
held at the Pentagon, that a meeting would be held that
night at the Washington City Church of the Brethern,
Washington, D. C. The evening meeting would "recap" the
activities of the day.

b6
b7C

On June 16, 1965, Special Agents (SAs) of the
Federal Bureau of Investigation (FBI), observed approximately
sixty-five persons present at the meeting held in the basement
of the Washington City Church of the Brethern, Fourth and North
Carolina Avenue, S. E., Washington, D. C., at 6:55 p.m. Among
those attending this meeting were the following individuals who
were publically introduced as speakers at the Pentagon Speak-
Out on June 16, 1965:

> Gordon Christiansen
> William C. Davidon
> Staughton Lynd
> Bradford Lyttle
> William H. Meyer
> A. J. Muste

DECLASSIFIED BY 6855
ON 7/27/77 DmL/GSL

Many of the unidentified persons attending the above
evening meeting had been observed by SAs of the FBI participating
in the demonstration at the Pentagon Speak-Out on June 16, 1965.

A. J. Muste presided over the meeting and recounted
his impressions of the Speak-Out at the Pentagon.

In August, 1964, a source described A. J. Muste
as National Chairman of the Committee on Non-
Violent Action, 325 Lafayette Street, New York,
New York.

APPROPRIATE AGENCIES
AND FIELD OFFICES
ADVISED BY ROUTING
SLIP(S) OF DECLASSIFICATION
DATE ___ DmL/REC ENCLOSURE   100-   916

Figure 2.1: FBI memorandum indicating the bureau's agents were closely watching the
pacifists participating in the Speak-Out at the Pentagon on 16 June 1965 and the follow-up
meeting held later that evening at the Washington City Church of the Brethren. Source:
Lynd's FBI file.

During this period, Lynd participated in numerous rallies, teach-ins, and planning meetings in New York and Washington, DC, and was crucial to many of the events he wrote about to the VDC. It was during meetings with the CNVA, WRL, the Catholic Worker organization, and other pacifist groups as well as with Bob Moses and other civil rights activists from SNCC that the idea for the Assembly of Unrepresented People slowly developed over June and July (document 1). The origins of the assembly emerged partially out of Tom Hayden's proposal in April after the SDS March on Washington to convene a new Continental Congress. Lynd, looking for a way to keep the momentum of opposition against the war going, kept Hayden's idea alive in various meetings with activists. In the spirit of cooperation, Lynd helped turn the CNVA, WRL, Catholic Worker, and Student Peace Union's originally planned conference at the White House on August 6 into the first event of a longer, four-day event designated as a broader Assembly of Unrepresented People. The idea was to commemorate the twentieth anniversary of the dropping of the atomic bomb on Hiroshima, "to confront" President Johnson and give him the Declaration of Conscience. Noting the failure of "traditional and conventional channels" in preventing escalation of the war, the original statement for the August 6 event urged that "those who have taken the stand of radical rejection of war in the atomic age set forth in the Declaration of Conscience are urged to give further expression to their concern" as fears mounted that nuclear weapons would be used in Vietnam.[2]

Planning for the Assembly of Unrepresented People opened the door for groups already in Washington, DC, over the summer to lobby Congress to come together and talk about coordinating their activities and connecting movements in order to build a broad-based coalition against the war. Lynd recalls that the first of a chain of encounters occurred when no more than half a dozen protesters tried to pass out literature on the steps of the Pentagon. A group of uniformed men asked them what they thought they were doing. Lynd replied, "You don't understand. We are just the first of thousands."[3] The crucial week of cementing the plans for the assembly evolved during a series of meetings in Washington beginning on the evening of June 16 connected to the Speak-Out at the Pentagon. Organized by the CNVA and WRL, the Speak-Out brought together roughly two hundred pacifists and civil rights workers who congregated on the steps of the Pentagon, made speeches, and handed out leaflets to soldiers and Pentagon civilian staff.[4]

Lynd was also part of a small group of people who met with Secretary of Defense Robert McNamara for thirty minutes inside the Pentagon. A poem by Paul Goodman captures the scene:

Staughton Lynd he said
to the Secretary of War,
"If on my little son
this can of gasoline I pour,

can you light a match to him?
do you dare?"
The master of the Pentagon
said nothing but sat there.

"Then how do you command
your soldiers to rain down
blazing gasoline
on little yellow children?"

This happened in America
in 1965
that people talked about
burning children alive.[5]

Even though the gathering at the Pentagon was small compared to other anti-war rallies of the era, the fact that the group had an impromptu meeting with Secretary McNamara is demonstrative of the power such small actions did have. Moreover, it also shows that the nascent movement against the war was interested in connecting with soldiers and civilian employees at the Pentagon. In fact, Lynd returned to the Pentagon the following day with other pacifists to leaflet and talk to the soldiers and employees there. A. J. Muste wrote about Lynd and the others' efforts at the Pentagon to Lucy Montgomery, a wealthy supporter of the civil rights and antiwar movements who was an activist in her own right, about another "exciting development": "On the Saturday following the Pentagon Speak Out a meeting of something like 30 or 40 persons active in CNVA, SDS, SNCC, WSP and other such groups held a week-end session. The possibility, in fact the near certainty, of a highly significant collaboration among the civil rights and antiwar groups has come out of that meeting."[6]

One of the key figures working with Staughton Lynd in these efforts was Bob Moses. Moses, who spoke with Lynd at the March on Washington in April, was now heavily invested in trying to connect the peace movement with the civil rights movement. Present during some of these meetings in New York and Washington, Moses set up a Washington office with other SNCC activists and CNVAer Eric Weinberger to help organize what they began calling the Washington Summer Action Project. In a letter to SNCC explaining these activities, Moses and others pointed to difficulties in the past in sharing resources between movements but nonetheless argued that the urgency of the moment called for such bold organizing. Noting the surge of activity in Washington over the summer and the intersections of the different movements, the letter insisted that "the only hope we have of checking Johnson's increasingly 'independent' and dangerous foreign policy is with the development of a deeply based 'critique' of his actions—one that he would be forced to heed."[7] Therefore, out the efforts of Parris, Lynd, the CNVA, and other peace and civil rights workers emerged the Assembly of Unrepresented People with the goal of bringing together the labor, student, antiwar, and civil rights movements for a series of workshops and direct-action initiatives in Washington, DC.

Meanwhile, the increased bombing of North and South Vietnam and the introduction of ground troops had not brought the Vietnamese revolutionaries to the negotiating table, and a new round of escalation was announced by President Johnson on 28 July 1965. During the president's second major speech on Vietnam, he announced a troop surge from the current number of 75,000 to 125,000 troops immediately and added that "additional forces will be needed later, and they will be sent as requested." The president added that draft calls were about to be increased from 17,000 a month to 35,000 and added, crucially, that the reserves would not be called up. At the time, the president believed that activating the reserves would have been more damaging politically than increasing the monthly draft calls. This decision set into motion the creation of a vast conscripted military the likes of which the United States had only seen four other times in its history (the Revolutionary War, the Civil War, World War I, and World War II).

In his speech, the president in no uncertain terms told the nation that "this is really war" and employed the Munich analogy—invoking the memory of British prime minister Neville Chamberlain appeasing Hitler in 1938 on the eve of Nazi Germany's seizure of Czechoslovakia—as evidence as to why the United States needed to act. "We have learned at a terrible and a brutal cost that retreat does not bring safety and weakness does not bring peace." Moreover, "we learned from Hitler at Munich that success only feeds the appetite of aggression. The battle would be renewed in one country and then another country, bringing with it perhaps even larger and crueler conflict, as we have learned from the lessons of history." According to Johnson, "aggression unchallenged, is aggression unleashed."[8] This use of the Munich analogy was a common argument utilized in both private and public statements by administration officials to justify US escalation and would be refuted by Lynd throughout the war. By the end of 1965, the number of American troops in South Vietnam increased to over 180,000 after President Johnson's July troop surge. In November, General Westmoreland requested an additional fifty-three battalions to be sent to South Vietnam, total-ing 440,000 troops by the end of 1966.[9]

Dramatic photographs of the antiwar movement were a central feature of the 20 August 1965 edition of *Life* magazine. Red paint was splashed across the clothes and faces of Staughton Lynd and David Dellinger as they marched to the US Capitol to declare peace with Vietnam as part of the Assembly of Unrepresented People. It should be noted that Bob Moses, walking arm in arm with both Dellinger and Lynd as a symbol of the coming together of the peace and civil rights movements, was cropped out of the photograph. The reverse page captured two other key resistance activities.[10] The day after Johnson's much-vaunted July 28 speech, Chris Kearns, a Catholic Worker and a pacifist, burned his draft card in a demonstration outside the Whitehall Induction Center in New York City. The event sparked outrage in Congress as Representative L. Mendel Rivers and Senator Strom Thurmond introduced identical bills outlaw-ing the willful destruction or mutilation of draft cards punishable by five years in prison and a $10,000 fine.[11] On the West Coast, marching under the banner of "Stop the War Machine," Vietnam Day Committee activists engaged in the kind of civil disobedience Staughton Lynd advocated in Berkeley in May by attempting to stop troop trains throughout early August. One leaflet handed out—entitled "Stop the Troop Train"—read, "To oppose the immoral war in Vietnam and to block the war machine is moral. . . . We are not demonstrating against the soldiers. We consider the soldiers to be our brothers—brothers who have been conscripted against their will forced to kill by a government which has forgotten how to tell the truth. We want to stop the war machine and tell the soldiers what is really going on in Vietnam."[12]

Throughout the fall, the antiwar movement slowly gained momentum with more demonstrations while the Johnson administration and members of Congress began a more concerted attack against movement leaders and groups associated with protests against the draft. First, the International Days of Protest against the Vietnam War brought out one hundred thousand people in one hundred US cities and several thousand more in countries around the world during the weekend of October 15 and 16. On the Friday, Lynd spoke in front of a crowd of three hundred in Philadelphia over the shouts of counterdemonstrators yelling "traitor," "draft dodgers," and "assassin." Lynd said he supported those of draft age who could not conscientiously fight in Vietnam. The following day, he flew to Berkeley, where he spoke at a rally of fifteen thousand gathered for a teach-in and march on the Oakland Army Terminal. The marchers were confronted by the Hells Angels and stopped by the Oakland police before they could spread their message to the soldiers en route to Vietnam.[13] At a rally of twenty-five thousand in New York City, David Miller, a twenty-two-year-old activist of the Catholic Worker movement, burned his draft card, thereby becoming the first to challenge the new draft-card mutilation law. In Ann Arbor, over thirty students from the University of Michigan held a sit-in at the local draft board in opposition to the Selective Service System.[14]

In response, the US government went on the offensive, accusing the antiwar movement of prolonging the war by giving North Vietnamese combatants the impression the American public was divided over the war. On October 18, Attorney General Nicholas Katzenbach launched an investigation into what he called the "beat the draft" movement. Talking to reporters in Chicago, Katzenbach stated there were "some Communists involved" in the antidraft movement and that he was initiating an investigation against the Students for a Democratic Society and the National Coordinating Committee to End the War in Vietnam, which was created at the Assembly of Unrepresented People.[15] The president, recovering from gallbladder surgery at Bethesda Naval Hospital, speaking through press secretary Bill Moyers, endorsed the Justice Department's investigation into communist infiltration of the movement. "The president feels it is possible for our adversaries to misread events in this country and to take and put into these events greater and broader support for a particular position than is justified by the feeling of the American people at large," Moyers told the press. Moreover, he stated that President Johnson believed that if the Vietnamese were given the impression that there was a sizable antiwar opinion in the United States, this would cause America's foes to fight harder and would prolong the war.[16]

Senators on Capitol Hill were more incendiary in their public statements. Senator Frank Lausche (D-Ohio) announced that the demonstrators were "harmful to the security of our country" and that they were "the product of communist leadership. Countless innocent, uninformed youth of the country are participating in them not knowing that they are following the flag of the Reds and bowing to the voices of the Communists."[17] At a speech at the national convention of the Defense Supply Association, Senator Thomas Dodd (D-Connecticut), chairman of the Senate Internal Security Subcommittee, denounced the protests as "tantamount to open insurrection" and argued that "we have to draw a line, and draw it soon, and draw it hard, between the right of free speech and assembly and the right to perpetrate treason."[18]

Before the weekend protests, Senator Dodd released a 235-page report arguing that the movement "has clearly passed from the hands of the moderate elements who may have controlled it at one time, into the hands of communists and extremist elements who are openly sympathetic to the Vietcong and openly hostile to the United States, and who call for massive civil disobedience, including the burning of draft cards and the stopping of troop trains. This is particularly true of the national Vietnam protest movement scheduled for October 15–16." The report singled out Staughton Lynd and twenty-five individuals (including Lynd's parents, Robert and Helen Lynd) as leaders of the movement with ties to international communism or harboring communist sympathies. A November 19 Gallup poll demonstrated that 58 percent of Americans believed that the communists had been involved in the demonstrations against the Vietnam War.[19]

Parallel to the wild fabrications in Washington about the nature and intentions of the nascent antiwar movement, the war continued unabated and with increased brutality. The use of napalm increasingly caught the attention of those opposing the war, highlighted in the speeches and writings of Staughton Lynd throughout 1965 and after. On the morning of November 2, a friend of the Lynds and fellow Quaker Norman Morrison read one such account of the use of napalm in the pages of *I. F. Stone's Weekly* where the harrowing survival of Father Currien was recounted. The French Catholic priest was found in a hospital by the French journalist Jean Lartéguy; Currien told Lartéguy of how he barely survived the US bombing of his village with napalm near Duc Co in the Central Highlands close to Pleiku. The area was controlled by the NLF, and after a firefight between the NLF and the US-backed South Vietnamese Army, US planes were called in to destroy the village. "I have seen my faithful burned up in napalm," the priest told Lartéguy. "I have seen the bodies of women and children blown to bits. I have seen all my villages razed. By God, it's not possible! (*C'est pas Dieu possible*)."[20]

Struggling with the US escalation for months, Norman Morrison was pushed into further despair by the priest's account. He decided to drive from Baltimore to Washington, DC, with his infant daughter, Emily, douse himself in kerosene, and light himself on fire in front of the Pentagon in protest of the war. Witnessing Morrison's self-immolation, Secretary of Defense Robert McNamara watched on in horror as onlookers rushed to rescue the infant child. The tactic, utilized by Buddhist monks in South Vietnam to protest repression by the US-backed regime, had a profound effect on individuals like Secretary McNamara, Staughton and Alice Lynd, and also, as Staughton would discover later when traveling to North Vietnam, on countless Vietnamese people struggling for independence.[21]

Staughton Lynd was at the forefront of these events. Documents in this chapter demonstrate how persistently the scholar-activist continued to offer justifications for the more radical tactics employed by the movement, while also becoming a prescient critic of American escalation.

Document 1

CALL FOR AN ASSEMBLY OF UNREPRESENTED PEOPLE

The Assembly of Unrepresented People brought together the energies of different groups and individuals looking to connect the various movements agitating in Washington over the summer of 1965. Held on the twentieth anniversary of the bombings of Hiroshima on August 6 and of Nagasaki on August 9, the assembly brought together perhaps two thousand people over the four days of events. It was at the assembly that Alice Lynd attended a workshop organized by the Central Committee for Conscientious Objectors calling for volunteers to become involved in draft counseling. Alice agreed and shortly thereafter put up a draft counselor sign as one entered the Lynds' apartment on 26 Court Street, five blocks from the Yale campus.[22] The two major commitments established at the assembly were the creation of the National Coordinating Committee to End the War in Vietnam and an agreement to organize the International Day of Protest against the war in Vietnam for October.

The following is the widely circulated leaflet inviting people to attend.[23]

1965

CALL FOR AN ASSEMBLY OF UNREPRESENTED PEOPLE
in Washington, D.C., August 6-9

> *"I like to believe that the people in the long run are going to do more to promote peace than our governments. I think the people want peace so much that one of these days governments had better get out of their way and let them have it."*
>
> --- President Dwight D. Eisenhower, Aug. 31, 1959

WE DECLARE PEACE

IN MISSISSIPPI and Washington the few make the decisions for the many. Mississippi Negroes are denied the vote; the voice of the thirty per cent of Americans now opposed to the undeclared war in Vietnam is not heeded and all Americans are denied access to facts concerning the true military and political situation. We must make it plain to the Administration that we will not be accomplices to a war that we did not declare. There can be no doubt that the great majority of the people of the world do not approve of the presence of American troops in Vietnam. We who will come to Washington on August 6 through 9 cannot in any sense represent this majority, but we can let our voices be heard in a symbolic *Assembly of Unrepresented People to Declare Peace.*

AUGUST 6 is the twentieth anniversary of the dropping of the first atomic bomb on Hiroshima; August 9 the anniversary of the Nagasaki bomb. Therefore, we choose August 6, 7, 8, and 9 for a new attempt to draw together the voices of nonviolent protest in America; not only those who have for so long been calling for an end to the Cold War, but also those whose protests focus on racial injustice, inquisition by Congressional committees, inequities in labor legislation, the mishandling of anti-poverty and welfare funds and the absence of democratic process on the local level. We invite not only those now active in organized protests but ministers, members of the academic community, teachers, women, professional people, students, people from the newly formed community groups in slums and rural areas, industrial workers, anyone who wishes to symbolically withdraw his support from the war and who wishes to explore the possibilities of inter-action inherent in this community of concerned people.

Norma Becker
Bob Swann
Donna Allen
Bob Parris
Mel McDonald
Carl Bloise
Peter Kellman
Barry Weisberg
Dena Clamager
Steve Weissman

Stephen Amdur
Eric Weinberger
Walter M. Tillow
Carl Oglesby
Ed Hamlett
Jeffrey Gordon
Jimmy Garrett
Courtland Cox
Dave Dellinger
Ray Raphael

Sandra Adickes
Francis H. Mitchell
John Porcelli
William Hartzog
Barbara Deming
Mack Smith
Staughton Lynd
Dennis Sweeney
Russ Nixon
Florence Howe
Paul Lauter

Activities of the Four Days

WHITE HOUSE CONFERENCE

August 6: A demonstration at the White House will center around the Declaration of Conscience which has already received over 6,000 signatures; it declares the signers' complete refusal to assist in the carrying out of the war in Vietnam and the Dominican Republic. Those of the signers who can come to Washington will constitute the core of the demonstration; non-signers will be welcomed. The Declaration has been sponsored and circulated by the Committee for Nonviolent Action, War Resisters League, Student Peace Union and the Catholic Worker. These groups will therefore have full responsibility for the conduct of this aspect of the four-day assembly. There may be nonviolent civil disobedience by some of the signers.

❖   ❖   ❖   ❖   ❖   ❖

August 7 and 8 will be the heart of the *Assembly of Unrepresented People.* They will be devoted to workshops, probably carried out in the open on the grass surrounding the Washington Monument.

❖   ❖   ❖   ❖   ❖   ❖

PROGRAM WORKSHOPS

August 7: The *Assembly* will divide itself according to the section of the protest movement which claims the greatest attention of each individual.

There will be groupings of community people and staff who have been working at the local level on organizing the poor to have a voice in the lives of their communities and in the administration of federal antipoverty funds.

There will be another grouping of people whose interest and work center on the Mississippi Freedom Democratic Party's attempt to have Congress unseat the five improperly elected representatives from their state.

There will still be other groupings to discuss the recent threats of destructive investigation by the House Un-American Activities Committee of elements of both the peace and civil rights movements.

We hope that there will also be present representative groupings from the ranks of organized labor to discuss labor's attempt to have repealed the so-called "right-to-work law" provisions of the Taft-Hartley Act.

A special workshop on *religion and social action* will be held on the 7th for ministers and lay people.

There will be workshops on Free Universities and Student Unions.

Additional workshops on other aspects of nonviolent direct action will be scheduled to meet the interests of those present.

CONSTITUENCY WORKSHOPS

August 8: Vietnam. There will be workshops of teachers, members of the academic community, women, professional people, students, people from local communities, union members and other "constituency groupings" to plan how they can work in the summer and through the year to stop the war. There will be a large evening meeting.

A Declaration of Peace drawn up by the initiators of the demonstration will be circulated in the workshops for use on the 9th.

August 9 ("Governments had better get out of their way and let them have it."): Those members of the *Assembly of Unrepresented People* in a position to face possible arrest and willing to pledge themselves to nonviolent behavior during the course of the demonstration will assemble and walk toward the Capitol with the intention of convening the *Assembly* in the chamber of the House of Representatives and thus deny that Congress has the right to declare war in our names. If stopped along the way we will sit down and declare the *Assembly of Unrepresented People* in session. One of the group will rise and begin to read the Declaration of Peace circulated in the workshops on the 8th. If, as seems likely, the person reading is arrested before the Declaration is fully read, another person will rise and continue reading. The *Assembly* will be open to the reading of additional declarations of peace that individuals or representatives of organizations may bring with them. We hope that this demonstration will serve as a symbol of the desire of the people of the world to express their opposition to the Vietnam war in a democratic fashion.

To implement this plan, we suggest that one focus for community organization between now and August 6 be discussion of what the government *should* do in Vietnam. The results of these discussions could be embodied in declarations of peace which representatives would bring to Washington. Some groups, particularly those farthest away from Washington, may want to create assemblies at state capitals and city councils on August 9.

Preparation for the *Assembly* will be coordinated at 107 Rhode Island Ave., NW, Washington, D.C. Address correspondence to Eric Weinberger or Bob Parris. Before and after the *Assembly* related activities will go on in Washington concerning Vietnam, FDP, 14-B, HUAC and community organization. Volunteers are urgently needed. We can probably provide free housing.
(A few hundred dollars are needed for office expenses. Checks to Washington Summer Action are requested.)
Printed by the Grindstone Press

Figure 2.2: The front and back of the flyer used to promote the Assembly of Unrepresented People in the summer of 1965. Courtesy of Bruce Hartford at the Civil Rights Movement Archive, www.crmvet.org.

Figures 2.3 and 2.4: Marchers gathering at the National Mall in Washington, DC, before departing to the US Capitol as part of the final day of the Assembly of Unrepresented People, 9 August 1965. *Left to right:* David Dellinger, Staughton Lynd, and Bob Moses with other unidentified individuals. Courtesy of Rowland Scherman and the Rowland Scherman Collection (PH 084), Special Collections and University Archives, University of Massachusetts Amherst Libraries

Figure 2.5: Staughton Lynd shortly after being splattered with red paint by right-wing counter-demonstrators on the way to the US Capitol as part of the Assembly of Unrepresented People, 9 August 1965. Courtesy of Rowland Scherman and the Rowland Scherman Collection (PH 084), Special Collections and University Archives, University of Massachusetts Amherst Libraries.

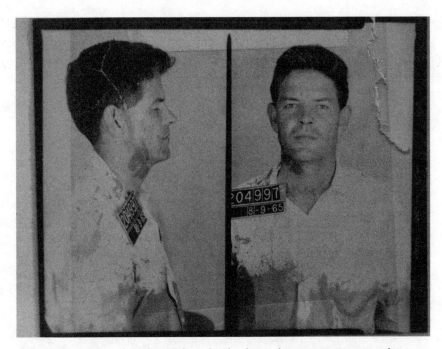

Figure 2.6: Staughton Lynd's mug shot taken by the Washington, D.C., Metropolitan Police after his arrest for disorderly conduct outside the US Capitol Building on 9 August 1965. Photograph courtesy of the National Archives and Records Administration. Source: Senate Internal Security Subcommittee, Name files, ser. 2, box 64, 8E2a/8/2/4, National Archives and Records Administration I, Washington, DC.

Document 2

"COALITION POLITICS OR NONVIOLENT REVOLUTION?"
JUNE–JULY 1965

Staughton Lynd responds to Bayard Rustin's February 1965 article in *Commentary* magazine, "From Protest to Politics: The Future of the Civil Rights Movement," in which Rustin implores African Americans to embrace a new coalition strategy in the struggle for freedom. For Rustin, "the civil rights movement is evolving from a protest movement into a full-fled *social movement*," and this required broadening the base of support and a change in tactics. "The future of the Negro struggle depends on whether the contradictions of this society can be resolved by a coalition of progressive forces which becomes the *effective* political majority in the United States. I speak of the coalition which staged the March on Washington [of 1963], passed the Civil Rights Act, and laid the basis for the Johnson landslide—Negroes, trade unionists, liberals, and religious groups."[24]

For Lynd and other radicals who worked closely with Rustin, this article was part of a string of recent actions that brought Rustin not only closer to the cautious center in American politics but also to outright hostility toward the movement he had led since his youth. Specifically for Lynd, he took issue with Rustin's cautioning the Mississippi Freedom Democratic Party to compromise at the 1964 Democratic National Convention and accept only two delegates when the new party sought greater representation for African Americans in the state. Moreover, Rustin was a signatory to a letter on the eve of the SDS March on Washington that called into question the participation of communists and Trotskyists and advocated an independent peace movement that excluded these individuals and groups.[25] Rustin, who was still an editor of *Liberation* magazine, upset his coeditors David Dellinger and A. J. Muste, who in turn asked Lynd to write a response to Rustin's article for the magazine. Below is Lynd's response, which created a fierce debate within pacifist and social democratic circles.[26]

Bayard Rustin's "From Protest to Politics: The Future of the Civil Rights Movement," an article which appeared in *Commentary* magazine for February 1965, has been widely criticized in radical publications. Ronald Radosh wrote an effective response in *Freedom North*, and Stanley Aronowitz will comment in a forthcoming issue of *Studies on the Left*.

The gist of the radical critique of Rustin might be summarized as follows:

1. Rustin writes that "the objective fact is that Eastland and Goldwater are the main enemies." In so doing he exaggerates the liberalism of the Johnson coalition, even asserting that Big Business, forced into the Democratic Party by Goldwater, "does not belong there."

2. Not only does Rustin urge that direct action be abandoned for politics, he argues also that independent political action is only rarely appropriate. The accurate perception that Negroes need white allies leads him to the conclusion that one must choose between existing aggregations of political forces: "The issue is which coalition to join and how to make it responsive to your program."

3. Thus, by exaggerating the Johnson coalition's capacity to solve fundamental social problems and by underestimating the need for independent action by Negroes, Rustin arrives at a stance which (in Radosh's words) "leads to a dissolution of the old Rights movement, as well as assuring that any new Movement will not develop in a more radical fashion." The effect of his advice would be to assimilate Negro protest to the Establishment just as labor protest was coopted at the end of the 1930's, in each case leaving the poorest, least organized parts of the population out in the cold.

I agree with Radosh's analysis, but I think it is not sufficiently fundamental. Fully to appraise Rustin's *Commentary* article, one must see it as the second in a series of three Rustin actions during the past year. First was his attempt to get the credentials committee offer of token seating accepted by the Mississippi Freedom Democratic Party delegates at Atlantic City (August 1964). Second was the article (February 1965). Third was the effort to undermine and stop the March on Washington against the war in Vietnam (March–April 1965). In this perspective, the most basic criticisms of his article should be these: 1. The coalition he advocates turns out to mean implicit acceptance of Administration foreign policy, to be coalition with the marines; 2. The style of politics he advocates turns out to mean a kind of élitism which Bayard has been fighting all his life, in which rank-and-file persons would cease to act on their own behalf and be (in the words of "From Protest to Politics") "merely represented."

In opposing the March on Washington against the war in Vietnam Bayard Rustin has permitted himself to drift into that posture which once evoked epithets such as "labor lieutenant of capitalism." Exaggerated as such labels may have been, they designated something real. There were in Europe and there are now in America pacifists and socialists who always support their own government in its international confrontations when push comes to shove. Such Americans

WE ARE NOT AT WAR WITH THE PEOPLE OF VIETNAM   57

insist on condemning Washington and Moscow "equally," but end up supporting the U.S. government which "after all" and "on the whole" stands on the side
of "freedom." They specialize in advising revolutionary movements overseas to
be nonviolent, forgetting that American arms and aggression play a major role
(as in Vietnam) in driving peaceful protest toward insurrection. They cultivate
the concept that the President is a man of peace misled by his advisors, who if
only one could reach him, would surely turn on the military-industrial complex
and overcome. Theirs is the stance of telling Washington what *they* would do
were *they* in power. If there is to be protest, so they say, let it be decorous protest
which (as Norman Thomas said in his April 22nd letter to the *Times*) "goes off
well," i.e., poses no serious embarrassment to the good man in the White House.

The basic error in this analysis seems to me the assumption that there now
exists what Michael Harrington calls "*de facto* coexistence" between the United
States and world revolution. Rustin and Harrington confine their analysis to
domestic problems, as if believing that foreign affairs are frozen and can be
forgotten. But as Harrington conceded in *Partisan Review*: "'escalation' of the
Vietnamese—or any other—crisis would ... end talk of the War on Poverty, and
of the Great Society." That escalation has occurred.

Coalitionism, then, is pro-Americanism. It is what Sidney Lens has called
"two-and-a-half campism." It is a posture which subordinates foreign to domestic politics, which mutes criticism of American imperialism so as to keep open
its channels to the White House, which tacitly assumes that no major war will
occur. But war is occurring in Vietnam, major enough for the innocent people
which it has killed. How can one reconcile virtual silence on Vietnam with the
screams of Vietnamese women and children?

Coalitionism is also élitism. Its assumption is that major political decisions are
made by deals between the representatives of the interests included in the coalition. Negro protest, according to the Rustin formula, should now take on the
role of such an interest. And men like Rustin will become the national spokesmen who sell the line agreed-on behind doors to the faithful followers waiting
in the street.

This was the meaning of Atlantic City. What was at stake, as it seemed to
the S.N.C.C. people there, was not so much the question, Should the compromise be accepted? as the question, Are plain people from Mississippi competent
to decide? Rustin, Martin Luther King and Roy Wilkins answered the latter
question: No. The decision, they insisted, involved "national considerations."
In some sense the destiny of America rested in the hands of those who made this
decision. Hence it should be made wisely, by the leaders, and put over to the
delegates from Mississippi.

But what those delegates and their S.N.C.C. associates learned at Atlantic City was simply no longer to trust these "national civil-rights leaders." They learned, as Mrs. Hamer put it on her return, that hypocrisy exists all over America. They learned, so Robert Parris told the *National Guardian* dinner in November, that the destiny of America was *not* in their hands, that they should seek their own objectives, "let the chips fall where they may."

So as some sunk deeper into the coils of coalitionism, S.N.C.C. people have joined with Students for a Democratic Society this winter in laying a new emphasis on "participatory democracy." Democracy, they say, means ordinary people making decisions for themselves. It means the staff of an organization making decisions rather than an executive committee, it means the organization itself working itself out of a job so that new popular organizations take over Freedom parties, Freedom schools.

All this Bayard Rustin used to believe. Direct action is inseparable from the idea that everyone involved in a movement has some ultimate responsibility and initiative. Decentralization was the hallmark of the early *Liberation*, which Bayard helped to found. Participatory democrats, as they move from direct action into politics, insist that direct action must continue along with politics, that there come into being a new politics which forces the representative back to his people, and politics back to life.

There is very little point in criticizing the coalition strategy suggested by Rustin unless one has an alternative to offer.

The Nonviolent Alternative

I think the time has come to begin to think of "nonviolent revolution" as the only long-run alternative to coalition with the marines. The civil-rights movement, so often called a revolution, is thus far no more a revolution than the trade-union movement of the 1930's. Presumably the definition of a revolution is that the direction of society's affairs shifts from one group to another, and that the economic foundation of political power is transformed so as to make this shift permanent. A revolution in this sense—and not merely public works planning by an Administration whose power rests on private ownership and lack of planning—seems to me required both to prevent war and to satisfy the needs of the other America. But is talk of revolution merely what Rustin calls moral gesturing?

So long as revolution is pictured as a violent insurrection it seems to me both distasteful and unreal. The traditional alternative, the Social Democratic vision of electing more and more radical legislators until power passes peacefully to the

Left, seems equally illusory. However, the events of the past year—the creation of the Mississippi Freedom Democratic Party and the protest against the war in Vietnam—suggest a third strategy. One can now begin to envision a series of nonviolent protests which would from the beginning question the legitimacy of the Administration's authority where it has gone beyond constitutional and moral limits, and might, if its insane foreign policy continues, culminate in the decision of hundreds of thousands of people to recognize the authority of alternative institutions of their own making.

Robert Parris has sketched out such a scenario as a possibility in Mississippi. What, he has asked, if Mississippi Freedom Democratic Party voters elected not only legislators but public officials as well? What if the Negroes of Neshoba County, Mississippi began to obey the instructions of the Freedom Sheriff rather than Sheriff Rainey? What if the Freedom Sheriff impaneled a Freedom Grand Jury which indicted Sheriff Rainey for murder?

The value of these imaginings is that they break up the concept of "revolution" as a monolithic, unitary event, and remind us that revolution begins as the decision of individuals to say, No, and take a first step. Even the most violent revolutions involved a larger component of nonviolent civil disobedience than is often recognized. Masses of poor men who defy constituted authority typically lack weapons, and succeed only when they convince the government's soldiers not to fire on them but to join them. Thus Trotsky presents the crux of the Russian Revolution as an encounter between mounted Cossacks and unarmed poor people rioting for bread: when the soldiers decided to join the rioters, the revolution was essentially won. St. Éxupery, writing of the Spanish Civil War, describes two peasants, one in the Nationalist army and one in the Republican, whose units were stationed on opposite slopes of a valley and who as night fell hurled to each other across great distance single words which sought to persuade: "Liberty," "Brotherhood." This is how real revolutions, as distinct from plots and insurrections, succeed or fail. Camus was wrong in presenting revolution and rebellion as mutually exclusive: no popular revolution is possible which is not composed of hundreds of smaller rebellions. Thus the American Civil War, our closest approach to revolution, began with solitary decisions to defy Congress and the Supreme Court and to succor fugitive slaves.

Needless to say all this makes sense only if our situation is desperate. I think it is desperate. If it was desperate in Mississippi when perhaps two dozen people were murdered over a period of five years, what is it in Vietnam where a hundred thousand lives have needlessly been thrown away since 1954? If there are, in Camus' phrase, "limits" inherent in human nature to permissible government policy, what more can we do after what we have done in Vietnam? If Vietnam

is permissible, can anything be forbidden? And how many more secret unde-
bated Presidential decisions will it take to convince us that a constitutional crisis
exists in America, that we have moved into a twilight zone between democratically delegated authority and something accurately called "fascism"? When the
President sent troops into the Dominican Republic he called in Congressmen to
tell them, he explained, before they read about it in the newspapers. As the *New
York Times* has pointed out, government management of the news, characteristic
of previous temporary crises such as the U-2 and Bay of Pigs affairs, has in connection with Vietnam become settled public policy over a period of months and
years. I believe we should have seen that America could not endlessly practice
Seven Days in May in underdeveloped countries all over the world, making
and unmaking governments at the behest of generals and C.I.A. agents, without these habits crossing the Rubicon between foreign and domestic politics to
become our political style at home as well. I think the situation is desperate.

Yet nonviolence offers rational hope which can forestall desperation issuing
in apathy or senseless violence. The situation of the Administration is more desperate than ours, and its present policy is the blind lashing-out of the cornered
and frustrated, who see no orderly method to achieve their goals. On the other
hand, few as we are our aspirations run along the grain of the hopes and strivings
of the majority of mankind. International public opinion constitutes some check
even on an Administration which has determined to go it alone without friends.
When suffragettes were over and over again imprisoned and mishandled on the
streets of Washington during World War I, public opinion was aroused, some
high government officials resigned, and women's suffrage was enacted into law.
If students chained themselves to the Capitol this summer in wave after wave
of massive civil disobedience, even the Johnson Administration would be con-
strained in its choice of means.

A Continental Congress

What then is to be done? Let me offer an imagined scenario, comparable to
Parris' for Mississippi, which without presuming to define a "position" or lay
down a "line" may help our thinking converge toward common action.

Suppose (I take this idea from Tom Hayden) there were convened in
Washington this summer a new continental congress. The congresses of 1774
and 1775 came about on the initiative of committees of correspondence of the
individual colonies. The continental congress of 1965 might stem from the initiative of the community union in a Northern ghetto, or the Freedom Party of
a Southern state. Suppose, at any rate, that such a call goes out, saying in effect:

This is a desperate situation; our government no longer represents us; let us come together at Washington to consult on what needs to be done.

Already there are in Washington Freedom Democratic Congresswomen who are, in a sense, tribunes of all the unrepresented people in America. As the actions of the Administration systematically exclude Congress from effective decision-making, the category of the unrepresented comes to include not only those (like 95 per cent of adult Mississippi Negroes) who cannot vote, but the rest of the American people who no longer have decision-makers that represent them. Although Mrs. Hamer and Mrs. Gray have held no "freedom legislative hearings" and introduced no "freedom bills," their presence is a symbol of the determination of the American excluded to have some say in what their government does.

The continental congress goes one step further. The act of convening it would stem from a conviction that even the victory of Mrs. Hamer and her colleagues would have little significance if the Congress which they joined no longer had effective power. The continental congress would be the coming-together of project and community union representatives who, were they one day to be elected to Congress, might refuse to go on the ground that Congress has given up its power.

Just as the American colonists organized Provincial Conventions and a Continental Congress to take the place of the colonial legislatures and the British Parliament, so the continental congress of 1965 would seriously and responsibly begin to debate the policies of the United States. The discussions which have failed to take place in the Senate about Vietnam, would take place here. Resolutions would be adopted and the form of treaties ratified; emissaries of the congress could seek to make direct contact with the people of other countries. In effect the continental congress would begin to govern.

The transfer of allegiance would apply, to begin with, only to specific acts. Those refusing to pay taxes might pay them to the continental congress. Those refusing to serve in the army might volunteer their labor to community projects under congress sponsorship. Some, with or without the explicit authorization of a congress majority, might initiate systematic civil disobedience in their own communities or in Washington (just so in 1774 Massachusetts moved out ahead of the Continental Congress and began to organize its own government and to prepare for war). Professors might organize a committee to hold foreign policy hearings, since the Senate Committee on Foreign Relations has failed to do so. Men of spiritual authority from all over the world might be convened as a parallel Supreme Court, to assess guilt and responsibility for the horror of Vietnam.

The pressures on American policy-makers suggest an iron drift toward more and more blatant repression at home and abroad. Yet even if this is so, all is not lost. Six months ago the air-conditioned nightmare seemed secure and invulnerable. Liberals congratulated themselves that America had turned its last corner, integrating the Negro into the happy permanent societal consensus. This was an illusion. America's situation was less secure. Johnson was less rational, the American people were less brainwashed, than they seemed six months ago. Now we know: whom the gods would destroy they first make mad; but also: we can overcome.

At the April 17th march in Washington it was unbearably moving to watch the sea of banners and signs move out from the Sylvan Theater toward the Capitol as Joan Baez, Judy Collins and others sang "We Shall Overcome." Still more poignant was the perception—and I checked my reaction with many many others who felt as I did—that as the crowd moved down the Mall toward the seat of government, its path delimited on each side by rows of chartered buses so that there was nowhere to go but forward, toward the waiting policemen, it seemed that the great mass of people would simply flow on through and over the marble buildings, that our forward movement was irresistibly strong; that even had some been shot or arrested nothing could have stopped that crowd from taking possession of its government. Perhaps next time we should keep going, occupying for a time the rooms from which orders issue and sending to the people of Vietnam and the Dominican Republic the profound apologies which are due; or quietly waiting on the Capitol steps until those who make policy for us, and who like ourselves are trapped by fear and pride, consent to enter into dialogue with us and with mankind.

Document 3

"INSIDE STORY OF THE QUAGMIRE," JULY 1965

Established in New York City in the summer of 1965, *Viet-Report: An Emergency News Bulletin on Southeast Asian Affairs* produced independent analysis and reporting on the Vietnam War. Founded by Carol Brightman, *Viet-Report* published several editions a year and ran until 1968. Over the summer and fall of 1965, *Viet-Report* had a print run of over eighty thousand copies and was distributed by various pacifist and political groups throughout the country.[27]

Staughton Lynd is listed as a member of the advisory board of *Viet-Report* and contributed to its first edition the following book review essay of David Halberstam's *The Making of a Quagmire* and Wilfred Burchett's *Vietnam: Inside Story of the Guerrilla War*. An excerpt from Lynd's speech at the Berkeley Teach-In from May offering different proposals to the movement is also printed in this first issue of *Viet-Report*.

The Making of a Quagmire. By David Halberstam. Random House. 323 pp. $5.95.

Vietnam: Inside Story of the Guerrilla War. By Wilfred Burchett. International Publishers. 253 pp. $4.95.

These books have been widely read and widely reviewed, and a non-specialist's contribution to their evaluation must be limited. Yet, there are two questions which I have not seen adequately posed and answered. First, do these views which are, as Bernard Fall put it, "literally" from opposite sides, corroborate or contradict each other? And, recognizing that Halberstam's volume reflects to a considerable extent the ideas of most lower echelon Americans in Vietnam, what light does it throw on the thinking which prompted escalation?

About Christmas time 1963 Burchett and Halberstam were at the front lines of the guerrilla war in the Mekong Delta near Saigon, on opposite sides. Did they see the same thing? Essentially, yes. Burchett saw the Saigon government nominally in control of villages while actually at the mercy of surrounding guerrillas, a situation he calls living "integrated with the enemy."

An American "senior adviser" described the tactic to Halberstam. "I don't think we've even begun to see the enemy's real capacity—I think they're playing cat and mouse with us. Many of these hamlets have never been hit by the VC, and the reason is that they don't have to hit them—they control them already."

Burchett and Halberstam also concur in their descriptions of the critical battle of Ap Bac in January 1963, the battle in which the Diem government lost the military initiative temporarily afforded in 1962 by the strategic hamlet program and the use of helicopters. Indeed, Halberstam offers a particularly dramatic illustration of the congruence of his own reporting and Burchett's view from the other side, when he states that the most accurate evaluation of Ap Bac was an after-battle analysis by the Vietcong, which fell into the hands of the Saigon government. Halberstam writes:

> . . . I and my colleagues felt that in general this document was a much more accurate and perceptive description of the war and the forces at play in it than any American statement we had ever read. It predicted that the Americans would become bogged down in a frustrating, unrewarding war; it described prophetically the built-in contradictions of the American-Diem relationship; and it noted that though the Government had a vast military superiority at the time, the Vietcong retained "absolute political superiority." We were all a bit chilled by its acute analysis.

More complex is the question of Vietcong terror. Burchett quotes a Vietcong guerrilla to the effect that assassination of village officials is directed only against particularly cruel administrators, and only after they are invited to stop working for the Saigon government and have refused. Halberstam's first reference to terror suggests that in 1960 the Vietcong began to systematically eliminate bad and corrupt officials together with some unusually able ones as well, making a particular target of school teachers. "Again and again the story was the same: brutal murders, decapitation of village officials in front of an entire village." Subsequently, however, when Halberstam describes not what was told him but what he observed in the Delta in 1962–1963, he gives a rather different impression:

> When they [the Vietcong] attacked, they attacked only the symbols of the Government: the armory or command post of the hamlet, the hamlet chief or the youth leaders (who were particularly hated because they were Nhu's men). They rarely harmed the population, and so the people of a village, who saw that the Government had not kept its promises and could not protect them, often sided with the Vietcong after a raid.

For confirmation that this is the more accurate picture of Vietcong terror, see Malcolm W. Browne, *The New Face of War*, pp. 102, 104, 109. Not merely the facts, but the tone and context of these two passages vary greatly; so much so, that the attack on officials as described in the latter passage begins to remind one of the use of violence against Vichy collaborators by the French Resistance.

In general, Burchett and Halberstam diverge most when either writes about matters he did not personally observe. Burchett's account of the political crisis in

1963 which led to the overthrow of the Diems—"The suppression of the Buddhists would have gone unnoticed had it not been for official U.S. dissatisfaction with Diem"—seems mechanical beside Halberstam's richly detailed version. According to him, the conflict between Diem and the Buddhists was provoked "by a series of coincidences" and came to include political as well as religious grievances only because of the Saigon government's prideful and authoritarian response to the first mild Buddhist protests. On the other hand, when it comes to the origin of the present Vietnamese war, Halberstam is content to say: "The new Indochina war was not a spontaneous uprising from the South. It was part of a systematic and calculated conspiracy on the part of the Communist government in Hanoi to take over the South." Burchett discovers the opposite. One of his principal objectives in once more going behind the Vietcong lines was to determine as best he could exactly how the armed uprising originated; personal interviews with persons directly involved proved to him that it started as a series of isolated military actions in response to intolerable repression by Diem without authorization from any central body in South Vietnam, let alone Hanoi. As I. F. Stone notes, in Halberstam's account "The real roots of discontent are touched on only peripherally."

Fall has written of Burchett's book: "Some of the descriptions of life in the 'liberated zones' have an evident ring of truth and are fully corroborated by what line-crossers or deserters tell us." This observation was dramatically confirmed by the recent defection of Do Van Dau, apparently the highest-ranking National Liberation Front personage to come over to the Saigon government. In an interview published in the *New York Times* of May 23, this informant said among other things: 1. That "the local people were sympathetic to the Vietcong," and had no complaints about NLF troops, who behaved most correctly in the villages; 2. That "the self-defense militia that Dau said the villagers hated were local military units recruited by the Government to protect its fortified hamlets"; 3. That "he thought the Vietcong, even without planes, 'would still win, because they already have two-thirds of the population in the South with them and they are skilled in guerrilla tactics.'" All three observations are emphatically corroborated by *both* Burchett and Halberstam (as to the behavior of Vietcong soldiers in the villages, for example, see Halberstam p. 91).

Halberstam's concluding chapter must therefore be regarded as an extraordinary illustration of the irrational logic of American policy. This hard-headed and painstaking reporter arrives at a set of conclusions markedly at variance with the evidence patiently accumulated throughout the book. Reflecting on the alternatives available to us, he realizes at one point:

> *American combat troops would create exactly the same situation as the French had; they would turn the entire population in favor of the Vietcong.*

In another place he concludes:

> The [strategic] hamlet program was what Homer Bigart referred to as
> 'another American gimmick,' one more attempt to change what was unal-
> terable under the Diem regime: that the Vietcong were more effective with
> the peasants, were more dedicated and had better leadership. Vast amounts
> of American resources went into the program; so committed were we to
> it that there was general agreement in those days that if the effort failed, *it
> would be clear that our side had nothing to offer the peasants* (my italics) and that
> the Government was bankrupt at the rural level.

Nevertheless, the man who wrote these sentences also writes that America
should stay in Vietnam "playing our part of the bargain as best we can."

If Halberstam's inconsistency can be grasped from within, current American
policy will be understood for the desperate thing it is. He himself provides
the clue. Referring to President Kennedy's escalation of the conflict in 1961,
Halberstam comments, "the essence of our policy was: *There is no place else to go.*"
Even after the Kennedy escalation failed (the burden of Halberstam's book is the
documentation of that failure), Johnson's escalation could still seem attractive
because frustrated American advisers felt they had never had a chance to show
what they could do if really in charge. Halberstam says that "anyone watching so much bravery squandered during those months could not have helped
wondering what would happen if that talent were properly employed." In other
words, both the American-on-the-spot who knew the Vietcong were winning
and the Pentagon planners who believed their own propaganda that they were
not, are drawn ultimately to the same place—limitless escalation—because they
saw no alternative. Yet, with his extraordinary occasional insight into American
motives, Halberstam notes that this lure may be deceptive, and that if his evaluation of the military situation erred, it was not in being too pessimistic but in
being too optimistic about the possibility of victory.

The hero of this book is Lieutenant Colonel John Vann, who resigned from
the armed services when the Chiefs of Staff refused to consider his detailed
demonstration that the war in Vietnam was being lost; that, for example, low
casualty figures interpreted by the Pentagon as evidence of Saigon success simply meant that the Diem troops "were doing very little fighting at all." The man
who blocked consideration of Vann's ideas was General Victor Krulak, the man
now commanding our marines in Danang.

There is of course somewhere else to go than toward escalation. Burchett
says that there "is only one way out: complete withdrawal from Vietnam."
Halberstam rejects this course on grounds of "honor." If he better understood
the background of the story whose foreground he so brilliantly narrates, he

would recognize that we asked ourselves into Vietnam and play there the role of the Hessian mercenaries who fought George Washington. (This is not an idle comparison. The *New York Times* of June 2 stated that 25,000 South Koreans are reported scheduled for shipment to Vietnam this month.) Halberstam mentions bitterly the young civil rights worker who congratulated him on his coverage of America's "colonial war." The young man had it right. And it is hardly comforting to be told that the man who in 1961 sponsored the neo-colonial strategy of "counter-insurgency" and who, once counter-insurgency had failed, directed the new strategy of using American ground troops, belong to "what is known in Washington as the 'Never Again Club' . . . a phrase meaning that its members never again wanted to place American combat troops on the mainland of Asia without atomic weapons."

Document 4

"WITHDRAWAL IN RETURN FOR FREE ELECTIONS,"
5 SEPTEMBER 1965

Staughton Lynd writes this letter to the editor of the *New York Times* in response to an editorial of 25 August 1965, in which the editors of the *Times* outline just "how far Washington has moved in its readiness to facilitate peace talks." Specifically referring to the appearance on CBS of Secretary of State Dean Rusk, United Nations ambassador Arthur Goldberg, and national security adviser McGeorge Bundy, the editors argue that "Washington and Hanoi seem to be within negotiating distance" except for the two conditions Hanoi places on the opening of talks: (1) that the National Liberation Front represent South Vietnam in negotiations, and (2) that Hanoi demands a coalition government in South Vietnam, meaning de facto communist control. For the *Times*, the editors conclude, "Ways undoubtedly can be found to narrow these differences once Hanoi decides, as Washington clearly has, that it too wants a negotiated settlement."[28]

To the Editor:

Does the United States really want a negotiated settlement in Vietnam? The present differences between the Johnson Administration and the National Liberation Front negotiating positions seem to be:

As *The Times* has observed, the United States still does not see the necessity of dealing directly with the N.L.F. To understand the position in which this places N.L.F. leaders one might recall the indignation felt by John Adams, John Jay and Benjamin Franklin in 1782 when the English Government attempted to make peace behind the backs of Americans with America's French allies.

The Johnson Administration is apparently now willing to contemplate what the United States rejected in 1956—namely, free elections. But North Vietnam and the N.L.F. now apparently feel that the people of South Vietnam have "voted with their feet" by giving much stronger support to the alternative administration of the N.L.F. than to the Government at Saigon; hence they demand the creation of a coalition government with key ministries controlled by the N.L.F.

Evidently the United States insists that its troops remain in South Vietnam during the negotiating process to insure fair play and to afford protection to those closely connected with the Saigon Government. On the other hand the N.L.F., fearing that American troops would be used as in Santo Domingo to influence the outcome of negotiations, demands either the physical removal of troops, agreement on a timetable for their withdrawal, or some combination of the two, before negotiations begin.

I suggest that if the United States is serious in returning to the principle of self-determination—that is, if we are truly prepared to see South Vietnam go Communist if that is what its people desire—the obstacles to a negotiated peace which these three differences present are not insuperable.

The United States is on strong ground in asking for free elections, since this was a part of the Geneva Agreements to which the N.L.F. and North Vietnam say they wish to return. The presence of American troops and American military bases also violates the Geneva Agreements.

Could we not offer to negotiate directly with the N.L.F., suggesting that the United States would agree to a phased withdrawal of the American military presence in return for N.L.F. agreement to free elections under international supervision?

26 August 1965

Document 5

"REVOLUTION AND THE CITIZEN'S MORAL RESPONSIBILITY,"
REMARKS AT THE TORONTO INTERNATIONAL TEACH-IN,
11 OCTOBER 1965

Staughton Lynd participated at the International Teach-In at the University
of Toronto, which was simultaneously broadcast on the radio in Canada and
the United States. Estimates vary over the weekend teach-in, but roughly
four thousand people were in attendance to hear Lynd speak, and up to one
million listened on the radio on both sides of the border.[29] Organized by a
teach-in committee of University of Toronto students and faculty, the event
featured other speakers such as Robert Scalapino (professor of political sci-
ence, University of California at Berkeley), Zbigniew Brzezinski (professor
of government, Columbia University), Cheddi Jagan (former prime minister
of the British colony of Guiana and leading Latin American Marxist), and
Lord Fenner Brockway (a British Labour Party politician).[30]

There is another American poem, by Robinson Jeffers, which begins:

"As this America settles heavily to empire
And protest, like a bubble in the molten mass,
Sighs and goes out; and the mass hardens;
Shine, perishing republic."

I confess that I speak in such a mood: as a citizen who, in a revolutionary world,
belongs to that once-revolutionary nation which now seeks to crush revolutions
outside itself and in the process destroys its own revolutionary past. I feel separated by a great distance from those American liberals who sense what it means
for women to be burned alive and children to be torn apart by hand grenades
as they cower in underground shelters, but who, like the Pope in *The Deputy*,
believe that stopping Communism has the highest priority and so sadly do
nothing.

There are persons who find it easy passionately to condemn American intervention in Santo Domingo because there were no Communists there; but who
find Vietnam, where to my mind America's violation of justice and morality
is just as clearcut and on a far greater scale, very complex—because there are
Communists.

As teachers and as students we are asked to imagine our lives as intellectuals
under a future Communist regime. But somehow for those who ask this question

it is enough to say the magic word "communism" to blur the present reality of the South Vietnamese lawyer sentenced to 20 years hard labor in August for leading a peace demonstration, and the three youths shot on the soccer field at Danang 11 days ago for the same crime.

These, we are told are "mistakes." I am reminded of Russians who visiting this country shortly after Stalin's death described his misdeeds with the same word: "oshibki," mistakes.

And I raced through my Russian-English dictionary to find the Russian word for "sin." As a historian, I have no doubt that when the Twenty First Century writes the history of Vietnam, they will call it a sin.

I feel despair about the apparent American belief that our armed services and Central Intelligence Agency can make and unmake governments all over the world but that democracy at home, somehow sealed off from such unpleasantness, will not be affected.

As an American citizen I feel it would be a grotesque presumption to give advice to those whom my government bombs and burns. An American citizen speaking on this subject must first ask forgiveness; and next, address himself to the specific responsibility of the citizen who is an American.

Yet I should like to say one word addressed to citizens of any nation. At a given historical moment some nations will be more closely aligned with the aspirations of mankind while others tend to work against the grain of men's hopes. But citizens of every nation should feel the challenge of the words: Above all nations, humanity; should aspire to the vision in a happier day, of America's Tom Paine: My country is the world, my countrymen are all mankind. Today, even those nations most entitled to sympathy and admiration of mankind—such as revolutionary Vietnam—should feel pressure from world public opinion to observe rules of war which represent the cumulative conscience of humanity. Despite my sense of shame for being an American citizen in the year 1965, I feel I must say this.

An American citizen's primary responsibility, however, is at home. How should he act? To what philosophy of political process should he adhere? What models, what guidelines exist for him to follow?

One such model is religious pacifism. Personally, I am a Quaker and a conscientious objector. In a time when any war can become a nuclear war, and all wars increasingly involve innocent civilians, the pacifist position ought to challenge every potential soldier. Yet as a historian I find that many corollary assumptions traditionally asserted by pacifists are untrue. It isn't true that in all conflict situations both sides are equally to blame. Nor is it true that violence never accomplishes anything constructive.

For those who are not religious pacifists and who live in nations like Canada, England or the United States, the problem is often felt to be simple. Surely in a democracy what one should do is petition, demonstrate and vote on behalf of one's convictions, in the faith that sooner or later public opinion and governmental decision-making will respond. But the problem is not so simple. This model too has its difficulties. Here are three:

1. Today decisions of a single nation can have catastrophic consequences for all mankind. Does one nation have the right to decide, simply because it decides democratically, that the rest of the world should be annihilated? It does not. Were the United States Congress formally to declare war in Vietnam, would that oblige an American citizen to support the war? Not as I see it. This is the first difficulty with the democratic model.

2. Serious question arises as to how democratic these democracies any longer are. Consider America's decision to bomb North Vietnam. During the 1964 Presidential Campaign Mr. Johnson said "so we are not going North." Hard as it is to believe, that was just one year ago. Mr. Johnson was elected, according to analysts such as Theodore White, above all because voters felt that his opponent was too warlike. Three months after his election the President made a secret decision to do what he had said in the campaign he would not do. There was no emergency as in Korea to lend possible justification to such secrecy. Congress failed to debate the matter, as its constitutional responsibility to declare war required it to. To this day the Foreign Relations Committee of the House and Senate have not held public hearings. For two months the President even refused to explain his decision; and since then we have had a series of shifting explanations which show no decent respect for the opinion of America, let alone the opinion of mankind.

   Is this democracy? When the executive acts so fast and loose with democratic procedures, is the citizen bound to write letters and petition, to pretend that business is as usual, to act as if a constitutional crisis did not exist? I think not. This is the second difficulty with the democratic model.

3. The third difficulty springs from the rulings of the Nuremberg Tribunal after World War II. There the United States said to German soldiers that they should have disobeyed orders to commit war crimes or crimes against humanity. I cannot see that this principle is affected by whether or not that order is the product of a democratic political process: whether for example, it issues from an officer commanded by the President in turn instructed by a Congressional Declaration of War. And it is clear that

American servicemen have committed in Vietnam some of the actions explicitly defined at Nuremberg as war crimes and crimes against humanity. For example, *Time* magazine for Aug. 6, 1965—the 20th anniversary of Hiroshima—states on p. 29 that marines have begun to kill prisoners. Chris Koch reports from Vietnam that we have begun to bomb the Red River dykes. Yesterday's newspaper states that American forces will henceforth use gas warfare routinely. It can be argued that a literal interpretation of the Nuremberg proceedings obliges a citizen to allow himself to be drafted and to refuse to commit such an action only when actually ordered to do so. But even if one accepted this interpretation as binding, which I do not, does this mean that there is no such thing as a point when barbarous practices become characteristic of an entire war? An American serving in the Air Force must assume that he will be ordered to bomb unprotected villages containing unarmed women and children on the suspicion that guerrillas may be there, for this has become the routine of the Air Force in Vietnam. I would find it quite in accord with the spirit if not the letter of Nuremberg for a conscientious and responsible American to refuse to have anything to do with the Air Force, even to disaffiliate himself in every possible way from the entire war effort.

Thus the third difficulty of the democratic model is that in Vietnam it runs head-on into certain ethical imperatives which since Nuremberg also have some force at law.

What then is to be done, if one is not a religious pacifist and is a citizen of a nominally democratic society fighting a war like America's war in Vietnam?

To my mind the most difficult problem stems from the fact that our responsibility is not merely to denounce the war; not merely to disaffiliate ourselves personally from it; but to stop it. This raises questions which go far beyond the familiar conundrum: When is it just to break an unjust law? What we are driven to confront is the phenomenon of an entire government acting in a manner which has been variously described as arrogant and self-righteous or, by Walter Lippmann, as an attempt to be policeman for the world. Other centuries described the same phenomenon with phrases such as "drunk with power," "possessed by a spirit of evil" and—this was how the Declaration of Independence put it—responsible for a long train of abuses exhibiting a fixed malevolent design. In a nutshell: Some of us feel that America's ill doing borders on that which in classical democratic theory has justified revolution. Yet it is clear that a majority of American citizens, at least for the moment, more or less support President Johnson's Vietnam policy. How should democrats respond to this dilemma?

I find that the theory and practice of nonviolent civil disobedience offer one path forward. In acting nonviolently the aggrieved citizen brings at least the immediate consequences of his action on himself, not on others. He does not coerce the majority. By putting his body in the way, metaphorically or tangibly, the nonviolent demonstrator asks his fellow-citizens to wonder why someone should act so bizarrely. He asks them, by his own willingness to absorb inconvenience or suffering on behalf of nonconformist beliefs, to reconsider the rationale of their policy. The fabric of law has grown through such actions. When Star Chamber asked John Lilburne to testify against himself he refused, saying that he knew this was against the law of God and he thought it was against the law of England. And thus the law of England changed.

When conventional channels of protest have been clogged—and I believe my President in his hubris has seen to that—then nonviolent disobedience can be brought to bear on public decision-making, too. There is a spectrum of possible actions ranging from the individual's refusal to pay taxes or serve in the armed forces, through demonstrations appealing over the head of one's government to world public opinion, to acts of obstruction such as blocking troop trains or climbing aboard Polaris submarines. In a nation which lacks the responsiveness of a parliamentary system and in which Congress has, for the moment, abdicated its duty, actions of this kind may seem the only possible way to express a decisive vote of no-confidence and to seek a change in administration.

Such action need not be wholly negative. Those who feel with anguish that their government has not only done what it should not have done, but also left undone that which it should have performed, can proceed to fill that vacuum with their own acts. Let me suggest three such acts. This could mean young Americans going to North Vietnam to rebuild hospitals and schools destroyed by American bombing, and to act while they are there as inadvert hostages. It could mean deliberately defying the Logan Act to negotiate directly with the National Liberation Front.

Americans might today make peace with the NLF on behalf of those who feel themselves unrepresented by our delinquent Congress. Conceivably they could go to Vietnam and bring home an agreement signed both by Americans and by representatives of the NLF. This agreement could be presented to a parallel Congress, a new Continental Congress of freedom parties, student groups and ghetto community unions for ratification, and then nailed to the doors of the Capitol in Washington.

First steps of some sort are available to all of us. The one certain moral responsibility of a citizen in a revolutionary world is that, whatever his beliefs, he should speak them with his life. In Thoreau's words, we must vote the whole of ourselves; in his words also, we must be men first and Americans at a late and convenient hour. To do this may mean going into a kind of exile within one's own country. We may be stripped of the rights of citizenship, like Eugene Debs for protesting World War I. Then we can respond as Debs did: They have made me a citizen of the world. Only he can become a citizen of the world who is ready to fight for humanity within his own country.

Beneath all questions of strategy, then, emerges the question of creating an opposition life-style, of learning how to live day by day in a way which begins to build a radically new society. Immediately this means, how should one respond to the draft? And I should like to make this suggestion that in addition to asking young men to consider going to jail rather than fighting, we create a parallel selective service system; that outside every induction center there be a table where a young man (or woman) can sign up for two years of service at constructive work in America or abroad; so that rather than blankly oppose the selective service system, we begin to create a planned economy of our own, offering the young people of America the challenge to what William James called the moral equivalent to war, an initiation into an adult society which meets and respects their desire to serve rather than ignoring or destroying it; and that when called for induction, those so registered actually begin to perform the tasks for which they volunteered, compelling the American Government, if it insists on conscripting their bodies, to drag them away from planting trees and building dams, from treating the sick and bringing aid to the afflicted. Thus could we take the first step to bring to pass the great vision of that line from a play of the Nineteen Thirties. "Someday they'll have a war and nobody will come."

Document 6

"MR. LYND ON VIETNAM," 4 NOVEMBER 1965

Lynd originally submitted this letter to the *New York Times*, but it was rejected for publication. He then submitted the letter in its entirety to the *Yale Daily News*. Here Lynd responds to the various charges lobbed against the antiwar movement in the aftermath of the International Days of Protest in October.

To the Chairman of the *News*:

Two major charges have been brought against those who demonstrate against the war in Vietnam. First, it is said that the demonstrators actually prolong the war by encouraging Hanoi and the N.L.F. to decline negotiations in the hope that anti-war sentiment in the United States will grow. Second, the demonstrators are charged with reckless disregard for democratic process and the authority of law.

Why do Hanoi and the N.L.F. decline to negotiate? On Oct. 15 Max Frankel of the *Times* described their reasoning as follows: Hanoi "contends that the real United States objective is the more-or-less permanent division of Vietnam into two states and a long military occupation of South Vietnam," while the N.L.F. "would not participate in arrangements that did not win for them some kind of political legitimacy." Despite the United States government's claim that it has repeatedly offered to negotiate "unconditionally," it remains the case that the United States still refuses to deal directly with the N.L.F. Further, the United States has failed to make it unmistakably clear that if free elections under international supervision were to result in an N.L.F.-dominated government in South Vietnam, we would (as we did not in 1956) acquiesce in the results. Nor has the United States unequivocally stated that it would be prepared to withdraw all or part of its armed forces in South Vietnam before such elections were held.

Under these circumstances, it seems not quite fair to blame Communist refusal to negotiate on American demonstrators alone. A member of my faith (the Quakers) who talked with representatives from Hanoi and N.L.F. this summer reported: "They will fight until they are crushed or are victorious before they will agree to continued U.S. military presence in Vietnam. If U.S. military withdrawal is firmly assured and somehow guaranteed, they will negotiate on timing of the withdrawal, a general referendum, etc."

Actually, the American government's decision to abandon efforts to negotiate for the time being, to defer all thought of a pause in bombing, and to resign itself to a long war was reported by the *Wall Street Journal* (Oct. 14), the *Times* (Oct. 15) and the *New York Herald Tribune* (Oct. 15) before the recent weekend of demonstrations. The demonstrators are saying in effect that the possibilities of negotiation have not been exhausted and that this decision is premature.

As to democratic process and legality. Congressmen in particular should consider the substantial lack of democracy and illegality in American decision-making about this war. There has been no declaration of war, as required by the United States Constitution. Article I, Section 8 of the Constitution does not say that the declaration of war shall be "on recommendation of the President," or "by the President with advice and consent of Congress." In the words of Justice Jackson in *Youngstown Sheet and Tube Company v. Sawyer* (1952): "Nothing in our Constitution is plainer than that declaration of war is entrusted only to Congress."

President Johnson rests his escalation of the war in Vietnam on the Tonkin Bay Joint Resolution of August 6–7, 1964 (H.J. Res. 1145) which states in part: "[Congress] approves and supports the determination of the President, as Commander-in-Chief, to take all necessary measures to repel any armed attack against the forces of the United States and to prevent further aggression." It is altogether unclear whether in February 1965 either armed attack against American forces or aggression from North Vietnam existed on anything like the scale of the American response. But apart from that, H.J. Res. 1145 also stated that any steps taken by the President should be "consonant . . . with the Charter of the United Nations and in accordance with its obligations under the Southeast Asia Collective Defense Treaty."

The Charter of the United Nations is a presently effective treaty binding upon the Government of the United States as part of the "Supreme Law of the Land." The Charter (Chapters I, VII) directs its members to refrain from the threat or use of force, and gives the Security Council responsibility to "determine the existence of any threat to the peace, breach of the peace, or act of aggression." The major exception to these provisions is Chapter VII, Article 51: "Nothing in the present Charter shall impair the inherent right of individual or collective self-defense if an armed attack occurs against a member of the United Nations, until the Security Council has taken measures to maintain international peace and security." This clause is clearly inapplicable to American action in Vietnam, for: (a) The 1954 Geneva Conference expressly stipulated that neither North or South Vietnam were independent sovereign states; (b) South Vietnam is not a member of the United Nations.

Chapter VIII, Article 53 of the Charter authorizes the Security Council to utilize regional arrangements for enforcement action. This might appear to justify United States action under the SEATO treaty. But again: (a) The immediately following sentence states that "no enforcement action shall be taken under regional arrangements or by regional agencies without the authorization of the Security Council"; (b) The United States has not sought formal SEATO approval of its Vietnam action because the SEATO Treaty requires that there be no dissenting vote among the signatories respecting action under the Treaty, and France, a signatory, has refused to support America's intervention.

Even if the United States Congress had declared war, and even if the United States had secured approval from the Security Council of the United Nations, many demonstrators would argue the legality of their refusal to take part in this war by appealing to the judgments of the Nuremberg Tribunal. One of the "war crimes" defined by Article 6 of the Charter of the Tribunal was "murder or ill treatment of prisoners of war." *Time* magazine for Aug. 6, 1965 (the twentieth anniversary of the bombing of Hiroshima) states on p. 29: "The marines have begun to kill prisoners." It should also be noted that the Geneva Convention of 1949 on the Treatment of Prisoners of War and War Victims, signed by the United States (1955) and South Vietnam (1953), extends to "conflicts not of an international nature" (i.e. civil wars); and that failure of the enemy to observe the rules of war does not justify the other belligerent in non-observance, for according to the Nuremberg Tribunal these rules of war are binding even against a non-signatory "as declaratory of international law."

It has happened before in American history that conscientious men whom history books now praise as heroes have deliberately broken American law in the name of a "higher law." Such was the case when abolitionists defied the Fugitive Slave Law of 1850 and the Supreme Court's Dred Scott decision (1857), which stated that Negroes never had been or could be American citizens. Today, civil disobedience against the war in Vietnam has the legal sanction of the United Nations Charter as part of the supreme law of the land, and of the Nuremberg Tribunal.

The great majority of demonstrators deeply sympathize with the plight of their fellow-citizens in the armed services in Vietnam, and do not wish to avoid danger or sacrifice. They are attempting to say by their actions: This war is illegal, immoral, and contrary to the cherished American principle of self-determination; and it must stop.

Staughton Lynd
Asst. Prof. of History

Document 7

"MAKE LOVE NOT WAR: THE CAMPAIGN AGAINST THE DRAFT," DECEMBER 1965

Staughton Lynd participates in an exchange in *Liberation* on the movement against the draft with two members of the Students for a Democratic Society (SDS): national secretary Paul Booth and Richard Rothstein, member of the national staff. At this point, after the successful March on Washington the previous April, SDS stepped back from a national campaign against the Vietnam War and the draft. This left the door open to much confusion about the organization's future plans and encouraged the growth of independent student and non-student organizations to oppose the draft. In addition to Lynd, Booth lays out the SDS plan to organize draftees to apply en masse for conscientious objector status, and Rothstein describes the efforts of the organization to respond to the investigation launched by the Justice Department in October. The following document describes a third strategy, proposed by Lynd.

No task is more urgent for the anti-war movement than clarifying its response to the draft. I should like to offer ten propositions for discussion:

1. The draft brings the war to American young men as a decision to be made, as a moral question. The task for the anti-war movement is to help those exposed to the draft to understand their individual plights as parts of a general, political problem; to break out of their isolation and act together, politically—but *not* to dull or smother a deeply personal immediate response of moral outrage.

2. Most young men who oppose the war in Vietnam are conscientiously opposed to this war only. They may be clear in their minds that they *would* fight in a just war; or, in the existential manner of the New Left, they may feel that they have light to act only in the present situation and do not know how they would respond to a hypothetical future war.

3. It is important, even for those who reject the Selective Service System entirely, to seek to have the legal definition of conscientious objection broadened to include men like David Mitchell whose objection is to a particular war or a particular (e.g. imperialist) kind of war.

4. Protesters should *be* conscientious. Young men should be encouraged to ask for Form 150 if they conscientiously object to the war but are unsure

whether the draft board will give them I-Ostatus. They should not be encouraged to use Form 150 to make it difficult for the Selective Service System to function; if one wishes to prevent a troop train or draft board from functioning, one should do so openly and forthrightly.

5. We need to convince American public opinion that we are not mere refusers, that we are willing to expose ourselves to danger in socially-useful service. I think this is important psychologically for the individual draft refuser also. I believe that for many struggling with the draft the charge of "slacker" and "traitor" gets under the skin more than they may readily concede.

6. This does *not* necessarily mean serving in the Peace Corps, or doing any other task, however constructive in itself, as an employee of the United States Government or under its direction.

7. Nor does a willingness to do positive self-sacrificial service necessarily mean willingness to perform alternative service, however constructive in itself, under the Selective Service System.

8. Nevertheless, I believe a way can be found whereby young men exposed to the draft could express their refusal to fight in a positive as well as negative manner. Suppose we created a parallel selective service system. Suppose that across the street from every draft board and induction center there were a table where young men could register for two years of constructive work: work which might be in the United States or abroad (including Vietnam); work which the registrants might already be doing, in radical activity North and South; above all, work which the registrant would most want to be doing, war or no war, which is, so far as he can tell, his genuine "vocation" for the next two years. Suppose that such parallel registration were available both to men applying also for governmental permission to do their chosen work as alternative service under the draft, *and* to persons conscientiously refusing to have anything to do with the Selective Service System. Finally, if such parallel registrants were called for induction and still felt conscientiously obliged to refuse to fight in Vietnam, suppose that they inducted themselves into the moral equivalent of war (if they had not previously done so) by proceeding—preferably in groups—to do that constructive work which they themselves had chosen, so that if the government came to jail them, it would find them engaged in activities such as teaching children or registering voters.

9. Women in the movement have particular problems of guilt because of the draft. They, too, could register for constructive work with the parallel Selective Service System.

10. For many, constructive work, even if self-chosen and non-governmental, will seem inadequate; for them, full-time, all-out, frontal opposition to the war itself will be the only acceptable vocation in the present movement.

Document 8

"AN EXCHANGE ON VIETNAM," 23 DECEMBER 1965

Staughton Lynd replies to an article in the *New York Review of Books* titled "The Vietnam Protest," by Irving Howe, Michael Harrington, Bayard Rustin, Lewis Coser, and Penn Kemble. The authors of the article were critical of the efforts of the radical antiwar movement for engaging in tactics that would alienate other Americans who supported the war or who were just beginning to ask the tough questions about the conflict. The authors presented a set of proposals that would bring together the broadest coalition of "the labor, Negro, church, and academic communities" who otherwise supported the Johnson administration. The article took specific aim at the use of slogans, the effort to organize the movement "around a full-scale analysis of the Vietnam situation," or "assign historical responsibility for the present disaster to one or another side" as individuals or groups were capable of doing this themselves. Moreover, the heart of the article was critical of the use of civil disobedience and comparisons with the civil rights movement and urged those opposed to the war to use this tactic as a last resort. Furthermore, the authors drew a distinction around the pacifist tradition of conscientious objection to all wars and the current rumblings of the draft resistance movement to apply for the status. The authors were critical of groups applying for CO status who were not absolute conscientious objectors and argued for maintaining the difference "between individual moral objection and a political protest movement." Finally, the article presented what the authors believed could be a common set of proposals to organize a protest movement around:

a) We urge the U.S. immediately to cease bombing North Vietnam;

b) We urge the U.S. to declare its readiness to negotiate with the NLF, the political arm of the Vietcong;

c) We urge the U.S. to propose to Hanoi and the Vietcong an immediate cease-fire as a preliminary to negotiations;

d) We urge that the U.S. recognize the right of the South Vietnamese freely to determine their own future, whatever it may be, without interference from foreign troops, and possibly under United Nations supervision;

e) We urge Hanoi and the Vietcong to accept a proposal for a cease-fire and to declare themselves ready for immediate and unconditional negotiations.[31]

In this article, Lynd argues that there is one basic issue, which the statement under consideration wholly ignores. That issue is when will the United States withdraw all the troops that the Vietnamese consider a hostile foreign force that is occupying their country?

To the Editors:

In their statement on "The Vietnam Protest" (*NYRB*, Nov. 25) Messrs. Howe, Harrington, Rustin, Coser and Kemble spoke of "a few professors" who shared with a larger number of students the tendency to "transform the protest into an apocalypse, a 'final conflict,' in which extreme gestures of opposition will bring forth punitive retaliation from the authorities." I believe I am one of the professors they have in mind, and I wonder if I may have the opportunity to respond?

First let me say that I for one welcome a variety of forms of protest, including those recommended by your correspondents. One reason I believe that extreme forms of protest during the summer and fall have been helpful is that, far from leading to the disappearance of more moderate dissent, they have stimulated it. Witness the forthcoming SANE-sponsored march on Washington, the newly-formed committee for Reappraisal of Far Eastern Policy, and indeed, your correspondents' statement. Many persons who last Spring were silent are now taking a more forthright position.

However, just as Mr. Howe and his colleagues see dangers in blocking troop trains or advocating resistance to the draft, so I see dangers in their proposals. They say that the protest movement should urge that the United States immediately stop bombing North Vietnam; that the United States declare its readiness to negotiate with the NLF; that the United States propose an immediate cease-fire as a preliminary to negotiations; that the United States "recognize the right of the South Vietnamese freely to determine their own future, whatever it may be, without interference from foreign troops, and possibly under United Nations supervision"; and finally, that Hanoi and the NLF accept the proposed cease-fire and declare their readiness to negotiate.

The central weakness of these proposals is their vagueness as to the withdrawal of American troops. Last spring, before the massive build-up of American forces in South Vietnam, it may have been sufficient to call for an end to bombing and direct negotiation with the NLF. Now that 160,000 American servicemen are there any negotiating proposal must make it crystal clear that a cease-fire would not mean the indefinite presence of United States troops. Clarity on this point is the more urgent because of several recent statements by high-ranking decision-makers. On October 12 the *New York Times* reported a statement by Senator Stennis that United States' troops would have to stay in

Vietnam "possibly for 15 years or longer" after the fighting ends. On October 26 the same newspaper reported a statement by the Army Chief of Staff, Gen. Harold K. Johnson, that United States troops might have to stay in Vietnam after the shooting stops to protect "the security of the people and the process of nation-building." The general was quoted as saying: "Even if the level and scope of hostilities in Vietnam were to decline, a sudden phasedown in our strength would not necessarily follow."

Note especially that, according to this same *Times* article, General Johnson also said that he favored a start on peace talks. The experience of Santo Domingo warns how troops which stay on after a cease-fire can be used as a club to influence "the process of nation-building." For this reason, even if President Johnson were to adopt as his own the proposals of "The Vietnam Protest," they would undoubtedly be rejected by the other side. Once more the President would say that his peacemaking efforts had been rebuffed. When the enemy's refusal to negotiate on this basis became evident, bombing of North Vietnam would be resumed; meantime the far more terrible bombing of South Vietnam would go on unchecked. In effect, by offering proposals which Hanoi and the NLF were bound to reject the authors of "The Vietnam Protest" would have assisted the President self-righteously to continue the war.

Mr. Howe and his collaborators base their proposals on the understandable conception that "the central need of the moment" is "an end to the bloodletting." But those against whom the United States fights apparently do not view the situation this way. They want, literally, liberty or death. For three times the length of America's War for Independence they have struggled to oust foreign intruders. They will not stop fighting if that means de facto American domination of South Vietnam. According to Neil Sheehan, writing from Saigon for the *New York Times* on October 23, de facto domination is precisely what the United States intends: the Johnson Administration, Sheehan says, has made it clear to Hanoi "that it will not countenance a Communist South Vietnam or the creation of any coalition regime in Saigon which *might* [italics mine] lead to a Communist seizure of power." As I see it, the difficulty with the program suggested in "The Vietnam Protest" is that it offers Hanoi and the NLF no concrete assurances that if the people of South Vietnam desire a Communist government, the United States will let them have it.

Your correspondents have much to say about the "impotence" of those who oppose the war by direct action and civil disobedience, about our "failure to affect the actual course of events." But to offer negotiations on conditions which (however reasonable they may sound to a broad coalition of concerned Americans) are sure to be rejected by the other side, is also a formula for futility.

Now I readily concede that it will not be easy to explain to the American people why the United States must offer unilateral withdrawal of its troops if there is to be peace in Vietnam. To explain this requires just that "full-scale analysis of the Vietnam situation" which Messrs. Howe *et al.* believe to be impossible in a broadly-based protest movement. But at this point, is it not they who have yielded to "impatience"? There is no shortcut to the truth. Most of those known to me who have taken the lead in direct action against the war have also spent night after night, week after week, on lecture platforms around the country presenting a "full-scale analysis of the Vietnam situation." May we not ask at least that Mr. Howe and his associates join us in this effort?

The authors of "The Vietnam Protest" deplore sectarianism yet they propose to ban from their coalition anyone who gives "explicit or covert political support to the Vietcong." There follows the remarkable statement that this condition is "both a tactical necessity and a moral obligation." May I inquire why it is immoral to desire a Vietcong victory? I had thought that, just as during the American Revolution there were many Englishmen who hoped for a victory by the American colonists, so it would be only natural to expect that *some* sincere opponents of the Vietnam War should actively sympathize with the National Liberation Front. It seems that in excluding such persons Messrs. Howe *et al.* have in fact implicitly assumed a "full-scale analysis of the Vietnam situation" which others are required to accept unarticulated and unexamined.

The authors of "The Vietnam Protest" are at pains to distinguish civil disobedience against the war in Vietnam from civil disobedience in the Southern civil rights movement. This section of their argument concludes with the assertion that Southern civil rights demonstrators, in contrast to Vietnam war protestors, "acted in behalf of the legal norms and moral values to which the nation as a whole had given its approval." Isn't it the point that the nation had "given its approval" to racial equality in just that insubstantial sense in which it might now be said to have "given its approval" to the doctrine of loving one's enemies? In other words, isn't the effort in the one case as in the other to make the nation live up to concepts which it had endorsed in the abstract but which it had failed to practice?

Finally, I passionately object to the deprecation of those who blocked troop trains in California as "the action by a small minority to revoke through its own decision the policy of a democratically elected government." From where I sit, it was President Johnson and his Tuesday luncheon club—a very small minority indeed—who revoked through their own decision the policy to which they had pledged themselves in the 1964 election campaign ("so we are not going North") and to implement which the voters had elected them. Earlier in their

presentation, the authors of "The Vietnam Protest" insist that the escalation policy "has never been seriously debated in Congress or candidly presented to the
country." Nonetheless, it seems we are to regard it as "the policy of a democratically elected government."

This, in the words of Kipling's elephant child, is too much for me. I shall
continue to say "No" as an individual in every way open to me, at the same time
urging others to do likewise.

Staughton Lynd,
Department of History
Yale University

Document 9

"THE SUBSTANCE OF VICTORY," JANUARY 1966

Lynd comments on the 27 November 1965 Committee for a Sane Nuclear Policy (SANE) march against the Vietnam War. Uneasy with the more radical antiwar rallies and marches, the Committee for a Sane Nuclear Policy organized the March on Washington for Peace in Vietnam to show that moderate Americans opposed the war also.

Taking out a full-page spread in the *New York Times* on November 23, SANE put forth its arguments against the escalation of the war, proposals to end it, and an analysis of the conflict to date. "We see no gain coming from the war in Vietnam. We see only the growing victimization of the Vietnamese people, the erosion of a better society at home and the clear possibility of a world conflict." SANE implored the Johnson administration to take actions that "could lead more quickly to negotiations," which included calling for a cease-fire, halting the bombing of North Vietnam, and stopping the shipment of additional combat forces to South Vietnam and asking the same of the North Vietnamese. Moreover, in order to build such an agreement, the United States also needed to indicate its acceptance of the 1954 Geneva Accords as the basis for peace, negotiate with all parties to the conflict including the NLF, agree to the creation of a new representative government in South Vietnam, and agree that the United Nations or other international coalition would oversee the peace in Vietnam.[32]

Controversially, the march organizers released a list of "authorized slogans" and deployed up to three hundred monitors who walked through the crowd to encourage compliance with the requested decorum. The *New York Times* reported that "all the signs authorized by sponsors of the march stop short of calling for immediate withdrawal of troops." The *Times* included the list of accepted slogans: "self-determination—Vietnam for the Vietnamese," "Stop the bombings," "Talk with the N.L.F. and Hanoi," "Respect 1954 Geneva accords," "Representative government in Saigon," "New actions to speed negotiations," "Supervised cease-fire," and "Cease-fire—negotiate—bring the G.I.'s home."[33]

The SANE march on November 27th helped to keep dialogue about peace alive in the country. It showed that extreme acts of protest have not destroyed moderate forms of dissent, but stimulated them: thus, the SANE march, Americans for Reappraisal of Far Eastern Policy, the National Council of Churches statement, the *New Republic* demand for American withdrawal.

But there is a problem which the program of the SANE march didn't reach. In asking de-escalation leading to negotiations, SANE stayed away from the question of bringing American troops home. The other side, however, will certainly reject proposals of negotiation which do not give assurance as to American military withdrawal. Their fear is that a ceasefire without troop withdrawal would legitimize America's military presence, help to bring about a *de facto* partition of Vietnam. It is an understandable fear, for recently such policy-makers as Senator Stennis and the chairman of the Joint Chiefs of Staff have said that after an end to hostilities American troops might remain in Vietnam for years to "assist" in the process of nation-building." *New York Times'* correspondents Neil Sheehan, writing from Saigon, and Max Frankel, writing from Washington, agree that the actual American war aim is to keep Communism out of South Vietnam, even if that means rebuffing offers to negotiate, violating agreements to hold free elections, or keeping American troops in Vietnam indefinitely. On the SANE picket line I ran into Richard Dudman of the *St. Louis Post Dispatch*, a newsman who has tried to write the truth about the war, and he concurred in this picture of American intentions.

The problem, then, is that what America might conceivably offer (cease-fire and negotiations preceded by a pause in bombing of the North) would very likely be rejected by Hanoi and the N.L.F. unless the offer gave explicit guarantees about American troop withdrawal: for they want not merely peace, but control of their country's destiny at any cost (what Americans once called liberty or death); whereas President Johnson, even if he became convinced that his present course was mistaken and withdrawal admirable, would have to face accusations of "selling out" if after American withdrawal South Vietnam went—as it surely would go—Communist.

On each side there is emotion which deepens the dilemma. With the N.L.F. it is bitterness based on having relied on Western promises in the 1946 and 1954 negotiations only to see those promises callously broken. With the United States it is pride in never having lost a war and fear lest failure to win decisively in Vietnam open the dikes to Communism elsewhere. Neither side wants merely to save face, to achieve something with mirrors. Each side wants the substance of victory: control of South Vietnam.

This is—we must face it—close to an impossible situation. How should one act in an impossible situation? Beyond Vietnam there is the larger, equally impossible problem: how to bring about decisive social change in a sick imperialist society so affluent that it easily buys off possible dissent?

What gives me hope to keep trying is faith that a fraternal society is possible (a belief about human nature) and confidence that a majority of mankind wants such a society (a belief about history). Believing these things, one endures: acting, and acting if necessary alone. When all organizations have crumbled and all programs have failed, there remains the contagion of example.

CHAPTER 3
TO HANOI AND BACK

Introduction

Departing on 19 December 1965, without permission from the United States government, Staughton Lynd, Tom Hayden, and Herbert Aptheker traveled from New York's JFK Airport to London, Prague, Moscow, Beijing, and on to Hanoi. Hayden was a founding member of the Students for a Democratic Society (SDS) and Aptheker a historian and a leading theoretician of the Communist Party United States of America (CPUSA). The origins of the trip lay in Helsinki, Finland, where from July 10 to 15, 1965, Herbert Aptheker participated in the World Peace Congress (WPC). At this time, Aptheker and the youth wing of the CPUSA, the W. E. B. DuBois Clubs, were approached by members of the Peace Committee of North Vietnam and invited to travel to Hanoi. Aptheker was specifically asked by the Vietnamese to invite two other guests who were preferably noncommunists, and this led him to invite Lynd in September, and he left it to Lynd to find the second person. At Yale after the tumultuous summer of 1965, Lynd first approached Bob Moses to see if he would be interested in traveling to Hanoi. According to Lynd, Moses was interested but eventually turned down the offer because of the consequences such a trip would have for the Student Nonviolent Coordinating Committee (SNCC). Facing the last-minute possibility that another person could not be found in time, Lynd asked Hayden if he wanted to join Aptheker and himself. The twenty-six-year-old agreed.[1] Incidentally, this was not the first time the trio were together, as they shared the same stage for a panel discussion titled "the African American Movement" at a "Socialism in America" conference at Yale University on 1 May 1965.[2]

Figure 3.1: Staughton Lynd outside the city of Nam Dinh inspecting US bombing dam-age. *Foreground (left to right):* Do Xuan Oanh, interpreter and member of North Vietnamese Peace Committee, and Staughton Lynd. *Background:* Unidentified Vietnamese guide with Herbert Aptheker. Photograph courtesy of Staughton and Alice Lynd.

The trip was part of the nascent effort by the Democratic Republic of Vietnam (North Vietnam) to engage in what Ho Chi Minh called "people's diplomacy," otherwise known as unofficial or informal diplomacy. Conceived during the independence struggle against the French beginning in 1946, the Vietnamese revolutionaries established information offices in several countries and sent del-egations of unofficial diplomats to conferences to connect with various social and political movements in communist and noncommunist countries in order to garner sympathy for the Vietnamese revolution and decolonization. Beginning in 1964, the DRV began in earnest to attract world attention to the growing struggle against the United States by sending Vietnamese delegations to various conferences to speak and interact with delegations from other countries. The result would be a massive effort on the part of many Western peace activists to make connections with Vietnamese revolutionaries at diplomatic missions in Paris and at various conferences held around the world in places like Canada, Sweden, Cuba, Czechoslovakia, and elsewhere throughout the war, and by traveling to Vietnam itself. As historian Mary Hershberger demonstrates, over two hundred American activists and intellectuals traveled to North Vietnam, and by 1969 an average of one American delegation was traveling to Vietnam per month.[3]

The Lynd-Hayden-Aptheker trip to Hanoi illuminates the complex interplay between Vietnam War diplomacy, Vietnamese people's diplomacy with the American peace movement, and the history of US national security policy and counterintelligence in the Cold War more broadly. The Federal Bureau of Investigation was first tipped off about the trio's journey on December 8 by an unnamed informant using undisclosed techniques who themselves obtained the information on December 4.[4] The FBI received further notice of the trip when on December 13 a coworker of Fay Aptheker, Herbert Aptheker's wife, surreptitiously "secured" their plane tickets and itinerary and promptly passed the information to the bureau the next day.[5] Such trips were possibly illegal under US law and set into motion a two-month investigation by the FBI into the motives and intent of Lynd, Hayden, and Aptheker in order to make a case for prosecution in federal court under four distinct criminal statutes: (1) conspiracy against the United States (18 USC §371), (2) violation of the Cold War–era travel restrictions to communist countries (8 USC §1185(b)), (3) misuse of a passport (18 USC §1544), and (4) the Logan Act, which criminalized negotiations "with intent to influence the measures or conduct of any foreign government or of any officer or agent thereof, in relation to any disputes or controversies with the United States, or to defeat the measures of the United States" (18 USC §953).[6] The State Department revoked Lynd's, Hayden's, and Aptheker's passports twenty-five days after they returned to the United States, stating in its official letter, "The Department's action is based upon information that you travelled to and in communist controlled North Vietnam in violation of the restriction imposed by the United States Government on the travel of its citizens to and in that area."[7] After its lengthy investigation by the FBI, submitted in two reports on 25 January and 1 March 1966 to the Department of Justice, the trio were not indicted under federal law. Regarding the Logan Act, the assistant attorney general confirmed that they "received no information which would be helpful in proving an intent to influence the measures or conduct of the United States." Specific intent was the chief stumbling block to proving misuse of a passport, and recent court decisions at the time on Cold War travel restrictions possibly prevented such a prosecution under this statute.[8] Added to the problems affecting indictment was Lynd's preemptive lawsuit launched in federal court challenging these very travel restrictions. Despite the lack of prosecution by the government, this did not mean, of course, there were no other repercussions.

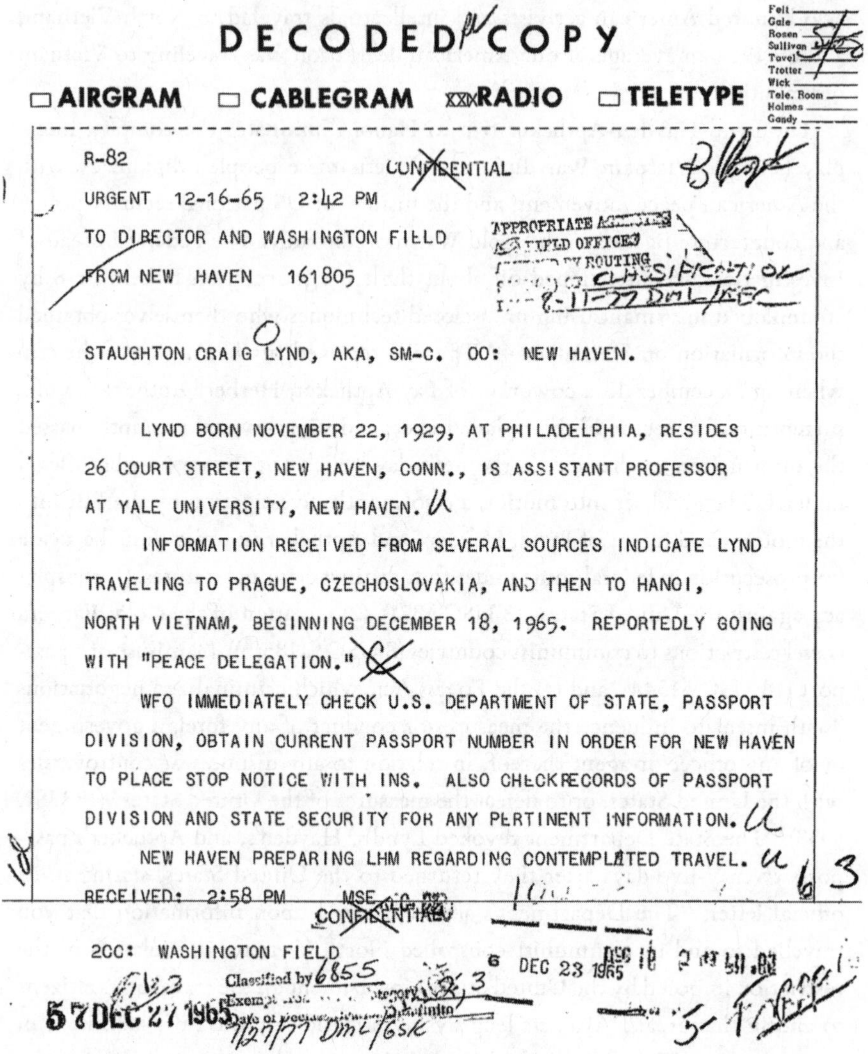
DECODED COPY

☐ AIRGRAM ☐ CABLEGRAM XXXRADIO ☐ TELETYPE

Felt
Gale
Rosen
Sullivan
Tavel
Trotter
Wick
Tele. Room
Holmes
Gandy

R-82 CONFIDENTIAL

URGENT 12-16-65 2:42 PM

TO DIRECTOR AND WASHINGTON FIELD

FROM NEW HAVEN 161805

APPROPRIATE AGENCIES AND FIELD OFFICES ADVISED BY ROUTING

STAUGHTON CRAIG LYND, AKA, SM-C. OO: NEW HAVEN.

LYND BORN NOVEMBER 22, 1929, AT PHILADELPHIA, RESIDES 26 COURT STREET, NEW HAVEN, CONN., IS ASSISTANT PROFESSOR AT YALE UNIVERSITY, NEW HAVEN.

INFORMATION RECEIVED FROM SEVERAL SOURCES INDICATE LYND TRAVELING TO PRAGUE, CZECHOSLOVAKIA, AND THEN TO HANOI, NORTH VIETNAM, BEGINNING DECEMBER 18, 1965. REPORTEDLY GOING WITH "PEACE DELEGATION."

WFO IMMEDIATELY CHECK U.S. DEPARTMENT OF STATE, PASSPORT DIVISION, OBTAIN CURRENT PASSPORT NUMBER IN ORDER FOR NEW HAVEN TO PLACE STOP NOTICE WITH INS. ALSO CHECK RECORDS OF PASSPORT DIVISION AND STATE SECURITY FOR ANY PERTINENT INFORMATION.

NEW HAVEN PREPARING LHM REGARDING CONTEMPLATED TRAVEL.

RECEIVED: 2:58 PM MSE

CONFIDENTIAL

2CC: WASHINGTON FIELD

DEC 23 1965

Classified by 6855
Exempt ...
Date of Declassification Indefinite

57 DEC 27 1965

Figure 3.2: Transcript of telephone report from FBI agent in New Haven to FBI headquarters. This is the first record in Lynd's FBI file reporting on his trip to North Vietnam. Source: Lynd's FBI file.

In public, there were many calls to prosecute the trio for treason, and government officials and commentators questioned their loyalty to the United States. Representative O. C. Fisher (D-Tex.) described the trio as "anti-American emissaries" who gave "aid and comfort to the enemy." As we have already seen, the language of treason was used by Yale University president Kingman Brewster when he criticized Lynd's address to a conference of Vietnamese intellectuals in Hanoi. Without Lynd's permission, the North Vietnamese released a text of Lynd's speech over Radio Hanoi, stating, in part, that US policy in Vietnam was "immoral, illegal and antidemocratic" and that the Johnson administration lied to the American public. While Lynd denied accusing Johnson of lying, he confirmed other aspects of the speech to the *New York Times*, stating in effect that he did not say anything in Hanoi that he had not already argued publicly in the United States. On January 19, Brewster released a statement arguing that Lynd "is entitled to these opinions; but the use of his presence in Hanoi to give this aid and comfort to a government engaged in hostilities with American forces seems to me inconsistent with the purposes of fact finding in the name of peace." As Carl Mirra demonstrates in his biography of Lynd, this controversy was a key domino to fall in Lynd's denial of tenure at Yale and blacklisting from the academy.[9]

As recent scholarship on DRV and NLF diplomacy demonstrates, after the Johnson administration escalated the war in February 1965 by instituting Operation Rolling Thunder, the North Vietnamese strengthened their resolve to fight and vowed to continue the struggle until military victory. This position was adopted because of the lessons of the Geneva Accords of 1954, which brought an end to the First Indochinese War with France but failed to bring the reunification of the temporarily partitioned North and South Vietnam through elections guaranteed to be scheduled in 1956. The US did not sign the Accords, the elections were abandoned, and the newly installed president of the Republic of Vietnam, Ngo Dinh Diem, fully supported by the Eisenhower administration, embarked on a campaign of violent repression against Vietnamese communists and political opponents in the South. Because of the failure of negotiations and reunification, anything short of an all-out military victory and withdrawal of US forces convinced Vietnamese officials that history would repeat itself as it had from 1954 to 1956. Utilizing newly opened Vietnamese archives, scholars of Vietnamese policy making and diplomacy skillfully demonstrate that, between 1965 and 1967, North Vietnam was committed to a military victory and its administration officials ruled out negotiations with the United States unless the US were to unilaterally halt the bombing of North Vietnam and accept the DRV's Four Points of April 1965 (see appendix D) as a basis for negotiations. While there was much debate among leaders of the Democratic Republic of Vietnam—with a faction calling for negotiation and another calling for military victory—the twin goals were the reunification of Vietnam under the auspices of the 1954 Geneva Accords and the establishment of socialism in the North, with the maximal goal of consolidating socialism in all of Vietnam. Moreover, the DRV and NLF did not trust US overtures for negotiations, as the US held out one hand with offers of peace and escalated the war in the North and South with the other. Without these core US concessions, which the Johnson administration was not prepared to make, the North Vietnamese rebuffed American efforts to negotiate until the the North Vietnamese softened their negotiating position toward the end of 1967.[10] A key question remains from this episode, despite the consensus on Hanoi's stiffening position: Would the North Vietnamese have agreed to negotiate if its demands were met—that is, if the US had uncondi-tionally stopped bombing North Vietnam, recognized the NLF, and signaled its willingness to deescalate by beginning to withdraw troops?

These facts were made painfully clear to Lynd as he talked to DRV and NLF representatives in Prague, Moscow, and Hanoi. En route to North Vietnam from China, Lynd wrote on his recently acquired Czechoslovakian typewriter, "Thus far, my impression is that no gimmick, no diplomatic skill, no offer of discrete concessions, and no amount of military power can bring this dreadful war to an end. The 'other side' wants one thing, and they will fight to the death for it: America must decide to withdraw."[11] Despite public statements to the contrary from the US government, Lynd came to understand more fully that the war was going to be a long and bloody one and that immediate withdrawal of American troops was the most realistic alternative to the course the Johnson administra-tion was then pursuing. These facts strengthened Lynd's resolve to argue, as he had throughout 1965, for immediate withdrawal of US troops when continuing to debate liberal peace advocates, social democrats, and conservatives such as William F. Buckley because of the realities on the ground in Vietnam. To Lynd, calls for a cease-fire and negotiation without a commitment on the part of the US to withdraw troops and stop the bombing would result in no concessions from the Vietnamese. This was an American-centric view of the conflict, and calls for face-saving measures or questions of prestige should not be precondi-tions to negotiations. This is crucial for trying to understand Lynd's mindset, especially as emerging critics of the war like Arthur Schlesinger Jr. were argu-ing that it was irresponsible to call for withdrawal even as the war began a new round of escalation at the end of January 1966.[12]

Outside of the expanding works on Vietnamese official diplomacy and peo-ple's diplomacy, there is now a well-established body of scholarship on diplo-macy during the presidency of Lyndon Johnson.[13] The critical year in question, 1965, was replete with public statements by all sides in the conflict and secret diplomacy. At the time Aptheker was invited to Hanoi in mid-July, President Johnson had not yet announced the troop surge and increased draft calls, and the administration was largely winning the public relations battle, convincing the media and the American people that the United States sought only peace in

Vietnam. On April 7 at Johns Hopkins University, the president announced that the United States was open to "unconditional discussions," and much effort was made by the president and Secretary of State Rusk over the spring and summer to argue that Hanoi's "aggression" was the true obstacle to peace. Since the beginning of the bombing, there were numerous public calls for a halt or pause of bombing North Vietnam and negotiations from Western allies such as Canada, Britain, France, United Nations secretary general U Thant, the Non-Aligned Countries, and many others. One effort in this direction was the five-day bombing pause in May code-named Sunflower, that Secretary of Defense Robert McNamara called in December 1965 "a propaganda effort."[14] It would not be until the end of 1965 that the administration publicly clarified its negotiating position by releasing its own fourteen-point plan for peace, which Dean Rusk described as putting "everything into the basket of peace except the surrender of South Vietnam." According to Vietnamese officials, the Fourteen Points (see appendix F) were an insult and were not taken seriously.[15]

On the other hand, the DRV released its Four Points on 8 April 1965. The Four Points were a thorn in the side of Johnson administration officials, and the question of whether these were preconditions that must be accepted in advance or set out as a basis of discussion was endlessly debated in the White House and State Department. Point three was the most difficult for US officials to interpret because it appeared as if the North Vietnamese were demanding that the NLF would take control over the government of South Vietnam and it would fall to communists. Moreover, the United States would never accept point three, or recognize the NLF, because of the damaging signal it would send to their allies in Saigon.[16] This was the Cold War logic of American policy makers. The North Vietnamese attempted to clarify the Four Points by creating the XYZ Channel in May 1965 between North Vietnamese commercial representative Mai Van Bo and US government representative Edmund Gullion in Paris, France. These meetings were abruptly called off by North Vietnam in September 1965.[17]

The Lynd-Hayden-Aptheker trip to Hanoi in late 1965 occurred at a historic moment in the Vietnamese conflict where it was possible to avoid further escalation of the war. The stakes were high, and each side dug in its heels. The United States believed that it could win the war—maintaining an independent government in South Vietnam, stopping infiltration of soldiers from North Vietnam into the South, and stopping the spread of communism in the region—through an increased bombing of North and South Vietnam, which eventually enveloped Laos and Cambodia. By bombing North Vietnam, attacking critical infrastructure, and hindering social and economic development, leaders in Washington believed the US would erode the will of the Vietnamese to fight. By contrast,

the North Vietnamese were convinced that they could defeat the Americans
through a military and diplomatic strategy that would, on the one hand, engage
US forces in large conventional battles while the People's Liberation Armed
Forces (PLAF) of the NLF would fight a protracted guerrilla struggle in the
jungles of Vietnam. On the other hand, the DRV and NLF would seek the sympathy of world opinion and increasingly open its doors to the Western peace
movement by engaging in people's diplomacy.

October 1965 to January 1966 was a crucial period in the escalation of the
war, as the Johnson administration saw proposals for increased escalation of
the conflict from the Joint Chiefs of Staff (JCS), General Westmoreland, and
hawks in both the Democratic and Republican Parties. In late October in an
Oval Office meeting, the JCS proposed to President Johnson a swift and decisive
bombing strike against strategic targets in North Vietnam (including Hanoi,
Haiphong, and other joint military and civilian targets and infrastructure such
as roads, railways, and bridges). Johnson rejected such a sweeping strike for fears
of starting World War III with China and the Soviet Union. The first major conventional battle between US troops and the North Vietnamese People's Army
of Vietnam (PAVN) in the Ia Drang Valley from November 13 to 19 served as
a wake-up call to the Military Assistance Command–Vietnam and policy makers in Washington. Although the PAVN lost 1,300 soldiers to the Americans'
300 soldiers killed in action, it was clear that US forces could not sustain these
casualties without larger numbers of troops in the field. In response, General
Westmoreland doubled his request for troops from 100,000 to 200,000 (from
twenty-eight battalions requested in September to now fifty-three battalions).
This would bring the number of US troops in South Vietnam to 440,000 by the
end of 1966.[18]

In response to the doubling of Westmoreland's troop request, President
Johnson sent Secretary McNamara to South Vietnam to confer with the military leadership and report back. Upon his return to Washington, McNamara
wrote to President Johnson on November 30, 1965, that the United States
was not winning the war, and on the contrary, the communist forces were on
the offensive. In this regard, McNamara recommended sending more ground
troops to South Vietnam and increasing the bombing of North Vietnam. Before
these escalations could be advanced, McNamara advised the president to pursue "a three- or four-week pause in the program of bombing the North before
we either greatly increase our troop deployments to Vietnam or intensify our
strikes against the North." According to McNamara,

> The reasons for this belief are, first, that we must lay a foundation in the
> mind of the American public and in world opinion for such an enlarged

phase of the war and, second, we should give North Vietnam a face-saving chance to stop the aggression. I am not seriously concerned about the risk of alienating the South Vietnamese, misleading Hanoi, or being "trapped" in a pause; if we take reasonable precautions, we can avoid these pitfalls. I am seriously concerned about embarking on a markedly higher level of war in Vietnam without having tried, through a pause, to end the war or at least having made it clear to our people that we did our best to end it.[19]

Over the next few weeks, Johnson, Rusk, McNamara, McGeorge Bundy, and other advisers debated the merits of a second bombing pause; ultimately they decided to pursue a temporary halt in bombing over the Christmas holiday. The original thirty-hour pause was extended to thirty-seven days and expanded to the administration's first "Peace Offensive," which lasted from 24 December 1965 to 31 January 1966.

While the administration was contemplating escalating the war, in mid-November CBS journalist Eric Sevareid released a bombshell article in *Look* magazine describing conversations he had with Adlai Stevenson, US Ambassador to the United Nations, just days before Stevenson's untimely death in July 1965. In his conversation with Sevareid, Stevenson outlined that in 1964 the UN secretary general U Thant had facilitated talks with a Russian emissary who arranged with Ho Chi Minh to agree to open peace talks in Rangoon, Burma (now Yangon, Myanmar). Sevareid reported that this effort was delayed and ultimately scuttled by the US.[20] The article presented information that corroborated the UN secretary general's cryptic comments in February 1965 to the press: "I am sure that the great American people, if only they knew the true facts and the background to the developments in South Vietnam, will agree with me that further bloodshed is unnecessary." Without providing details, U Thant argued that the opening of "discussions and negotiations alone can create conditions which will enable the United States to withdraw gracefully from that part of the world. As you know, in terms of war and hostilities, the first casualty is truth." If U Thant put the onus on the United States to engage in negotiations and ultimately withdraw from Vietnam in February 1965, the Sevareid article opened the window further for legitimate questions about the truthfulness of the statements coming from the White House and State Department. The Sevareid article created a dilemma in Washington, as Washington spent considerable political capital over 1965 painting North Vietnam as inflexible and unwilling to engage in "unconditional discussions."[21]

The State Department's response to the article, and Secretary Rusk's comments in particular, laid the groundwork for Lynd, Hayden, and Aptheker to clarify the negotiating position of the North Vietnamese. A State Department press statement argued, "The North Vietnamese regime has made it clear again and again that it will not enter into any discussions unless the conditions it has set down for settlement are accepted as the basis of negotiation. These conditions, amounting to a surrender of South Viet-Nam to Communist domination . . . include the withdrawal of United States Military Forces and acceptance of the program of the Viet Cong." Rusk maintained at a press conference on November 26 that

> Hanoi, in their well known four points, has indicated its basic position on Viet-Nam. They have refused to accept the suggestion that their points can be discussed along with all other points presented by other Governments. They, therefore, exclude in advance the position which they know the United States will take, namely, that North Viet-Nam must stop its aggression against South Viet-Nam and discontinue its effort to impose the program of the National Liberation Front on South Viet-Nam by force.[22]

US government public statements and news articles like Sevareid's created much confusion about the state of Vietnam War diplomacy. Before leaving the United States, Lynd drafted a memorandum for Hayden and Aptheker titled "Things Which Need Clarification about the N.L.F.-Hanoi Negotiating Position." For Lynd, there were two main issues: (1) the political future of South Vietnam as envisioned by the NLF and (2) whether the DRV demanded that the United States withdraw all troops from Vietnam before negotiations.[23] Before leaving the United States, Hayden and Lynd issued the following statement: "We have no assurance that we can add anything to American understanding of the other side's approach to peace. The recent bombing of Haiphong and the danger that this dreadful war may be further escalated, however, confirms us in the feeling that we should try."[24] Lynd also announced that he would be reporting his findings in *Viet-Report*, and indeed the magazine devoted considerable space for Lynd's interviews, statements, and analysis.

It is worth briefly noting the effects the Lynd, Hayden, and Aptheker mission to Hanoi had on the Johnson administration's peace offensive. I have written about this aspect elsewhere, and so I will summarize the main findings.[25] First, when Lynd returned to the United States on 9 January 1966, he told reporters at a press conference that the US had not made direct contact with the North Vietnamese. This created a controversy the following day when the White House press secretary, Bill Moyers, told the press it was a "safe deduction" that the US had indeed contacted Hanoi but provided no further details. Internally, this led members of the Johnson administration to acknowledge that there were not enough direct contacts between the United States and the Democratic

Republic of Vietnam. This was the reality: there was a lack of direct contacts between the United States and the Democratic Republic of Vietnam during the much-vaunted "Peace Offensive." In total, there were three direct but low-level US to DRV contacts in Paris, France, Rangoon, Burma, and Moscow and two third-party contacts sanctioned by the United States through a Polish government intermediary in Hanoi and in Vientiane with the Laotian president. These low-level contacts and third-party efforts were not exploited to their full potential, and indeed the most fruitful contacts in Rangoon and Vientiane were thwarted when the US resumed bombing.

Second, Washington believed that the bombing pause over North Vietnam was a sufficient signal to Hanoi that it was willing to open negotiations. However, the US continued to bomb South Vietnam. During this time, the Johnson administration refused to recognize the National Liberation Front and argued that it was not an "independent entity" because it was controlled by the DRV. If this was the case, it was surely a confusing signal to Hanoi. The reality of course was much more complicated, and the NLF was not simply a puppet of the DRV despite receiving substantial assistance. The DRV protested the continued military operations in the South to Lynd, in its public statement on January 4, and to Ambassador Kohler on January 21 and January 24. Moreover, the longer the bombing pause went on the more voices emerged calling for an end to the bombing of South Vietnam and for the US to recognize the NLF. This much was confirmed after Lynd's speech in Washington on January 24. As seen from Washington, this was simply unacceptable, and the sentiment was expressed in a memorandum from the president's special adviser Jack Valenti after Lynd's speech at the Washington Hilton hotel was reported in the media. The Associated Press reported, "Prof. Staughton Lynd of Yale said tonight that he was in telephone contact with the Communist-led National Liberation Front of South Vietnam only three days ago and that President Johnson could do the same if he wished."[26] In response to Lynd's statement, Valenti wrote to the president, "The minute we resume, there will be two vital points we must nail down, else the doves, the Lynd-liners and the *Times* will shriek": Did Hanoi respond, and is there hard evidence that Hanoi took advantage of the pause by increasing infiltration of troops and supplies to the South? According to Valenti, the "Lynd-line" was, "Stop the bombing forever—recognize the Viet Cong—(and soon, it will be: organize a Popular Front or coalition government, then get troops out and let the Vietnamese decide their own fate. This will surely come next as the line)."[27]

Third, in Lynd's own speeches by late January and into February he continued to refer to articles in the press that demonstrated there was a lack of conventional military attacks by North Vietnamese forces in South Vietnam (see documents 5 and 6 in this chapter, as well as chapter 4, documents 3 and 4). Lynd argued that this was perhaps a signal to Washington that it was standing down during the bombing halt. In various high-level national security meetings and in memoranda from top officials, administration officials reflected on this fact and argued that the lack of conventional PAVN attacks in the South did not help their case for resuming the bombing. If President Johnson and his top officials were serious about finding a peaceful settlement to the conflict in January 1966, they could have taken this as an opportunity to open the door for more high-level negotiations. Nonetheless, the bombing was resumed on January 31 despite the fact that administration officials knew there was a decrease in PAVN conventional attacks during the bombing pause.

Finally, the direct channels of communication between Washington and Hanoi became a liability to Johnson administration officials who were pushing for a resumption of the bombing. By the end of the third week of the pause, the principal members of the president's inner circle—McNamara, Rusk, and Bundy—were pushing for the direct channels to be closed so that the bombing of North Vietnam could resume. While the direct channel in Rangoon was still open and President Souvanna in Laos was speaking with DRV diplomats, the US moved to close the channels so that it could resume bombing. The striking fact is that both these channels *were still open* when the bombing was resumed and top-level decision makers knew full well that these lines of communication were not given enough time to work.

Since this chapter presents perhaps the most controversial and consequential episode of Lynd's antiwar praxis during the Vietnam War, I have spent a considerable amount of space explaining the context. I have also included further documentation on each side's approach to a negotiated settlement, which are referred to in this introduction and throughout the materials in the appendixes: (1) the Geneva Accords of 1954, (2) the National Liberation Front of South Vietnam's Five Points of March 1965, (3) the North Vietnamese Four Points of April 1965, (4) the government of the Republic of Vietnam's Four Points of June 1965, and (5) the United States government's Fourteen Points of December 1965.

During the three weeks between his return from Hanoi and the United States' resumption of bombing North Vietnam, Staughton Lynd was under constant pressure to report on what he and his companions had learned during their trip. He did not have a single stump speech that he repeated in successive presentations, but inevitably there was some repetition from one text to the next. When faced with a choice, the editor has chosen to preserve the integrity of the historical record.

Figure 3.3: Cover of *Viet-Report*, January 1966. The image shows the airplane journey Staughton Lynd, Tom Hayden, and Herbert Aptheker took to get to and from Hanoi. The January 1966 edition of *Viet-Report* included extensive reporting on the trio's trip to North Vietnam. Courtesy of Archives & Special Collections, University of Connecticut Library.

Document 1

A REFUGEE IN THE NORTH, INTERVIEW WITH
NGUYEN MINH VY, 3 JANUARY 1966

Staughton Lynd, Tom Hayden, and Herbert Aptheker arrived in Hanoi on December 28 after spending the first nine days traveling and talking to various representatives of the Democratic Republic of Vietnam and the National Liberation Front in Prague, Moscow, and Beijing. In Hanoi, the group met with North Vietnamese officials, leaders of youth groups, women's groups, trade unions, peasants and workers, intellectuals, and an American prisoner of war who was shot down over North Vietnam. These events are explained in more detail in Staughton Lynd and Tom Hayden's *The Other Side* and Herbert Aptheker's *Mission to Hanoi*, both released in 1966.

This interview with Nguyen Minh Vy, a Southern Vietnamese revolutionary who regrouped to the North, was conducted by Lynd and translated by Do Xuan Oanh. Lynd would reference the interview in numerous speeches recounting his trip.

Figure 3.4; Staughton Lynd and Herbert Aptheker meeting Nguyen Minh Vy on 3 January 1966. The photograph appeared in the January 1966 edition of *Viet-Report*. Courtesy of Archives & Special Collections, University of Connecticut Library.

Hanoi, January 3.—A conversation with Nguyen Minh Vy, a member of the DRV National Assembly representing the South Vietnamese Province in which the new

American base at Cam Ranh Bay is located, and Secretary of the DRV Peace Committee. These are Prof. Lynd's notes of that conversation. Viet-Report *reprints them without alteration, both to minimize interpretation and to preserve freshness.*

For people of South Vietnam struggle means existence itself. 2,000,000 died of starvation up to 1945.

DRV led whole country in struggle against French. Not all territory South occupied by French. Many large liberated areas in central and southernmost South Vietnam. 1946–1954 half population South Vietnam free. Land distributed. This explains Ho's prestige in South Vietnam. For peasant, independence means to safeguard the land he has received. Thus, for peasants, existence and independence are the same thing.

There was also a sort of resistance administration in the cities. Present DRV minister of public health was chairman of resistance administration in Saigon and Cholon. His orders carried out. Prestige resistance administrative committee grew as resistance itself triumphed.

Regroupment required persons in liberated areas to obey hostile administration. Leaving for regroupment was sad. Ho was obliged to issue a special appeal to the population of South Vietnam to carry out the Geneva Agreements. "South Vietnamese compatriots have to sacrifice their immediate interest for long term interest of peace and independence."

People of South Vietnam understood Diem from the beginning. He had been an agent of French, had committed many crimes since 1930 under label of exterminating Communism. He made people understand that the most patriotic people are Communists.

Everyone knew that Americans had assisted the French. As the resistance struggle drew to a close it was clear that French were not principal aggressors.

So how did the people feel when they had to accept a hostile administration, when revolutionary administration withdrew, when the whole army regrouped to North? They were very anxious. They knew beforehand what Diem would do. During the first years the U.S. was more clever than the French, by its policy of neo-colonialism. But our people understood that very well and experience taught them more.

The Diem administration was terrible. Even Kennedy finally turned against it but he had eulogized Diem in 1960 campaign. What did Diem do? He was a former feudal official. Obviously he defended the rights of the landlords, the *compradores*. It was logical for him to give land back to landlords. Then there were the reprisals against former resistance members. U.S. State Department says we left our men behind. But we called resistance against French a people's resistance because everyone participated. The Geneva Agreements required all armed men to withdraw but it couldn't mean all members of the resistance because then the whole population would have had to leave. And this is why the Agreements stipulated no reprisals against those who resisted. It was similar in the North, where very many who cooperated with French are still in DRV.

We believed that since Geneva was an international agreement there was much probability it would be carried out. But we suspected the Americans. The fact that Bedell Smith [undersecretary of state and chief US negotiator during the Geneva Conference] made a separate statement at Geneva was a warning.

What is the basic problem? The implementation of provisions about unity: that is to say, to hold 1956 elections. There is variety between North and South but not significant. South Vietnam has a warmer winter. Hundreds of thousands of South Vietnamese in the DRV feel when winter comes that they would like to go South. Perhaps it is like Florida.

For the thousands of years of our history there was never such terror as under Diem. I was arrested by the French. But they imprisoned only persons who had committed concrete crimes. After imprisonment one could live a normal life. Diem arrested people on ideological grounds. If you were a former resistance member that made you automatically a Communist. They said, tear down the picture of Ho, tear down the red flag, and we'll set you free. Otherwise we'll imprison you forever.

In the six years 1954–1959, 150,000 were killed. Torture was unimaginable. Under the French Poulo Condore [prison camp] was only for men. Diem put men and women together. Then there was the 10/59 law. People were imprisoned, even killed, for the intention of committing crimes. That is why some Western journalists spoke of "McCarthyism," but McCarthy would have been envious of Diem.

I am luckier than others because my wife is with me. Majority who regrouped left wives behind. Diem had the cruel policy of forcing these wives to abandon their husbands. If they didn't do this it meant that they still loved Communists.

Then the strategic hamlets. In an industrial country it is easy and good for people to be concentrated. In North Vietnam villages are nucleated, people within a fence of bamboo trees. In South Vietnam people are dispersed, especially in the Mountains. Mountaineers lived completely freely. They don't like anyone to sow troubles in their lives. They have their own gardens, their own fields, their own fish ponds. Each individual has his own economy. They are self-sufficient in rice, fish, clothing.

What will happen when these people are concentrated? They must have permission to go out to till land. They went out in the morning and came in at evening, like buffaloes and oxen. There was forced labor. Taxes. Their sons were taken for the army. If they protested they were called Communists. They couldn't bear it. This was the reason for the fall of Diem. Diem tried to use the experience of Algeria and Malaya. The French had even had agrovilles in Vietnam, but fewer.

Houses were burned to drive people into the hamlets. For a Vietnamese peasant a house was built three generations before. They were very very poor. A house was passed from father to son for generations. Two things Diem did were most shocking to the people: he dug up the graves of ancestors, and he burned houses. He also cut down fruit trees, for example orange trees which must be grown for many generations to bear fruit.

If you resisted you were killed. Following the imperialists, Diem killed people to make an example of them. If you asked to live in your former house you were considered a Communist and killed. Until 1959 the struggle only meant to urge implementation of Geneva, to demand assurance of freedom rights, to demand land. The main thing was to demand to be alive. Diem regime did not give you a hope of living otherwise.

When Americans say Diem was "inefficient" what they mean is he couldn't win the people. Diem was not only anti-Communist but against everyone. Many people said if someone else than Diem had been in power it would have gone better for the Americans. No. Anti-aggression feeling was deep in the blood. No one who acted as an agent for foreign aggressors could stand. Our people are very sensitive to this. Ky [prime minister of the Republic of Vietnam and later vice president] was a French pilot in the early 1950's. Generally speaking the present officials of the Saigon government were officers in the French army. How can they say they're patriotic? For Vietnamese people the question is not "For or against Communism?" but "For or against foreign aggression?" I can say without fear of having to correct myself that all those who supported the French or now support the Americans are not anti-imperialist. Diem pled for the imperialists as cleverly as anyone could.

In 80 years of French rule 2,000,000 died of starvation. In 5 years of Diem 150,000 were killed and nearly 1,000,000 arrested.

How was this question related to the Americans? The U.S. government created and equipped the Diem administration to fight our people. Diem was replaced by someone like him. Ky considers Hitler his hero.

How do people in North Vietnam feel about the South? It is not like the Sudan. Regroupment sent hundreds of thousands of South Vietnamese to North. They can't stand to look at half their country on a map. If the South is covered, the country seems to lack legs and feet. If the North is covered, it seems to lack a head. Unity does not mean Northern encroachment. Not only history but Geneva recognized unity. There are not the two nations Dean Rusk often speaks about.

How is the South waging its struggle? There is one thing which I can say because I am a Southerner. It is often said that the South Vietnamese can fight only because of the existence of the North. But there are 14 million South Vietnamese. There are only 6 million Cubans. And what's the population of Santo Domingo? But if they can't stand things they find a way to do something about it.

People of South Vietnam desire independence the more because they once had it. They are like a hungry man who has tasted a cookie and found it good, and will not be satisfied to have it taken away or with another kind of cookie.

The arms of the guerillas are very primitive. Thus they have used bamboo tubes for running water and by putting in powder and using a nail as a detonator, made a mortar that is effective at 10 meters.

American troops can't cope with the situation. Why? Why does the NLF and its army grow so rapidly? Western press says this is because of terrorism. It isn't true. Diem was the greatest terrorist: if it is terror which wins people Diem should have won them.

There is no reason for the NLF to use terror. It must win doctors, teachers, intellectuals, not let them go. Their strength lies in the fact that they can establish a front.

I want you to understand what is in our heart. When we say peace it is not a mere word. For the sake of peace I left my home to regroup in the North in 1954. That's why I said the South Vietnamese were struggling for the very right to live. It's not because they are bellicose. If peace, independence, and unity are guaranteed there will be peace at once. These are fundamental things.

The South Vietnamese people have their own method of struggle. It limits the effectiveness of American weapons. B-52's don't work. They use close-in fighting. For example, I'll tell you a story about bamboo spikes. American troops are very mobile. We agree with that. But at the last moment they must go on foot at least 500 meters and any number of spikes can be put in 500 meters. Radar and electronics can't detect them. Most effective are prods but then you can't be mobile. At Pleime U.S. troops took 7 hours to go 1 mile.

Helicopters can't land in jungle, tanks don't work in swamps.

The logistics of supply are very simple for us. The local population helps.

Regarding the Cao Dai, Hoa Hao, Binh Xuyen—present situation is different from under French. First two are religious sects. French won support of all by saying that Communists are against religion. But members of these sects are

peasants and also Vietnamese. They have seen that it's not profitable to follow
Diem and the Americans. And they have the experience of not gaining anything
from the French, not to speak of the fact that the people regarded them as traitors. People have had experience and now realize that the Front is not against
religion, the Americans are.

Americans have had many plans. First they were going to pacify the country
in 18 months, then they fell back on key points. First they used puppet troops,
then American troops. I think that winning the war by increasing the number
of troops is an obsolete idea.

The support of the world's people is developing. We know the difficulties
of the American people are not the same as ours. We often say to each other:
What made [Norman] Morrison burn himself? This speaks for the holiness
and nobility of his death. Johnson advises us not to overestimate the American
movement, that it represents only a minority, etc. But we think it's great and are
confident it will develop with every passing day.

Document 2

"THE OFFICIAL INTERVIEW" WITH PHAM VAN DONG, 5 JANUARY 1966

On 5 January 1966, Lynd, Hayden, and Aptheker met with North Vietnamese prime minister Pham Van Dong for ninety minutes at his executive residence. The Vietnamese requested before the meeting that the trio submit a series of written questions to which the prime minister would respond in his official capacity. Outside of these questions, Lynd and Hayden provided an extended transcript of their discussion in chapter 7 of *The Other Side.* According to this unofficial transcript, verified with Vietnamese translators, this crucial exchange was not part of the official text:

> *Question*: Since December twentieth when President Johnson said he would "knock at any door," has the United States attempted to make direct contact with the D.R.V.?
>
> *Answer*: No.
>
> *Question*: Do you mean that no D.R.V. ambassador anywhere in the world has been contacted by the United States, as well as that there has been no direct communication with Hanoi?
>
> *Answer*: In that broader sense of the question, the answer is still No.[28]

This response by Pham Van Dong would cause a public relations problem for the Johnson administration when Lynd reported this denial upon arriving to the United States on 9 January 1966.

Hanoi, January 5—An interview, in writing, with Premier Pham Van Dong of the DRV. The translation is official.

Question 1: What is your comment on the idea that the Democratic Republic of Vietnam and the National Liberation Front refuse all offers to negotiate? Is it not the case that the DRV and the NLF set conditions for negotiations? What must the United States do before there can be negotiations?

Answer: I am not going to answer in the place of the South Vietnam National Front for Liberation.

As far as the Government of the DRV is concerned, may I quote a few sentences from the January 4, 1966 statement of our Foreign Ministry. These sentences are:

"It is the unswerving stand of the Government of the DRV to strictly respect the 1954 Geneva Agreements on Vietnam, and to correctly implement their basic provisions as concretely expressed in the following points: (i.e. the four-point stand of the Government of the DRV, made public on April 8, 1965)

A political settlement of the Vietnam problem can be envisaged only when the U.S. Government has accepted the four-point stand of the Government of the DRV, has proved this by actual deeds, at the same time has stopped unconditionally and for good its air raids and all other acts of war against the DRV.

Question 2: What is the meaning of the third point of Premier Pham Van Dong, "the internal affairs of South Vietnam must be settled by the South Vietnamese people themselves, in accordance with the program of the NLF"?

Answer: The third point is a very important one in the four-point stand of the Government of the DRV from which it can by no means be dissociated. The U.S. authorities have recently stated that they do not accept this point. Thus they recognize neither the sacred right to self-determination of the people of South Vietnam, nor the National Front for Liberation, the sole genuine representative of the people of South Vietnam. In short, they do not accept the four-point stand of the Government of the DRV, which means they are still pursuing a policy of aggression in South Vietnam.

Question 3: If the United States withdraws its troops, would the DRV withdraw its troops from South Vietnam?

Answer: The so-called "presence of the forces of the DRV in South Vietnam" is a sheer U.S. fabrication in order to justify their war of aggression in South Vietnam.

Question 4: Exactly how would the creation of a national coalition government in South Vietnam and the eventual reunification of South with North Vietnam come about?

Answer: The setting up of a national coalition government in South Vietnam is an internal affair of the people of South Vietnam. It is to be settled by the people of South Vietnam in accordance with the program of the NLF. This program provides for the establishment of "a broad national democratic coalition administration including representatives of all strata of people, nationalities, political parties, religious communities, and patriotic personalities. We must wrest back the people's economic, political, social and cultural interests, realize independence and democracy, improve the people's living conditions, carry out a policy of peace and neutrality and advance toward peaceful reunification of the Fatherland."

The reunification of Vietnam is an internal affair of the Vietnamese people, it is to be settled by the Vietnamese people in the two zones. On this subject, it is said in the program of the NLF:

> The urgent demand of our people throughout the country is to reunify the Fatherland by peaceful means. The NLF undertakes the gradual reunification of the country by peaceful means, on the principle of negotiations and discussions between the two zones on all forms and measures beneficial to the Vietnamese people and Fatherland.

And the program of the Vietnam fatherland Front reads in part:

> To achieve in favorable conditions the peaceful reunification of our Fatherland, we must take into account the real situation in the two zones, the interests and legitimate aspirations of all sections of the population. At the same time, we must conduct negotiations to arrange the holding of free general elections in order to achieve national unity without either side trying to exert pressure on, or trying to annex the other.

Question 5: Would the Geneva Conference be reconvened?

Answer: In reply to this question, I would like to quote a sentence from the April 8, 1965 statement of the Government of the DRV about our four-point stand:

> If this basis is accepted, favorable conditions will be created for the peaceful settlement of the Vietnam problem, and it will be possible to consider the reconvening of an international conference of the 1954 Geneva Conference on Vietnam.

Question 6: It is often said by the United States Government that the NLF is an agent of the DRV, and that the DRV is controlled by the Chinese People's Republic. What is your reply?

Answer: This is a vile fabrication designed to slander the Vietnamese people, the NLF, the DRV and the PRC (People's Republic of China).

The NLF is the sole genuine representative of the people of South Vietnam, it enjoys great prestige among the people of South Vietnam and in the world, it is now leading the infinitely heroic and certain to be victorious fight waged by the people of South Vietnam against U.S. imperialist aggression. The U.S. refusal to recognize the NLF shows all the more clearly that the U.S. Government is bent on pursuing the war of aggression in South Vietnam, consequently, it will sustain even heavier defeats.

The DRV is a socialist, independent and sovereign country. Its relations with the brotherly PRC are founded on the principle of mutual equality, cooperation and mutual aid. These are relations between comrades-in-arms, as close with each other as lips and teeth.

Document 3

STAUGHTON LYND STATEMENT AT KENNEDY AIRPORT ON RETURN TO THE UNITED STATES, 9 JANUARY 1966

Arriving back in the United States on 9 January 1966, Staughton Lynd read the following statement, cowritten with Tom Hayden, in front of a throng of reporters and television cameras. There was much speculation in the media whether the trio would be arrested upon their arrival, and in view of the uncertainty, Alice Lynd arranged to meet a lawyer from the American Civil Liberties Union (ACLU) at the airport.

IN HANOI ... THE PEACE THAT IS NOT OFFENSIVE

On January 9 Staughton Lynd, Thomas Hayden and Herbert Aptheker returned from a three-week fact-finding mission to Prague, Moscow, Peking and Hanoi. Professor Lynd traveled as a correspondent for Viet-Report. Thus, for approximately one week, the American press had a correspondent in Hanoi.

It is not that U.S. news media were not interested in the war as seen from North Vietnam. On the contrary, virtually every major media made handsome offers for the story. But why hadn't you gone after the story yourselves, we asked. Some blamed it on Hanoi. Three were clearer: Washington would be displeased. Has Washington's pleasure or displeasure become a significant—or decisive—factor in American press coverage of the Vietnamese War? It is natural that the Administration should try to "manage the news." What is not natural is that the Press should cooperate, to become in effect a Court Press.

Figure 3.5: A photograph of Staughton Lynd, Tom Hayden, and Herbert Aptheker having a meal with their Vietnamese hosts. The photograph appeared in the January 1966 edition of *Viet-Report*. Courtesy of Archives & Special Collections, University of Connecticut Library.

---

9 January, 1966

Mr. Hayden and I wish first to explain why we will limit our comments this evening to the written statement I am about to read, rather than answering questions. Having in mind the experience of the Italian professors whose words as quoted in the press were repudiated by Hanoi, we fear the possibility of unintentional distortion which could lessen the usefulness of the report we have brought back from Vietnam.

For example, it would be a distortion to say or imply that we return with a dramatic concession or an explicit peace feeler. We feel we do bring back with us significant clarifications of the NLF and DRV attitudes toward some of the more controversial among President Johnson's 14 points. We ask the cooperation of the press, in the interest of the concern for accuracy and responsibility which you share with us, to report our statements in this regard as what they are, namely, clarifications rather than concessions.

The first half of the remainder of our statement will deal with the pause in bombing and the reaction of DRV to that pause. Then we will return to some of the specific points at issue between the United States on the one hand, and the NLF and DRV on the other.

Among the significant North Vietnamese commentaries on what is termed in Hanoi the United States peace offensive, have been a statement by the Voice of Vietnam radio on Dec. 30, authoritative articles in Nhan Dan for Dec. 31 and Jan. 3, and the statement by the DRV Foreign Ministry on Jan. 4. We also discussed the new American initiatives with many persons, among them Premier Pham Van Dong in our interview with him on Jan. 5.

We think that as seen from Hanoi there is a deep inconsistency in the United States policy between a peaceful posture looking toward a negotiated settlement, and an interventionist posture which has in view the permanent partition of Vietnam and an expanded war. This two-sidedness makes United States policy seem hypocritical and suspect to the Vietnamese, who hear overtures of peace but also pledges to stay in Vietnam, who know of the pause in bombing but also observe a daily military build-up in the South.

For those to whom we talked in Vietnam, the record of events in recent weeks proves clearly the continuing inconsistency of American policy. American ambassadors have gone all over the world to "knock on any door" seeking peace. But Premier Pham Van Dong, in response to our questions, stated unequivocally that the United States government had not made contact with the government of the DRV, either at Hanoi or through DRV ambassadors in other capitals, since President Johnson spoke of knocking on any door Dec. 20. We assume that the United States, in keeping with previous policy, has not sought to make contact with NLF representatives either. To those with whom we spoke in Vietnam, it appears that the United States knocks on all doors except the doors of those whom it is fighting. They wonder if the United States is searching for peace or mainly attempting to soften its image before negative public opinion abroad and at home.

To be sure, there is now a pause in the bombing of North Vietnam. But the Vietnamese remind us that the last pause was followed immediately by expansion of the war. During the current pause, while the United States has waited for a so-called signal from Hanoi, Vietnamese sources have emphasized that President Johnson's words are accompanied by escalation in the South. According to these sources, the day after President Johnson spoke of knocking on any door the Department of Defense admitted the widespread use of toxic chemicals and authorized "hot pursuit" by American troops into Cambodia. A week later, when President Johnson announced his 14 points, 4000 new American troops of the 25th division arrived at Pleiku. Hanoi sources also point to the arrival in Saigon between Dec. 21 and Jan. 1 of the Chief of Staff of the United States Army, the chairman of the Joint Chiefs of Staff, the Secretary of the Army, and the Secretary of the Air Force. Experience suggests to them that such conferences immediately precede new escalation.

The North Vietnamese do not trust an offer to negotiate unconditionally which, as they see it, represents only one side of America's two-sided policy. They want to know if the United States has clearly decided that Vietnam should be united, rather than partitioned. They want to be sure that the United States has finally abandoned any plan to make South Vietnam a military base for the United States in Southeast Asia. Thus "Observer" stated in Nhan Dan for Jan. 3 that the so-called unconditional negotiations offered by the United States in fact contain four conditions: 1. United States troops will stay in South Vietnam as long as the United States thinks it necessary; 2. South Vietnam must be an independent sovereign state; 3. The United States refuses to recognize the NLF; 4. "The North Vietnamese people are not allowed to support the patriotic struggle of their compatriots in the South."

In our view, the United States does make such policy demands regularly, and they do conflict directly with its other stated aim of unconditional discussions and its denial of any ambition to occupy part of Asia.

President Johnson's 14-point program appears to come close to the diplomatic statements of the NLF and DRV, especially in accepting the Geneva Agreements as a basis of settlement, in denying any desire to keep troops indefinitely in South Vietnam, and in approving reunification.

However, the North Vietnamese see two crucial inadequacies in the new United States peace position. First, they wonder how the United States can accept the Geneva Agreements as the basis for settlement but treat the DRV four points merely as a matter which could be discussed. Hanoi considers its four points to be the essence of the Geneva Settlement, especially the provisions requiring withdrawal of all foreign troops from Vietnam and leaving all political solutions to the self-determination of the Vietnamese people.

Secondly, the United States realizes that the NLF must be in some sense a party to any final negotiation, but the United States defines the NLF simply as an arm of Hanoi. Premier Pham Van Dong told us that his government "can by no means be dissociated" from the third point in its four-point program, which calls for settling the affairs of South Vietnam in accordance with the program of the NLF. The Premier said that what this point involved was the principle of self-determination at the heart of the Geneva Agreements. Like many others with whom we spoke, the Premier insisted on the independence of the NLF from the DRV government in Hanoi. At one point in our talk he indicated his own surprise at the apparent strength of the NLF and its success in dealing with the United States forces.

Thus the negative response of the DRV to the bombing pause appears to stem, first, from observation of warlike acts in South Vietnam which have accompanied the pause, and second, from uncertainty as to whether the United States has really given up its plans for an indefinite occupation of South Vietnam and decided to return to the Geneva Agreements.

So long as American policy remains obviously two-sided, we can understand the realistic suspicion of Premier Pham Van Dong, who told us: "What is the reason for the peace offensive? To win public opinion, particularly American public opinion. Only by so doing can President Johnson escalate the war."

We feel it would be tragic, and quite frankly, irresponsible on the part of the United States government, to regard Hanoi's response to a temporary bombing pause as a conclusive demonstration that an honorable negotiated solution cannot be found with the NLF and the DRV. Our conversations in Vietnam convinced us that many ingredients of an honorable solution exist.

As you know, we have cabled Senator Fulbright asking to report our findings, at any time and under any conditions, to the Senate Committee on Foreign Relations. We sent this cable because we consider it our responsibility as American citizens to make available to the appropriate agency of the government the information we have obtained.

We hope to present to the Senate Committee on Foreign Relations the full text of our questions to Premier Pham Van Dong and his written answers, together with a summary of our interviews with the Premier and with other NLF and DRV spokesmen. Both these texts will be made public no later than Sunday, January 16, when we expect to make a public report at the Manhattan Center in New York City.

However, because of the urgency of the problems involved, we also consider it our responsibility to state now what we regard as some of the key points in Premier Pham Van Dong's answers to our questions.

1. In his written answers, the Premier repeated the statement in the Foreign Ministry release of Jan. 4, namely, that a "political settlement of the Vietnam problem" could be envisaged "only when the United States has accepted the four-point stand of the Government of the DRV, has proved this by actual deeds, at the same time has stopped unconditionally and for good its air raids and all other acts of war against the DRV."

   In our interview, we asked the Premier what actual deeds the government of the DRV had in mind. He replied that that was something for the United States government to decide.

   In the context of our other conversations, this response appears to clarify significantly the DRV attitude toward American military withdrawal. On the one hand, as we were told over and over again, the NLF and DRV require, as a precondition to negotiations, an unambiguous *decision* by the United States to withdraw all its troops from Vietnam. On the other hand, they would seem to be prepared to leave the United States considerable freedom in choosing how to demonstrate by concrete steps that this decision has been made. Every indication is that there is no explicit requirement of the physical withdrawal of all United States troops prior to negotiations.

2. The Premier categorically denied the presence of "forces of the Democratic Republic of Vietnam in South Vietnam," terming it a "sheer fabrication."

   We think that this denial has not previously been made in such absolute terms by the highest governmental authorities in the DRV. In response to a similar question from reporter Felix Greene only a few weeks earlier, President Ho Chi Minh only said that the United States is "fabricating false information" to "cover up" its aggression.

   Premier Pham Van Dong's answer seems even more interesting since we prefaced our questions by saying that we would not report having asked any question that the Premier chose not to answer. We see little reason for Premier Pham Van Dong to make such a statement if it can be proven false by American authorities.

3. It has been widely assumed in the United States that the DRV is no longer open to the possibility of reunification of North and South Vietnam by means of a free general election. In response to a question about this, Premier Pham Van Dong referred to a passage in the program of the Vietnamese Fatherland Front, which says in part: "we must conduct negotiations to arrange the holding of free general elections in order to achieve national unity without either side trying to exert pressure on, or trying to annex the other."

4. In response to a question about the possible reconvening of the Geneva Conference, Premier Pham Van Dong quoted his words of last April to the effect that once the DRV four points had been accepted "it will be possible to consider the reconvening of an international conference of the type of the 1954 Geneva Conference on Viet Nam." We might add that one of the DRV ambassadors to whom we spoke en route to Hanoi commented that determination of the "role and composition" of an international supervisory commission would be an appropriate task for such a conference.

Throughout our interview Premier Pham Van Dong, like so many others to whom we spoke, insisted that while the people of Vietnam were prepared to fight as long as need be to win their independence, none wanted peace more than they. If there was one message which person after person charged us to bring back to the people of the United States, it was this: Tell the American people we make a distinction between them and the American government. Explain to them that we have been fighting for twenty-five years and that many of us, having regrouped to the North under the Geneva Agreements, have not seen or heard from our families in ten years. Who could want peace more than we? But there can be no real peace unless there is independence. An end to this war, they never failed to add, would be in the interest both of our people and of yours.

At one point in our interview with Premier Pham Van Dong, he said to us: If you have the opportunity to see President Johnson, please ask him for me, why is he fighting us? We wonder if the American people are sure of the answer to this question. Before we launch a new and more terrible round of escalation, should we not stop to consider whether the possibilities of peace have really been exhausted? The present American peace initiative is not yet seen as such by the Vietnamese. They see it through suspicious eyes, for it is accompanied by American military build-up in the South and by continued United States references to the permanent partitioning of Vietnam. Until these policy inconsistencies have been resolved, we believe it is tragically unfair to brand our antagonists as intransigent or to conclude that an honorable negotiated settlement is impossible.

Figure 3.6: Herbert Aptheker, Tom Hayden, A. J. Muste, and Staughton Lynd at the Manhattan Center in New York City, 16 January 1966. Photo: Getty Images.

Document 4

ADDRESS OF PROFESSOR STAUGHTON LYND AT WOOLSEY HALL, YALE UNIVERSITY, 17 JANUARY 1966

Staughton Lynd wasted little time preparing to challenge the "Peace Offensive" and report his findings from North Vietnam. Preparations were underway to complete the January 1966 edition of *Viet-Report*, which would appear in the middle of the month. On January 14, Lynd debated the war with Arthur Schlesinger Jr. and other New York intellectuals in New York City. His first major report back was organized by the Fifth Avenue Peace Parade Committee at the Manhattan Center in New York on January 16 in front of a crowd of five thousand people.[29]

The following text is Lynd's presentation at Yale University's Woolsey Hall. Speaking to an overflow crowd of three thousand and simultaneously broadcast live on WYBC radio, Lynd was introduced by Yale's chaplain, William Sloane Coffin. The event was cosponsored by Coffin's newly formed organization, Americans for the Reappraisal of Far Eastern Policy, as well as the Yale-New Haven Committee for Peace in Vietnam, Yale SDS, the Yale Socialist Union, the Divinity School Social Action Committee, *Yale Daily News*, and the Young Democrats. In addition to Lynd's talk, the January edition of *Viet-Report* was distributed hot off the presses and dominated by the trio's firsthand reporting.[30]

Figure 3.7: Staughton Lynd at Woolsey Hall. Courtsey of Alice and Staughton Lynd.

During the week in which I have known about this meeting I have thought of it as an opportunity to report, in a rather personal way, to the Yale community. However, I confess that now that the moment is here what fills my mind is this morning's lead story in the *New York Times*, indicating that the United States will probably escalate the war further when the Lunar New Year ends a week from today.

What I do and say, and what you think of me, and whether Yale in the end fires me or keeps me, and whether I lose my passport or spend five years in jail, and how my doings affect alumni contributions, and whether or not I am considered a traitor—all these are really insignificant things compared to what we may do to the people of Vietnam ten days from now. (The one thing I want most to express tonight is that if bombing is resumed next Monday the Administration may be able to say that it has given Senator Fulbright his thirty day pause, but the Administration will not have exhausted the possibilities of peace; the peace offensive will have been revealed to be what the other side suspected from the outset, a public relations maneuver; and we will all be the losers.) I say this because, as Sanford Gottlieb reported yesterday on the basis of talks with NLF and DRV spokesmen in Algiers and Paris, it is clear that during the first week and a half or two weeks of the bombing pause Hanoi responded with understandable skepticism. Only now, as Gottlieb says, may there be the beginnings of curiosity and new interest. How tragically premature, therefore, to choose this moment to say that our tentative conclusion is that the knocks have had no answer and the lull must soon end. To leak that information on the eve of the Vietnamese New Year is once more to exhibit the mistaken idea of threatening our antagonist into negotiation which underlay the mistaken escalation of the war one year ago.

Nevertheless, before sharing with you the diary of my trip—and that is what the bulk of my talk tonight will consist of—I want to say just one word about myself and Yale.

I empathize very deeply with those students and alumni who must feel that one man's casual self-dramatizing gesture destroy the patient anonymous work of thousands who have sought to make this institution grow. I understand too that precisely because Yale has a president committed to academic freedom, it is in a curious sense I and not the University that has freedom of action, I who am free to take my perhaps bizarre initiatives and the University which must somehow answer the phone calls. I feel around me in the college community many who distrust my motives and dislike my actions in the most fundamental way but who, because of a strong sense of decency and fairness, do their level best to tolerate someone whom they find nearly intolerable.

I have at least some sense of these feelings, and because I do I have over and over wondered whether I should offer my resignation so that the University, if it chose to retain me, would be doing so altogether of its own free will.

Thus far I have not decided to offer my resignation, and the reason is that thus far I have concluded that the presence here of someone like myself may have some educational value.

I think what happens in education is that people learn from each other's lives. No doubt books are important, but I suspect much less important than they may appear in the midst of an exam period. Even the books which I recall most vividly are those, like Edmund Wilson's *To the Finland Station* or Ignazio Silone's *Bread and Wine*, which suggested to me the possibility of kinds of men, kinds of lives that I had never dreamed of.

If this is true, if what really happens in education is that we learn from each other, then there is some value in maximum variety amongst ourselves. The Chinese, so we were told in Peking, believe in the need to learn from negative examples as well as positive examples. If I am a negative example for most of you, well good, there is still something to be learned from me. One hundred and twenty-five years ago the abolitionists were the carriers of such noxious habits as indiscriminate law breaking; the arrogant insistence on inserting one's personal effort when the efforts of governments seem to have failed; denunciation of American policy in foreign capitals; the annoying tendency to mix one good cause with a host of other more disreputable reforms; the use of harsh and insulting language about men in government; and an irritating tendency to appear not from the dregs of society but from among those vines of ivy which, it may seem to some, would better have been used to throttle them at birth. One hundred and fifty years ago the president of this University, Ezra Stiles, shortly before his death hailed the French Revolution and wrote that Americans should have the right to assemble even to overthrow their government. Two hundred and twenty-five years ago three English desperadoes, Goffe, Dixwell and Whalley, had the audacity not merely to help kill a king but, with unpardonable bad taste, to inscribe their names in three streets which surround this respectable institution in a veritable revolutionary encirclement.

If there are to be such lamentable departures from the glass of fashion and the mould of form which is the Yale man, why not have them in the flesh, hideous living examples of the way which right-thinking persons must not trod? Or to be serious: If we really believe what we say about the free play of all ideas, should we not believe even more strongly in the unrestricted encounter of different sorts of men?

★ ★ ★

Monday, December 20, the day President Johnson offered to knock on any door and travel anywhere in search of peace, Herbert Aptheker, Thomas Hayden and I flew to Czechoslovakia en route to Hanoi.

We were to meet many persons who had regrouped to the North under the provisions of the 1954 Geneva Agreements, expecting a two-year separation from their families until the nationwide election in 1956 which the Agreements required. The election, of course, never came. For these Southern exiles, reunification is something more than an abstract dogma.

We flew from Prague to Moscow Dec. 23rd and went to the North Vietnamese Embassy. Ambassador Kinh emphasized what we would hear repeatedly from others: that the United States offer of "unconditional negotiations" is felt to contain several implicit conditions. One is that the United States insists on keeping troops in Vietnam so long as it believes them necessary, which the Vietnamese say violates the Geneva Agreements. Another implicit condition, from the standpoint of the other side, is that the United States demands the permanent partition of Vietnam. The Vietnamese say this, too violates the Geneva Agreement's stipulation for reunification elections in 1956. Finally—and I believe this to be the key to the whole situation—the Vietnamese stress the refusal of the United States government to deal directly with the NLF. They ask: How can we say that we have knocked on every door if we fail to knock on the door of those we are fighting?

One thing Kinh said was hopeful, however. Asked whether the DRV would permit international supervision of a future peace settlement, the ambassador replied that his government has always recognized the International Control Commission and reported violations to it. As for the future role and composition of the ICC, that could be determined by an international conference composed of the same parties as at Geneva.

Perhaps the most impressive interview of our whole trip was with the Front representative in Moscow, Dang Quang Minh. This 56-year old man, another member of the NLF central committee, was first imprisoned in 1930. During the Japanese occupation of Vietnam in World War II he was again imprisoned for five years. As he spoke harsh thoughts to us in a musical, almost inaudible voice, one had the sense of having penetrated through a fog of bureaucratic arrangements and travel plans to the very mind of the Vietnamese revolution.

Minh said the problem is that the United States still hopes to occupy South Vietnam. America, he continued, knows that counter-insurgency "special war" has failed, knows that 1965's "escalation" has failed, but still does not understand the strength of "people's war." Therefore, according to Minh, the United States still hopes to improvise a victory.

From Minh's point of view, the NLF has already made significant concessions. The Geneva Agreements provided for reunification in two years; now, said Minh, the Front is willing that much more than two years go by before North and South Vietnam are united. Further, the Front envisions a coalition government for South Vietnam which would include all "patriotic" mass organizations and all individuals who reject American aggression. Such a coalition government would not ally with Moscow or Peking but would, according to this spokesman, pursue a neutralist foreign policy.

Having conceded this much, Minh said as we drank tea and peeled oranges, the Front would not concede more.

Finally Minh struck a note which would predominate in our talks when we reached Hanoi. "The South Vietnamese cherish peace more than any other people in the world," declared the grim veteran. "The desire for peace may be seen in the fact that in the intervals of fighting we continue to build. The war cannot prevent the people from building a new life. In the past five years we have helped fourteen minorities to create written alphabets. 2,000,000 hectares of land have been distributed to individual farmers." But, he added (as they all add), there can be no real peace until we are independent.

Next we flew to China and saw a high official in the peace committee. It is too simple to say that Peking is a land of uniformity. True enough, most people wear blue quilted suits. True again, the sheer number of people in the streets suggests a mass society. But there are all physiological varieties: the high-cheeked Mongolian sitting cross-legged atop his cartload of cabbages; the round-face unarmed police girl directing traffic; the soldier, in his olive uniform with red star, scanning the wall newspaper; the teen-agers playing basketball in the courtyard of their school as we stroll down a nearby alley. Everywhere is the pulse of purposeful activity. Walking before breakfast the next day, Tom and I passed a group of women energetically singing before starting the day's work. Later in South China, our airport bus passed at six in the morning group after group of young men jogging along the roadside to keep fit.

More pictures which stay in the mind are hundreds of volunteers digging a new Peking canal on Sunday afternoon, and other hundreds, that same afternoon, skating on the ice near Peking University.

When we finally visited the Museum of the Revolution, a high official of the Chinese Peace Committee acted as our guide. He had called on us Christmas afternoon, said that he studied at Berkeley in the 1930's, asked me if my father was the famous author of *Middletown*, and invited us to supper. Supper led to the museum trip, the museum trip to an enormous lunch. Through it all our host talked, and for the first time I felt I had some sense of what makes China's foreign policy tick.

He began by saying that China felt close to Vietnam because many Vietnamese and Korean revolutionaries, including Ho Chi Minh, had fought in the Chinese Revolution. Among the Chinese, he went on, there is discussion of questions such as: Is our foreign policy right when all rich countries are against us? China is poor and yet we give much foreign aid, isn't this wrong?

"We answer the first question this way: We are Communists and belong with the weak oppressed people. If the rich like us, something is wrong. And to the second question we say: We can only be free when all are free."

As to Vietnam, the Peace Committee leader continued, our position is very simple. We support the four point program of the DRV and the five point program of the NLF. And when we say support, we mean support. Our determination to help the Vietnamese people won't be deterred by the United States threat of bombing China.

"We expect bombing," he said. "The United States says to us: Behave or we will bomb you. That gives us two choices. One, capitulate, Two, to say to them, Go ahead and bomb all you want. Come in, destroy all the pots and pans, cups and saucers, factories, Peking. But we will fight."

Next we flew to Hanoi. Our ten days in Hanoi led us to believe that sooner or later the United States would see what the French and Japanese had seen before us: that the cost of staying was excessive and it was time to go. Two other, related points were underlined by conversations in North Vietnam with dozens of persons ranging from Premier Pham Van Dong and five visiting heroes of the NLF army to ordinary workers and peasants and, last but not least, the interpreters who we came to know best of all. First that whatever the nature of the tie between Hanoi and the Front, the NLF struggle in the South has strong local roots which we will neglect at our peril. Second, that the negotiating position of the United States as clarified by President Johnson's Fourteen Points and the negotiating position of the DRV as clarified for us by Premier Pham Van Dong, were so close that peace seems tantalizingly near.

Nguyen Minh Vy, who comes from that part of South Vietnam where the American army is building a huge military base at Cam Ranh, spoke of the Diem regime:

> "For the thousands of years of our history there was never such terror
> as under Diem. I was arrested by the French. But they imprisoned only
> persons who had committed concrete crimes. After imprisonment one
> could live a normal life. Diem arrested people on ideological grounds.

If you were a former resistance member that made you automatically a Communist. They said, tear down the picture of Ho, tear down the red flag, and we'll set you free. Otherwise we'll imprison you forever."

Vy went on to speak of the strategic hamlets in which, between 1961 and 1963, the United States sought to enclose ten million of the fourteen million people in South Vietnam:

> "In South Vietnam people are dispersed, especially in the mountains. The mountaineers lived completely freely. They have their own gardens, their own fish ponds.
>
> What will happen when these people are concentrated? They must have permission to go out to till the land. They went out in the morning and came in at the evening, like buffaloes and oxen. There was forced labor. Taxes. Their sons were taken for the army. If they protested they were called Communists. They couldn't bear it. This was the reason for the fall of Diem."

Vy described the beginning of resistance:

> "Houses were burned to drive people into the hamlets. Two things Diem did were most shocking to the people: he dug up the graves of ancestors and he burned houses.
>
> If you resisted you were killed. Following the imperialists, Diem killed people to make an example of them. If you asked to live in your former house you were considered a Communist and killed. Until 1959 the struggle only meant to urge implementation of Geneva, to demand assurance of freedom rights, to demand land. The main thing was to demand to be alive. The Diem regime did not give you a hope of living otherwise."

"For the people of South Vietnam," Vy asserted, "the struggle means existence itself."

This was also what we heard from the NLF "heroes." Incredibly youthful in appearance ("we look younger than we are," an aide in the DRV Peking embassy remarked), barely coming up to our shoulders, these enemy soldiers told us their personal stories.

Ta Thi Kieu, a girl, 26 years old, from Ben Tre province:

> "In my village land had been distributed during the resistance against the French. In the beginning our struggle against Diem was political. We protested against jailings, against impressment for the army. But the more we carried out political struggle the more terrorism and suppression increased. At first we had only bamboo sticks, booby traps, no rifles. The villagers divided the land, helped each other in production."

"If you were in our position," said Kieu, "you would have no other way than what we are doing."

Le Chi Nguyen, 29 year old demolition expert, a member of the regular (as distinct from the guerilla) NLF forces:

"The Front never forces young people to join the army. It is the puppet army which does this. We young people felt that we would never be slaves. That's why we stood up with sticks and stones in our hands. Joining the army is the aspiration of the people."

As we were leaving the soldiers, Nguyen grasped my hand with an iron grip, looked at me in the eyes and said: Tell the American people we don't want to kill the American soldiers. We distinguish between the American people and the American government. I feel love for the young Americans who are in your army willingly, and I feel sadness about having to kill them.

During these and other conversations the pause in American bombing had begun. Eagerly we searched newspaper and radio summaries, quizzed our interpreters, questioned each government official whom we met. What was the Hanoi response to the pause?

As seen from Hanoi there is a deep inconsistency in United States policy between a peaceful posture looking toward a negotiated settlement, and an interventionist posture which has in view the permanent partition of Vietnam and an expanded war. This two-sidedness makes United States policy seem hypocritical and suspect to the Vietnamese. They hear overtures of peace but also pledges to support the Saigon government. They know of the pause in bombing but also observe a military build-up in the South. And so they wonder: Which is the real American policy, and which the make-believe? Past experience has led them to expect that a military lull is likely to be followed by new escalation.

Does this make a political settlement hopeless? I think not. For the fact is that, unless the Vietnamese were lying to us, many of the obstacles to negotiations supposed to exist in the United States are more apparent than real.

For example, Premier Pham Van Dong insisted in written answers to our questions that while Vietnam welcomed the assistance of China, it made its own decisions. As if to demonstrate this flexibility, the Premier quoted the program of the Vietnam Fatherland Front (a North Vietnamese equivalent of the NLF) which specifically calls for free general elections to determine whether North and South should be united, without pressure for annexation from either side.

Our ninety minute interview with the Premier came on January 5, in the flower-surrounded presidential palace. Again there was tea; again interpreters; again the three unauthorized Americans; but this time the speaker was the second most powerful man in the nation we are fighting. "The Vietnamese people," stated Premier Pham Van Dong, "feel they are fighting for a just cause against barbarous aggression. This is the central reality. The same thing happened when you fought against the British. It is very simple."

Like so many others, the Premier insisted that the Vietnamese passionately want peace. "This building," he said pointing to the room around us, "might be destroyed and that would be a loss. But our grief is about the children, the women, the old and young people who are killed. We feel pain in our heart because of these sufferings." One wondered why the killing had to continue. The Premier answered: "But peace at what cost? All the problems lie here. We must have independence. We would rather die than be enslaved."

As a succession of planes whirled us back past Nanking, Wuhan and Peking, past Irkutsk, Omsk and Moscow, past Prague, Zurich and Paris, and so to New York City, the question kept recurring: Both sides now take their stand on the Geneva Agreements; both sides favor the eventual withdrawal of all foreign troops; both sides favor free general elections to reunify North and South; is peace really impossible?

★ ★ ★

Since we have been back, nothing has been said or done to us by way of legal reprisal. We regard our trip as intended not for negotiation but for clarification. Like Felix Greene, Lord Fenner Brockway, William Warbey and other fact-finders who have talked directly with the DRV and NLF, we asked questions and brought back a report about the answers. Our hope is that the government will choose to regard our trip as an expression of the President's intent to knock on any door and travel anywhere in search of peace. In this spirit, we cabled from Hanoi to Senator William Fulbright asking for an opportunity to present our findings to the Senate Committee on Foreign Relations.

A telegram has been received from Senator Fulbright, as follows:

> YOUR GROUP'S REQUEST HAS BEEN CONSIDERED BY THE COMMITTEE, BUT THERE ARE NO PLANS TO HEAR YOU. IF YOU HAVE NOT ALREADY DONE SO I WOULD SUGGEST THAT YOU PASS ON TO THE STATE DEPARTMENT ANY PERTINENT INFORMATION OBTAINED DURING YOUR TRIP TO NORTH VIETNAM.

We are disappointed that the United States Senate, with its ultimate constitutional responsibility for war and peace, has shown so little interest in direct contact with the only Americans who have been to Hanoi in recent months. We have wired Senator Fulbright:

URGE YOUR COMMITTEE RECONSIDER DECISION.
IMPOSSIBLE TO CONVEY FULL SENSE OF FINDINGS THROUGH
INTERMEDIARY. HAVE SPOKEN JAMES LEONARD STATE
DEPARTMENT AND TOLD HIM OF FURTHER INFORMATION
ESPECIALLY CONCERNING NLF WHICH WISH TO PRESENT
DIRECTLY TO YOU. WE AGREE WITH YOUR PROCEDURE IN
DOMINICAN CRISIS OF COLLECTING FACTS INDEPENDENTLY.
WE ARE RELEASING QUESTIONS AND ANSWERS ALSO
INTERVIEW WITH PREMIER PHAM VAN DONG WHICH WE
THINK INDICATE IMPORTANCE OUR INFORMATION. WILL
HOPE TO HEAR FROM YOU FURTHER.

I would like to report on my conversation with Mr. Leonard, Deputy Director of Research on the Far East for the State Department. At the request of the Department Mr. Leonard flew to New Haven Thursday January 11 and we talked for two hours.

One reason for our trip to North Vietnam was the belief that the American people do not clearly understand the peace terms of the other side. I suspected that the United States government shared some of these same confusions. Mr. Leonard confirmed that this was so. He said that there was "endless debate" within the State Department as to the meaning of the third point in the four point program of the North Vietnamese government. He indicated also that the government has no clear understanding of what the Democratic Republic of Vietnam means by "acceptance" or "solemn recognition" of its four point program.

Conversation with Mr. Leonard therefore deepened the conviction which was at the heart of our journey: that if there is unclearness about what one's antagonist means, an appropriate procedure is to go ask him.

Mr. Leonard also emphasized that the United States government cannot simply accept the other side's four point program, as this would suggest unconditional surrender by the United States. He said that for the same reason the United States cannot perform "actual deeds" of de-escalation, as required by the DRV and NLF, unless similar deeds are performed by the other side.

I am convinced that direct contact with the DRV and with the NLF might help to resolve these essentially procedural problems. For example, one can imagine the following scenario:

The DRV preconditions, as stated in the Foreign Ministry statement of Jan. 4 and in Premier Pham Van Dong's answers to us Jan. 5, include three elements. First, bombing of North Vietnam must be ended permanently and unconditionally. Second, the United States must accept the DRV four points as a basis of negotiation. Third, the United States must demonstrate its sincerity by "actual deeds."

These preconditions can be accepted without loss of face by the United States if the United States continues the direct contact with the DRV, which, according to Mr. Moyers, has already begun; and if, as Senators Church, McGovern, Cooper and others have suggested, the United States agrees to deal directly with the National Liberation Front.

Bombing could be ended without a humiliating public announcement if it could be privately communicated to the DRV government that the pause will go on indefinitely.

Since the DRV regards its four points as a summary of the 1954 Geneva Agreements, conversation with DRV representatives could lead to acceptance of the four points in the form of a joint announcement by the two governments that the Geneva Agreements would be the basis of forthcoming negotiation.

As to actual deeds, Premier Pham Van Dong and Colonel Ha Van Lau, liaison officer of the DRV government to the International Control Commission, told us that it is up to the United States which deeds it takes. The physical withdrawal of American troops prior to negotiation is not required. Colonel Lau told us that one possible actual deed would be recognition of the NLF, a step involving no military de-escalation at all.

Talking with the NLF might also resolve the main American hesitation in accepting the DRV four points. This hesitation concerns the third point, which calls for settling the affairs of South Vietnam in accord with the program of the NLF.

Mr. Leonard and I agree that this point is unclear. Premier Pham Van Dong's answer to our second written question suggests that one meaning of point three is simply recognition of the NLF. I believe that if the United States were to agree to deal directly with the NLF, we might find that other aspects of the NLF program would become more negotiable.

Thus from every point of view our essential message to the American people and government remains: to make peace, you must knock on the doors of those whom you are fighting; to make peace, you must be willing to reason together with your antagonist; to make peace, we must initiate and deepen direct contacts with both the DRV government and the NLF.

Yet it is essential to add that the decision demanded of the United States is more than a decision to talk. It is also a decision to withdraw. Although the other side does not require physical withdrawal of all troops as a precondition to talking, it does insist that before negotiations we decide to leave and leave soon.

Why must we withdraw? Because we do not have and never did have any business in having one single soldier in Vietnam.

I need not tell you that I believed this before my trip. I believe it more strongly now.

Try for a moment, by way of recapitulating my remarks tonight, to view the situation as it seems through their eyes. The rhetoric is not of Communism but of nationalism. The slogan is not "Socialism in one country" but, quite literally, "Liberty or death." As we were told over and over Vietnamese history appears to those who live there as one long struggle for independence and nationhood. The last phase, which began when Ho Chi Minh sat in the jungles of Vietnam with an American lieutenant and asked him how the Declaration of Independence began so that he could use those words in the declaration which Ho was then, in the summer of 1945, writing for his own people—the last phase of war against the French and the United States merely continues the centuries-long effort against the Chinese. When we asked what Ho meant when he said that Vietnam would help the United States withdraw on a red carpet, we were referred to the invasion of Vietnam by the Ming dynasty in the 15th century when, having captured the Chinese general staff, the victorious Vietnamese built boats so that the Chinese could go home without loss of face.

Are we quite sure that this perspective is irrelevant? When the NLF interpreter in Prague had carefully explained to us the position of the Front on amnesty, he added: "But if the sky should fall after you withdraw, that would still be a Vietnamese problem." Premier Pham Van Dong explicitly denied that there were forces of the DRV in South Vietnam, but the undertone was unmistakable: If they were there they would still be Vietnamese soldiers in their own country, unlike your troops.

Arthur Schlesinger told me Friday night that he thought the pause had been supported by two groups: the military, who saw the pause as a pretext for new escalation; and the Kennedy wing of the Democratic Party, who believe we should get out. Schlesinger himself said that, in contrast to last spring, he now believes no more American soldiers should be sent to Vietnam. He agreed with my statement that the NLF rebellion began spontaneously in the South and was not ordered from Hanoi. He stated further that bombing whether in the North or the South had always seemed to him mistaken. He thinks the way ahead now would be by a phased withdrawal of troops over a period of one or two years. On the one hand this would meet the other side's belief that there can be no free elections in South Vietnam so long as American troops are there. On the other hand a phased withdrawal would, as Schlesinger put it, give the non-Communist elements a "fighting chance" to create a permanently neutral rather than Communist-oriented South Vietnam.

It is this sort of thinking which, so the morning papers indicate, may have lost out now, if indeed it ever was seriously heard.

I believe this week our nation faces a choice which will affect all of our lives for decades. It is more than a decision about what to do in Vietnam. It is a decision about what sorts of behavior are appropriate for this country. My case, ultimately, is that the United States will stand or fall not because of power, not because of guns or money, but because its policies express the dream of brotherhood on which this nation was founded; that if we continue using more or less toxic chemicals, more or less toxic gases, and savage indiscriminate bombing on unarmed women and children we will hand to our antagonists what Premier Pham Van Dong called "the great truth of our time ... that men must be brothers"; that the means we have allowed ourselves to adopt cannot be effective in a world which has accepted our dream of brotherhood as its own. When, in Wendell Phillips' words, a whole nation sets itself to do evil, there is a place for you and me who, standing outside politics, say the things which politicians think they cannot say and so make it possible for them to say them; who, with no doubt a childlike simplicity of approach, affirm that the way to make peace is to talk to the people you are fighting; and who, in a country on the verge of collective madness whose misdeeds must someday come before a court more authoritative than itself, persist in responding: Lord, not I.

Document 5

"WHAT SHOULD THE UNITED STATES DO IN VIETNAM?" A SPEECH AT THE WASHINGTON HILTON HOTEL, 24 JANUARY 1966

At the invitation of Women Strike for Peace (WSP), Staughton Lynd discusses the latest developments of the Johnson administration's "Peace Offensive" as it relates to his findings in Vietnam. Significantly, Lynd addresses the several controversies prompted by his public statements and what would be meant by "direct contact" with the enemy. Moreover, he discusses a telephone call he made to representatives of the National Liberation Front in Prague for their latest statement on negotiations in preparation for this speech. According to a report in Lynd's FBI file, an overflow crowd forced WSP organizers to hastily organize two sessions in front of a total of nine hundred people.[31] While Lynd was heavily surveilled during each speech he gave, it appears that this was the only speech to be recorded by the FBI.[32]

The selection from Lynd's diary has been removed. The text of the diary can be read in his address to Yale University in document 4 of this chapter. Other materials from this speech have been presented in earlier speeches by Lynd and have been kept, underlining their importance.

During the last month, millions of people in this country and around the world have dared to hope that peace might be possible.

Now the President, the Secretary of State and other Administration spokesmen tell us: For a month we have made every possible effort on behalf of peace. We have offered to knock on any door, to go to any place, to talk with any group about peace in Vietnam. We have offered unconditional discussions. We have clarified our war aims. But from the other side no response has been forthcoming. Reluctantly, therefore, we must prepare to fulfill our commitments and to continue to resist aggression, with whatever manpower the task requires.

This, roughly, is the American government's assessment of the purpose and result of its celebrated peace offensive.

I disagree fundamentally with this assessment. Conversations with spokesmen of the North Vietnamese government and the National Liberation Front in Prague, Moscow, Peking and Hanoi suggest the following evaluation:

1. Despite the bombing pause, the United States government has continued to escalate the war. Thus it has authorized "hot pursuit" into Cambodia,

admitted the use of toxic chemicals, and landed in South Vietnam since December 20 *new* troops approximately equal in number to the *total* number of North Vietnamese troops allegedly there. The message signaled by our military actions has been a confused message, and it would be tragically unfair and premature to draw conclusions from the DRV and NLF response thus far.

2. Neither by word nor deed has the United States government indicated a readiness to knock on the door of those with whom we are fighting: the National Liberation Front. This confirms the other side in its suspicion that the United States government still insists on controlling the political destiny of South Vietnam. When Administration rhetoric refers to knocking on any door, speaking with any group, but Administration action declines direct contact with its immediate antagonist, how can it expect its peace offensive to be regarded as sincere?

3. Accordingly, I believe that the Vietnamese people, the American peace movement and world public opinion, are justified in saying to the United States government that if the "peace offensive" stops now it will rightly be regarded as a public relations maneuver; and that if the Administration wishes the world to believe that it has exhausted the possibilities of peace, it must:

4. Continue the bombing pause indefinitely, to give the DRV and NLF time to digest the United States initiative.

5. Clarify this initiative by military de-escalation in South Vietnam as well as North Vietnam.

6. Unequivocally declare its readiness to talk directly with the National Liberation Front about the concrete political circumstances under which the United States would withdraw its troops from Vietnam.

Let me say a word more about the meaning of direct contact.

Mr. Moyers and a variety of auxiliary sources have apparently agreed that on December 29 an American official passed a note to an official of the government of North Vietnam. If it is true, it is welcome news. But it seems to me at least that the transmission of one letter hardly fulfills the December 20 promise to pursue peace relentlessly, not just to be available for it but to find ways and means of bringing the enemy to the conference table. Nor does it mitigate in any way the failure to make contact with the NLF.

Our trip illustrated the possibility of talking—not just passing notes, but talking—with the other side. If President Johnson wished to knock on the NLF door, he could do so by simply picking up the telephone. I know this because I did it myself last Friday morning. Wishing to inquire before tonight as to the Front's most recent statement of its position, I placed a call after breakfast to the NLF office in Prague. Within an hour and a quarter I was speaking to a Front representative who, incidentally, was fluent in English.

I am not so simple-minded as to suppose that wars can be ended by after-breakfast telephone calls. But somehow, someway there must be a beginning in dialogue with our antagonist. Words on paper and the good offices of third parties just cannot take the place of direct conversation. Therefore, in all seriousness I ask whether President Johnson has the right to order a resumption of bombing, the doubling of American troops, and the general escalation of the terrible mutual slaughter in Vietnam, until he has picked up the phone.

I might add that the representative of the Front to whom I spoke, while making it quite clear that his words were not definitive, said that so far as he knew there had been no American effort to make direct contact with the NLF.

World public opinion supports the demand that the United States government talk directly with the Front. An open letter of European intellectuals took this position before our group left the United States December 19. Last Thursday, January 20, the Secretary General of the United Nations expressed the same thought. On January 22 the *New York Times* reported Secretary Rusk's belief that world response to the United States peace offensive had been "overwhelmingly favorable"; and yet a story on the next page of the same paper for the same day stated that in Japan, the Asian nation most sympathetic to the United States, "most Japanese seem to feel that Washington is unrealistic in trying to exclude the National Liberation Front from attending the peace negotiations as a full participant."

The 14 points enunciated by President Johnson just after Christmas revealed a hopeful flexibility about many aspects of a peace settlement, particularly in endorsing the eventual reunification of North and South Vietnam. But on this question of dealing directly with the NLF the Administration showed no flexibility at all. It still clings to the notion that the Front can make its voice heard as part of a North Vietnamese delegation, as if to forget the insistence of John Jay, John Adams and Benjamin Franklin in 1782 that England make peace with them not with their French ally.

The Administration's refusal to recognize the NLF stems from its theory that what we face in Vietnam is "aggression from the North." But that theory commands less and less support from responsible observers, even in the United States. Arthur Schlesinger, Jr., one of the Administration's two principal defenders at the National Teach-In here last May, stated in New York ten days ago that the war in South Vietnam began as a spontaneous uprising against the Diem regime. Columnist Richard Starnes, one of the harshest critics of peace activity here in Washington last August, wrote last Friday:

> "Diem was almost wholly a creation of Washington, and particularly of the CIA. There has never been any shred of credible evidence that any significant numbers of South Vietnamese ever vowed allegiance to Diem. . . . Moreover, the fact is that substantial North Vietnamese intervention did not take place until *after* the Diem regime refused to hold the elections that had been the bedrock of the Geneva accord. . . . The State Department's white paper of February 1965 tried to prove that there had been significant North Vietnamese intervention, and failed significantly."

Parenthetically, one wonders why, if Washington is as eager as it says it is to discern some North Vietnamese "response," Robert McCloskey confidently brushed aside the fact that no contact with North Vietnamese troops has been reported in South Vietnam since the peace offensive began. I continue to believe that this may have been why Premier Pham Van Dong, in his written answers to our questions, went out of his way so categorically to deny the presence of any DRV "forces" in the South.

In his January 21 press conference Secretary Rusk gratuitously referred to the "so-called National Liberation Front" and then asserted that "the overwhelming majority" of the South Vietnamese people "want something other than what the Liberation Front has been offering." This statement flies in the face of ex-President Eisenhower's assertion in his memoirs that 80% of the people of Vietnam would have voted for Ho Chi Minh at the end of their war with France; it contradicts Senator Russell's statement on television last summer that a majority of the people of South Vietnam would probably vote for Ho if a plebiscite were held today; and it is hard to reconcile with Senator Mansfield's report that total Vietcong strength is "steadily increasing despite . . . serious casualties" and that while "the majority of the population remains under national government control . . . dominance of the countryside rests largely in the hands of the Vietcong." While we were in North Vietnam, an authoritative article by "Observer" in the Hanoi *People's Daily* quoted Walter Lippmann as follows:

> "the Secretary of State has conditioned our withdrawal from Vietnam with the establishment in Saigon of a stable and sure government which has nothing to do with the Vietcong who are now occupying more than half the country. Such a condition practically means that we shall never withdraw from Vietnam."

In sum, then, the major thing which the United States peace offensive has left undone is recognition of the NLF. So long as we refuse this, we keep not just the

Front but Hanoi as well from coming to the conference table. The third point in
North Vietnam's four point proposal for peace settlement is settling the affairs of
South Vietnam in accord with the program of the NLF. Does this mean acceptance of the full Front program, or would the other side be satisfied if the Front
were guaranteed inclusion in any peace talks and any future South Vietnam
government? Dr. James Leonard, Deputy Director of Far Eastern Research for
the State Department, told me on January 11 that there is "endless debate" in
the Department about this question. It is presumptuous to suggest that if we are
confused about the meaning of point three that we try asking those who wrote
it? Is it impossible that if the United States accepted point three in its minimal
sense of direct dealing with the Front, other aspects of constructing a government in South Vietnam might suddenly become more negotiable?

We received a strong impression on our trip that such flexibility does exist
in the negotiating position of the other side. We were told in Prague that there
were many ways and means of creating the national coalition government
for which the Front program calls. In Hanoi it was emphasized that once the
American intention to withdraw was clear, then—these are the words of DRV
liaison officer to the International Control Commission—"some points in a
political settlement could be negotiated" and "concrete details can be discussed."
Both the Front program and the declaration of the first Front Congress in 1962
explicitly call for South Vietnamese elections by universal suffrage and secret
ballot, with all political parties and mass organizations guaranteed the right
to present candidates. Premier Pham Van Dong, in his written answers to our
questions, explicitly envisioned free general elections to decide the question of
reunification.

Are our own goals really so far from these that we can in good conscience
further escalate the carnage without more effort at clarification than one melo-
dramatic month affords?

If the first major failure in the United States' peace offensive has been its
failure to knock on the NLF door, the second key inadequacy has been the
Administration's vagueness about the withdrawal of American troops. Would
American troops at once be withdrawn as soon as we were certain that no DRV
troops were in the South? Or, as both Secretary Rusk and Mr. Moyers have suggested since the peace offensive began, would American troops remain until we
were assured that the government of South Vietnam would not go Communist?

This ambiguity was stressed by Hanoi radio on December 30. Commenting
on the President's Fourteen Points, the broadcast conceded:

> they said they agreed to hold "negotiations without preconditions," to "talk
> at any time, anywhere and with any government"; that they were ready

to implement the 1954 Geneva Agreements on Vietnam and approved the reunification of North and South Vietnam; they also declared that it is possible to discuss the four-point stand of the Government of the Democratic Republic of Vietnam along with the other proposals put forth by the US or its henchmen; that the South Vietnam National Front for Liberation might explain its viewpoint at the conference table; they also proposed a ceasefire from both sides when the talks begin, and so on and so forth.

"But," Hanoi radio continued, "there is one and the most fundamental thing which they have never mentioned: the withdrawal of US troops from South Vietnam."

By this the Vietnamese do *not* mean physical withdrawal of all troops before negotiations. What they *do* mean is that the presence of American troops in their country seems to them an outrageous violation of the principle of self-determination; and in particular, that no election could be free so long as foreign troops remained.

I came to understand through my trip that this attitude toward foreign troops is no mere negotiating position, but has deep roots in Vietnamese history. Secretary Rusk is wont to speak of North and South Vietnam as "neighbors." The Vietnamese find this singularly insulting. They say that quite apart from the Geneva Agreements, which stipulates clearly that the 17th parallel is provisional, history and culture make Vietnam "one country, one people." The rhetoric of North Vietnam is more nationalist than Communist; their slogan, quite literally, is "liberty or death." The war against ourselves is viewed as a continuation, not only of resistance against the Japanese and French, but of a centuries-long struggle for nationhood and independence against China. We were ceaselessly reminded that the Chinese and Vietnamese languages are quite different; that the Vietnamese have their own style of music, architecture, cooking and family life; that—as they put it—"we take advice from every one but (here usually comes a little laugh) we make our own decisions." When we asked what Ho meant when he said that Vietnam would help the United States withdraw on a red carpet, we were referred to the invasion of Vietnam by the Ming dynasty in the 15th century, when, having captured the Chinese general staff, the victorious Vietnamese built boats so that the Chinese could go home without loss of face.

Americans must understand that Communists can also be nationalists. They are people who feel as strongly about home and family and the good things of life as we, but to quote Ho again, they will fight for twenty years if need be to expel all foreign troops. I recall the interpreter in Prague who carefully explained the NLF stand on amnesty, and then added: "But if the sky should fall after you withdraw, that would still be a Vietnamese problem."

Since we have been back, nothing has been said or done to us by way of legal reprisal. We regard our trip as intended not for negotiation but for clarification. Like Felix Greene, Lord Fenner Brockway, William Warbey and other fact-finders who have talked directly with the D.R.V. and N.L.F., we asked questions and brought back a report about the answers. Our hope is that the government will choose to regard our trip as an expression of the President's intent to knock on any door and travel anywhere in search of peace. In this spirit, we cabled from Hanoi to Senator William Fulbright asking for an opportunity to present our findings to the Senate Committee on Foreign Relations.

A telegram has been received from Senator Fulbright, as follows:

> YOUR GROUP'S REQUEST HAS BEEN CONSIDERED BY THE COMMITTEE, BUT THERE ARE NO PLANS TO HEAR YOU. IF YOU HAVE NOT ALREADY DONE SO I WOULD SUGGEST THAT YOU PASS ON TO THE STATE DEPARTMENT ANY PERTINENT INFORMATION OBTAINED DURING YOUR TRIP TO NORTH VIETNAM.

We are disappointed that the United States Senate, with its ultimate constitutional responsibility for war and peace, has shown so little interest in direct contact with the only Americans who have been to Hanoi in recent months. We have wired Senator Fulbright:

> URGE YOUR COMMITTEE RECONSIDER DECISION. IMPOSSIBLE TO CONVEY FULL SENSE OF FINDINGS THROUGH INTERMEDIARY. HAVE SPOKEN JAMES LEONARD STATE DEPARTMENT AND TOLD HIM OF FURTHER INFORMATION ESPECIALLY CONCERNING NLF WHICH WISH TO PRESENT DIRECTLY TO YOU. WE AGREE WITH YOUR PROCEDURE IN DOMINICAN CRISIS OF COLLECTING FACTS INDEPENDENTLY. WE ARE RELEASING QUESTIONS AND ANSWERS ALSO INTERVIEW WITH PREMIER PHAM VAN DONG WHICH WE THINK INDICATE IMPORTANCE OUR INFORMATION. WILL HOPE TO HEAR FROM YOU FURTHER.

What would I say if I could speak to Senator Fulbright's committee? Something like this:

When I spoke on January 11 with James Leonard, Deputy Director of Far Eastern Research for the State Department, Mr. Leonard stressed that the United States cannot simply accept the other side's four point program. He said such acceptance would suggest unconditional surrender. He added that for the same reason the United States cannot perform "actual deeds" of de-escalation, as required by the DRV and NLF, unless similar deeds are performed by the other side.

I am convinced that direct contact with the DRV and NLF might help to resolve these essentially procedural problems. For example, one can imagine the following scenario.

The DRV preconditions, as laid down in the Foreign Ministry statement on Jan. 4 and in Premier Pham Van Dong's answers to us Jan. 5, include three elements. First, bombing of North Vietnam must be ended permanently and unconditionally. Second, the United States must accept the DRV four points as a basis for negotiation. Third, the United States must demonstrate its sincerity by "actual deeds."

These preconditions can be accepted without loss of face by the United States if the United States continues the direct contact with the DRV which, according to Mr. Moyers, has already begun; and if, as Senators Church, McGovern, Cooper and others have suggested, the United States agrees to deal directly with the National Liberation Front.

First, bombing could be ended without a humiliating public announcement if it could be privately communicated to the DRV government that the pause will go on indefinitely.

Since the DRV regards its four points as a summary of the 1954 Geneva Agreements, conversation with DRV representatives could lead to acceptance of the four points in the form of a joint announcement by the two governments that the Geneva Agreements would be the basis of forthcoming negotiations.

Finally, as to actual deeds, both Premier Pham Van Dong and Colonel Ha Van Lau said that it is up to the United States what deeds it takes. Colonel Lau told us that one such actual deed might be recognition of the NLF, a step involving no military de-escalation at all.

A scenario very much like this was suggested to me ten days ago by Arthur Schlesinger.

Schlesinger told me that he thought the pause had been supported by two groups: the military, who saw the peace offensive as a pretext for new escalation; and liberal Senators like Robert Kennedy, who believe we should get out. Schlesinger himself said that bombing, whether in the North or South, had always seemed to him mistaken. He stated further that, in contrast to his attitude last spring, he now believes no more American soldiers should be sent to Vietnam. He thinks the way out now might be a phased withdrawal of troops over a period of one or two years. On the one hand this would meet the other side's belief that there can be no free elections in South Vietnam so long as American troops are there. On the other hand a phased withdrawal would, so Schlesinger said, give the non-Communist elements a "fighting chance" to create a permanently-neutral rather than Communist-orientated South Vietnam.

It is this sort of thinking which, so each day's papers indicate more clearly, has lost out now if indeed it was ever seriously heard.

What then is to be done? Were I to have an opportunity to speak to Senator Fulbright's committee, I would now add roughly the following:

You, gentlemen, have deeply disappointed the American people by your failure to exercise your constitutional responsibility over war and peace. Article I, Section VIII of the Constitution gives to Congress and only to Congress the power to declare war. Yet this Congress has permitted the President to land 200,000 soldiers in Vietnam without even public hearings by the Senate Committee on Foreign Relations, let alone a responsible Congressional debate.

I would go on to say that the Congressional resolution of August 1964, from which the President derives his power to act, explicitly requires the United States to act in conformity with the Charter of the United Nations. Yet, in contrast to the action of President Truman in 1950, one year after escalation of the war in Vietnam the United States has still not formally brought the problem before the only body legally authorized to designate a threat to world peace. I would tell Senator Fulbright that many many Americans agree with the opinion expressed by Mariner Eccles, former chairman of the Federal Reserve Board, on Jan. 3, that the United States is in Vietnam "as an aggressor in violation of our treaty obligations under the United Nations Charter."

Then I would call attention to the Nuremberg Tribunal. On that occasion the United States sent German soldiers and decision-makers to death and life imprisonment for what we carefully defined as "war crimes" and "crimes against humanity." Among these crimes were indiscriminate destruction of civilian populations, and torture and murder of prisoners of war. It is common knowledge that actions of this kind take place in Vietnam. On August 6, 1965, the twentieth anniversary of the bombing of Hiroshima, *Time* magazine stated: "the marines have begun to kill prisoners." We claim that our chemicals are not toxic and our gases are not lethal, but on Jan. 13 the *Brisbane Courier Mail* reported that Corporal Robert Boutwell was killed despite the protection of a gas mask when trapped in a tunnel amid the fumes of so-called tear gas grenades. What of the women and children crouching in such tunnels without gas masks? Everyone knows that American bombers routinely decimate unprotected villages on the mere suspicion that guerillas may be among the population. Perhaps it will help us understand the NLF rejection of the United States peace offensive if we read again its Jan. 5 statement that the United States has introduced in South Vietnam "a mobile bacterial and chemical warfare institute and thousands of tons of noxious chemicals and gases strictly banned by international law," that in the first seven months of 1965 seven hundred square kilometers of crops were destroyed by toxic chemicals, that between December 7 and 14 forty-six thousand people were affected by chemicals sprayed in Ben Tre province alone.

Senator Fulbright, I would continue, many of us who have been freely denounced as law-breakers feel that in refusing to commit such acts we obey the higher law of the Nuremberg Tribunal. Such a one is David Mitchell, who rests his refusal to be drafted on the twin grounds that Congress has not declared war and that the Vietnam war violates the Nuremberg judgments. Others are the twenty-nine young men who go before an appeals court in Ann Arbor tomorrow for sitting-in at a draft board October 15. Their plea? That this is an unconstitutional and aggressive war, in violation of the Nuremberg Tribunal. Still others are the 7000 persons, myself included, who have signed the Declaration of Conscience against the War in Vietnam. Among the signers are religious figures like Daniel and Philip Berrigan, scientists such as Linus Pauling, literary personalities such as Harvey Swados and Maxwell Geismar; also included are W. H. Ferry, Eric Fromm, Milton Mayer; not the least are Bayard Rustin, organizer of the March on Washington, Robert Parris, organizer of the Freedom Democratic Party, and James Bevel, organizer of the Selma to Montgomery March.

All these persons have signed the following Declaration of Conscience against the war in Vietnam [see chapter 1, document 1].

Senator, I would conclude we, who have committed ourselves to this Declaration honor the brave men on both sides of the war. But we are not at war with the people of Vietnam. If the war escalates, it will escalate without us.

Document 6

STAUGHTON LYND AND TOM HAYDEN, "THE PEACE THAT MIGHT HAVE BEEN," FEBRUARY 1966

On 31 January 1966, President Johnson ordered the resumption of bombing of North Vietnam and the end of the "Peace Offensive." Below, Staughton Lynd and Tom Hayden respond.

What Clergy Concerned About Vietnam have called the government's "appalling lack of candor" is nowhere more evident than in Secretary Rusk's insistence that Hanoi made no positive response to the peace offensive.

Each side asserts that it pays more attention to the other's "actual deeds" than to mere words. Judged by this standard, the other side's de-escalation during the peace offensive was at least as substantial as that of the United States.

Between December 20 and January 31 the United States:

1. Increased its troops in South Vietnam from 180,000 to 197,000, thus adding more *new* troops during the peace offensive than the *total* of 14,000 North Vietnamese soldiers which the Mansfield Report says are in the South.

2. Spread the war into the whole of Indo-China by authorizing "hot pursuit" into Cambodia on December 21 and subsequently conceding the bombing of Laos from bases in Thailand.

3. Also on December 21, admitted the continuing use of toxic chemicals in South Vietnam. (The Jan. 5 response of the NLF Central Committee to the peace offensive stated: "from December 7 to 14, 1965, while prattling about 'peaceful negotiation,' the US imperialists carried out massive poison sprays, notably in Ben Tre province, where 46,000 persons were affected, mostly women—including expecting mothers—, aged people and children, tens of thousands of hectares of rice and other crops were destroyed, and a great number of domestic animals killed.")

4. Continued bombing in South Vietnam. On the day when Mr. Moyers says the United States handed the North Vietnamese government a note (December 29), North Vietnamese sources say that B52 bombers flew 322 sorties.

To those on the other side with whom we spoke in Hanoi between December 28 and January 7, United States ".knocking" during the peace offensive still appeared done more with bombs and bullets than with the hand of peace. Experience has led them to tune out our words and watch our actions. They called the peace offensive a public relations maneuver because the bombing pause in the North was more than offset by new escalation in the South.

What of the military actions of Hanoi during the peace offensive? On January 5, in a written answer to a written question, Premier Pham Van Dong categorically denied the presence of DRV "forces" in South Vietnam. The answer puzzled us. We had carefully explained to the translator that we would not report having asked any question which the Premier chose not to answer. We were told that the customary practice of the North Vietnamese government was to deny the presence in the South of specific units, such as the 325th regiment. We knew that in response to a similar question from Felix Greene only a few weeks earlier, President Ho Chi Minh had said only that the United States was "fabricating false information." Why had the Premier gone out of his way to give us so blunt and sweeping an answer?

A possible answer suggested itself when, after our return, American media repeatedly confirmed the fact that no contact with North Vietnamese troops had been reported in the South since early November. Perhaps the strongest statement appeared in the *New York Herald Tribune* for January 29, the day the President ordered the resumption of bombing: "Communist regular forces continued to make themselves scarce. A high military source in Saigon said there were indications that some units of the North Vietnamese Army had pulled back across the South Vietnamese border into Laos and Cambodia. The source also told *United Press International* that the Reds have been ordered to scale down their activities and avoid large battles with Americans."

In the face of this evidence Mr. Rusk told his press conference January 31 that "they made clear their negative view by deeds as well as words ... we have not seen a reduction of activity in the South."

Conveniently for the Secretary, the bodies of a number of dead enemy soldiers "dressed in the khaki uniforms of the North Vietnamese Army" were reportedly found January 29 and appeared in the January 30 headlines. How these uniforms were distinguished from the khaki uniforms of the regular NLF troops, which we saw for ourselves in Vietnam, was not made clear. At lunch on January 31 one of the most respected newsmen in the United States told us that the finding of those bodies on the eve of the bombing's resumption, after three months of no contact with North Vietnamese soldiers, simply strained his credulity.

What kept the United States from exploring the possibilities opened up by these surprisingly flexible responses was, of course, its bleak refusal to knock on the door of those whom it is fighting. On this head the President's 14 points did not approach the other side's position even verbally. Military de-escalation in the South as well as North was the first missing element in the government's peace offensive. The second missing element was an unequivocal declaration of American willingness to talk directly with the NLF about the concrete political circumstances under which the United States would withdraw its troops from Vietnam.

In his state of the Union message President Johnson seemed to move beyond the rigidity of point 13 when he referred to the possibility of talks with "any group." But he also reaffirmed American commitment to the Saigon government, a point emphasized by Hanoi in a response which could have been regarded as a request for clarification. According to the *New York Times* for January 30, Secretary of State Rusk appears to have clarified the ambiguity by going to Saigon and telling General Ky that the United States would never deal directly with the NLF.

Document 7

SPEECH AT TRAFALGAR SQUARE, LONDON, ENGLAND, 5 FEBRUARY 1966

In the midst of the brewing controversy in the United States over Lynd's visit to Hanoi, he was asked by the British Broadcasting Corporation to take part in a debate on the show *24 Hours*. Afterward, Lynd addressed an antiwar rally at Trafalgar Square organized by the British Council for Peace in Vietnam. Below is an excerpt of this speech.

When one recalls that in April 1917 the United States went to war so that American citizens might have the right to travel unmolested to England, even in the midst of general European war, it is rather ironic that the United States Government should question my coming to England at the invitation of BBC television and speaking on a panel with four professors and three MPs.

The right to travel freely is part of the larger right to free inquiry on which free societies such as England and the United States ultimately depend. The United States government stands in particular need of such assistance today.

Deliberate deception by the highest officials of our government, episodically practised in connection with the U-2 incident of 1960, the Bay of Pigs invasion of 1961, and the Cuba missile crisis of 1962, has in Vietnam become settled public policy. Mr. Arthur Schlesinger now concedes that he lied about the Bay of Pigs invasion, and Mr. Arthur Sylvester, information officer at the Pentagon, justifies such prevarication as in the public interest.

I believe that the United States government has once again deceived the people of the United States and of the world in its explanation of why bombing was resumed.

At his press conference on January 31, Secretary Rusk stated that there had been no positive response to the peace offensive from Hanoi, either by word or deed. However, on Saturday, January 29, the day President Johnson gave the order to resume bombing, the *New York Herald Tribune* carried a dispatch from Saigon which stated that, according to a high military authority there were indications that some North Vietnamese troops had been pulled back into Laos and Cambodia, and added that intercepted messages revealed that both North Vietnamese troops and NLF troops had been instructed to avoid contact with American soldiers.

The President and the Secretary say bombing was resumed because North Vietnam continued its so-called aggression from the North during the peace offensive by rebuilding roads and bridges in North Vietnam, and sending more men and material to the South. But the *New York Times* for February 4 carried an article by Neil Sheehan from Saigon which said: "There is no confirmation here of statements in Washington that the North Vietnamese moved 5,500 men into South Vietnam during the pause, nor of statements that the North Vietnamese were now infiltrating 4,500 men a month into the South."

The North Vietnamese crimes during the peace offensive, it would seem, is that they rebuilt the facilities which had been destroyed by American bombers during the preceding ten months and continued to give material aid to their fellow-countrymen south of the 17th parallel. Against this one must set the fact that during the period of the peace offensive the United States landed more new troops in South Vietnam (17,000) than the *total* number of North Vietnamese troops there, according to the Mansfield Report (14,000); and that the moment the Lunar New Year ended the United States launched its largest offensive operation since the Korean War, appropriately titled "Operation Masher."

I submit that what these facts suggest is that during the peace offensive, just as before and after it, the United States, not North Vietnam, was the principal aggressor south of the 17th parallel.

If we ask, Why did Hanoi not respond more positively to the peace offensive? I can tell you, from having been there, that what impressed them was that the day after President Johnson said he would knock on any door for peace, the Defence Department authorized hot pursuit into Cambodia and admitted the continuing use of toxic chemicals, and the day after the President enunciated his 14 points, 4,000 new troops of the 25th Division arrived in Pleikhu and B52 bombers carried out more than 300 sorties in the South.

The American government was ushered into existence by a declaration which stated that a decent respect for the opinion of mankind required facts to be submitted to a candid world. It has lost that respect. It is acting in a different spirit. Its present policy in Vietnam is as ruthless to the truth as it is ruthless to human beings. I for one shall have nothing to do with that policy.

Figure 3.8: Staughton Lynd posing for the media with his passport stamped "Cancelled" after a hearing at the State Department in Washington, DC, in March 1966. Lynd's passport was originally stamped "Cancelled" upon returning from London, England, at the JFK Airport in New York one month earlier. Courtesy of Getty Images and the Bettmann Collection.

Document 8

EXTRACT FROM TRANSCRIPT, "IN THE MATTER OF
THE PASSPORT APPEAL OF STAUGHTON CRAIG LYND,"
DEPARTMENT OF STATE, WASHINGTON, DC,
24 MARCH 1966

Upon Staughton Lynd's return from London on February 5, immigration officials seized Lynd's passport and stamped it in large red block letters: "CANCELLED." As is mentioned in the introduction to this chapter, the State Department notified Lynd on February 2, the day he left for London, that his passport was revoked. Lynd had not received the letter and traveled to England under the shadow of possible government retribution. Lynd told the press at the airport that "I intend to uphold my right to travel. It is an elementary and constitutional right." He also told reporters that before his trip he was informed by the ACLU to issue a statement of protest to US Customs officials if anything should happen upon his return.[33]

Below is an extract from Lynd's passport hearing inside the Department of State during his administrative hearing appealing the cancellation of his passport. Lynd had also filed suit in federal court challenging the revocation of his passport and the US government's restriction on travel to communist countries. Here Lynd explains why he made the trip to North Vietnam.

Transcript of Hearing
Department of State
Thursday, March 24, 1966
10:30 am

MR. BROOKS: Do I understand the answer essentially to be—and I don't want to misquote you at all—but is it that Professor Lynd reserves the right to travel in restricted areas without using a passport?

MR. CARLINER: That is correct.

MR. LYND: He reserves the right is a rather dry, legal form. I think it is the case that I am, on the whole, an open and honest person, not an indiscriminate lawbreaker, and as a matter of fact, not even a world traveler.

This was the first trip outside the United States too since I was eight years old. Nevertheless, as a historian I must say that there are circumstances when men have broken laws. I think, in the judgment of history, I think the judgment of history is that they acted rightly.

An example would be the Abolitionist's Movement when Congress passed the Fugitive Slave Act requiring all citizens of the North to give assistance in the return of fugitive slaves, a law upheld in the Supreme Court in the Dred Scott case of 1857.

Now, travel, as I see it, involves the right of freedom of speech under the first amendment. My personal concern with the kind of traveling we have been considering throughout this long day involves something more [than] that to wit: the contact between persons who are separated by war.

It is my interpretation of the rules of the Nurnberg Tribunal after World War II that there are circumstances in wartime, particularly if the acts there are war crimes, and are crimes against humanity, which not merely permit whatever country they may belong to to refuse certain kinds of orders and to break certain kinds of laws and think it is a valid inference from the spirit of the Nurnberg Tribunal that just as there may be circumstances in which, under the rules of that Tribunal, an individual is obliged to say "no" to an order.

There may be positive acts which he feels called upon to undertake to bring an end to war crimes, crimes against humanity and to bring an end to war and it was in this spirit of peace making that we undertook our Christmas journey. Indeed, our trip, began the day before President Johnson spoke about knocking on anybody's door in the spirit of peace.

I think the trip had positive results. I think that there is a certain amount of evidence that responsible journalists in the State Department itself feel that the trip had positive results.

Among the evidence which I expect to produce, I would mention, for example, a column by Warren Rogers in the Baltimore Press for January 13 in which he says, "In this case the State Department is inclined to take a less than serious view. The report that the three travelers brought back is considered important by the State Department. It is especially significant in light of other contacts the Department has had with the contacts which officials hope may eventually point the way to the kind of solution to the Vietnamese that they are hoping for."

I would like to mention just one other piece of evidence at this time as to the constructiveness of our trip. It is a column by Seymour Topping, the foreign correspondent of the *New York Times*. In the *Times* for February 4 it referred to the written answers from Premier Pham Van Dong to our written question as one of a series of documents which, in his opinion, have helped analyze and clarify the peace terms of the other side and this was the purpose and only purpose of our journey so that, while I must say that I have no present plans for another journey to one of the forbidden countries, indeed, my present plans call only to responding to such countries as England and Norway. Nevertheless, I cannot imagine a circumstance in which I would feel more legally obligated to make the kind of journey I did in December and January and it is with all this in mind that I have to answer the question in the way counsel indicated.

CHAPTER 4

WHAT WOULD VICTORY BE?

Introduction

When President Johnson resumed bombing over North Vietnam on 31 January 1966, it was a fateful *choice* that locked in an escalation that more than doubled the previous year's military effort. Although the first bombing run over North Vietnam was more restrained than the Joint Chiefs of Staff advocated, 132 attack sorties nonetheless struck the DRV and obliterated any efforts at peace that could have been pursued further in Vientiane and Rangoon. While pursuing peace proved difficult during the bombing pause, it was not helped by the United States' continued military actions in South Vietnam and Laos. For example, the US flew 8,000 attack sorties over Laos to interdict soldiers and supplies along the Ho Chi Minh Trail in January 1966 alone. This was double the amount flown over Laos in the last quarter of 1965. In 1966, the rate of escalation was astounding, as bombing sorties were more than tripled in North Vietnam from 25,000 in 1965 to 79,000 in 1966. In South Vietnam, US attack sorties increased from 37,645 in 1965 to 124,686 in 1966. In total, during the Americanization of the Vietnam War by the Johnson administration from 1965 to 1968, the US flew 565,686 sorties in South Vietnam and 304,345 in the North; this equaled 2.2 million and 643,000 tons of bombs respectively.[1]

For Staughton Lynd, meeting this renewed challenge of escalation required more than selecting and campaigning for "peace candidates" in the 1966 mid-term elections or the growing calls from elected officials in the Senate and from certain liberal wings of the peace movement for an "enclave strategy" in South Vietnam. For instance, the February edition of *Harper's* magazine featured an article by retired lieutenant general James Gavin calling for the US forces to withdraw to selected coastal enclaves and hold those positions, using US air and naval power in the South, and stopping the bombing over North Vietnam.

This strategy would allow the US to engage in an international settlement either through the United Nations or a reconvening of the Geneva Conference. Gavin's article sparked debate in all corners of American politics, both inside and outside the government, which led to Gavin being calling as lead witness in the televised hearings of the Senate Foreign Relations Committee (SFRC), headed by Senator J. William Fulbright. As we will see, the hearings themselves proved highly influential, and the enclave strategy would be endorsed by several leading "dove" senators, including Fulbright and George Kennan.[2]

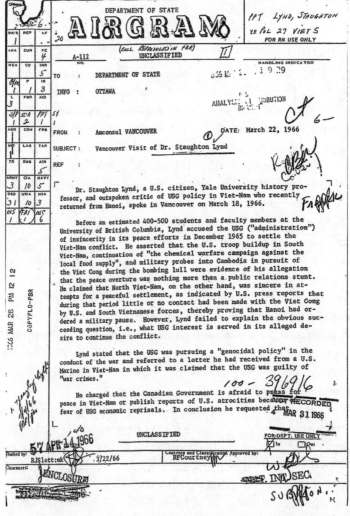

Figure 4.1: An Airgram from the American consulate in Vancouver, British Columbia, reporting on Lynd's talk at the University of British Columbia on 18 March 1966. Source: Lynd's FBI file.

While Lynd welcomed the convening of the Fulbright hearings, he nonetheless found the emerging proposals emanating from the growing list of the war's critics as lacking understanding of the urgency and crisis of the moment. Once the bombing of North Vietnam resumed, Lynd understood that the war would again be escalated beyond the bounds of morality and domestic and international law. To meet this challenge meant building a larger, mass movement against the war, specifically targeting the Selective Service System. Speaking at the Second International Days of Protest on 26 March 1966, Lynd told separate protest rallies in Madison, Wisconsin, and Chicago that the North Vietnam Peace Committee commented that they were "puzzled" more young people in the United States were not "refusing to serve in your army." Lynd went on to criticize SDS for failing "to emphasize an anti-draft program" and a group known as the May Second Movement for starting the "We Won't Go" pledges in 1964 and then "suddenly [backing] away from it." He called on those in attendance to start thinking about the upcoming national Selective Service exams in May and June "when young men will be invited, after being fingerprinted, to do well on a test so that the person in the next chair will be killed." He concluded: "The most obvious and tragic failure of the movement against the war in this last year has been its failure to develop a responsible program against the draft."[3] As later chapters will explore, Lynd was a leading figure in developing such a movement.

While the mood and temper of the early months of 1966 were ones of anguish and sometimes solitude in the antiwar movement, a period of soul-searching among early critics of the war for more effective tactics and strategies, a flurry of activity nonetheless demonstrated that the movement was widening its base as new organizations emerged and new voices entered the fray. On January 6, the Student Nonviolent Coordinating Committee (SNCC) issued its first public statement against the Vietnam War and support for draft resisters, the first civil rights group to do so. While debate within SNCC developed over the fall of 1965, the killing of Sammy Younge, a twenty-one-year-old Navy veteran and civil rights activist, in Tuskegee, Alabama, for trying to use a whites-only bathroom at a gas station, pushed the organization to finally release its statement. Citing its right to dissent from US government foreign policies, SNCC called into question the sincerity of the United States in its calls for freedom and free elections for the people of South Vietnam when African Americans benefitted from neither at home. The statement read in part,

> Samuel Younge was murdered because United States law is not being enforced. Vietnamese are murdered because the United States is pursuing an aggressive policy in violation of international law. The United States is

no respector of persons or law when such persons or laws run counter to
its needs and desires.

SNCC concluded by encouraging people to refuse to cooperate with the
Selective Service System and stated that "the civil rights movement and other
human relations organizations is a valid alternative to the draft. We urge all
Americans to seek this alternative, knowing full well that it may cost them their
lives—as painfully as in Vietnam."[4]

The National Emergency Committee of Concerned Clergy about Vietnam—
formed in the aftermath of government criticism of antiwar dissent in October
1965 and later renamed Clergy and Laymen Concerned about Vietnam
(CALCAV)—used the thirty-seven-day bombing pause to create a national
organization by pushing Protestant, Catholic, and Jewish faith leaders and con-
gregations to call for an end to the bombing and negotiations to end the war in
Vietnam. Lynd's colleague at Yale, William Sloane Coffin, was at the forefront
of the national effort to build the committee. The determination paid off with
165 local chapters created by the end of January and numerous local actions for
peace in Vietnam undertaken as a result.[5]

A major boost to the movement came in February 1966 when former US
Army master sergeant and elite Green Beret Donald Duncan published an
explosive article in *Ramparts* magazine arguing "the whole thing was a lie!" The
same month Lieutenant General James Gavin was writing and testifying about
respectable and face-saving plans for the US to exit Vietnam, Duncan was writing and speaking about the abject failure of US military strategy and the mis-
truths belying US public positions. "We weren't preserving freedom in South
Vietnam," Duncan wrote. "It's not democracy we brought to Vietnam—it's
anti-communism" and anti-communism was "a lousy substitute for democracy."
A member of the Army's Special Forces, Duncan engaged in counterinsurgency
operations in the jungles of South Vietnam for eighteen months in 1964–1965
and returned to the United States deeply affected by his experiences. As a result,
Duncan communicated his experiences with an authority few antiwar activists at
this point could claim.[6] Duncan exposed extremely sensitive classified information such as the joint US–ARVN (Army of the Republic of Vietnam) commando
raids into Laos under Project Delta and the ultrasecret Studies and Observation
Group raids into North Vietnam in 1964, which tried to subvert and sabotage the
DRV before full-scale US escalation commenced. Therefore, Duncan challenged
the Johnson administration's narrative about why it was fighting in Vietnam,
especially the main argument that it was North Vietnamese aggression that was
to blame for the conflict, and wrote candidly about torture and the killing of
prisoners of war, the culture of the armed forces, and the racism inherent in US

operations in Southeast Asia. He argued that the South Vietnamese resistance was an indigenous movement and that the effect of the bombing was imperiling the stated mission. For these reasons, the US should get out of Vietnam. It was a powerful indictment and one that led to an espionage investigation of Duncan by the FBI.[7] Lynd specifically referred to Duncan's revelations in what would become a controversial speech at Carleton University in Ottawa.[8]

Throughout the remainder of the war, Duncan acted as a bridge between the intersecting movements of veterans, active-duty GIs, and the civilian antiwar movement. One early manifestation of this was a full-page advertisement in the *Chicago Daily Defender* sponsored by Veterans for Peace in Vietnam, to which Staughton Lynd was one of the signatories. Featuring a picture of Donald Duncan in uniform, the caption read, "Let's Stop the Killing in Vietnam!" The statement read,

> We are veterans of the U.S. armed forces.
> Our experience with the agony of war gives us a special responsibility to speak out about the war in Vietnam, which may bring World War III.
> Blind support for our government's policy is not patriotism. True patriotism means the courage to question, and to insist that our policies be just and worthy of our great country.
> We believe the war in Vietnam is illegal, immoral, unjust and unnecessary.
> We are destroying Vietnam in an attempt to wipe out the "Viet Cong." But the "Viet Cong" are native South Vietnamese who have been fighting occupying armies for 25 years. They control most of the countryside and are supported by a large part of the population (80% according to former President Eisenhower).
> We are told that we are resisting "invaders from the North," and that we are protecting the "independence" of South Vietnam. But the 1954 Geneva Agreements providing for a free nation-wide election, which we promised to honor and then violated, speak not of a North and a South Vietnam, but of a single, unified Vietnam.
> No Chinese or Russian troops are in Vietnam, but over 200,000 U.S. troops are preventing the Vietnamese from settling their own affairs.
> We are told that we must fight in Vietnam, or tomorrow we will be fighting closer to home. Whatever government the small nation of Vietnam chooses does not threaten our security. What does threaten our security is our involvement in an unjust war on the other side of the world.[9]

These were all welcome developments for the burgeoning antiwar movement. However, the most important development during this period was the opening of debate about the war initiated by Senator Fulbright and his decision to use the forum of the SFRC to broadcast nationally televised hearings on the Vietnam

War. Fulbright was the leading figure in the Senate in August 1964 pushing through the Tonkin Gulf Resolution, a decision he came to regret and perhaps an important impetus for initiating the hearings. After the resumption of the bombing of North Vietnam, however, demands for the hearings grew from other members of the SFRC when President Johnson rebuffed the bipartisan letter from fifteen senators calling for an extension of the bombing pause and separate calls for the SFRC to be consulted before the resumption of bombing. In the president's brisk response to the letter, Johnson informed the senators he was "guided in these matters by the [Tonkin Gulf] resolution of the Congress approved on Aug. 10, 1964." In an especially encouraging development, the days leading up to bombing in late January saw Fulbright and Senator Wayne Morse questioning the legality of the resumption of bombing. In an open but not televised SFRC hearing with Secretary Rusk on January 28, Fulbright argued that he could find no legal justification in either the Tonkin Gulf Resolution of 1964 or the Southeast Asia Treaty Organization (SEATO) treaty of 1955 for the renewed bombings of North Vietnam. The following day, Morse introduced a resolution calling for rescinding the 1964 justification for the war and "a full and complete investigation of all aspects of United States policies in Vietnam." The *New York Times* reported from an unnamed source that the president's "senior advisers are said to have told him that it would take six or seven years of military action in South Vietnam to bring about a satisfactory solution there." Many of the senators who originally voted for the 1964 resolution began to argue that it was being used by the administration beyond its intended scope and that they did not intend it to be used as a "blank check" for US military action in Southeast Asia. However, the president, Rusk, and Bill Moyers reminded the critics that the resolution read "that the Congress approves and supports the determination of the President, as Commander in Chief, to take all necessary measures to repel any armed attack against the forces of the United States and to prevent further aggression."[10] In response to these developments, Senator Fulbright called for the hearings and tied them to the $415 million foreign aid supplemental request that was to be voted on by the Congress. The final decision for the televised hearings came on February 3. The hearings themselves heard from retired lieutenant general James Gavin on February 8, George Kennan on February 10, General Maxwell Taylor on February 16, and finally Secretary Rusk on February 18.[11]

Not to be outdone, President Johnson ordered his team to hastily organize a conference in Honolulu with South Vietnamese prime minister Nguyen Cao Ky and Chief of State Nguyen Van Thieu to focus on the social, economic, and political aspects of the war—what was called "the other war" or the pacification war—and to have various US cabinet-level officials attend the meetings as well. Johnson specifically organized the Honolulu conference to divert attention from the opening of the Fulbright hearings, as McGeorge Bundy told historian and Fulbright biographer Randall B. Woods in an interview that the meetings were "a big farrago, meant to take the spotlight off the hearings."[12] While focusing on nonmilitary aspects of the war at these meetings, Johnson nonetheless approved General Westmoreland's request of two hundred thousand more troops to South Vietnam and issued a "Final Declaration" that ensured that South Vietnamese leadership, the US Congress, and the American people understood that the Johnson administration was fighting in Vietnam to guarantee a stable, viable, noncommunist government in South Vietnam at all costs.[13] One consequence of the Honolulu conference was the closing of the Rangoon channel when the North Vietnamese harshly condemned the Final Declaration on February 21. Citing the resumption of bombing, increased troops, support for the government of South Vietnam, and the Honolulu Declaration, the DRV informed the US ambassador, "The American government is doing its utmost to intensify and expand its aggressive war in Vietnam and Indochinese countries, bringing it to a new stage, seriously endangering peace and security of the countries in this region."[14]

Throughout 1965, Staughton Lynd argued that direct action against the war would force moderates off the sidelines to take positions on the war and open new avenues for other kinds of dissent. These developments in early 1966 demonstrate that the agony of the war and the more radical demands of immediate withdrawal from Vietnam were forcing the debate. Some of the major elements that Lyndon Johnson's personal adviser Jack Valenti referred to as the "Lynd-line" were beginning to make headway on Capitol Hill and demonstrating that the reality of the conflict was no longer to be concealed by the various public pronouncements of administration officials. For instance, on January 24, as Tom Wicker of the *New York Times* argued, Senator Fulbright "moved sharply away from the Administration position by advocating that the Vietcong be invited to participate in peace negotiations. He said he believed the absence of such an invitation might be the main obstacle to negotiations."[15] Senator Robert F. Kennedy went even further at the close of the Fulbright hearings by arguing that the NLF should be admitted "to a share of power and responsibility" in any South Vietnam government because this was "at the heart of the hope for a negotiated settlement." The *New York Times* noted that this was the most controversial of all proposals to date and an even clearer break with the administration than that proposed by Fulbright a month earlier. The *Times* also reported that Robert Kennedy's proposal, behind closed doors, was perhaps shared by half the members of the Senate and that Senator George McGovern went on the record saying that "two-thirds of the Senators favor a course that would get the United States out of Vietnam short of abject withdrawal." Two days later, Fulbright gave "qualified support" to Kennedy's proposal, noting that the NLF should be treated as an "independent entity" and "must be one of the principal parties" during negotiations. In response to these developments, National Security Adviser McGeorge Bundy and Assistant Secretary of State George Ball opposed the idea of a coalition government. Ball told the press that this would quickly lead to "a Communist government in Saigon."[16]

On a personal level, Staughton Lynd approached the renewed escalation with a recharged sense of commitment to the struggle against the war. Now an international, as well as a national, protagonist against the war, Lynd entered the new semester at Yale facing increased scrutiny for his political activities by students, his colleagues in the History Department, the administration, and especially alumni who were calling for his dismissal publicly and privately. Under such circumstances, in the daily professional life of a university academic, to continue to push the boundaries of what was considered the normal behavior of a "Yale man" in the face of colleagues who questioned the intentions and even patriotism of Lynd's actions, took some courage, a strong sense of confidence, and awareness of the gravity of the situation. Alice Lynd told biographer Carl Mirra that these events led her to believe that Staughton was "miserable" at Yale.[17] Despite these difficult circumstances, pressures that would force others to self-censor themselves or retreat to the comforts of their offices or classrooms, Lynd persisted in his opposition to the war.

Document 1

IN RESPONSE TO THE FULBRIGHT HEARINGS, FEBRUARY 1966

While Staughton Lynd, Herbert Aptheker, and Tom Hayden were still in Hanoi, they cabled Senator William Fulbright that they would be willing to testify before the Senate Foreign Relations Committee about their findings in Vietnam. As we have seen in Lynd's speeches on January 17 at Yale and on January 24 in Washington, DC, the response was negative. In the proceeding weeks, crucial in the escalation of the war in Vietnam, pressures mounted for a congressional debate on the war and the legality of it without a declaration of war. Upon the announcement that Senator Fulbright would be launching televised hearings on the war in Vietnam, Staughton Lynd wrote this short and previously unpublished response. The piece was found in Lynd's papers at Kent State University.

What ought one do, what can one do in this desperate situation? Discussion has begun in Congress and Senator Fulbright courageously voted to rescind the Tonkin Bay Resolution. But I believe it would be disastrous to argue that dissent has now made its way back into the conventional political process, and that the time for direct action is over. What is the scenario which leads from Congressional debate and a modest increase in the number of dissenting Congressmen to withdrawal from Vietnam?

If Congressmen want to stop the war, they will have to take much more courageous steps than any yet contemplated. To begin with, sooner or later they will have to stop talking about enclaves, about negotiations without withdrawal, about NLF representation as one of many forces in a South Vietnamese coalition government, and accept the necessity of American negotiation with the NLF on the basis of (1) phased but rapid and complete American withdrawal, (2) a South Vietnamese government whether formed by election or coalition which will include groups not now in the NLF but in which the NLF will have a major role.

Next, Congressmen who really mean to stop the war will have to be prepared to vote "No" on appropriations bills. The power of the purse is the legislature's historical weapon against the executive. Understandably, for human as well as political reasons legislators hesitate to vote against appropriations for equipment which might save an American life. Sooner or later, however, they will have to face the fact that the way to save American lives in Vietnam is to bring the troops home, and that to do this they must refuse appropriations designed to put more troops in Vietnam and escalate the war.

Ordinary citizens can help Congress to do this, I believe, not merely by writing letters to Senator Fulbright, not merely by asking next fall's candidates to pledge themselves to de-escalation, not merely by running peace candidates ourselves in some constituencies, but also by acting out in our own lives the thing we ask our Congressmen to do. We ask them not to vote money for the war. We should ask ourselves whether we can conscientiously pay taxes to support the war. We ask them not to put more soldiers in Vietnam. We should ask ourselves whether we can conscientiously go.

I believe there is no alternative to such direct action even after dialogue has begun within conventional channels. Remember the abolitionist movement which after a Sumner, a Stevens, a John Quincy Adams began to speak up in Congress still required brave men and women to take direct action to rescue individual fugitive slaves.

Of course it will be said that we give aid and comfort to the enemy, something the President has very nearly said about the chairman of the Senate Committee on Foreign Relations. We must just hold fast to the knowledge that those whom we seek to aid and comfort are all the suffering human beings in Vietnam.

Figure 4.2: Lynd speaking in front of the Lincoln Statue on Bascom Hill at the University of Wisconsin–Madison at the Second International Days of Protest in Madison, 26 March 1966. Photograph courtesy of the Wisconsin Historical Society, Madison, Wisconsin.

Document 2

"HOW THE AMERICAN LEFT CAN CHANGE THE SYSTEM: TEXT OF ADDRESS AT 26 MARCH DEMONSTRATION OF PROTEST AGAINST THE WAR," 26 MARCH 1966

At its first convention from November 25 to 28, 1965, the National Coordinating Committee to End the War in Vietnam agreed to organize a Second International Days of Protest against the War in Vietnam to be held March 25–26, 1966. This would be the last major event organized by the NCCEWV due to internecine rivalries between members of the Communist Party and the Socialist Workers Party that dominated the committee. Specifically, debates about calling for immediate withdrawal versus negotiations, as Lynd explains in the speech, became counterproductive if they led to the breakup of coalitions and the estrangement of people curious about joining the movement.

Searching for strategies to keep momentum through the winter months, generally considered low times of organizing by activists, the Second International Days of Protest were not as successful as the first series organized in October 1965. This led some commentators to believe the movement was losing steam. Despite this, the protests turned out over one hundred thousand in the streets of New York, San Francisco, and Chicago and in up to one hundred other cities in the United States and thirty countries around the world. The protests were organized locally by grassroots coalitions, which was actually more demonstrative of the growth in the movement.[18] Staughton Lynd, for instance, addressed rallies in Chicago and Madison, Wisconsin, on the same day on March 26.

Below is the text of Lynd's speech. A portion explaining different debates within the movement about tactics and strategy has been edited out in the interest of space. The text of the speech is from Lynd's papers at Kent State University.

Last spring at the April 17 march and at the Berkeley teach-in late in May, the movement against the war in Vietnam laid down a number of theoretical perspectives and suggested a variety of immediate actions. On April 17 Paul Potter, president of Students for a Democratic Society, said that the war was the product of a "system," and told us that the system must be named and changed. On Nov. 27 at the Thanksgiving March Carl Oglesby, by then the new SDS president, named the system "corporate liberalism," meaning by this that American capitalism had appropriated both the rhetoric and the personnel of the American liberal tradition to assist it in appropriating about half the world's goods. As to changing the system, Oglesby has this to say:

> "Those allies of ours in the government—are they really our allies? If they are, then they don't need advice, they need constituencies; then they don't need study groups, they need a movement. And if they are not, then all the more reason for building that movement with a most relentless conviction."

This is where we are. We know we need a movement, both to stop the war in Vietnam and to change the system of corporate liberalism.

I think that history, believe it or not, has some help to offer as we struggle with the problem of power.

The only successful revolutionary movement in this country since 1776 was abolitionism. Like the civil rights movement, abolitionism began with a decade of direct action and emphasis on morality, then went into politics. Like the civil rights movement, abolitionism enormously strengthened its appeal when it linked the cause of the slaves to other causes, and in particular opposition to the Mexican War. (Even so mainstream a politician as Abraham Lincoln gave aid and comfort to the enemy throughout the Mexican War by continually asking President Polk on just what spot that war began.)

Like the civil rights movement, abolitionism broadened its appeal not only by moving in the direction of a multi-issue program but also when the civil liberties of abolitionists were attacked—petitions to Congress gagged, Elijah Lovejoy killed defending his press in Illinois—and liberals not much concerned about slavery moved in to defend the First Amendment.

I think there are three lessons of abolitionism we should learn and learn well. The first is that direct action should not be abandoned when politics begins. Abolitionists in Congress acted with more fervor about fugitive slaves because other abolitionists, out of Congress, were helping individual fugitive slaves who knocked on the door in the night. Similarly: If we expect our representatives to risk their political lives by voting against appropriations bills for Vietnam and voting with Senator Gruening to keep draftees from going to Vietnam against their will, then I think you and I must show our representatives the way by taking the risks involved when we, personally, refuse to pay taxes and when we, personally, refuse to serve in Vietnam.

The second lesson is to remember that the people most unrepresented in current American decision-making are the people of the world outside the U.S., above all the Vietnamese people, just as the abolitionists considered that their first constituency was the Southern slaves. Tom Hayden put it this way in a speech at Nashville on the Southern day of protest Feb. 12:

"Before Garrison, abolitionists tended to view Negroes—much as Americans view Vietnamese—as simple, docile people now and then agitated by a minority into a rebellion. Garrison undertook to look at the slave question as the Negro looked at it. Garrison and Phillips opposed calls for a moderate long-term approach. Almost overnight a movement grew up to challenge the doctrines of gradualism. Garrison and others demanded immediate abolition: (1) As the only moral demand from the viewpoint of the oppressed. (2) As a demand which made friendly relations in the future more possible if the slave realized what a full change of heart had come over his former oppressor. (3) As a necessary demand, because anything else was liable to postpone change by giving the slaveholders an excuse.

"The abolitionists too were charged with demanding change overnight; but Phillips said: 'The cause is not ours, so that we might rightfully postpone or put in peril the victory by moderating our demands...Our clients are three millions of slaves standing as dumb suppliants at the threshold of our world. They have no voice but ours to utter their complaints.'"

The third lesson is to be wary of assuming that the poor will take humane positions on foreign policy. A problem for the abolitionists was that the Northern working-class was not much interested in emancipating Negroes who might become competitors for Northern jobs. This sentiment of Northern workers toward the Southern Negro can be compared with the sentiment of workers in the industrial West today toward exploited workers and peasants in the underdeveloped world.

Thus it was not true that in 1835 a Northern workingman who voted for Jackson and advocated public education, the right to strike, and universal suffrage necessarily cared about slavery. In fact, that same Jackson was just then closing the Southern mails to abolitionist literature and planning to annex Texas. Likewise, I think it is not true in 1966 that a person who is organized around democratizing the poverty program or the right to vote will necessarily come to care about Vietnam. I think he may, particularly if he is Negro, particularly as the draft calls grow. But in the meantime I believe students and intellectuals have a moral obligation to go out all by themselves on this issue of the war, not waiting to take a stand because the working class or the ghetto has not produced a mandate. Participatory democracy means among other things respecting the integrity of each individual to grow in his own way. I think that means not forcing one's views on others; and that it also means being true to oneself.

But I would like to come at the same problem more hopefully by referring to the experience of the Mississippi Freedom Democratic Party. Clearly Atlantic City was a traumatic experience for the Southern civil rights movement and clearly it has not yet securely found a new sense of direction. Where did we go wrong in the winter of 1964–1965? I speak of this with hesitation since in a variety of senses I can't call myself part of the "we": I was not in Mississippi after the summer, I am not a Negro, I am not now in the Deep South trying to pick up the pieces.

Nevertheless, I should like to venture the opinion that the congressional challenge was a mistake. It was a mistake because it was directed more toward energizing national opinion than toward building the movement locally: in other words, it was the same kind of mistake many of us have often attributed to bureaucratic coalition-builders. During the summer there was a growing conviction among persons working at the local level that the precinct meetings organized to mount the MFDP challenge at Atlantic City should be transformed into precinct movements which would formulate local programs and run local candidates. I think this is what is now happening in Alabama in the work of Stokely Carmichael and the Black Panther party. I think it didn't happen in Mississippi because the focus came to be Washington, D.C., rather than Washington County.

Now this has a very interesting connection with the problem I just posed about the attitudes of the poor toward foreign policy. The movement had no foreign policy orientation in the summer of 1964. I urged that foreign policy discussion be kept out of the Freedom Schools for just that reason. But in the almost two years since then concern about the war has grown in Mississippi, just as in the ghettoes of the North. Many people remember the Korean War and what American Negroes who fought in it came back to. Paul Lauter met a Mrs. Ida Mae Lawrence who wrote a poem about the war which ends: "Maybe the people there can't register, just like us." She understood the central issue of self-determination perfectly. She saw that there was a connection between unrepresented people in Vietnam. And what blocked and impeded this developing consciousness of ordinary people was precisely the effort to play the electoral politics game.

I remember how moved I was when at the church in Neshoba County after Schwerner, Chaney and Goodman were killed, Bob Moses said in August, 1964: "Their bodies were found the same day the President ordered the bombing of Vietnam; the lesson of all these deaths is that men must stop killing." But it seemed to me queer when the MFDP then went to Atlantic City saying that it was more loyal to President Johnson and the Democratic Party than the Mississippi regulars. And it seemed to me queerer still when just at the time of the Assembly of Unrepresented People a SNCC veteran, working with the MFDP in Washington, told me that he agreed personally with the Negroes in McComb who called on other Negroes to refuse the draft; and he agreed personally with the concept of the assembly, but he had to say the opposite publicly because it was important to win the votes of liberal congressmen.

Meantime the intellectual, Bob Parris [Moses], continued his personal exploration which took him into the anti-war movement, then to Africa, now back into the Negro community but organizing around the war. The people and the intellectual were growing in harmony, but the politicians tried to slow them both down.

Let's think about this more broadly. I maintain that what it means is that there is a natural connection between the kind of community organizing which builds consciousness, builds people's faith in themselves, doesn't expect overnight results, assumed that sooner or later these calls will join into an American resistance movement but doesn't force the process, uses electoral politics as a device to make discussion visible as well as a tool for acquiring power—between that and the Thoreauvian acts of solitary intellectuals like myself. Whether I can put into words what the connection is, is something else again. But I want to try.

I think what is key is that the intellectual and the poor person in Mississippi or Newark, act personally. They are concerned with ends, not like the politician with means (otherwise known as votes). Both have in view—and I think anyone who worked in the South will bear me out on this—both the Negro Baptist fieldhand in Mississippi and the intellectual activist have in view an ideal community, they have a vision of how people ought to relate together. In the back of the minds of each is a picture of a blessed community, something like a family but bigger, something like a seminar except that people act as well as talk, something like a congregation except that people work together as well as pray together.

I don't mean to be sentimental. I recognize the iron law of history which holds that the most valuable comrades are the hardest to get along with. Yet I don't think you can build a movement on hate. In my experience the most militant people have also been the quietest. In my experience he who thinks the policeman can become a brother is less likely to get hit on the head. The toughest nuts among us, I have noticed, will shyly confess in an odd moment that what really keeps them going is the vision of a band of brothers standing in a circle of love.

This vision of a good society which I contend lingers in the imagination of the alienated poor, and recurs to the imagination of the alienated intellectual, this vision of community simplifies many knotty strategic problems. It makes the fundamental strategic assumption that if enough people want such a society they will sooner or later find a way to achieve it. The really important thing is that in the meantime we not lose hope, that we stay together, that we deal with each other in an honest and kindly manner, that we share our resources with one another—socialism is a very natural idea for poor students, as it is for poor people of any kind—in the faith, or to use a newer expression, that we keep our eyes on the prize and hold on.

It's not a new vision. It is a very old idea that God gave the good things of this world to his children to share as in one family: that the idea of someone owning a field, or owning a portion of downtown Chicago, that the idea of private property is blasphemy. It is a very old idea that society should be made new on the model of the family, so that we would bear each other's burdens as brothers and sisters and like the early Christians, have all things in common. What does it have to do with Vietnam? Ultimately, whether this war stops will depend on how many of us feel how strongly another very old idea, an idea which has been espoused mainly by alienated poor people and alienated intellectuals—namely the idea that states may have quarrels with each other but that people don't, the idea that wars will end when the soldiers fraternize; Paine's idea of being a citizen of the world, the words which Garrison put on the masthead of the *Liberator*, which Debs said before going to jail in World War I.

But it's Utopian, I hear someone cry! Even if people can live that way in little groups they cannot change the structure, cannot solve the problem of power! Romantic, putschist, bohemian, nihilist, anarchist, petty-bourgeois, undisciplined, counter-revolutionary, counter-productive, and for the birds! And I answer with C. Wright Mills in his letter to the New Left: Whatever else it may be, it's not that.

The vision of community natural to alienated poor people and alienated intellectuals is not utopian because it is not pie in the sky. It doesn't put off action until tomorrow. Its creed is: If not now, when? and If not you, who? It is the faith which says each of us must act as best he can in response to each day's moral outrage, not waiting till the party decides its perspective for the coming period. Confronted with a need for new strategy, such as we have today, it seeks that strategy not by a meeting on 14th Street with internal bulletins, caucuses, and parliamentary hassles, but by sending individuals out into the field until some seed strikes fertile soil and persons begin to gather around a Moses in Mississippi because that person has found a new way to take hold.

This vision is not utopian because it implies and increasingly says that folk who care about this country had best be organizing a resistance movement to hold the line against the increasing repression which we anticipate—as this war escalates, as fighting revolution in Vietnam leads on to fighting it all over the third world, and American becomes a two-bit gangster with his back against the wall blazing away at an increasing number of Indians coming over the hill, resolved, finally to take one or two of them with him or perhaps even all since he has a nuclear button— to organize a resistance movement against these endless wars and the domestic repression which will come to complement the external fascism of the horror in Vietnam; to organize a resistance movement which will some day be in the position really to bid for power. Call that utopian if you like. But then tell me your scenario for how running a congressman in Berkeley and a senator in Chicago leads on to changing American capitalism and stopping American imperialism.

For students and intellectuals, Mills left a special mandate. In his essay on the decline of the Left, he said: "We must become internationalists again. For us, today, this means that we, personally, must refuse to fight in the Cold War, that we, personally, must attempt to get in touch with our opposite numbers in all countries of the world—above all those in the Sino-Soviet zone of nations. With them we should make our own separate peace." You can call that utopian if you like, but be careful, for it's an invitation to treason.

For myself, having joined with 300 others to declare peace with the people of Vietnam last August in Washington, I take this occasion to say again that I am not at war with the Vietnamese people; that while I deplore the absence of public discussion symbolized by the absence of a congressional declaration of war, if Congress declared war I would still not be at war with the Vietnamese people; that as long as this war lasts I will not voluntarily pay taxes; and that as I and most of you said long ago in signing the Declaration of Conscience, I wish to encourage others who can conscientiously do so not to serve in Vietnam. The purpose of such action is not only for its own sake, as a witness, but also to stimulate discussion, to confront people with actions which make them think.

We spend a good deal of time in the peace movement arguing about the slogan "negotiation" as over against the slogan "withdrawal." I think these slogans represent a real difference in appraisals of the war. He who advocates "negotiation" is likely to feel that both sides are more or less equally guilty; that the main purpose of the peace movement should be to stop the bloodshed; that the war in Vietnam is a tragic aberration from an American foreign policy that is fundamentally well-intentioned. He who advocates "withdrawal" is likely to feel that the U.S. is the aggressor and that NLF violence cannot be compared with the near genocidal practice of America; that the NLF is right in feeling that much as it wants peace, peace would lack substance so long as American troops and bases are in Vietnam; and that the war in Vietnam is not a mistake or aberration but the characteristic product of an essentially imperialist and counter-revolutionary foreign policy.

When the matter is put thus, as a difference in theoretical perspectives, I wholeheartedly agree with the position: "Bring the troops home now." But what remains unclear to me is what difference the question of slogans makes in how we act. If advocating withdrawal has as its tactical corollary splitting the peace movement then I think it is destructive, and I have an idea that some who pursued such splitting at the NCC Thanksgiving convention in Washington might in retrospect agree. If advocating withdrawal means a style of work in which preserving a hard core of militants ideologically pure becomes more important than reaching out to new constituencies, I'm against it. So far as I'm concerned it is more important for people to seek ways to withdraw their support from U.S. foreign policy through action than to waste all of our time haggling about whether the ten letters spelling the word "withdrawal" should or should not appear on a sign which somebody carries in a parade. Personal draft refusal by one man builds the movement more than a hundred paper victories in committees.

As the discussion spreads, as our strength grows, there will be many tactical and organizational problems. But what is essential is that we have a clear common sense of what it is we are doing. I believe what we are doing is developing a broader and broader, deeper and deeper, consciousness that this society needs to be fundamentally changed, and that the war in Vietnam is the concentrated expression of its moral bankruptcy and contempt for democratic procedures. I believe we are encouraging people to find what ways they can to translate this vision of a good community into their daily lives; but at the same time cautioning that without structural changes the room for institutional maneuver is small and the resources are in other hands, so that we must all be ready for a long pull of semi-exile in our own country. I believe we are seeking to break through Camus's distinction between rebel and revolutionary, and like the guerrilla who fights with one hand and with the other redistributes land and wipes out illiteracy, ourselves learn to be militant nonviolent revolutionaries while at the same time seeking to start the good society in our own lives, here and now.

I believe we are trying to develop in ourselves and others a conscience of mankind as a whole in its wonderful unity and variety, its non-antagonistic contradictions which men of the future will spend their lives savoring and exploring; but at the same time to remind ourselves and others that to be a citizen of the world here and now means drawing on oneself the wrath of the antidisestablishmentarian nation state. I believe we are carrying to our fellow-countrymen the paradoxical message that a brotherly society is possible and a Fascist state is probable; that men can live at peace but that nuclear war with China is very likely; seeking not to confuse ourselves or others, but to draw hope from the vision so as to be able to give back courage when our time in jail arrives.

I believe, as Carl Oglesby said at the *National Guardian* dinner last autumn, that the war in Vietnam may be the supreme test of this country's moral character. And I believe that we can meet that test, and that we shall overcome.

Document 3

"THE RESUMPTION OF BOMBING," MARCH 1966

In the below article published in the March 1966 edition of *Liberation*, Staughton Lynd sets out further evidence that Hanoi and the NLF may have sent Washington a signal during the bombing pause and "Peace Offensive" by de-escalating militarily.

Let us scrutinize for a moment the decision to resume bombing.

The order to resume bombing was given at 6 p.m., Saturday, January 29. That same day the Pope appealed for an approach to peace through the United Nations. That same day the text of Ho Chi Minh's response to the peace offensive was published in the American press: a text, incidentally, whose distinguishing characteristic was its more explicit emphasis on the need for direct contact between America and the N.L.F. That same day, also, a Saigon dispatch appeared in the *New York Herald Tribune* which said:

> Communist regular forces continue to make themselves scarce. A high military source in Saigon said there were indications that some units of the North Vietnamese Army had pulled back across the South Vietnamese border into Laos and Cambodia. The source also told United Press International that the Reds have been ordered to scale down their activities and avoid large battles with Americans.

One would have thought that the Pope's appeal, or Ho Chi Minh's letter, or the Saigon dispatch, might have led a President as concerned for peace as President Johnson says he is to pause just a moment before sending on their way again the metallic doves. Not at all. Everything proceeded according to plan. And at his press conference Monday, January 31, Secretary of State Rusk declared:

> They made clear their negative view by deeds as well as words ... We have not seen a reduction of activity in the South (*New York Times*, February 1, 1966).

Does this mean that the *Herald Tribune* story was exceptional, that there were no other indications of military de-escalation by Hanoi? No. One story after another during January 1966 noted the fact that there had been no contact with North Vietnamese troops in the South since November. On Thursday, February 3, the *Tribune*, in another Saigon dispatch, stated:

> The South Vietnamese High Command said in Saigon yesterday that the Viet Cong's main force still has launched no offensive operations

since before the Christmas ceasefire. U.S. military headquarters said that although the allied forces launched a record number of probing patrols during the last week—including Operation Masher—they encountered fewer instances of Viet Cong resistance than in any one-week period of the last five months.

A U.S. military spokesman also confirmed an earlier South Vietnamese report that regular North Vietnamese units believed to have been infiltrated into the South last year have not initiated any major battle since November.

The next day, February 4, a *New York Times* dispatch from Saigon stated that Washington reports of heavy North Vietnamese infiltration during the peace offensive were unconfirmed in South Vietnam.

Is it merely my private speculation that the other side may in fact have de-escalated in response to the pause? By no means. Roger Hilsman, former Assistant Secretary of State for Far Eastern Affairs and State Department intelligence chief, told the House subcommittee on Far Eastern Affairs February 1 regarding the North Vietnamese troops in the South that "there is evidence they pulled back at least into the mountains during the bombing pause—which may be a signal" (*I. F. Stone's Weekly*, February 7, 1966). Note that I make no mention of the fact that on January 5, 1966 the North Vietnamese prime minister told Mr. Aptheker, Mr. Hayden and myself there were no North Vietnamese troops in the South, and that after the interview we were told that this was the most categorical denial yet to be made by so high a governmental source. I do not mention this, because it is taken for granted in this country that if there is a conflict in testimony between, say, Premier Pham Van Dong on the one hand, and Mr. William Moyers on the other, it must be Mr. Moyers who is telling the truth. So I prefer to quote such sources as the *New York Herald Tribune*, the *New York Times*, and the former head of intelligence for the United States State Department. And I suggest that these sources indicate that the United States government may have monstrously misused the truth in justifying resumption of bombing on the basis of alleged escalation by the North.

Remember that in his State of the Union address on January 12 President Johnson said: "We'll respond if others reduce their use of force." Set beside this the evidence for de-escalation just presented. Then add this. When on January 25 the President offered a group of Congressmen the evidence which justified resumption, it included the fact that more than 200 trucks were photographed in the southern area of North Vietnam between December 31 and January 31, "most of them" heading for what was said to be the gateway of the Ho Chi Minh Trail. That comes to an average of fifteen trucks per day (*I. F. Stone's Weekly*,

January 31, 1966). On February 1, 1966, the *Baltimore Sun* stated that Pentagon sources "held that North Vietnam had not gained any military advantage from the suspension." The same day the *Washington Post* said: "Officials believe there was increased infiltration of men and supplies during the bombing pause, but the figures they cited do not clearly demonstrate this." The story continued that the Pentagon estimate of enemy numbers at the end of the pause was "about the same" as Senator Mansfield's estimate of their numbers before the pause began.

I think the testimony of history is that nations are unlikely to give up power as rapidly as is necessary unless they are prodded by citizens who in effect resolve to live by the standards of the future as if they were now in force. Have major moral changes ever come about in any other way? Socrates acquiesced in the judgement of his society that he should die, but he refused to stop questioning the assumptions of that society in wartime so as to avoid the hemlock. Because Luther could not do otherwise, the principle was established that each man, in communion with his Bible and his God, must be the final evaluator of religious truth. Because in Thoreau's phrase, American abolitionists resolved to be men first and Americans at a late and convenient hour, slavery was abolished in this country. And, I think, because there was a Quaker Norman Morrison and a Catholic Roger LaPorte, because their sacrifice lays upon all of us, not as scholars but as human beings, the obligation to live beyond ourselves, to take risks we thought unriskable, to burn bridges we thought unburnable—there may yet be peace in the world.

Document 4

"TO SPEAK THE TRUTH," MARCH 1966

Staughton Lynd addresses the criticisms and allegations made by Yale's president Kingman Brewster about Lynd's trip to North Vietnam and statements to a gathering of Vietnamese intellectuals. Brewster made the statement on 19 January 1966 in response to questions from the editors of the *Yale Daily News* as well as many others within the Yale community. While Brewster's statement is too long to produce in full, the relevant paragraphs include,

> While I would not have approved of his trip, I could condone it as an exercise of a citizen's right to dissent, to travel, and to pursue the dictates of his own conscience.
>
> I have quite recently reaffirmed my conviction that as long as a man is in good faith, as long as he is not in default with respect to his teaching and scholarly obligations for which he is employed, then the long-run interests of this University, indeed the long-run charge which this University bears from its own tradition, makes it unthinkable that we should penalize a faculty member for his political position.
>
> So, I would have disagreed with, but would have condoned, Mr. Lynd's stated purpose to find facts in the cause of peace, even if it tested the outer limits of passport regulations.
>
> However, Hanoi radio reported, and Mr. Lynd reportedly confirmed, that while in Hanoi he publicly asserted that the Johnson administration lies to the American people and that the United States policy is immoral, illegal, and anti-democratic. He is entitled to these opinions, but the use of his presence in Hanoi to give this aid and comfort to a government engaged in hostilities with American forces seems to me inconsistent with the purposes of fact finding in the name of peace.
>
> I think Mr. Lynd's disparagement of his country's leadership and policies while in Hanoi damaged the causes he purports to serve. By this irresponsible action I believe he has done a disservice to the causes of freedom of dissent, freedom of travel, and conscientious pacifism.[19]

For any assistant professor, facing an upcoming review for tenure, such comments from the president of their university would give most people pause. Instead, Lynd decided to respond publicly to Brewster's allegations below.

After my return from Vietnam President Brewster of Yale said that a speech I made in Hanoi gave "aid and comfort" to the enemy. A little later Secretary

McNamara stated that for him to testify publicly before the Senate Foreign Relations Committee would be "giving aid and comfort to the enemy," and President Johnson added that open testimony would be "aiding the Communists and aiding the enemy" (*New York Herald Tribune*, February 8, 1966). Now, "aid and comfort" is a phrase from the law of treason. People get shot for committing treason. The use of these words by President Brewster and President Johnson gives a certain existential pertinence to our inquiry.

When I said in Hanoi that American policy in Vietnam was "illegal, immoral and antidemocratic," I said something which to the best of my knowledge as a scholar and historian was true. I believe I can document each contention.

Not only am I convinced that what I said in Hanoi was true, I had said it before on many occasions in the United States. Indeed I opened my very brief remarks in Hanoi by observing that I would attempt to say essentially what I had said at the March on Washington against the war in April 1965.

I was speaking to a conference of intellectuals. The thrust of my remarks was that the common belief of all intellectuals, in whatever country they may live, is that truth is a great power.

Thus the truth, or at least a conscientious effort to tell the truth in an address to fellow-scholars, in President Brewster's eyes verges on treason. But when Arthur Schlesinger, Jr. recently said that he, when in government during the Bay of Pigs crisis, had deliberately lied, but that he hoped he would be forgiven for acting in the public interest, I noticed no statement from the President of Harvard condemning Mr. Schlesinger for violating the most elementary precept of intellectual integrity. It would seem then, that for one historian to lie in Washington is almost patriotism, while for another to try to tell the truth in Hanoi, is almost treason.

Clearly I am personally involved in this matter and, whether by the canons of law or scholarship, should not be judge in my own cause. But I invite someone more detached than I to carry further an exploration. Does truth become untruth depending on the place it is uttered? Can it ever be contrary to an intellectual's profession to try to tell the truth? Does there not exist a tension between a scholar's commitment to an idea of truth which knows no frontiers, and a citizen's commitment to his country? If there is such a tension, has not President Brewster drastically oversimplified the dilemmas involved in dealing with it?

The problem of the intellectual's responsibility—or as Benda put it, the intellectual's honor—presents itself the more sharply because of the United States government's habitual lack of veracity about Vietnam. In the U-2 episode of 1960, in the Bay of Pigs invasion of 1961, in the Cuba missile crisis of 1962, the American government lied, but its deception was temporary, episodic. What was most dangerous was that during the missile crisis Mr. Arthur Sylvester, then and now public relations officer for the Pentagon, said that deception could be in the public interest (the same phrase which rubbed off on Mr. Arthur Schlesinger). The fruits of Sylvesterism in Vietnam are common knowledge. Carl Rowan, while head of the United States Information Service, referred to the public's "right *not* to know during a period of undeclared war." The general manager of the *Associated Press* has said: "News restrictions imposed by the Pentagon raise serious questions as to whether the American people will be able to get a true picture of the war in Vietnam" (*New York Journal American*, April 15, 1965). What was episodic in 1960–1962 has now become routine; so much so that when in the midst of the peace offensive we learn that American bombers over Laos were not (as U.S. officials had steadfastly maintained) flying reconnaissance but were in fact dropping bombs, it hardly perturbs us anymore. What is inexplicable, however, is that in the face of such manhandling of the truth we expect the other side to place some confidence in our words. They don't. They watch only our actions: In the weeks of the peace offensive the United States conceded the use of toxic chemicals, authorized hot pursuit into Cambodia, admitted the bombing of Laos from bases in Thailand, and landed in Vietnam more new American troops than the total number of North Vietnamese troops there according to the Mansfield Report.

Document 5

"DID HANOI RESPOND?" MARCH–APRIL 1966

Below Staughton Lynd gives a further accounting of the failure of the "Peace Offensive" and the choice to resume bombing by the Johnson administration. Lynd refutes, point by point, the public statements of US officials for why it had to resume bombing. The article appeared in the March–April 1966 edition of *Viet-Report*.

The U.S. government makes the following assertions about its celebrated Christmas peace offensive:

- The United States exhausted every possible means of communicating its initiative to the other side. In President Johnson's words, it knocked on every door.

- To prove its sincere desire for peace, the United States accompanied its words by the concrete deed of halting the bombing of North Vietnam for 37 days.

- As on other occasions when the United States has sincerely offered to negotiate, the other side responded negatively or not at all. Explaining the resumption of bombing, Secretary Rusk stated: "they made clear their negative view by deeds as well as words" (*N.Y. Times*, 2/1/66).

- Reluctantly, and after waiting until the last possible moment consistent with the safety of American servicemen in Vietnam, the United States resumed bombing and further escalated the war.

It is true that the United States stopped bombing North Vietnam. With that exception it is my considered view, both as a professional historian and as one who had some opportunity for firsthand observation, that the American government's picture of its peace offensive essentially distorts the truth and conceals the fact that major responsibility for the continuation of this dreadful war rests on the United States.

To begin with, it is clear—at least so far as the public record is concerned—that the United States did not make direct contact with the National Liberation Front during the peace offensive. Thus it knocked on all doors except the door of those whom it is fighting.

This failure is of exceptional importance. The government of North Vietnam, both in conversations with us and in its public statements, laid down three preconditions for peace talks. The first was permanent and unconditional cessation of bombing in the North. The second was acceptance of the four points set forth by Premier Pham Van Dong in response to President Johnson's Johns Hopkins speech. The third called for certain unspecified "actual deeds" to prove American sincerity.

The first, second and fourth of Premier Pham Van Dong's four points are literal restatements of the 1954 Geneva Agreements pertaining to withdrawal of foreign troops, dismantling of military bases, and reunification of North and South Vietnam. They do not require physical withdrawal of American troops prior to peace talks. As Premier Pham Van Dong made clear to us, reunification would be by free election just as the Geneva Agreements stipulated. There is no conflict between points 1, 2 and 4 of the four-point basis for negotiations proposed by the North Vietnamese government, and the 14 points enunciated by President Johnson on December 27.

The problem lies with the North Vietnamese third point. This concerned the government which would rule South Vietnam prior to reunification elections, a subject about which the Geneva Agreements are silent. The North Vietnamese third point means at least that the United States must negotiate directly with the National Liberation Front. But the thirteenth of President Johnson's 14 points, as interpreted by government spokesmen, clings to the idea that the Front can make its views heard only as part of a Hanoi delegation.

This is the one area in which the negotiating positions of the two sides differ. Both Premier Pham Van Dong and Colonel Ha Van Lau, DRV liaison officer to the International Control Commission, made it clear to us that the North Vietnamese government did not wish to specify what "actual deeds" the United States might perform to prove its sincerity, but Colonel Ha Van Lau added that one acceptable act would be recognition of the National Liberation Front.

Thus, during the bombing pause, the first North Vietnamese condition—a permanent cessation of bombing—could have been met simply by continuing the status quo; the second condition—acceptance of the DRV four points as a basis for negotiations—could have been met by a willingness to recognize the National Liberation Front as an independent participant in negotiations; and that same act would have satisfied the North Vietnamese demand for an "actual deed." Nothing stood in the way of peace except American refusal to do what President Johnson pledged on December 20 that he would do, namely, knock on *any* door.

Our "Concrete Deed"

Consider the second element in America's self-image: the notion that the United States did demonstrate its sincerity by an actual deed, namely, the bombing pause. North Vietnamese sources have emphasized that America's bombing pause in the North was accompanied by continued escalation in the South. (See, for example, Premier Pham Van Dong's interview with us in the January *Viet-Report*.) The North Vietnamese called our attention to the following timetable of American actions:

- *December 21*: The Defense Department concedes that toxic chemicals are being used to poison South Vietnam's food supply. "Hot pursuit" into Cambodia is authorized.

- *December 21–22*: Harold Johnson, Chief of Staff of the U.S. Army, and Earl Wheeler, Chairman of the Joint Chiefs of Staff, arrived in Saigon. On January 1 they are joined by the Secretaries of the Army and Air Force. In Vietnamese experience, such gatherings usually precede fresh escalation.

- *December 28*: 4,000 new American troops of the 25th Division arrived in Pleiku.

- *December 28–29*: B-52 bombers launched 322 sorties in South Vietnam.

Since we left Hanoi the Vietnamese press added that prior to the resumption of bombing in North Vietnam on January 31, the American press exposed the fact that U.S. bombers based in Thailand were bombing Laos, and that the total number of *new* American troops which arrived in South Vietnam during the peace offensive was greater than the 14,000 North Vietnamese troops in South Vietnam claimed by the Mansfield Report.

Taken together, American refusal to talk with the National Liberation Front and the continued U.S. buildup during the bombing pause convinced the Vietnamese with whom we talked that the peace offensive was a public relations maneuver and that the United States was not yet prepared to consider withdrawal from Vietnam.

On January 3, "Observer" in the Hanoi's *People's Daily* pointed out that on December 30, Secretary of State Rusk had made plain what the 14 points of December 27 really meant. The Vietcong would have to lay down its arms. By "free elections," this article continued, Secretary Rusk meant "South Vietnam to be placed under the rule of a Saigon regime rigged up by themselves." In support of this interpretation, "Observer" quoted Walter Lippmann as follows: "The Secretary of State has conditioned our withdrawal from Vietnam on the establishment in Saigon of a stable and sure government which has nothing to do with the Vietcong who are now occupying more than half of the country. Such a condition practically means that we shall never withdraw from Vietnam."

Premier Pham Van Dong summed up the North Vietnamese critique of the peace offensive in his interview with us January 5. He said: "The essence of the

United States peace offensive is the idea of negotiation from strength. There is nothing new in it. Absolutely nothing new. What is the reason for the peace offensive? To win public opinion, particularly American public opinion. Only by so doing can President Johnson escalate the war" (*Viet-Report*, Jan. 1966).

Now that the peace offensive is over, American officials themselves cynically state that the North Vietnamese evaluation was correct. Seymour Topping of the *New York Times* writes: "Official planning in Saigon no longer takes account of any possibility of peace negotiations with the Vietcong. It is felt that the President's 'peace offensive' was undertaken to demonstrate that the Communists are not interested in negotiations and to assuage public opinion. The President is said now to be bent on action to break the back of the Communist-led insurgency." Topping continues: "Officials here did not weigh seriously the issues raised in the exchanges between President Johnson and Senator Robert F. Kennedy, over his proposal on the role of the Vietcong. Air Vice Marshal Nguyen Cao Ky...is planning to hold elections late next year, but the 10-member governing Military Directory says it has no intention of allowing the Vietcong to vote or to put up candidates" (*N.Y. Times*, 2/26/66).

The Making of Unfacts

I turn now to the third and fourth American allegations about the peace offensive: that bombing was resumed reluctantly after it had become clear that North Vietnam was intensifying its effort in the South rather than de-escalating in response to the United States initiative.

President Johnson ordered the resumption of bombing at 6 PM on Saturday, January 29. Three things had happened earlier that day which might have led a President concerned for peace to postpone his decision. First, the text of Ho Chi Minh's letter to several heads of government was made public, along with the text of Premier Pham Van Dong's written answers to our written questions. This material was not abusive in tone or intransigent in content. It contained several indications of flexibility on matters of importance, such as the process of reunification.

Second, the Pope appealed for arbitration under the auspices of the United Nations. The appeal may have suggested to President Johnson that he combine resumption of bombing with an approach to the United Nations, which up to that time he had steadfastly ignored. That this approach was one more public relations gimmick appeared the next week. UN diplomats, although unsympathetic to the timing of America's approach to the Security Council, nevertheless attempted to make something positive from the event by suggesting that the

UN call for reconvening of the 1954 Geneva Conference with full participation of the National Liberation Front. President Johnson destroyed this hope, too, by abruptly going to Honolulu to give visible and uncompromising endorsement to the government of Marshal Ky.

The third event which happened on January 29, which might have led another President to pause, was a dispatch from Saigon in the *New York Herald Tribune*. The story stated: *"Communist regular forces continued to make themselves scarce. A high military source in Saigon said there were indications that some units of the North Vietnamese Army had pulled back across the South Vietnamese border into Laos and Cambodia. The source also told United Press International that the Reds have been ordered to scale down their activities and avoid large battles with Americans"* (italics mine).

In his State of the Union address on January 12, President Johnson had announced: *"We'll respond if others reduce their use of force."* Throughout the peace offensive the American press reported a mysterious absence of contact between U.S. forces and the North Vietnamese soldiers said to be in South Vietnam. Despite this, at the end of the Buddhist Lunar New Year the United States launched its largest offensive operation since the Korean War, appropriately named "Operation Masher." The January 29 story in the *Tribune* indicated that almost a week after this provocation, enemy forces in general and North Vietnamese forces in particular were still seeking to avoid frontal contact with American troops. Yet the bombing was ordered anyway, and on January 31 Secretary of State Rusk blandly ignored the evidence for enemy de-escalation and asserted that the other side had not responded to the peace offensive by word or deed.

Had the President waited, he would soon have had confirming evidence for enemy de-escalation. On February 1, Roger Hilsman, former chief of intelligence for the State Department and Assistant Secretary of State for Far Eastern Affairs, told the House of Representatives Subcommittee on Far Eastern Affairs that "there is evidence they [the North Vietnamese regular troops] pulled back at least into the mountains during the bombing pause—which may be a signal" (*I. F. Stone's Weekly*, 2/7/66). On February 3 the *N.Y. Herald Tribune*, in another Saigon dispatch, stated:

> "The South Vietnamese High Command said in Saigon yesterday that the Vietcong's main force still has launched no offensive operation since before the Christmas ceasefire.
>
> "U.S. military headquarters said that although the allied forces launched a record number of probing patrols during the last week—including Operation Masher—they encountered fewer instances of Vietcong resistance than in any one-week period of the last five months.

"A U.S. military spokesman also confirmed an earlier South Vietnamese report that regular North Vietnamese units believed to have been infiltrated into the South last year have not initiated any battle since November."

The next day a *New York Times* dispatch from Saigon added that Washington reports of heavy North Vietnamese infiltration during the peace offensive were unconfirmed in South Vietnam. This substantiated stories that even Pentagon briefings on the day bombing was resumed "held that North Vietnam had not gained any military advantage from the suspension" (*Baltimore Sun*, 2/1/66).

I submit that this evidence demonstrates scandalous insincerity and deliberate deception on the part of the United States government in making its decision to resume bombing. Despite solemn statements by President Johnson that the other side has never responded to American peace initiatives, the fact is that the government of North Vietnam has responded to each of these U.S. initiatives [see "American Counter-Diplomacy in Vietnam," *Viet-Report*, March–April 1966, p. 9] and *by its military de-escalation in December and January gave precisely the response demanded by the United States as a condition for negotiations.*

Document 6

EASTER SPEECH AT TRAFALGAR SQUARE, LONDON, ENGLAND, 11 APRIL 1966

An advertisement for the upcoming British Campaign for Nuclear Disarmament–sponsored Easter Monday Rally at Trafalgar Square in London presented its speakers list, which included among others a giant puppet show, David McReynolds, and "Professor Staughton Lynd (if the US Government permits)."[20] As it turned out, the US government did permit Lynd to travel to London, issuing him a ninety-day passport for the trip.

The State Department felt it had little choice but to issue Lynd the temporary passport. After his passport was revoked in February, Lynd filed a lawsuit in federal court on March 14 that sought "to enjoin and restrain the enforcement of the withdrawal of his passport and to obtain an order directing the Secretary of State to issue him a valid passport at least for the period from 4/7/66 to 4/18/66." This summary comes from the FBI, who followed the Lynd travails closely. In a hearing in front of US District Judge Oliver Gasch on March 30 regarding Lynd's civil claim, the judge ordered that the lawsuit could not proceed until he had exhausted the administrative remedies within the State Department's passports office. Therefore, Lynd's administrative hearing was held two days later in Washington at the Department of State, where the cancellation of his original passport was validated because Lynd refused to promise he would not use it to travel to restricted countries. Lynd did so out of principle and also because he was engaged in a lawsuit challenging these Cold War travel restrictions. Lynd did indicate, however, he would make such assurances in the context of being issued a temporary passport for his trip to London. The Department of Justice was advising the State Department and the FBI that even with such assurances, Lynd should not be given a temporary passport because he had already violated the Cold War area restrictions. On the eve of Lynd's appeal of the administrative ruling, it was reported "that while the Board of Passport Appeals and the Secretary of State had held that the withdrawal of Lynd's passport should not be cancelled, the State Department will issue Lynd 'limited travel documents' for his trip to England." The FBI's legal attaché in London reported that Lynd arrived in London on April 10 and returned to the United States on April 11.[21]

Below is the text of Lynd's handwritten speech.

I would like to begin by thanking you for not sending English troops to Vietnam.

Then I would like to ask for your help in ending this terrible war in which my government is the principal murderer and your government is the principal accomplice.

I ask this on behalf of the American peace movement, and in the name of the great spirits of our own common radical tradition: in the name of Price and Priestley, who defied your government to defend our revolutionary war; in the name of the British textile workers who endured hunger and unemployment during our Civil War to support the abolition of American slavery; in the name of William Morris, and Gene Debs, and Keir Hardie and their dream of a society of brothers; in the name of Brockway and Brailsford and their long struggle to free India; in the name of Schwerner and Goodman and Chaney and the many others who have died for Freedom Now in the other America. I ask it in the name of the American soldiers in Vietnam.

As when the sun never set on the British empire we acted on occasion as your conscience and critic, so in this high noon of American empire: don't underestimate what it means when England says it understands and sympathizes with America's external fascism, don't underestimate what it would mean were you now to wash your hands of it. In 1954 on the eve of the Geneva conference, England stopped Dulles from using atom bombs at Dienbienphu. Today the plans are already drawn for dropping bombs on Hanoi and Peking. We can't stop it alone. Won't you please help us?

When Aptheker, Hayden and I went to Hanoi at Christmastime, our purpose was to clarify the negotiating position of "the other side," very much as Fenner Brockway, Felix Greene and James Cameron had sought to do earlier in the year. And I think that to a modest extent we did this. Once again it was made clear that the Front and the North Vietnamese government do *not* require the withdrawal of all American troops before negotiations; that the other side *does* anticipate free elections both in South Vietnam and to determine the question of reunification of North and South; and that so long as America talks of knocking on any door but refuses to talk with its actual antagonists, the NLF, the other side will regard so-called peace offensives as public relations maneuvers. Since Christmas, of course, United States support for the Ky government against the demand of South Vietnamese students and Buddhists for—for what?—why precisely for free elections, has exposed the utter hypocrisy of the Johnson Administration for all to see.

So I think our trip did something to explode the falsehood put forward both by my government and yours to the effect that the other side has been bleakly intransigent toward peace initiatives from Washington and London. In fact it was they, not me, who made the offer through U Thant in the fall of 1964 which

Mr. Rusk rejected without explanation because his sensitive antennae told him it was spurious. In fact when in April 1965 President Johnson finally got around to telling the American people why he had broken his campaign promise in February, the North Vietnamese responded within 24 hours with its 4 points. In fact, when America for 5 days in May stopped bombing N. Vietnam, there *was* a response by the other side through Paris; and when President Johnson stated at his July 13 press conference that candor compelled him to say that our repeated peace initiatives had met with no response, he added one more to the series of barefaced lies which have characterized his entire conduct of the war. And in fact, as I said when I was last here in Trafalgar Square, the evidence is very strong that during the recent peace offensive, while America was widening the war to Laos and Cambodia, announcing the routine use of toxic chemicals, and putting more *new* American soldiers in South Vietnam than the total number of North Vietnamese soldiers there according to the Mansfield Report, the other side was in fact de-escalating, breaking off contact with US troops and withdrawing some units from South Vietnam.

So much for negotiating positions. But when we returned to the States and had a few nights' sleep, I began to realize that the most important thing about our trip was that through us the US peace movement had made face-to-face contact with the people whom our government had designated our enemies. By doing this we broke through the official stereotypes with which our governments seek to make us hate persons whom we have never met. According to that stereotype, the Vietnamese is a dark-skinned little man in black pajamas who can live for a week on a ball of glutinous rice—whatever glutinous rice is—and doesn't mind being tortured or burned to death because Orientals have no feelings. But we met human beings whose feelings were at least as close to the surface as our own, men and women who broke into tears as they tried to tell us of the suffering of their people.

The US could not fight its dirty wars in Vietnam if it permitted its citizens to encounter directly the human beings they are ordered to kill. This is why free travel is so important. And it must be free travel not only of Englishmen and Americans to Vietnam and China, but of Vietnamese and Chinese to England and America. I challenge the US government to let the South Vietnamese demonstrators—young men and women who do not assassinate village officials but use the nonviolent techniques of the American civil rights movement, high school and college students who are asking not for Communism but for peace and freedom, brave friends who are risking their lives in defying a military government which my government supports—I challenge the US government to let them come to America and present their case. If they are as Washington says about them as about us hooligans and Communists, how about letting us see the dreadful reality with our own eyes?

I challenge the British government, too. The last time I was here the rally ended with a march on the American Embassy and Mr. Wilson said in Parliament, why don't the demonstrators make demands on Hanoi as well? To which the natural response would seem to be: If you would recognize the N. Vietnamese government and provide us a North Vietnamese embassy in London to march to, we'll be glad to do it. I understand Mr. Michael Stewart said at the Oxford teach-in that it was the pride of Englishmen to hear all sides. Well, then, how about giving visas for representatives of the NLF to come to England and join the conversation? Or have we departed so far from the standard of John Milton that the only acceptable winds of doctrine are those which blow from the West?

Internationalism is an essential creed of both the pacifist and the socialist. And though the pacifist and socialist take hold of the idea from different angles, what it comes down to for them both is the proposition that we have got to respond to the destruction of our Vietnamese brothers and sisters as if they were our own flesh-and-blood; we have got to take our stand like Tom Paine, who belongs to both England and America, and say: I am a citizen of the world and my countrymen are all mankind. We have got to recognize that for the Christian and the socialist there is a loyalty higher than the loyalty to party or to state; that above all nations is humanity; that Henry Thoreau was right when during the shameful war against Mexico he resolved to be a man first and an American at a late and convenient hour.

For you and for us, Englishmen and Americans, I think this means that we must reach out our hands to the poor and oppressed all over the world and raise a united protest against the governments of both of our countries. Together we must face the fact that our policy in Vietnam and your support for it are not mistakes or exceptions; but characteristic products of Anglo-American bipartisan foreign policy which has been fundamentally counterrevolutionary since at least World War II. Of course there are important differences between England and America, between Kennedy and Johnson, between a Labour government and a Tory: but I first heard of napalm when Labour used it in Malaya and it was Kennedy who organized the US Special Forces in Vietnam.

We have got to face up to the long run failure of European and American socialism to defend the exploited of the third world against exploitation and war. Politically, therefore, we have got to develop a kind of campaigning which makes foreign policy a central issue, a kind of voter who does not out of mistaken deference leave international decisions to his national establishment, a

kind of candidate who is prepared to work 10 years for a seat in parliament or
Congress, and give it up in a day rather than support a Vietnam.

Finally, above and beyond politics, I think you in England, us in America,
must find the courage to say to our governments:

> Gentlemen of power, brothers of Whitehall and Washington, friends of
> Wall St. and Threadneedle St.—
>
> We don't own bananas in Guatemala or copper in Rhodesia, and we're
> not going *to* war for them.
>
> The dust which dropped on Palomares dropped on us as well, and we
> have nothing to defend east of Suez.
>
> We don't believe in an America which consumes half the world's pro-
> duce, and we're not content with a welfare state which ends at the ocean's
> edge and becomes a warfare state beyond it.
>
> It's your Cold War.
>
> We're signing off from it.
>
> You started it.
>
> But we intended to end it and we shall overcome.

CHAPTER 5

TREASON?

Introduction

S taughton Lynd was first interviewed by the Federal Bureau of Investigation on 13 August 1953 because he was suspected of being a communist or a communist sympathizer. Even though Lynd was never a member of the Communist Party, for one to face such accusations during the late 1940s and up until the late 1960s was equal to being considered disloyal or even a traitor to the United States. In subsequent FBI reports and the various other files compiled on Lynd, these allegations followed him everywhere within the national security state bureaucracy for twenty years, and there were personal consequences.[1]

On 20 October 1953, Lynd was drafted into the United States Army as a noncombatant medic, having been granted conscientious objector status (1-A-O). Lynd recalled that while he was in the Army, the Viet Minh had launched its decisive battle against the French at Dien Bien Phu in March 1954, and he wondered, as was speculated at the time, whether he would be sent to Vietnam. This would not come to pass, as the US refused to intervene militarily, and Lynd was booted out of the Army on April 26, less than seven months after being inducted. He was undesirably discharged under US Army Regulation 615-370: Disloyal and Subversive. According to a report in Lynd's FBI file, the discharge was based on several factors: while Lynd was a student at Harvard, he was a member of American Youth for Democracy and the John Reed Club; he "was believed to be a Communist sympathizer"; he "included considerable Marxist philosophy in papers submitted while a student at Harvard"; he was described by an informant as "at least an idealistic Communist"; he sought to review the Communist Party publication *Masses and Mainstream*; he "was believed to be a member of the Communist Party"; he was described "as 'a dangerous type Communist' who would be disloyal to the United States in the event of an emergency affecting this nation"; his father, Robert, had close connections to the

Communist Party; and his mother, Helen, was "a hyper-modern educator who follows the Communist Party line."

CONFIDENTIAL
DEPARTMENT OF THE ARMY
OFFICE OF THE ADJUTANT GENERAL
WASHINGTON 25, D. C.

IN REPLY REFER TO
AGPO-XD 201 Lynd, Staughton C.   18 February 1954
US 55 435 330 (11 Feb 54)

SUBJECT: Allegations

TO: Private Staughton C. Lynd, US 55 435 330
        2131st ASU, Medical Replacement Training Center
        Camp Pickett, Virginia

1. Derogatory information has been received in this office which reveals the following:

That you —

a. In 1947 and 1948, were an officer in American Youth for Democracy and John Reed Club at Harvard University. The American Youth for Democracy is cited as subversive and Communist by the Attorney General of the United States. John Reed was one of the earliest Communist leaders in the United States.

b. Were believed to be a Communist sympathizer.

c. Included considerable Marxist philosophy is papers submitted while a student at Harvard University.

d. Were described as "at least an idealistic Communist".

e. Appeared at the Russian Research Center, presumably at Harvard University, requesting interviews for the publication "Masses and Mainstream" which is cited as the successor to New Masses, a Communist magazine.

f. Were believed to be a member of the Communist Party.

g. Were described as "a dangerous type Communist" who would be disloyal to the United States in the event of an emergency affecting this nation.

h. Have a father, Robert, who:

(1) Was reportedly closely connected with the Communist Party.

CONFIDENTIAL

CONFIDENTIAL

AGPO-XD 201 Lynd, Staughton,C.   18 February 1954
US 55 435 330 (11 Feb 54)

            (2) In 1944, 1946, 1947 and 1948, registered in New
York City as an affiliate of the American Labor Party. The American Labor
Party is cited by the House Committee on Un-American Activities as being
under Communist control in New York City.

        i. Have a mother, Helen, who:

            (1) Was described as a hyper-modern educator who
follows the Communist Party line.

            (2) In 1944, 1946, 1947 and 1948, registered in New
York City as an affiliate of the American Labor Party.

        j. In 1949, were a member of the Independent Socialist
League which is cited as subversive by the Attorney General of the United
States.

        k. In 1949, were a member of the Socialist Workers Party
which is cited as subversive and Communist by the Attorney General of the
United States.

        l. Attended meetings of the Socialist Youth League which
is cited as subversive and Communist by the Attorney General of the United
States.

    2. You are advised that you have thirty (30) days in which to make
rebuttal in writing of the above mentioned allegations.

    3. This letter has been classified to prevent embarrassment to you.
However, should you desire to obtain legal advice, permission is granted to
disclose the information contained herein to your counsel notwithstanding
the security classification of this letter.

    4. In the event of a failure to reply, or upon submission of an inad-
equate reply, the allegations may be used as a basis for discharge.

    5. Your reply should be made direct to The Adjutant General, Washington
25, D. C., Attention: AGPO-XD, and forwarded in the attached envelopes.

    6. Place your reply in the envelope which is stamped CONFIDENTIAL, seal
and place in the lined envelope that is NOT stamped confidential. Do not indicate in any way on the outside envelope that it contains confidential matter.

        BY ORDER OF THE SECRETARY OF THE ARMY:

                                            Adjutant General

2 Incls
   Envelopes (2)

CONFIDENTIAL

Figure 5.1: An 18 February 1954 US Army memo to Staughton Lynd outlining several
allegations that eventually led to his dishonorable discharge for disloyalty and subversion.
Courtesy of Staughton and Alice Lynd.

Lynd's undesirable discharge, along with 720 others, was overturned after the US Supreme Court decision in *Harmon v. Brucker*, 355 US 579 (1958).[2] The decision allowed Lynd to claim the GI Bill, and he applied to the doctoral program in history at Columbia University.

Therefore, long before Lynd's opposition to the Vietnam War, he was caught up in the McCarthyite anti-communist crusade—named after Senator Joseph McCarthy, who used baseless accusations to tarnish anyone who was a member of the Communist Party or, in the case of Lynd, was placed under immense scrutiny for perceived communistic writings, leanings, sympathies, friends, or relatives. Separate from McCarthy's tactics was the use, or misuse, of the House Un-American Activities Committee (HUAC), which led to hundreds of Americans being called to testify against themselves or others. In Lynd's case, his associations and political beliefs got him an undesirable discharge from the Army, which could have had a negative impact on his future because of the taint of being dubbed a communist. While certain of the excesses associated with Joseph McCarthy were rolled backed after 1954, when McCarthy was himself censured by the Senate, the effects lingered into the 1960s. Many individuals engaging in antinuclear, women's rights, gay and lesbian rights, antiwar, civil rights, and various other causes were labeled communists in order to discredit them in the eyes of the public. HUAC continued to call witnesses, until it was renamed in 1969 and ultimately disbanded in 1975, including Tom Hayden (2–3 December 1968) and David Dellinger (4 December 1968). A major component of the post-1945 national security apparatus was J. Edgar Hoover and the FBI, whose mission included the stifling of dissent and connecting it to disloyalty, un-Americanism and anti-Americanism. The FBI was central in rooting out subversive elements in the United States long before Senator McCarthy and long after, and this is the reason historian Ellen Schrecker prefers the term "Hooverism" to "McCarthyism" to describe this process of post-1945 anti-subversion and counterintelligence.[3]

When Lynd faced accusations in 1965 and 1966 of being a communist, un-American, anti-American, or a traitor for his activism against the Vietnam War, they were designed to discredit and sanction him. In some corners of the liberal establishment and the national security state, this meant getting him denied tenure at Yale. Marching in Washington, DC, on 9 August 1965, Lynd was dramatically splashed and smeared with red paint by right-wing counter-protesters to leave no doubt that Lynd was a "Red." When he was arrested in front of the Capitol building and booked by the Metropolitan Washington Police for disorderly conduct, his mug shot still bore the red smears on his shirt and face. This mug shot made its way into Lynd's Senate Internal Security Subcommittee File, and he was also the subject of a growing HUAC investigation. Both congressional committees, central to the McCarthyite and Hooverite crusade, followed Lynd's activities closely. As is mentioned in the introduction to this collection, Lynd was singled out as a leader of the antiwar movement in a lengthy Senate report that, among other things, argued that the movement had been taken over and led by communist elements. The chairman of HUAC received numerous letters from congressional representatives asking for information on Lynd, to which the committee happily replied. Among other open-source intelligence on Lynd, HUAC would pass out a statement by Representative John M. Ashbrook given on the eve of the Assembly of Unrepresented People to smear the organizations and individual participants. When it came to Lynd, Ashbrook argued, "Professor Lynd appears to be indiscriminate in the type of Communist organizations he supports," citing articles and speaking engagements with communist- and Trotskyist-associated organizations and publications covered extensively in Lynd's FBI file.[4] The dangers of McCarthyism/Hooverism was that the burden of proof was on the accused and not the accuser to prove they were not, indeed, a communist; which incidentally Lynd never was.

The accusations would only intensify after Lynd returned from Hanoi. As we have seen, Lynd, Hayden, and Aptheker wrote to Senator Fulbright that they would be willing to share the information they gathered with the Senate Foreign Relations Committee. Outraged by the thought of such a testimonial in the center of the US government, Senator Lausche openly warned of "the grave mistake" such an invitation would invite if "these men were honored with the right to appear before the committee." Lausche continued that "their love is for Communist China and North Vietnam, and distrust and hatred for the United States." To leave no doubt in the minds of the committee, and the American public, Lausche proclaimed that they are "not promoting the cause of the United States. They are not friends of our country. Nor should they be listened to. Especially should they not be allowed to desecrate the chambers of this Capitol by their advocacy of conquest over our country in favor of communism."[5]

When Kingman Brewster, president of Yale University, accused Lynd of giving "aid and comfort" to the North Vietnamese, he did so citing the Central Intelligence Agency's Foreign Broadcast Information Service transcript of Lynd's talk over Radio Hanoi. As Carl Mirra explains, Lynd's speech was broadcast as far as Tokyo, where the agency recorded and transcribed it. This was not publicly available information, but nonetheless the CIA's record of the broadcast made it into a growing file of complaints about Staughton Lynd in Brewster's files. The CIA itself had a file on Lynd even though the agency was expressly forbidden to collect information on American citizens under its own charter. Despite the CIA's withholding pages and redacting much of the information, Lynd's file begins in May 1965 with newspaper clippings from the Berkeley Teach-In and a copy of the Declaration of Conscience and a poster of the Speak-Out at the Pentagon in June 1965. On 23 August 1965, the agency acquired Lynd's arrest file stemming from the Assembly of Unrepresented People, and on December 28 the FBI notified the CIA that Lynd was in Hanoi.[6]

It was for similar reasons that Lynd was targeted by the national security state that his relationship with Yale was becoming increasingly tenuous during 1966. Lynd's trip to North Vietnam touched a nerve to be sure, but so did his continued calls for civil disobedience and nonviolent revolution, which became more focused on building a mass movement against the draft in 1966. It is worth pausing here to reflect on what Lynd was saying in public that caused growing consternation at Yale. Lynd not only opposed the Vietnam War, but his analysis of the roots of the conflict was also in sharp contrast to that of his liberal and conservative colleagues. Lynd argued that the crisis in Vietnam was central to US post-1945 foreign policy and therefore not a mistake or an aberration. In this regard, Lynd's criticism struck at the heart of the structure of the Cold War and the pervasive anti-communist consensus that gripped both Republicans and Democrats, conservatives and liberals alike. Lynd criticized both US foreign policy and its domestic counterpart of political repression and stifling of dissent in the name of loyalty and patriotism, of which he was intimately aware. Crucially, this critique, especially during the Johnson administration, indicted the liberal establishment, of which Yale was a valued member, as Lynd himself pointed out in his speech at Berkeley in May 1965. It was this Berkeley speech that led Kingman Brewster to contact Lynd to clarify a newspaper account of the speech because he himself was particularly sensitive and sympathetic to being misquoted.[7] I will spend the remainder of this introduction discussing the fallout of the fourth and last time Brewster asked Lynd to clarify a newspaper account of a speech. This episode will be covered in document 1 of this chapter and illuminates the intersection of Lynd's radical critique of the war and political repression by the national security state and the liberal establishment. But first, a little context.

After Lynd's passport was revoked in February 1966, he made several trips to Canada—Montreal, Ottawa, Vancouver—in February and March to give speeches about his recent trip to North Vietnam and the failed "Peace Offensive." During his speech at the Student Union for Peace Action (SUPA) teach-in at Carleton University in Ottawa on 2 March 1966, Lynd criticized Lyndon Johnson's and Dean Rusk's continued use of the Munich analogy to justify US escalation of the war in South Vietnam and the bombing of North

Vietnam. Munich was a shorthand for the widespread belief that British prime minister Neville Chamberlain had naively believed Hitler's lies in 1938 on the eve of Nazi Germany's conquest of Czechoslovakia and therefore was directly responsible for emboldening Nazi Germany and its conquest of Poland in 1939. Therefore, the Johnson administration used the Munich analogy to argue that if it did not intervene in Vietnam and challenge North Vietnamese aggression, communism would spread throughout Southeast Asia and embolden other communist forces throughout the world. In this sense, the much-vaunted domino theory by the Eisenhower administration in the 1950s was a derivative of the Munich analogy. To directly challenge this analogy, as Lynd did throughout the war and in Ottawa, was to argue that the United States was the aggressor in Vietnam and therefore in violation of the UN Charter and the Nuremberg principles of 1950. To make such an argument during the Cold War, with the legacy of World War II still fresh in the minds of many Americans, verged on treason and was certainly cast as unpatriotic. So too was the question of US war crimes in Vietnam, which Lynd discussed in this speech as well, citing Master Sergeant Donald Duncan's recent exposé in *Ramparts* magazine. To argue that the US was the aggressor in Vietnam and that war crimes and crimes against humanity were being committed, which violated the precedent set at the Nuremberg Tribunal in 1945–1946 and the Nuremberg principles of 1950, was simply a bridge too far for most of the liberal establishment and the media. As David L. Schalk argues in his comparison of intellectual debates during the French war in Algeria and the American war in Vietnam, appeal to the Nuremberg precedent engendered "passionate disagreements among American intellectuals" because of its origins and connotations with Nazi criminality. As the documents in this collection demonstrate, Lynd was a central figure in these debates and such arguments were related in part to the US government's constant argument, echoed in the media, that the North Vietnamese were the aggressors in South Vietnam.[8]

The account of Lynd's speech in one local newspaper took this argument out of context and removed the criticism of the Munich analogy as *the basis* for his concluding remarks. With the sensational headline "'We're the Nazis'—Yale Professor. LBJ Compared to Hitler" in the *Ottawa Journal*, the account led readers to believe that Lynd was making a direct comparison between the crimes of Nazi Germany and the alleged crimes of the US in Vietnam. According to former Yale History Department chair John Morton Blum, the article outraged the US ambassador to Canada, a Yale alumnus, who sent it directly to Brewster. This led Brewster to call a meeting with Blum and Edmund Morgan, who recruited Lynd to Yale, to discuss the article and what to do with the junior professor. Therefore, in the timeline to the untenure of Lynd, as recounted by Lynd's biographer Carl Mirra, this event is particularly important as a contributing factor to Lynd being pushed out of Yale.[9]

According to Blum's memoir *A Life with History*, Brewster received the article around the same time Lynd gave his Easter Monday speech at Trafalgar Square in London. Brewster used the opportunity to ask the history chair to convene a meeting with Lynd to ask if he had missed any of his classes at Yale given his busy speaking schedule throughout the United States, England, and Canada. The meeting would be a pretext for Blum to ask Lynd to clarify the newspaper account. When Lynd stated that the quotations were essentially correct, while making some contextual corrections, Blum told the younger historian that, on a personal note, he found his antiwar activities "strident and extreme" and reported this information back to the university president.[10] This might seem insignificant or harmless; after all, there were numerous letters to Brewster about Lynd's antiwar activities and Lynd's speech in Hanoi, unlike this event, that led the president to issue a public statement condemning the history professor. However, Blum devotes nearly three pages of his 298-page memoir to Lynd, and one of these pages focuses specifically on this incident in the context of a broader discussion about why Lynd did not receive tenure at Yale. It is also significant because, as he points out, the newspaper article recounting Lynd's speech was sent to Brewster by the US ambassador to Canada. This potentially adds some gravity to the situation given that Lynd was denouncing the US in a foreign country.

It is also important to understand what was "extreme and strident." In responding to a letter from William Sloane Coffin, who warned the Yale president he was concerned about recent comments he made about Lynd, Brewster wrote,

> I was disturbed by the fact that Lynd seemed to be getting so cavalier with his facts and extreme with his characterizations. As a result I thought he was losing many who had respected him even if they did not fully support his views. This seemed to me especially the case with the effort to create the impression that anyone could reach Hanoi at a high level just by picking up the phone; and the assertion that the Americans were purposefully killing and maiming civilian women and children. The gap between fact and word was ambiguous, the gap between fact and impression intentionally created seemed to be gross. I didn't like the technique when used by Senator McCarthy, and I don't like it any better when used by Lynd. However, I have not so far made any public mention of this, since I had hoped that you and his other admirers would persuade him to see the folly of these ways.
>
> As far as the epithets are concerned, I had in mind the ease with which he likened the United States Government to the Nazis when he was in Canada, and the label "murderers" in London. It is all too reminiscent of

Goldwater at his worst. If it falls outside the wide latitude for excuse which a politician enjoys, it most certainly falls well outside my notions of conduct fitting for a teacher and scholar. When a member of our faculty has achieved a notorious public identification with this University, I have no hesitation in letting the public know it if I believe his manner and style seem unfitting for his calling.[11]

Brewster clearly took exception to Lynd's characterization of the United States' actions in Vietnam and indicated that his detractors were losing respect for the younger scholar. For Brewster, himself a Navy veteran of World War II, these types of comparisons were irresponsible. There was simply nothing the United States was doing in Vietnam that could in any way resemble the actions of Nazi Germany. Moreover, while Brewster characterized Lynd as engaging in a McCarthyite tactic, what is clear from this episode is that Lynd was more accurately a victim of late-stage McCarthyism/Hooverism. While Brewster had "no hesitation in letting the public know" his disapproval of Lynd's public statements, he certainly believed it was unnecessary to inform the public that he received the CIA's readout of Lynd's speech in Hanoi or that he was informed about Lynd's remarks in Ottawa from the US ambassador to Canada.

The fact that the US ambassador to Canada, according to John Morton Blum, sent the newspaper article to Brewster should not be downplayed, nor should his affiliation with Yale. Throughout 1965 and 1966, there was a growing campaign to get Lynd fired from the university, and the action of an official representative of the US government sending such a newspaper article to Lynd's employer needs to be viewed in the same light; it was no longer simply disparate letters from irate alumni and members of the public. The second half of 1966 saw the coalescing of a more concerted campaign to get Lynd out of Yale. One June 15 letter from a group of Yale alumni to Brewster highlighted their belief that Lynd's association with the university was the only reason he received such "publicity." "Without the prestige of this association, Lynd would be just another shouting far leftist and most people would pay no attention to him.... Why should loyal Americans and Yale permit its name to be used in such degrading activities, pay his salary and furnish a renowned platform of freedom for Lynd to consort and aid the enemy?"[12] Perhaps this was the same group, or yet another one, who met in New York on 28 October 1966 "to formulate a plan to ease [Lynd] out of Yale University." This comes from a memorandum from an FBI special agent who was informed that a group of Yale alumni, including then current trustees, "were greatly concerned that Yale University might 'become another Berkeley'" and were trying to identify the right people "to effect [Lynd's] dismissal with no publicity."[13]

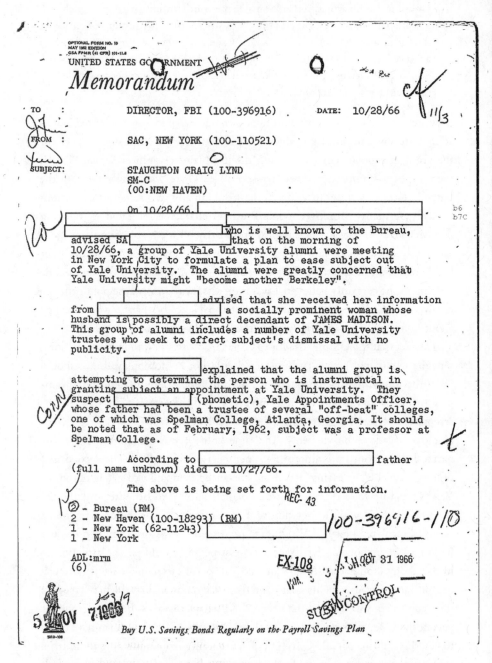

Figure 5.2: FBI memorandum from special agent in charge, New York field office, to FBI director J. Edgar Hoover, informing the director that a group of Yale alumni and trustees met to strategize how to get Lynd removed from Yale. Source: Lynd's FBI file.

While there is no direct evidence that there was any interference by the bureau in this particular case, the newspaper accounts of Lynd's speech were clearly making the rounds in FBI offices in the US embassy in Ottawa. Significantly, the FBI's legal attaché (legat) in the embassy forwarded the newspaper articles covering Lynd's speech at Carleton to J. Edgar Hoover on 4 March 1966, and the articles were passed on to the New Haven FBI field office. Lynd's speech was recorded, transcribed, and passed on to the bureau by the US Army attaché in Ottawa two weeks later.[14] Was the newspaper article that landed on the desk of Kingman Brewster and in the hands of John Morton Blum originally presented to the US ambassador during this dissemination process? The legal attaché's office routinely sent such articles back to the bureau. Ellen Schrecker notes in *No Ivory Tower: McCarthyism and the Universities* that FBI intervention to get professors fired was done secretly, and the sending of information, including press reports, "purposefully left few traces."[15] While this is speculation, what is clear is that the FBI, the US ambassador in Ottawa, Brewster, and Blum all found Lynd's speech "extreme and strident" and wanted to use it against him. Averell Harriman, President Johnson's personal peace envoy, also condemned Lynd's speeches in Hanoi, London, and Ottawa in an interview with the *Yale Daily News*.[16] To the national security state and leaders of the liberal establishment, this was unacceptable behavior for an American, let alone a Yale man, to compare the actions of the US to Nazi Germany in a foreign country and assert the US was committing war crimes during a speech condemning the Vietnam War. While Blum opposed the war in Vietnam, he "had no sympathy for the radicals' rhetoric or methods," and this inference was beyond the pale. The United States, despite all its faults, were the good guys, and to compare the actions of the US military, let alone President Johnson to Adolf Hitler, was heretical if not treasonous in the larger battle against communism.

It is true that this event did not lead to Lynd being fired, or even officially reprimanded. However, this latest conflict at Yale led to a break between Lynd and his colleagues and to the second time in six months that Yale's president questioned the professionalism of the junior faculty member. Had it not been for the US ambassador sending the article to Brewster, it seems unlikely that the president would have even read the sensational article from a local conservative Ottawa newspaper. As we will see in document 1 in this chapter, the much more widely circulated *Ottawa Citizen* covered the same speech, and the article did not even mention Lynd discussing Nazi Germany and was much more balanced in its appraisal. This intersection between national security state repression and liberal establishment outrage at Lynd crystallized during this crucial period, and there was no turning back. Informally in April 1966 and again formally in September 1966, Blum informed Lynd that because of budgetary constraints his chances for tenure were "minuscule." Lynd would not be under formal review for tenure by the History Department until 1968, and so Lynd took this announcement, coupled with the professional conflicts that emerged throughout 1966, as a signal he was being pushed out for political reasons. There were indeed budgetary concerns, as Blum explains in his memoir, but these were solved shortly after his chairmanship was over, and importantly, Lynd was not informed of the newfound financial stability in the department. By this time, the Lynds decided to move to Chicago in July 1967, and Staughton informed the History Department in 1968 he would not be returning for the final year of his contract. After years of speculation, Blum confirmed that financial problems were not the reason Lynd was denied tenure in 1968–1969.[17]

I have discussed this episode at some length to demonstrate the power of the Cold War anti-communist consensus and the marginalization Lynd and others faced when making radical critiques of the war. There was a weighty consensus among the champions of American liberalism at Yale, the national security state, and, as we will see, conservative commentators such as William F. Buckley Jr. that Lynd had crossed a line by 1966. If the publicity Lynd received was indeed due to the fact he was an Ivy League university professor, he used this platform to make unsettling arguments that shook the liberal establishment but also led to estrangement from his colleagues. This was a personal price Lynd was willing to endure in order to oppose what he viewed as an illegal, immoral, and unjust war. Conversely, because Lynd made these arguments and stood his ground on these crucial issues—traveling to North Vietnam to clarify peace terms of "the enemy," calling for civil disobedience and draft resistance, arguing the US violated international law and committed war crimes—he contributed to the unraveling of the Cold War consensus. It was precisely the brutality of the war in Vietnam that shattered the myth of American exceptionalism in the minds of many liberals by 1968 and 1969. In October 1969, Kingman Brewster joined with New Haven mayor Richard C. Lee in calling for unilateral withdrawal from Vietnam. In a press conference, the duo declared, "Our military presence has brought neither political freedom nor peace to South Vietnam. Rather, it has meant bombing and burning and maiming and dying—with no end in sight."[18] In November 1969 when the details of the My Lai massacre were revealed by Seymour Hersh—the horrific slaughter of 504 Vietnamese villagers in the hamlet of My Lai on 16 March 1968—Edmund Morgan, critical as he was of Lynd's actions and his speech in Ottawa in March 1966, wrote in the pages of the *New York Times* that US soldiers "have turned into monsters."

After the Second World War some of us found it difficult to believe that the German people did not know what their leaders were doing to innocent men, women, and children at Dachau and Auschwitz. None of us can deny that we know what we are doing to innocent men, women, and children in Vietnam—and I do not count Vietcong troops among the innocent.[19]

Reflecting on these statements from Brewster and Morgan, Lynd argued at an event at Yale University—titled "God and War at Yale" on 28 April 2005—that this language "was indistinguishable from that used by myself and others in the antiwar movement three or four years earlier."[20]

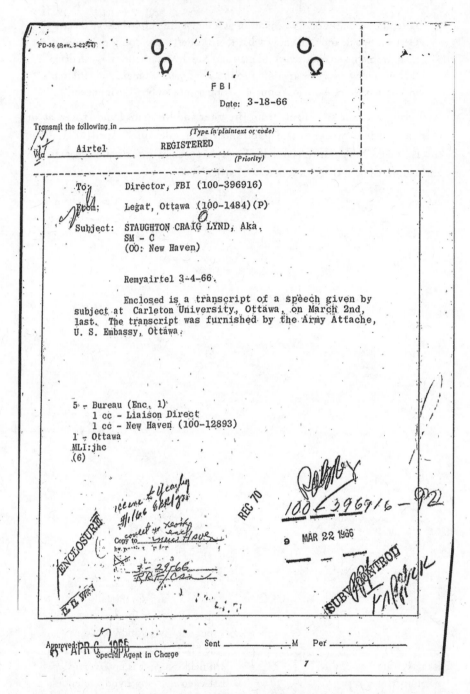

Figure 5.3: An Airtel from the FBI legation in Ottawa to J. Edgar Hoover, furnishing a copy of Lynd's speech at Carleton University. Note the transcript was provided by the US Army attaché in Ottawa and was forwarded to the FBI's field office in New Haven. Source: Lynd's FBI file.

Document 1

EXCERPT FROM TRANSCRIPT OF STAUGHTON LYND'S SPEECH AT CARLETON UNIVERSITY, 2 MARCH 1966

With Staughton Lynd's passport revoked, he gladly traveled to Canada on three separate occasions in February and March 1966 to "prove I can travel freely." Before his visit, the FBI field office in New Haven prepared information for the bureau's legal attaché in the US embassy in Ottawa "suitable for dissemination regarding Lynd's talk." In anticipation of the visit, the Canadian Department of Manpower and Immigration confirmed to the press that Lynd would be allowed to travel and speak in Canada after the controversial decision in March 1965 to bar US professor M. Q. Sibley for his advocacy of "free love."[21] Lynd's first trip on February 18 was sponsored by the Emergency Committee for Peace and Self-Determination in Viet Nam at Plateau Hall in Montreal in front of a crowd of 1,200 people. In the battle of headlines, Lynd appeared to be giving much the same speech he would give in Ottawa two weeks later. "I believe the United States government is systematically and deliberately committing war crimes, punishable under the judgment of the Nuremberg Tribunal, against the people of Viet Nam, is systematically and deliberately deceiving the people of America and the world about the nature of its policy; and is systematically and deliberately preventing the American people from using normal political channels to reconsider that policy," Lynd is quoted in the *Montreal Star* story with the headline "Ostracized Professor Cites Canada's Role." The other major English-language news headline covering the speech, "Prof. Hits 'Nazi' U.S.," by the *Toronto Telegram*, goes on to say, "The United States government was likened to Nazi war criminals 'punishable under the judgment of the Nuernberg [*sic*] tribunal,' by Yale professor Staughton Lynd, here yesterday."[22]

Lynd's second visit to Canada, organized by the Student Union for Peace Action (SUPA), proved to be much more consequential. At the time, Canadian peace groups were clamoring for information on Canada's role in the Vietnam War, and in this respect SUPA organized four days of antiwar activities in Ottawa with a teach-in at Carleton University on 2 March 1966 as part of the program. SUPA was demanding a debate in the House of Commons on Canada's role in the conflict, especially the selling of weapons to the United States. At this event, Lynd spoke to four hundred people, and two newspaper clippings were sent from the FBI legal attaché in Ottawa to the FBI in Washington and the New Haven field office. It is noteworthy that the article in the *Ottawa Citizen* does not even mention Lynd's references to Nazi Germany, as they are removed completely from its accounting: "The controversial professor accused the U.S. of insincerity and deception in resuming bombing of North Viet Nam after the year-end pause." Instead,

Doug MacRae focuses on Lynd's exchanges in the question and answer portion: "Among Prof. Lynd's statements to a packed house of 400 at Carleton was a charge that President Johnson is racially prejudiced and that this prejudice is reflected in U.S. policy." MacRae went on to quote Lynd stating President Johnson was "moderately prejudiced," citing statements Johnson made as a congressman in 1947 about "yellow dwarf[s]" with pocketknives threatening the United States in the Far East. According to the article, Lynd said "Anyone who thinks President Johnson has changed since then doesn't understand American politics" and that there was a "lower threshold of inhibitions in Americans in doing such things (war atrocities) to dark-skinned people than there is in doing them to Europeans." Even though these statements were quoted on racism and the United States, with Lynd talking about African Americans being killed at higher rates than white Americans in Vietnam and connecting these issues to the riots in American cities, this article clearly was not shared with Kingman Brewster at Yale because it does not mention his comments about Nazi Germany.[23]

The article in the *Ottawa Journal* shared with Brewster by the US ambassador was much more sensational. Written by Catherine Janitch, the article was captioned "'We're the Nazis'—Yale Professor" and headlined "LBJ Compared to Hitler." While Lynd's statements about racism were also quoted, the relevant paragraphs from the article read,

> An American professor Wednesday compared President Johnson's actions in Viet Nam to Hitler's actions in Europe and called on Canada for help as a "voice of sanity." ...
>
> ... Professor Lynd denounced the recent American peace offensive as a "big lie unequaled since the comparable deceptions by Hitler's Germany." ...
>
> ... "We, with our torture and murder of unarmed prisoners ... our scorched earth policy, our use of lethal gases and toxic chemicals ... we are the Nazis," he said.[24]

On March 18, the transcript of Lynd's speech in Ottawa, recorded and transcribed by the US Army attaché at the US embassy in Ottawa, was forwarded to FBI headquarters and New Haven. Comparing the speech to the newspaper article, it is clear Lynd is grossly quoted out of context. Removing Lynd's statement about the Munich analogy completely omits the raison d'être of Lynd's conclusion and comparisons with Nazi Germany. Here, the newspaper article makes it appear Lynd is making a direct comparison between Nazi crimes throughout the entirety of World War II with the United States' military actions in Vietnam.

Below is the relevant excerpt of Lynd's talk, taken from the transcript provided to the FBI. After outlining Lynd's conclusions from the peace offensive—similar to the articles "The Resumption of Bombing" and "Did

Hanoi Respond?" already included in this collection—Lynd summarized
the negotiating position of the United States vis-à-vis Hanoi throughout
1965. Here is the controversial conclusion to Lynd's speech.

I submit on balance that the statements of the United States Government about
its so-called peace efforts in 1965 constitute not just a series of lies, but a big
lie—unequalled since the comparable deceptions by Hitler's Germany.

The United States Government justifies its Vietnam policy by an analogy to German aggression in the 1930's. Well, I accept that analogy. I accept
it in the same sense that MSgt Donald Duncan, writing in *Ramparts* magazine for February 1966, accepts an analogy between the war in Vietnam and
the Hungarian Revolution of 1956. Duncan volunteered for the United States
Special Forces in Vietnam because "he felt frustrated and cheated that the United
States would not go to the aid of the Hungarians in 1956." At Fort Bragg, North
Carolina, he was taught how to make a prisoner talk by pressing his testicles
in a jeweler's vice and ironically in view of American charges about the Viet
Cong, that special teams should be set up to gain friends among the populace
by assassinating unpopular local officials. After 18 months in Vietnam, Duncan
concluded, we aren't the freedom fighters, we are the Russian tanks blasting the
hopes of an Asian Hungary.

Yes, President Johnson and Secretary Rusk, I accept your analogy to German
aggression in 1939, only we aren't the European resistance movement. We with
our torture and murder of unarmed prisoners, our saturation bombing of
unprotected villages, our scorched-earth policy, our use of lethal gases and toxic
chemicals, our imprisonment and execution of Vietnamese who peacefully protest these barbarities—we have made it quite clear who we are.

Our policy in Vietnam is in the words of Maurice Duverger, "an external
fascism," and we are the Nazis.

Document 2

"VIETNAM: WHAT NEXT?" INTERVIEW BY WILLIAM F. BUCKLEY JR., *FIRING LINE*, EPISODE 11, 23 MAY 1966

It was no secret William F. Buckley Jr. despised Staughton Lynd and wanted to see him ousted from Yale. Buckley, himself a Yale alumnus, was incensed by Lynd's "abuse" of the American radical tradition and especially his visit to North Vietnam. Immediately after Lynd returned from Hanoi, Buckley, in a nationally syndicated column, responded sardonically, "Why all the publicity?" Buckley believed that Lynd and his companions had not returned with any new information and that they were the guests of a "Communist totalitarian state." Most of the column focused on possible "sanctions" against Lynd, beginning first with the question of Lynd's professional responsibilities at Yale and his "globe trotting during class periods." However, whether it was the Logan Act or passport violations, there was no clear-cut answer for Buckley that Lynd would face legal penalties. "The resulting confusion is considerable," Buckley concluded. "In point of fact, Lynd et al have been giving aid and comfort to the enemy. In point of law, they are not traitors, and legal sanctions, as distinguishable from social sanctions, are inadmissible. Will the social sanctions be forthcoming?"[25]

It is clear from this episode of *Firing Line* that Buckley attempted to sanction Lynd, and the result is an informative back-and-forth. Buckley, the quintessential postwar conservative, defends the US in Vietnam and in Cold War policy more generally while Lynd challenges Buckley's justifications. Buckley's weekly television program, *Firing Line*, was still brand-new when Lynd was invited to talk about Vietnam. The program first aired on 4 April 1966, and Lynd was its eleventh guest—a demonstration perhaps of Lynd's growing national and international fame as an outspoken critic of the war in Vietnam.

Below is a transcript of the episode. Minor changes have been made to the text when verifying it with the video. A short back-and-forth on post-1945 US policy has been edited out, as the substance of the disagreement is more succinctly provided later in the transcript.

BUCKLEY: Staughton Lynd is Assistant Professor of History at Yale University; and as a scholar, his specialty is the Radical Tradition in America before 1900. As a citizen, he appears to be concerned to revive that tradition, or as some people might put it—myself for instance—to abuse that tradition. He styles himself a Marxist-pacifist-existentialist, and he is primarily known for his activities in connection with the Vietnam War.

Last winter he journeyed to Hanoi in the company of an American Communist official, and propagandized for the Viet Cong. Indeed, he is on record as hoping the Viet Cong will win the civil war. And he believes that 80 per cent of the Vietnamese would have voted in 1956 in favor of the Communist government there.

Mr. Lynd is the son of two famous scholars, both of them Socialists, authors of the sociological classics, *Middletown*, and *Middletown in Transition*. He is here today to argue, among other things, that the U.S. should pull out of Vietnam, and that the Viet Cong should take over the government of South Vietnam. But before we get into the specific subjects, I should like to ask Professor Lynd, who does believe that some wars are just, whether he can imagine a situation in which the U.S. would be justified in using military force against a Communist power? Mr. Lynd?

LYND: Well in fact Mr. Buckley, I almost feel obliged to begin by correcting one or two statements you made in your opening remarks, if I may.

BUCKLEY: Yes sir.

LYND: That is, I don't feel that the purpose or the consequence of our trip this winter was to make propaganda for the Viet Cong. I don't believe I've said that I favored a Viet Cong victory. It is, however, true, as you suggest, that I believe that the course the United States should now follow in that country is withdrawal.

And I feel this—to come back to the question you asked me a moment ago—because I think, in fact, what we have done is to read the situation in Southeast Asia as if it were a military invasion, like those of Nazi Germany in the 1930's, or indeed, like those of the Soviet Union in Eastern Europe after World War II, whereas I am inclined to think that it's essentially a civil war, rather than military aggression from without.

BUCKLEY: Well. In other words, the interview that appeared in the *Yale Daily News* quoting you as coming out in favor of a Viet Cong victory is incorrect. And I'm very glad to correct that.

LYND: It certainly is.

BUCKLEY: So you do not hope for a Viet Cong victory?

LYND: That's correct.

BUCKLEY: What were you doing in Hanoi, which might be construed as standing in the way of a Viet Cong victory?

LYND: Well, our purpose in going—mine at least—was to try to clarify, if we could, the approach to peace negotiations from the standpoint of the other side. Because there were—and I learned after coming back, this confusion exists in our government as well—there were a series of questions, such as, what do they mean when they say, settle the affairs of South Vietnam according to the program of the National Liberation Front? Do they, in fact, require the physical withdrawal of all American troops before negotiations? There were a series of such questions that seemed to me—and I think to many others in this country—unclear. And my own personal way of dealing with the anguish which I'm sure we all have about the war, was to feel that, as a historian, perhaps I could help somewhat in clarifying some of these issues.

BUCKLEY: Mr. Lynd, were you also misquoted when—in that same interview or perhaps a different one, which said—Mr. Lynd said that U.S. brutality in combat and deceit in negotiations were the main reasons of his protest?

LYND: I think that we find ourselves in Vietnam in a situation where, first, we are beginning to use military practices such as torture and the bombing of unarmed villages that are, I think, somewhat foreign to the American military tradition. And secondly, I think it is simply a matter of public record that our best correspondents, Bigart, Halberstam, and so forth, have corroborated, that the United States government has persistently been less than candid with us, the American people, about the situation in that country—soldiers described as advisors, and so forth and so on.

BUCKLEY: Well now, as a scholar, Mr. Lynd, it seems to me that you have been saying a number of things, on the one hand suggesting that your trip to Vietnam, had primarily a scholarly purpose, but on the other hand, suggesting also that you went over there freighted down with a number of value judgments which, as a scholar, it seems to me you ought to suspect. For instance, you say it's not part of the American military tradition to torture, and you leave an audience thinking all kinds of things.

Number one, that torture has not been a part of other wars, which is historically incorrect; number two, suggesting that innocent people haven't gotten killed in other wars, which is historically incorrect. We did more damage in Dresden in three days, I think, in 1945, to completely innocent people, than we would do at the current rate in North Vietnam over a period of ten years.

You're also suggesting, as a historical fact, that we are now engaged in torturing North Vietnamese soldiers, and that we are now engaged in wantonly destroying innocent people. Now that's an awful lot of value judgment, it seems to me, for a historian to throw out moments after introducing his own credentials as a scholar. How do you manage that?

LYND: Well, I'd be glad to present some of the evidence that I had in mind. I don't mean to say that torture or murder of unarmed prisoners is habitual or routine. That it has happened, I think is beyond question. For example in *Time* Magazine, August 6, 1965, the 20th anniversary of the bombing of Hiroshima, on page 29, there's a flat statement, "The Marines,"—referring, I think to the Chu Lai Base in South Vietnam,—"have begun to kill prisoners." As to the question of bombing, I think, again, that it's well-established that our bombers do go into villages in South Vietnam on the report of forward observers that the presence of some National Liberation Front soldiers in those villages is suspected. And secondly, that there are so-called free zones—that is, whole areas— of South Vietnam, within the National Liberation Front lines, where airmen are permitted to bomb at will. I just think there is some difference, both in quantity and quality between these practices and what has existed in earlier wars.

BUCKLEY: Well, let's leave it that the demonstration has not been made, A, and B, that it certainly hasn't been made with reference to scholarly standards. But let me ask you this: are you ...

LYND: Well, I wouldn't accept that. I mean, I'm speaking here ad lib on a television show; but I would say that Professor Bernard Fall, of Howard University for example, has in fact demonstrated by the most rigorous scholarly practices that such things occur.

BUCKLEY: That such things occur uniquely in the North Vietnamese war?

LYND: No, not that they occur uniquely, but that the quantity and quality of American brutality and our conduct of this war is on rather a new scale. I don't think that his scholarly credentials have been questioned.

BUCKLEY: Well, the question is hardly whether they are questionable, but whether or not it is possible to motivate such a phenomenon. What is it, according to your understanding, either as a scholar or as a human being, that requires the United States at this point in its rather humane history, to decide to take pleasure from killing people whom it is not necessary to kill in order to advance the strategic objective in South Vietnam?

LYND: I think that's the key question, with the exception of the words, take pleasure. Because I don't mean to imply that. And when I say it's the key question,

I mean I think it gets beneath the implication that there's something sadistic or enjoyable to Americans about doing these things; because I don't think that for a moment.

I think it's rather that, because we are fighting in a situation which we have wrongly pictured to ourselves as a case of outside invasion, but which is not in fact such, and because we are dealing in this case with a Communist-led movement which has substantial popular support—and the figure of 80 per cent, by the way, is President Eisenhower's, not mine—that because we don't have the sympathies of the people with us, as we so often have had in our previous wars, therefore we find ourselves driven to these practices, not because we enjoy them.

BUCKLEY: Listen professor, let's stop dropping these little statistical gems around the place. What Eisenhower said when he used the term 80 per cent was that 80 per cent of the people would have joined in any war against the French. He didn't say that 80 per cent were in favor of Ho Chi Minh. And the statistic seems to me so obtrusive, as even to occur to an ideologue. There were almost one million refugees, who having tasted the North Vietnamese regime, went down from the Northern part to the Southern part of Vietnam in 1954 and 1955. So let's be careful about these things. Now . . .

LYND: Well, what President Eisenhower said, in fact, in his book, *Mandate for Change*—and I don't have the quotation spread out before me—is that all those with whom he could consult said that at the time of the end of the war against the French, in 1954, the end of the eight year Viet Minh war against French occupation, 80 per cent of the people of Vietnam as a whole would have voted for Ho Chi Minh in an election.

BUCKLEY: Of course, as an alternative to Bao Dai. Ho Chi Minh had not started his rather systematic euthanasia of people who disagreed with him up until 1954. He was considered the George Washington of that area. There is no question at all but that when the brutality of his regime became manifest—and it was physically manifest to the estimated 60 per cent of the elite class who were liquidated in the ensuing five years that he was hardly a popular hero. He would only be a popular hero in a world populated by sadists. So I think these data are extremely deceptive. And I worry about the extent to which they seem to work on you.

LYND: Let's take another indication from another, I would say unideological, source, Senator Richard Russell, the Chairman of the Armed Services Committee of the Senate, who said on CBS Television—I believe it was last August in the *Face the Nation* program—that he felt it was altogether likely that in a free plebiscite in South Vietnam today Ho Chi Minh would be returned the victor, because his status, Senator Russell thought, was still that, as you suggest, as the George Washington of his people, the leader of their independence struggle, in the popular mind.

BUCKLEY: Well, in the first place, Mr. Lynd, it's a stupid statement. It's as stupid as saying that the majority of the French would have voted for the Nazis. In point of fact they did. They wrote the Vichy peace with their feet, because the alternative at that moment seemed to be death. And I have no doubt that there are still a lot of people in South Vietnam, maybe 80 per cent, and for all I know among the faculty of Yale University, who would rather be red than dead.

So Senator Russell's statement, if it was made exactly as you quote it, is a highly mischievous one, a highly immoral one, and a highly dangerous one. Because it really presupposes that there are rational reasons why people would decide to live under the manifest hideousness of the kind of regime presided over by Ho Chi Minh, which has caused some of the most intensive misery in the post war history of mankind, in North Vietnam, between 1954 and 1960.

But I wonder why, as you throw around these desultory quotations, why you thought that arriving in Hanoi, with a Communist cohort and Communist hosts, anybody would feel any obligation to tell you anything truthful?

Were you in a position where you could actually exercise your scholarly apparatus or did they simply treat you in Hanoi the way the average observer would have expected that they would treat you in Hanoi—simply, here is an American idiot, whom we are in a position to manipulate, because he's an idealist and we find that we can opportunise on his fine personal instinct and feed him all kinds of trash, which he can then go back and propagandize in the United States? What feeling did you have that you could come to terms with reality in Hanoi?

LYND: Well a number of other private citizens, Mr. Buckley—distinguished newsmen and public figures, Felix Greene; William Warbey, a British Member of Parliament; Lord Fenner Brockway of the British House of Lords, men whom I haven't at least ordinarily heard referred to as idiots, felt during the year . . .

BUCKLEY: I meant that in the Greek sense, you understand, a moral idiot.

LYND: Oh I see.

BUCKLEY: Yes.

LYND: Well, I would say that they were carrying out the traditional function of newsmen, to try to go to sources of information. Now admittedly, those aren't the only relevant sources of information. But on the other hand, sooner or later, if one wants to find out what the other side does mean by its peace terms, one has, it seems to me, to do exactly what President Johnson spoke of on December 20th, 1965, to wit: knock on any door, even the doors of people whom one doesn't particularly like, to ask them, in fact, what their very contradictory and ambiguous statements about troop withdrawal and the political future of South Vietnam mean.

BUCKLEY: Well are you willing, then, to concede that, having gone all the way to Hanoi, you came back with empty pockets?

LYND: No, I'm not.

BUCKLEY: Oh. What is it that you found out that we were not able to find out through the normal sources, or that, in fact, the sheer intelligence of our own apparatus was able to tell us, namely, that the North Vietnamese are not prepared to suspend the war until they have won it on their terms or until they find that the prosecution of that war is something that is intolerable. What did you find?

LYND: First of all, I think I understand more clearly than American mass media would have led one to understand why it was that the other side was so suspicious of the peace offensive. There may have been all kinds of spurious and devious and hidden reasons as well. But there's one reason rather on the surface of their think-ing which I think makes some sense. That is to say, they saw the bombing pause in North Vietnam, on the other hand they listed to us a whole series of measures of continued escalation in South Vietnam. And they said, in effect, how are we to know which of these two kinds of signal is the true American intention. And so we came back with the feeling which Secretary General U Thant has since underlined, that the bombing pause of North Vietnam at Christmastime in fact did not fully test the possibilities of American military de-escalation as a way to opening the door to negotiations, that if we want to test that hypothesis fully we will have to try a modest—I don't speak of full withdrawal now—but a modest de-escalation in the South as well as the North. Then, I think we can say to our-selves that the signal has gone through clearly to the other side.

In addition to that, if I might just quickly finish in answering your question, Seymour Topping the Far Eastern correspondent of the *New York Times*, early in February wrote a column in which he drew on our written question and answers exchanged with the North Vietnamese Prime Minister, as well as other sources, saying that he felt that now the North Vietnamese peace conditions were more clear that it was, in fact, not the case that they asked the withdrawal of all American troops prior to negotiations, and spelling out, in a number of other ways, what he said—this by no means ideological *New York Times* correspondent—was a more clear picture of their peace terms. And I think our visit made a modest contribution to that.

BUCKLEY: Mr. Lynd, you call yourself a Marxist. Surely, as a Marxist, you don't seriously believe that your little vacation to Hanoi would have mid-wifed some sort of dialectical reconciliation which would not have, otherwise, taken place. Surely, Hanoi isn't dependent on Yale's vacation schedule for deciding how to press its foreign policy, is it? And I don't mean to say that in the sense of trying to prick your balloon, because I am sure that you sincerely believe that you had something to do with the crystallization of this theretofore unknown truth.

But I am suggesting that your belief in it is a part of that syndrome of unreality that does govern your whole approach to these matters. You do understand?

I'm not at all confident, if I may say so, about the desirability of you and Mr. Aptheker, the Communist Historian, being sort of a second State Department, sent over to negotiate all situations in which we have run into a deadlock. But I do ask you—incidentally, let's not get into the fact that your trip was illegal or get into any of those sort of mechanical disqualifications—I'm sure you're as tired of them as I am.

LYND: Particularly, since the Supreme Court is still considering the question.

BUCKLEY: Well, the Supreme Court is still considering every question. It's illegal so long as the Supreme Court doesn't say it isn't illegal. It's against the laws of the United States. . . .

LYND: I mean to say that I think there are many dictatorships which in fact the United States does not react to with hostility, that it isn't only Communist dictatorships in Eastern Europe that have been spared, and that we have, in fact, been somewhat selective as to where we have intervened. And I was wondering what your criteria were as to what situations we should intervene in and what situations we should not?

BUCKLEY: I would be delighted to tell you what my criterion is. It's a singular, not a plural. I am in favor of intervention in the affairs of any nation which represents a threat or an extension of a threat to American freedom, and not otherwise. Now it seems to me clear that, by that criterion, intervention in Eastern Europe after the war was most definitely called for. And it was most certainly called for, I should think, under the moral inertia of the existing situation.

After all, we got into the war in the first instance—or the English did—in order to protect Poland. And Poland, was of course, was the last thing we bothered remembering. But I'm asking you because I'm interested—in you as an individual, and you as a generality—how do you view the Communist menace, and do you view it as something about which energetic action is called for, even as it was against the Nazis?

LYND: I think that, since the death of Stalin, the spread of Communism has been primarily through Communist assistance and leadership of indigenous revolutions, rather than through the marching of red armies across borders. I think this presents a different kind of situation to which we need to respond by different means, and primarily, by preventive economic and social measures to alleviate discontent of the kind that Mr. McNamara referred to in Montreal the other day.

BUCKLEY: What would you call the spreading of Communism to Cuba, which was post-Stalin by six years? Is this what you call an example of Communist didacticism taking over the democratic people? Or how do you stand on Castro, by the way? Because it will save me a lot of time if you are very much against him.

LYND: I certainly feel that it was primarily an internal revolution if that's what you mean, rather than a case of military aggression from abroad.

BUCKLEY: As a matter of fact it was not. I just thought I'd let you know that. It was not a social revolution. It was a political revolution. And I think that the people who marched with Castro would, every single one of them, almost unanimously, confirm me in my own judgment, who then left, when it became an ideological coup d'etat, a coup d'etat that was never tested by referring to the people, because it would be voted down manifestly.

LYND: Well, my own impression—I would like to enter on the record—is quite different. I think that the 12 men or whatever it was who went up to the mountains in Cuba, could not have developed the strength that they did had they not offered a program to the peasants as well as using merely political means.

BUCKLEY: Sure. They offered a program, none of which was carried out. And those parts that Castro went on to carry out were, of course, unrelated to the program that made him such a hero when he took over Cuba on the First of the year 1959. But now, in order not to try to myself commit the sin of being desultory, I am anxious to relate to your position on Cuba. And I'll give you a hint what my final thesis is going to be. My final thesis is going to be that you have a

very dim hold of reality. And it is that dim hold of reality that relates your muta-
tis mutandis to the people who, in the 30's, were asking us not to do anything
about Stalin, who were asking us not to object to the Stalin purge trials, who
were always there to defend the Soviet Union, and urge the American people
not to get heated about the subject.

If, after all, that human and intellectual phenomenon could have taken place
in the 30's, there's no reason in the world why it couldn't take place again in the
60's, and there is no reason that I know of why it couldn't have happened to you,
is there?

LYND: I think we are, however, both attempting to be truth-seekers, and not
to score debating points off each other; and I don't think that the use of epithets
and pejorative adjectives helps. Now the question I wanted to ask you was about
South Vietnam today. I have the impression that Marshall Ky's government in
South Vietnam is an unpopular one. Furthermore, without calling it the worst
dictatorship that has ever existed—which I don't mean to imply—that it is a dic-
tatorial one, that there is for example, a decree, now one year old, which says that
people agitating for peace or for neutrality in South Vietnam can be executed for
treason, that in fact, three persons were executed near our Marine base at Danang
last September, when they led a small demonstration in that town.

I want to ask you what you think about our policy of support for Marshall
Ky's government, and if a government would be elected in South Vietnam, as the
Buddhists and students are asking for, and that if that elected government were
to ask the United States to withdraw so that it could negotiate with the National
Liberation Front, what your attitude would be, how you feel we should respond
to such a demand.

BUCKLEY: You've got to understand I think, Mr. Lynd, that you do represent
the views of so small a percentage of the American people and you do affront
the general view so dramatically that they have got to reach—we have got to
reach—for some way of understanding you. Just as, no doubt, you feel that
you've got to understand us, the capitalist oppressors, the deceitful Johnson
Administration, the brutalitarians and so on and so forth.

You tend to use your epithets in sort of an Aesopian prose. That is to say,
when you're insulting me, you do it not ad hominem but you insult the government and the nation in which I have, from time to time, confidence, so that my
treatment of you as an individual, is merely a technique by which I can seek to
amplify what it is that goes on in your mind.

For instance, the very fact that you should now want to focus this discussion on how exquisitely apportioned is democracy in South Vietnam suggests to

me once again this evasion of reality. Who sat around here wondering whether Churchill was the most popular leader in England during the war? What they're worrying about in South Vietnam is how they're going to get food, or how are they going to go out and till their fields without getting beheaded by Viet Cong barbarians. This is the kind of thing they're worrying about in Vietnam.

And I don't care at all myself whether Ky is popular. All I care is that the area be pacified, that it be not added to the Communized zone, that we do not betray whatever chance there is for a little repose and hope and decency for these people.

LYND: I want to say, Mr. Buckley, that I'm not at all sure that it is the case that the general viewpoint which I represent is quite such a small minority as you suppose. I noticed in this morning's *New Haven Register* a Gallup Poll which said that 54 per cent of the American people favored United States withdrawal from Vietnam, if full scale civil war erupts in South Vietnam. And therefore, to get to a second point which you made, I think that what happens in South Vietnam needs to be of concern to us. And that when students and Buddhists and others demonstrate in the streets, non-violently, asking not for Communism or socialism but for the right to elect their own government, the United States needs to pay attention to that. And we can't brush that all aside in a way that I felt you were about to a moment ago.

BUCKLEY: Why didn't we pay attention to the Vichy government? The Vichy government told us to get out of the way, to forget the war, to leave France alone. Would you have taken the position that we should have acknowledged them as the rightful stewards of French destiny, or General De Gaulle who wanted to save his own land?

LYND: Well, I would have thought that, since our concern in South Vietnam is freedom, free elections, democracy, and since that's precisely what these demonstrators are asking for, that it would behoove us to try to respond to their demands as opposed to that of an outright dictator.

BUCKLEY: Professor Lynd, you can't have democracy without experience. South Vietnam has no experience in democracy; and for them to suppose that they can have democracy tomorrow in the middle of an enormous civil war, is something that you, as a historian, ought to be telling them they can't have. This is what they need to know, that elections in wartime were even suspended in the country of the mother of parliaments. There were no elections in England during the Second World War. Why should there suddenly be one in South Vietnam, which would probably be about the fourth election in its 2,000 year history?

LYND: But isn't it really up to them? I think that's one of the basic issues between us.

BUCKLEY: No. You know or should know certain things that they don't know.

LYND: You think I should?

BUCKLEY: Yes, I think you should. I think you should know, for instance, that there has never been a successful democracy in the history of the world that hasn't had a certain amount of experience with democracy. The so-called democratic nations of Africa instantly proved this. We also know that certain people are too volatile for democracy, even in Spain, which is an old civilization. Let's hope they get it in South Vietnam. But short of that, let's hope that at least we can spare them that hideous destiny of being taken over by the North Vietnamese Communists, who would usher in a reign of terror which we, I think, cannot morally or responsibly allow.

LYND: Now I don't mean to say that the states of Africa, for example, have had the same degree of preparation for self-government as the 13 colonies in 1776. Of course they have not. But on the other hand, I think it is the desire of people all over the world—and I would not be inclined to make your distinction between the volatile and the unvolatile—to make their own mistakes, to find their own way, to learn for themselves. And I just question whether if, in fact, a majority of the people of South Vietnam were to ask us to leave, were to say that they wished to negotiate with the National Liberation Front, whether we would have the right to overrule them.

BUCKLEY: Well, the supreme right, of course, is the safety of the state, that is to say, we have the right—everybody has the right—to commit suicide, or that is one way of viewing the extent of an individual's sovereignty over himself. But nobody has the right to ordain another person's suicide. I happen myself to feel that the case would be impossible to make that authorizes a nation to go Communist. Because in the course of becoming Communist that nation accepts a mandate to communize you and me.

And even though you might not feel that you wanted to resist this other than passively, I feel that I would. And therefore, my destiny is, to a considerable extent involved in South Vietnam, whereas it's not involved, for instance, in South Africa, except in a sense that all of us are brothers and we should act in a brotherly way towards each other. But that I think is the crucial distinction. And I'd like to remind you that there were saintly, angelic people defending the Stalin trials in 1939, and remind you that even some of the people that you associate with, for instance the socialist, Mr. David McReynolds, has said about you, as a result of your insistence on a sort of a revolutionary posture as regards human experience; "What Lynd has done makes him sound like a member of the old left"—this is a socialist speaking—"as if he had just emerged from a Communist Party meeting in the 30's, with the news that the Social Democrats were the true mass enemy."

I insist that to view reality with any sense of perspective, you have got to recognize that for you to be preoccupied with the extent with which Ky is a democratic leader, and utterly unpreoccupied with the ordeal of North Vietnam and Red China, suggests that you are basically dislocated as regards recent human experience.

LYND: But, you see, you've made an assumption which I don't think is the case. I have, for example, joined other American intellectuals in protesting the recent forced labor sentences for Soviet writers. I don't think it's true of myself as an individual or of the so-called new left in America generally, that it is simply the 1930's in new guise. I don't think there's that same application of a double standard. At least it's certainly not our intent that there be that.

BUCKLEY: It's a question of perspective, isn't it, not so much a question of a double standard. I don't doubt that you will protest any atrocity committed anywhere else. But I do note that you spend your energies in such a way as to give special focus to those discontents which oughtn't to be the principal discontents of any man whose moral sense of hierarchy is secure.

LYND: But you see Mr. Buckley, the people who are asking in South Vietnam now that we leave are not Communists, they're not even socialists most of them, they are Buddhists, neutralists, democrats.

Document 3

"CIVIL LIBERTIES IN WARTIME," CIVIL LIBERTIES AND WAR WORKSHOP, STATE UNIVERSITY OF NEW YORK, STONY BROOK, JUNE 19–22, 1966

In this talk, Staughton Lynd addresses several scenarios and complex issues facing draft-age men and their supporters looking to oppose the Vietnam War. He addresses these issues at the intersection of conscience and the law and whether the acts of lawbreaking are justified under the US Constitution. For Lynd, these were not abstract questions, as we have seen. In April 1966, the Lynds announced that they would again refuse to pay the portion of their income tax that went to the military. The statement argued that the US military was "clearly being used in violation of the US Constitution, international law and the United Nations' charter."[26]

The question of what opponents of the war could do who were not of draft age themselves came into sharp focus over the late spring of 1966 as students and teachers across the country were confronted with the question of how grades were being used to determine who was sent to Vietnam. With rising draft calls, the Selective Service director, General Lewis Hershey, suggested that student deferments be eliminated by 20 percent and implemented a renewed voluntary testing regime that originally existed from 1953 to 1961 to determine who got the coveted 2-S student deferment and therefore the comforts of campus life. This voluntary exam would help local draft board administrators determine whether someone received the 2-S deferment; however, it was not an ironclad guarantee they would receive it. In order to get the deferment, high school and university students needed a C average and a 70 percent on the voluntary Selective Service exam.[27] In response, the Students for a Democratic Society (SDS) organized their own counter-exam and picketing at universities across the country out front of the exams on May 14 and 21 and June 3. As Lynd explains in this talk, this placed students and teachers into direct conflict with the university system, as teachers were being asked to cooperate with the Selective Service System, which would have a direct impact on a student's life and the manpower needs of the military. The editors of the *New York Times* responded harshly to the students' protest. While noting the inequities in the draft and deferment system and calling for a "fundamental reappraisal" of the Selective Service System, they nonetheless labeled the opposition as "inexcusable" and "adolescent irrationality" that resulted in "temper tantrums aimed at those who want to assure the fairest possible treatment under existing conditions." Staughton Lynd responded to the editors by pointing out these were the actions of "mature citizens" who were engaging in "participatory democracy." In fact, Lynd argued that "the draft deferment examination stimulates personal

self-interest of the narrowest and most ignoble variety" and led to competition between students "so that they rather than he will be killed." For Lynd:
"Have we the right to refuse this demand when it touches matters literally
of life or death, when in effect it becomes a plea for no annihilation without
representation?"[28]

Lynd addressed these issues and others at his talk at the State University
of New York, Stony Brook. While on Long Island, he also spoke at a picnic
organized by the Long Island Committee to End the War in Vietnam at the
Westbury Friends Meeting House.[29]

Consider once more the familiar words of the preamble to the Declaration of
Independence. What does "inalienable" mean? Not that liberty cannot be taken
away from you; but the far more radical proposition that you cannot give up
liberty. From the standpoint of the Declaration of Independence men do not
surrender their rights in becoming part of society. They set up governments to
"secure these rights." Representatives, trustees for the rights of their constit-
uents, cannot give up their power of trusteeship: were Congress to make the
President a dictator the Declaration of Independence would render the act null.
Still less can representatives give away the underlying individual rights which it
is their duty to secure: were Congress and a requisite number of state legislatures
duly to abolish the First Amendment, from the standpoint of the Declaration of
Independence the action would have no effect at all on the rights of man. These
come not from Congress but from man's Creator, and "among" them—there are
presumably others which the Declaration does not pause to enumerate—are life,
liberty, and the pursuit of happiness. Thus Jefferson wrote to Francis W. Gilmer
on June 7, 1816 (*Writings*, ed. Ford, X, 32): "Our legislators are not sufficiently
apprized of the rightful limits of their power; and their true office is to declare
and enforce only our natural rights and duties, and to take none of them from
us ... The idea is quite unfounded, that on entering into society we give up any
natural right." Professor Leonard Levy has shown that Jefferson in office often
acted inconsistently with this text, but from the standpoint of the Declaration
this is only one more proof that the best of representatives should be mistrusted.

From the standpoint of the Declaration, the rights of man are not only "inalienable" but "self-evident." This does not mean that any two lawyers will agree
about them; but the far more radical proposition that common men, using
"common sense," can recognize and interpret their rights without the help of
lawyers. The Declaration's absolutistic stance on rights may seem a little distant
and archaic to us because clothed in the language of natural law and made part

of a scenario of social contract which we find unusable. Let us then redefine the rights of man in the language of Camus and Silone, Buber and A. J. Muste, men who discovered them anew under the hammer of Fascism and the shadow of nuclear war. Let us consider a right to be something inextricably part of man's being and experience, not given him by social artifice but in him by virtue of the fact of being human. Let us understand the rights to existence, freedom and joy to mean that there are certain things—such as burning little children to death with napalm, or sentencing novelists to hard labor—which must not be done to any person by any society under any circumstances.

Finally, the rights of man are universal: they belong equally to all men everywhere. The ancient ethical consensus to this effect has in our day begun to acquire legal form and weight. Justice Jackson and his colleagues at Nuremberg made it clear that if one presumes to create ex post facto law the least one can do is to affirm that in future this law will apply to oneself as well.

Let us examine some of the existential situations in which the Declaration of Independence currently encounters the nation state.

You are a young man of draft age. You have heard of the Nuremberg Tribunal: you get a copy of its findings, and read its definitions of "war crimes" and "crimes against humanity." You read about the war in Vietnam, and (to substitute my own experience for that of the hypothetical young man) you find in *Time* magazine for August 6, 1965, the twentieth anniversary of the bombing of Hiroshima, the statement on page 29 that "the Marines have begun to kill prisoners"; you quote this indignantly in a statement to the press and await public outcry; nothing happens. You read of the Spring 1965 decree of the Ky government which makes neutralism a capital offence: that is, which offers death to those who engage in "all direct or indirect actions aimed at spreading Communist policies, slogans and instructions by any individual or group of individuals influenced or controlled by Communists," "all moves which weaken the national anti-Communist effort and are harmful to the anti-Communist struggle of the people and the Armed Forces," "all plots and actions under the false name of peace and neutrality according to a Communist policy," "the diffusion, circulation, distribution, sale, display in public places, and the keeping of these above mentioned aims, either in printed form, drawings, photographic, or otherwise," and which goes on to say that "all associations, agencies, and organizations violating [the aforementioned] shall be disbanded and their properties confiscated" (American Friends Service Committee, *Peace in Vietnam*, pp. 104–105); you note that under this decree three men, including a Saigon lawyer, are sentenced to 10–20 years hard labor in August, and three other men in September are tied to posts on the Danang soccer field and shot; you wait for the outcry from even anti-Communist American liberals; nothing happens. Bearing in mind the Nuremberg definition of "wanton destruction of cities, towns or villages" as "war crimes," and "inhumane acts committed against any civilian population" as "crimes against humanity," you read Father Currien's account of the bombing of a village in South Vietnam by United States planes, without warning and indeed in contradiction to the explicit statement of a ground troop commander that "you and your faithful are no longer in danger," at a time when no one was in the village but "women, children and old people"; and then, if you are Norman Morrison, you drive from Baltimore to Washington that same afternoon and burn yourself to death.

If you are Norman Morrison, you try to understand your obligations under the international law of the Nuremberg Tribunal. Suppose torture and murder of prisoners are exceptional acts by United States servicemen; does that mean one should enter the armed services, and refuse to commit such a specific action only at the point ordered to carry it out? Suppose saturation bombing of unprotected villages either on suspicion of Vietcong presence or because the village is in a "free zone" where pilots may unload their bombs at will, is routine; does that mean one should refuse participation in the war at the point of induction, or only that one should refuse participation in the Air Force? Suppose one is not a draft-age young man but a teacher who has that concerned young man in your class; have you no obligation, or does the Nuremberg Tribunal indirectly impose on you the task of making your protest against war crimes and crimes against humanity? Could it even be argued that one's citizenship in a country committing such actions imposes an obligation, not merely to say No, but to become as best one can a peacemaker?

Return to the situation of the teacher. You are required to give grades which will be sent on by the administration of your university to Selective Service. You are disturbed, to use the language of a group of teachers at the University of Chicago, "about the effects on the educational process which may flow from linking students' classroom performance to their chances for induction," "by the notion that students deserve special preference with respect to selective service, or that academic performance should be a basis for distributing special privilege," "by the fact that this use of grades converts the University quite explicitly into an arm of the Selective Service System" and "by the fact that, by permitting our grades to be used in this way, we are actively cooperating in a war effort whose purposes we profoundly oppose." This group of teachers concludes "that the freedom of conscience of faculty and students who are opposed to the war effort" is violated by Selective Service use of academic grades as a basis for induction and deferment. Is this a legitimate invocation of conscience? If a university were to fire a faculty member who refused to send in grades, could he be defended under the First Amendment?

Consider, again, the draft-age young man. You do not belong to an historic peace church. You would have fought in World War II. Were it possible for you to serve in a nonviolent capacity in Vietnam, offering medical aid or relief and reconstruction or assistance in social revolution, you would gladly do so. Yet everything deepest in you objects to this particular war. If you are a Catholic you bring forward traditional criteria for distinguishing just and unjust wars: treatment of prisoners, treatment of the civilian population, and so on. If you are an atheist or agnostic, you nevertheless stand inarticulately horror-stricken before your draft board, wishing you had words to say that if (in the words of the Society for Ethical Culture) "the place where men meet to seek the highest is holy ground," this war is the reverse of all that.

You are an American Negro. In the SNCC newsletter you read Charley Cobb's poem:

so cry not just
for jackson or reeb
schwerner, goodman
or chaney
or lee

cry for all mothers
with shovels
digging at hovels
looking for their dead
cry for all the blood spilled
of all the people killed
in the Standard Procedure
of the country
which is not ours
but belongs
to those who run it
and can't be seen
but are very few
who
listen to each other
and not to us
cause we don't know
what it takes
that makes
Standard Procedure.

You stumble on a poem by Mrs. Ida Mae Lawrence, a leader of the group from the Mississippi Delta which recently sought to occupy the Federal Air Force base at Greeneville and Lafayette Park opposite the White House. It reads in part:

> What does we have against the Vietnams?
> Why are we fighting them?
> Who are really the enemy?
> Are Vietnam the enemy or we Americans enemies to ourselves?
> If we are the same as Vietnams why should we fight them?
> They are poor too.
> They wants freedom.

If you live in McComb, where the SNCC voter registration drive in Mississippi began in autumn 1961, you are upset when a young man active in that effort is drafted, sent to Vietnam, killed, and sent home in a coffin. You take part in drafting the statement of August 1965: "1. No Mississippi Negroes should be fighting in Vietnam for the White Man's freedom, until all the Negro People are free in Mississippi. 2. Negro boys should not honor the draft here in Mississippi. Mothers should encourage their sons not to go..."

What is the standing at law of all this pain? Does the First Amendment protect it? In January 1966 the staff of SNCC makes the connection with the right to dissent in the first sentence of its unanimous statement on the war: "The Student Nonviolent Coordinating Committee assumes its right to dissent with United States foreign policy on any issue, and states its opposition to United States involvement in the war in Vietnam..." The belief has consequences. The statement ends:

> We are in sympathy with and support the men in this country who are unwilling to respond to the military draft which would compel them to contribute their lives to U.S. "aggression" in the name of the freedom we find so false in this country...
> We ask: Where is the draft for the freedom fight in the United States?...
> We believe that work in the civil rights movement and other human relations organizations is a valid alternative to the draft. We urge all Americans to seek this alternative, knowing full well that it may cost them their lives, as painfully as in Vietnam.

Within days the problem of conscience blends into the problem of self-government as representative-elect Julian Bond is unseated. What part of the Constitution is applicable? The First Amendment? Or the guarantee of republican government?

You are under 35 and a socialist. The Attorney General of the United States asks the Subversive Activities Control Board to designate the WEB

DuBois Clubs of America as subversive. He knows that the Supreme Court has ruled that individual members of organizations so designated may not be required to register with the government. He himself has recommended the repeal of the law under which he acts. Yet he does act, and the immediate consequence is hooliganism in Brooklyn and dynamiting in San Francisco. What bearing has the First Amendment here? Can the Attorney General be forbidden to hold press conferences? Or required in such matters to proceed in private rather than in public? In *WEB DuBois Clubs of America v. Katzenbach*, Robert Havighurst, Ralph Di Gia, Dave Dellinger, Norman Thomas, Donna Allen, Carl Oglesby, James Bevel, Dagmar Wilson, the Rev. William Coffin, John Lewis and myself have joined other plaintiffs in seeking to enjoin the Attorney General from further proceedings under the McCarran Act "since free expression—of transcendent value to all society and not merely to those exercising their rights—will be the victim."

You are *not* a draft-age young man, a professor, a Negro, or a socialist. You are an American citizen and tax-payer who happens to fall into none of these categories. Yet your problem is more fundamental than that of any of the special categories of persons just described. You probably voted in November 1964 for a Presidential candidate who on half a dozen occasions had pledged himself not to "go North" and not involve American troops in an Asian land war. Three months later, in a situation that was not an emergency, disregarding peace overtures from the other side, making no appeal to the United Nations, without an explanation to the public and without a Congressional declaration of war, he did what during the campaign he had said he would not do. Congressmen feel inhibited from voting against appropriations bills for a war in which young Americans risk their lives, albeit without Congressional authorization. Lacking a parliamentary system of government, the perpetrator of this policy will doubtless enjoy the power to continue it six more years. What is the Constitutional remedy for *this* situation?

Several hundred of us, including professors at Columbia, Hofstra, Michigan, Haverford, Connecticut and Yale, had said in effect that this amounts to taxation without representation. We refuse to pay all or part of our taxes.

In such ways the question of the war comes to the doorstep of the potential draftee, the professor, the Negro, the radical, the ordinary tax-paying citizen.

As suggested at the outset, one way of articulating the problem is as a dialogue between conscience and law. President Woodrow Wilson in World War I provided a classic illustration of what happens when the first is simply subsumed in the latter. After asking Americans to be neutral in thought as well as deed, after proclaiming that a victor's peace would rest on shifting sands and that what the world must have was "peace without victory," President Wilson then turned around, called the war a crusade for democracy, resurrected the posture of unconditional surrender, and hounded out of existence Wobblies, socialists, pacifists and all others less agile than himself in changing the party line. So there *is* an inherent conflict between statesmen, conventionally-authorized executioners, and those who following Camus insist on striving to become neither executioners or victims.

But I think it is a fundamental and disastrous error to portray the problem of civil liberties in wartime as merely a problem of individual conscience. The other side of the question is that in wartime the state goes out of control. If the rising moon or a wayward flight of geese come through on the radar screen of the early warning network as ICBMs from the other side, the President has the apparent power to incinerate us all. I must testify that I object to any human being having the power to decree the death of 100,000,000 others. I appeal to you as lawyers: what does the inalienable right to life of my seven-year-old son or ten-year-old daughter signify if President Johnson can murder them whenever he decides to? There is a problem of democracy involved in the enormous present powers of the quasi-mobilized nation state which we must not shirk by addressing it as a problem of individual freedom only.

Consider freedom of travel. I suppose it can be defended as a right of conscience, as protected in that sense by the First Amendment. But I should like to pose the issue of freedom of travel in a more public context. I think freedom of travel is one of the last vestiges of control available to the ordinary citizen to prevent the executive from killing him at its discretion. Freedom of travel is essential if common men are to retain any say at all in the fashioning of foreign policy and the declaring of wars.

To make war the modern administrator requires stereotypes. *All* Germans must be seen as "Huns" (or alternatively, as decent essentially-Western folk manning a bastion against Communism); *all* Japanese must be regarded as little, yellow, buck-toothed fanatics (except of course those running the country since 1945); *all* Vietnamese (that is to say, all except those, if any, who would support Marshal Ky in a free election) are faceless schemers in black pajamas and conical hats who can live for a week on a ball of glutinous rice—whatever that is—and don't mind being tortured because they are stoical Asiatics.

But if you or I can talk to these people directly that stereotype may crumble. My personal experience, for example, was to observe a museum director, an interpreter, a factory manager—a variety of persons in official capacities— break down and cry in public, as they tried to describe the suffering of their country. This does not mean that all North Vietnamese officials cry in public.

It means that they are human just as we are, that their feelings are as close to the surface as our own. In Prague, an NLF interpreter said to us: "We know you say that we are faceless. But as you see, we do have faces."

Thus I want to suggest that whether or not actions such as taking an airplane to Hanoi or sitting in at a draft board can be considered "speech" under the First Amendment, the bureaucratic character of twentieth-century decision-making about foreign policy makes the protection of such actions by the Constitution indispensable to the protection of the natural right to life.

But you will respond: Going to Hanoi or sitting in at the Ann Arbor draft board is against the law, or more precisely, against the law as presently defined. And I respond with my most outrageous hypotheses: Deliberate lawbreaking through nonviolent civil disobedience is a valid and should become a routine form of democratic dialogue. Let me defend this on three grounds.

Accepted constitutional doctrine in the United States represents an invitation to hypocrisy. On the one hand we say, think and express yourself freely without consciousness of social obligation. But on the other hand we affirm, do not act on what you believe unless the majority agrees with you, that is, sanctions such action by law. The problem is not merely a personal one. Law itself has grown when individuals defied it. When John Lilburne was hailed before Star Chamber on the eve of the English Civil War, he refused to answer questions which might incriminate him, saying: I think my refusal is justified by the law of England and I know it is justified by the law of God. Thus it became part of the law of England. When the Dred Scott decision of 1857 gave Supreme Court approval to the Fugitive Slave Act of 1850 abolitionists defied the assertion of the highest constitutional authority that Negroes could not be American citizens, and deliberately broke the law. In less than ten years the Attorney General of the United States and the Fourteenth Amendment made their lawlessness into law. If in historical retrospect we find such actions good, as I suspect most of us would, how can we categorically condemn similar lawbreakers today?

No doubt you will respond: Am I not justifying the lawbreaking of persons with whom I agree while condemning the lawbreaking of, say, a Southern segregationist? No. If there is a Southern segregationist who is prepared nonviolently to disobey the legislation of recent years and go to jail for it, I support his action on the ground that he may have something to point out to me about those laws which I have not yet seen. Thus my second ground for proposing nonviolent civil disobedience as a legitimate form of democratic dialogue is that there simply *is* a difference between lawbreaking which is quiet, public, deliberate, and lawbreaking of one who snatches up a shotgun to shoot another in the back. The difference between nonviolent civil disobedience and other lawbreaking is that the nonviolent civil disobeyer does not, at least as an immediate consequence, injure anyone but himself.

Yet you may say: Is not the ultimate consequence of his action to weaken law, to weaken the fabric of conventions which keeps us sinful men this side of anarchy? No, I believe nonviolent civil disobedience strengthens law. Were it the case that all defiance of law was illegitimate, the right of revolution would also stand condemned and the doctrine of both the Declaration of Independence and Lincoln's First Inaugural would have to be discarded. Prudence indeed will dictate that just as peoples are more disposed to suffer than revolt, so one-man revolution also will not be undertaken for light and transient causes. Few men are prepared to court jail terms for the sake of an idea; those that are willing deserve our thanks. History will remember David Mitchell with gratitude when it has all but forgotten Lyndon Johnson.

For, if to paraphrase Lincoln one takes one's stand with the Declaration of Independence, statutory law will be seen as the declarer not the creator of rights, and the law written in the hearts of men will be viewed as the standard by which laws written on parchment and paper must be judged. The law of a given conventional jurisdiction has validity insofar as it enforces the rights of all men. Mankind as a whole, in a nuclear age, confronts all nation states as chronic criminals far more dangerous to the rights of man than the solitary nonviolent disobeyer. By saying, No, that disobeyer seeks to recall authority to common sense.

Document 4

"STATEMENT ON DRAFT RESISTANCE," BY STAUGHTON LYND AND CARL OGLESBY, 20 AUGUST 1966

In July 1966, Staughton Lynd attended a meeting in New Haven with eight draft-age men who were searching for a way to effectively oppose the draft that went beyond the impasse in the Students for a Democratic Society (SDS) and its refusal to commit to a national campaign opposing conscription. Out of this frustration came a statement of noncooperation with the Selective Service and a call for a mass draft card turn-in for November 1966. Of the eight, two were members of SDS, one was a member of the Committee for Non-Violent Action (CNVA), and three others had participated in the Mississippi Freedom Summer in 1964. At the meeting, some of the participants agreed to fan out across the United States throughout July to talk to people about building an antidraft movement and produce a report that they planned to deliver at the SDS National Council meeting in Clear Lake, Iowa, at the end of the summer. It was agreed that Lynd would help build support among those too old to be drafted.[30]

According to Lynd, this initiative by the New Haven group was the impetus behind drafting the below statement on 14 August 1966 and sharing it with Carl Oglesby while Lynd was visiting the younger radical. Oglesby had just ended his term as national president of SDS, and Lynd was searching "for a new statement, stronger, more detailed in its argument, and better publicized" than the Declaration of Conscience against the War in Vietnam. The finalized statement was twice as long as Lynd's draft, and both sought to circulate it as widely as possible. As events unfolded, both Lynd and Oglesby were not able to garner more than fifty signatures because their energies were focused elsewhere. Lynd published an even longer statement with the list of signatures in the October 1966 edition of *Liberation* (see document 5 of this chapter).[31]

A man's desire to support his country's government is natural and strong. In time of war, when his countrymen face death on battlefields, this desire grows all the stronger. But conscience may at some point be so deeply abused by acts of government that suspension of consent becomes the only alternative to dishonor.

Americans have had to confront more than once the staggering need to choose between obedience which disgraces conscience, and disobedience which restores it:

In 1846 Henry Thoreau went to jail rather than pay taxes to support war with Mexico.

In the 1850's abolitionists assisted the escape of fugitive slaves in defiance of federal law.

William James, Mark Twain and others denounced suppression of the Philippine independence movement which followed war with Spain in 1898.

Eugene Debs, A. Philip Randolph and others were jailed for opposing World War I.

So in other nations:

Martin Niemoeller was imprisoned and Dietrich Bonhoeffer executed for assisting the German Resistance movement against Hitler's regime.

In 1960 more than a hundred French intellectuals stated publicly that they supported and encouraged direct action, including refusal to fight, against their government's war in Algeria.

The war in Vietnam confronts Americans again with the choice these men were forced to make. To choose disobedience was never easy. It is not easy now. The verdict of an aroused nationalism is all too easily foreseen. But no nation has ever achieved a political conscience except as individual men chose to accept that verdict and endure what reprisals might come.

We understand that dissent is of itself no proof of wisdom or goodness, and we do not presume to anticipate the judgment of history. But what we know about the war in Vietnam persuades us that it is wrong in its purposes and barbarous in its effects. This belief makes impossible the moral luxury of acquiescence, and obligates us to take as forceful a stand as possible against the war which our government calls us to accept.

We want it to be known that we support and encourage such acts of opposition as the following:

1. Sending medical aid to all human beings who suffer in this war, including adherents of the National Liberation Front and the people of North Vietnam.

2. Protesting production of napalm and other instruments of chemical warfare.

3. Refusing induction, whether or not on a pacifist basis.

4. Refusing to fight in Vietnam after induction, whether or not on a pacifist basis.

5. Refusing to pay all or part of one's federal taxes.

6. Establishing peaceful and open contacts with the people of North Vietnam, the National Liberation Front, and mainland China.

And believing this to be a position honorable and necessary for ourselves as men and Americans, we invite others to join us in this declaration.

Document 5

"ESCALATION IN VIETNAM," OCTOBER 1966

When Staughton Lynd and Carl Oglesby's "Statement against the Draft" failed to garner much support due to the inability of either to make a push for signatures, Lynd decided to publish a longer version in the October 1966 edition of *Liberation* highlighting that 1967 would be a crucial year in resistance to the war in Vietnam.

Dramatic further escalation of the war is probable after the elections. President Johnson will want to do something decisive to remove the Vietnam issue from the 1968 campaign. The period of maximum danger, as analysts of the nuclear arms race used to say, will be the year between the November 1966 elections and the de facto beginning of the Presidential contest in the winter of 1967–1968. During this year there will be no elections to national office to focus on discontent, nor will there yet be a Presidential challenger around whom opposition can coalesce.

What then is to be done?

To begin with, three attitudes seem to me essential:

1. We must act in terms of the situation which we believe will exist six months from now, rather than in terms of the present moment. In Spring 1965 we anticipated that hundreds of thousands of American troops would be sent to Vietnam to fight for years, at a time when the Scalopinos and Schlesingers spoke of a modest commitment of American troops to blunt the anticipated Vietcong summer offensive. Because we were right in our forecast, our actions—the creation of the National Coordinating Committee, the International Days of Protest—were not left behind by events. Now it is incumbent on us to plan in terms of further escalation, very likely by invasion of North Vietnam, and quite possibly leading to war with China.

2. We must act on the assumption that the United States government acts in bad faith. It is painful to watch the *New York Times* grasp at every straw of the Administration's peace rhetoric, while at the same time it points out that the Administration's actions steadily escalate the war. We cannot afford such illusions. Ambassador Goldberg's proposals were not designed to end the war but to convince the world on the occasion of the convening

of the United Nations Assembly that the United States wants peace. Goldberg did not endorse U Thant's three points, but sought to give the appearance that he did. U Thant, Senator Fulbright, and one-third of the students of the Yale Law School call for unconditional cessation of the bombing of North Vietnam. But Goldberg offered an end to the bombing in exchange for assurances that North Vietnam would de-escalate its support for the National Liberation Front, a quite different proposal which seems fair and appropriate only if one accepts the American government's thesis that the N.L.F. struggle is aggression from the North.

3. We must not despair. One of the two or three things which most impressed Tom Hayden and myself in talking to spokesmen for the other side was their confidence that political contradictions—between the United States and its allies (de Gaulle), between the Saigon government and the populace it nominally controls (the Buddhist and student protest), between the American government and the American people—would offset the United States' apparent overwhelming superiority in military hardware. It isn't true that America's war in Vietnam cannot be lost. It can be and must be lost, that is, the United States must come to recognize that if France can withdraw with honor from Algeria, America can withdraw with honor from Vietnam.

During the critical year of (roughly) November 1966 to November 1967 I propose that the movement concentrate its energy on direct action against the war. But I propose that we do this *not* because I have abandoned hope that the war can be ended, but because I think that this will give the Romneys and Kennedys the best chance to end it by winning in 1968. I propose that we concentrate on direct action *not* because I think in hard times a man must at least keep his integrity through isolated personal deeds, but because I believe a mass movement can be built around a package of direct action programs.

I have in mind six kinds of direct action.

1. Sending medical aid to all human beings who suffer in this war, including adherents of the National Liberation Front and the people of North Vietnam.
   Brethren of the political Left, this is not mere ambulance-chasing. It is a kind of action which brings into tension the two principal components of the American tradition: patriotism and Christianity. At the same time that it challenges people to discard the mindset of "we" and "they," and to affirm that the human race is one family, it invites them to confront the U.S. government directly and to consider the necessity of civil disobedience on behalf of an unexceptional cause.

Specifically, a number of Quaker groups are sending relief to Vietnam to be divided in three equal parts among the Front, the North Vietnamese government, and the government of South Vietnam. The action defies the House Un-American Activities Committee and the Trading With The Enemy Acts. Nevertheless, by declaring their absolute determination to send relief whether or not permitted by the government, the New York Yearly Meeting has been licensed to send medical supplies through the Canadian Friends Service Committee. A third Quaker grouping, A Quaker Action Group, insists on the inalienable right to care for the sick without government regulation. Thus the potential donor has a variety of ways in which he may offer his charity, and is obliged to undergo the educational process of choosing.

The potentiality of this form of direct action to build mass support is suggested by the fact that at Yale the chaplain of the University, together with the local Young Friends and St. Thomas More groups on campus, have requested permission from the government to send tripartite relief through the Canadian Friends Service Committee.

And not quite incidentally, this action does a little something to atone for the suffering for which all of us Americans share responsibility.

2. Protesting production of napalm and other instruments of chemical warfare.

The possibility of building mass support around this form of direct action is amply indicated by the successful campaign at the University of Pennsylvania against chemical warfare research, and the September protest statement by leading American scientists. The forthcoming War Crimes Tribunal in Europe (about which I hope to comment in the next *Liberation*) will keep this issue alive. The American conscience, I believe, simply will not tolerate indefinitely a situation in which American planes nicknamed "Providers" destroy the food supply of hungry peasants, under the slogan "Only you can prevent forests."

3. Refusing induction, whether or not on a pacifist basis.

4. Refusing to fight in Vietnam after induction, whether or not on a pacifist basis.

"We Won't Go" remains the single best slogan around which to build opposition to the war, superior to "Bring The Troops Home" because it asks people to change their lives. Women and older men can participate in draft refusal by publicly advocating it. Draft refusal action can be politically effective if (a) many men act together rather than letting themselves be picked off one by one, (b) an initial action is conceived as the beginning of organization rather than a one-shot effort. The best way to support the Fort Hood Three is for more persons to do the same thing.

5. Refusing to pay all or part of one's federal taxes.

A new federal telephone tax, explicitly and solely to finance the war, opens up a modest form of tax refusal possible for masses of people. Thus far the tax has not been collected from those who refused to pay it.

6. Establishing peaceful and open contacts with the people of North Vietnam, the National Liberation Front, and mainland China.

Many continue to feel called to go to the scene of battle in order to be hostages or perform relief. As the war escalates, it may become more and more difficult to do so. But N.L.F. and D.R.V. personnel can be readily contacted in Europe; and participants in the movement can make greater efforts to seek out the Latin American revolutionaries who will be fighting the Vietnam wars of tomorrow.

Finally: Carl Oglesby and I have written a short statement in which we say that we "want it to be known that we support and encourage" these six kinds of direct action. The statement has been signed by (among others) Donna Allen, Dena Clemage, Dave Dellinger, Douglas Dowd, Ross Flanagan, Tom Hayden, Robert Greenblatt, Sidney Peck, Vincent Harding, Honey Knopp, David McReynolds, Stewart Meacham, A. J. Muste, Muriel Rukeyser, Mildred Scott Olmstead, Alan Krebs, Marvin Gettleman, Louis Menashe, Glenn Smiley, Ron Young, Julien Gendell, Thompson Bradley, Marjorie Swann, Dagmar Wilson, Howard Zinn, Hugh Fowler, Irving Beinin, Stanley Millet.

We shall overcome.

Document 6

"LYND CLARIFIES," 28 NOVEMBER 1966

In the fall of 1966, students at major universities began issuing "We Won't Go" statements. Unlike sitting in at a local draft board or participating in demonstrations, the statements required students to simply sign their names and make their intentions known that they planned not to cooperate with the draft. This stepping-stone tactic was designed to bring people into the movement, and it worked. In early November, thirty-two University of Chicago students drafted and signed the first of many We Won't Go statements, and it was published in the campus newspaper, the *Chicago Maroon*. The statement read, "The undersigned men of draft age are united in their determination to refuse military service in Vietnam, and urge others of like mind to join them."[32] The Chicago students inspired many other We Won't Go statements at colleges across the United States, including Cornell, Yale, and others.[33]

Thirteen Yale students issued their We Won't Go statement on November 22, the culmination of over a year of organizing on campus to initiate a more persistent antidraft campaign. The students released the statement on the same day they held an information session at Yale's Dwight Hall. The statement read,

> We the undersigned members of the Yale community are grieved that the war in Vietnam continues to grow. We are distrustful of our government's avowed concern for peace. We earnestly seek for ourselves a constructive role in bringing peace to Vietnam.
>
> Convinced that our government's present course of action is not in the best interests of either the United States or the people of Vietnam, we are united in our intention to refuse induction if drafted into the armed services that are participating in the current war. We choose to express our position publicly at this time in the hope that others of like mind will join with us to create a politically effective protest. We encourage all decisions of conviction and challenge each man to assess his position regarding the war.
>
> The thirteen signers published the statement in the *Yale Daily News* along with their telephone numbers so that they could be easily reached by anyone else wishing to join or who had questions.[34] Staughton Lynd also spoke at this meeting, announcing that he and Alice would be holding seminars at their apartment on conscientious objection.[35]

Below Lynd responds to mischaracterizations in the *Yale Daily News* about the Lynds' intentions to hold seminars on conscientious objection. He outlines a new conception of conscientious objection that takes into consideration one's commitments to international law and not just one's religious or moral convictions.

To the Chairman of the *News*:

I should like to correct certain errors in news stories concerning the remarks I made at a meeting November 22 in which a dozen members of the Yale community announced their intention to refuse induction if drafted.

Some reports have it that I offered a "cram course for conscientious objectors" or a seminar in "how to avoid the draft." I believe that Rev. Coffin, Dr. Shorrock of the Divinity School faculty, and others who were at the meeting will substantiate the fact that I did nothing of the kind. The *Yale Daily News* of November 23 stated correctly that I "proposed a seminar to help interested students come to a decision." I made it quite clear that (as the *New Haven Register* for November 23 correctly quoted me) it is my "personal position to support and encourage conscientious refusal of induction. My wife and I share a larger concern, though, that whatever decision a person comes to about the war he makes that decision after careful consideration of the alternatives. He should not make the assumption he has no choice."

The *Yale Daily News* made one error in reporting that I "criticized the walk-out of the Yale delegates from the conference at Antioch College." What I said was that the Yale delegation based its walk-out on a misunderstanding. When the conference voted to support a change in Selective Service law to make possible conscientious objection to a particular war, Mr. Davis and Mr. Rothchild walked out because they thought this would mean "operating under a completely voluntary system." They were, of course, mistaken. England presently uses the system which the conference recommended, and its adoption in the United States has been urged by highly respected figures such as Dr. John Bennett, president of Union Theological Seminary. A Selective Service system which made possible conscientious objection to a particular war would not make military service voluntary, but would change the criteria wherewith draft boards evaluated claims for conscientious objection. If, as Catholic theological training holds, there are morally just and morally unjust wars, then surely one can envision the possibility of a conscientious objection to a particular war—let us say, the refusal of a German soldier to fight in World War II—which was not based on pacifism and did not entail refusal to fight in all other wars.

Staughton Lynd
Assistant Professor of History

Document 7

"WAR CRIMES IN VIETNAM," NOVEMBER 1966

In this article in *Liberation*, Staughton Lynd addresses the recently formed International War Crimes Tribunal (IWCT or Russell Tribunal) founded and organized by famed British philosopher and early critic of the war Bertrand Russell and his Bertrand Russell Peace Foundation (BRPF). The Russell Tribunal was perhaps the most important expression of the global anti–Vietnam War movement, with participants from twenty-six countries, two formal tribunals (held in Stockholm, Sweden, in May 1967 and Roskilde, Denmark, in November–December 1967), and an edited collection publishing its proceedings. While Lynd would offer a more thorough critique of the tribunal in a later edition of *Liberation*, included in this collection, the following article addresses the possible positive benefits such an undertaking could have on the question of exposing war crimes in Vietnam and how this could aid the antiwar movement.

Specifically, Lynd discusses the controversial announcement in June 1966 by North Vietnam to try captured US pilots for war crimes and the parallel creation of the North Vietnamese Commission for Investigation of US Imperialists' War Crimes in Vietnam. When the Johnson administration escalated the air war over North Vietnam on June 30, striking petroleum, oil, and lubrication (POL) facilities in the Hanoi and Haiphong areas, this led to increased demands in North Vietnam to place US prisoners of war on trial and resulted in dramatic photos of US soldiers being marched through Hanoi on July 6 in front of tens of thousands of onlookers. United Press International and the Associated Press reported that the crowd was angry, shouting "down with the U.S. aggressors," "death to the American air pirates," and "Yankee go home." Photos of the parade circulated around the world, and the spectacle was widely condemned.[36] At the time, the Pentagon disclosed that 35 servicemen were "detained" by the NLF or DRV (including 22 pilots, 2 marines, and 11 army soldiers) and listed 233 as missing in action. Because of the secrecy around the official numbers, the Defense Department was not able to confirm the number held captive between North and South Vietnam.[37]

At this time (November 23) the factual situation regarding the war crimes tribunal is as follows:

Members of the tribunal met this week in London, as planned. Jean-Paul Sartre was chosen president with Vladimir Dedijer as chairman. During the next few months six teams of four persons each will visit Vietnam to investigate particular questions such as the use of toxic gases and chemicals. When the public sessions of the tribunal begin early in 1967 a number of witnesses from Vietnam will be present to supplement the reports of the investigating teams. Three Americans are expected to be members of the tribunal, among them a representative of S.N.C.C. and Dave Dellinger, *Liberation* editor now in Hanoi.

Many *Liberation* readers have undoubtedly felt some uneasiness about such questions as: Will the tribunal's judgments lead to more severe punishments, or even execution, for captured American pilots in North Vietnam? Will the tribunal be dominated by Communists and Communist sympathizers? Is it appropriate for persons radically critical of courts, jails, and retaliative penal systems in whatever country to participate in or support the tribunal? I have had all these questions and I would like to share my tentative answers.

I believe it is the intention of the tribunal to function as a grand jury rather than a petty jury, that is, to bring in an indictment rather than to render a verdict. The verdict will be rendered by that same "opinion of mankind" to which the Declaration of Independence appealed in 1776. In this country the verdict will be rendered by individual citizens who will make use of the findings of the tribunal in deciding whether to refuse induction into the United States Army, to refuse to fight in Vietnam after induction, to refuse to pay all or part of their federal taxes, to send relief supplies to "the enemy" despite contrary regulations.

This conception of the tribunal seems to me valid. It seems to me critical, however, that the jury—that is, ourselves—keep constantly in mind that it is we, not the tribunal or the North Vietnamese government, who are to render the verdict; and that the appropriate way for us to render that verdict, should we find the United States government guilty of systematic war crimes, is not by punishing someone but by increasing our own opposition to the war.

I express this caution because it is clear that the North Vietnamese themselves are struggling with the question of whether to punish their prisoners more severely. Whatever they decide will be (to quote Fanon) "psychologically understandable," and Americans have very little right to offer advice. Still, we can *act* in such a way as to communicate our wish that the Vietnamese on the "other side" continue their astonishingly humane treatment of prisoners.

Let me cite a few bits of evidence for the struggle going on in the minds of the North Vietnamese about how to treat American pilots. In June and July there *was* a growing demand for the punishment of American pilots; this was *not* wholly a fabrication of the United States government. In the *Vietnam Courier* for June 9 and June 16—before the bombing of Hanoi and Haiphong—headlines declared: "In North Vietnam The Population Demand Due Punishment To Those Coming To Sow Death and Ruin," "U.S. War Criminals Should Be Duly Punished."

Nowhere have I seen a demand for execution; but it should be recalled that the N.L.F. has announced its intention to "punish with a steady hand" a "very few [South Vietnamese] officers and thugs who deliberately follow the U.S. aggressors and massacre and murder the people" (*Vietnam Courier*, November 4, 1965). The other side is torn between anger at the individual captured pilots and recognition that the pilots fly on orders from Washington. This ambivalence was evident in an account of a procession of captured pilots through the streets of Hanoi (*Vietnam Courier*, July 7, 1966). On the one hand: "The Hanoians boiling hot with utter indignation gave vent to their hatred for the horde of assassins." But on the other hand: "These miserable and unfortunate American pilots [are] forced to commit crimes in Vietnam by the U.S. warmongers."

For the time being, restraint and humanity have prevailed. The *New York Times* for October 12, 1966 quoted State Department and Pentagon spokesmen to the effect that the pilots are receiving adequate care, with no torture or brainwashing: the same impression Tom Hayden, Herbert Aptheker and I received last Christmas-time in speaking to one captured pilot, and that Wilfred Burchett received a few months later when he spoke to three others (see his *Vietnam North*, chapter 2). The first document of the North Vietnamese Commission for Investigation of U.S. Imperialists War Crimes In Vietnam (*Vietnam News Agency Bulletin*, November 4, 1966) directs its condemnation at the United States government rather than individual pilots or soldiers.

Paradoxically, if we as individuals act on the basis of the Nuremberg principle and say "No" to the war, we will encourage the North Vietnamese government and the Front not to apply the Nuremberg principle to those individual war criminals they have captured: for our opposition will demonstrate that (as the other side tries to believe) there *is* a difference between the American government and the American people. But the paradox is only apparent. We can assume individual responsibility for trying to prevent future war crimes at the same time that we ask, by our action, that individuals not be punished for war crimes already past.

Document 8

SPEECH AT WE WON'T GO CONFERENCE, UNIVERSITY OF CHICAGO, 4 DECEMBER 1966

The initial signers of the University of Chicago "We Won't Go" statement against the draft followed up by organizing the We Won't Go conference at the University of Chicago on December 4. The conference was held at the same time a private conference on reforming the draft was held across campus cosponsored by the Ford Foundation and University of Chicago. At the We Won't Go conference, attendees discussed conscientious objection, draft dodgers, draft resisters, draft-card burning, fleeing the United States, those who had already refused induction, and those jailed for noncooperation. It would also address the "problems and frustrations" of the movement, the tactics and history of antidraft organizing, and the theory of noncooperation as a justifiable form of struggle.[38] Conference speakers included Staughton Lynd; Richard Flacks, a University of Chicago professor and cofounder of SDS; civil rights leader James Bevel of the Southern Christian Leadership Conference; Arlo Tatum of the Central Committee for Conscientious Objectors; John Otis Sumrall of the Congress of Racial Equality; Jeff Segal, who would eventually become national SDS draft coordinator; and David Mitchell, a draft resister sentenced to prison.

   Below, Lynd provides a historical analysis of draft resistance in a widely circulated speech.

Many if not most American young men who refuse to serve in Vietnam are not conscientiously opposed to all wars, but are conscientiously opposed to *this* war. They are not pacifists. But they are deeply convinced that America's war in Vietnam is—to use the language of the Fort Hood Three—illegal, immoral and unjust. In England such young men could be classified as conscientious objectors. In America, whether or not they would be willing to accept CO status, they do not have the option. The basic principle of their resistance is the idea that an individual should refuse to participate in an unjust war. This idea is old. For example, it was advanced in England in 1773 by Granville Sharp. Sharp was a clerk in the British defense department who resigned his position rather than participate in England's war against the American colonies; it was also he who, in 1772, won a legal decision that in the absence of positive law to the contrary, natural law prohibited slavery. The words of his 1773 pamphlet on *Manslaughter and Murder* show how old the so-called Nuremberg principle really is:

"Gentlemen of the Army are not obliged, indeed, to acquire a critical knowledge of the Law, but they must not forget that they are Men, as well as Soldiers; and that if they do not maintain the Natural Privilege of Men, (viz. that of thinking for themselves, and acting agreeable to the Dictates of their own Conscience, as Members of the Community), they are unfit for British Soldiers, of whom the Law requires an acknowledgement of her supremacy.

For the Law will not excuse an unlawful Act by a Soldier, even though he commits it by the express Command of the highest military Authority in the Kingdom: and much less is the Soldier obliged to conform himself implicitly to the mere opinions and false Notions of Honour, which his Superiors may have unfortunately adopted.—Even in public military Service, or war live Expeditions by National authority, the Law manifestly requires the Soldier to think for himself; and to consider, before he acts in any war, whether the fame be just: for, if it be otherwise, the Common Law of this Kingdom will impute to him the Guilt of Murder.

And though the Law does not actually punish such general Crimes, as may unfortunately have obtained, at any time the sanction of Government, yet the time will certainly come, when all such temporizing military Murderers must be responsible for the innocent blood that is shed in an unjust War, if they have rendered themselves accessories to it by an implicit, and therefore, criminal obedience to the promoters of it."

There is also an old and honorable American tradition of conscientious objection to particular wars on political grounds. Thoreau advocated civil disobedience toward both the Mexican War and the Fugitive Slave Law of 1850. *Civil Disobedience* is well-known; let me quote a few less well-known phrases from his 1854 essay, *Slavery in Massachusetts*:

"Show me a free state, and a court truly of justice, and I will fight for them, if need be, but show me Massachusetts, and I refuse her my allegiance, and express contempt for her courts." He also said: "I would remind my countrymen that they are to be men first, and Americans only at a late and convenient hour." Massachusetts should dissolve its union with the slave states, urged Thoreau, and individuals in Massachusetts should dissolve their "union with her, as long as she delays to do her duty."

As Thoreau opposed America's imperialistic venture against Mexico before the Civil War, so after the Civil War Charles Sumner urged civil disobedience, if necessary, to prevent American acquisition of Santo Domingo.

In 1862 the Union government under President Abraham Lincoln recognized Haiti, first black republic of the Western Hemisphere, independent by virtue of a successful slave insurrection since 1804 but for fifty-eight years diplomatically unrecognized by America. Then in 1870–1871 President Grant, reflecting the new mood of capitalist greed which enveloped the United States at the end of the Civil War, sought to annex Santo Domingo. Senator Charles Sumner, Massachusetts abolitionist and chairman of the Senate Committee on Foreign Relations, opposed the move.

According to Sumner, the facts were these. Emissaries of the President, unauthorized by Congress, secured an agreement from one Baez, for annexation to the US of Santo Domingo, the eastern half of the island of which Haiti constituted the western half. Baez, according to Sumner, had no popular support: he was "sustained in power by the Government of the United States that he may betray his country." He was, Sumner said, an American puppet. Warships were present when Baez and the American commissioners reached agreement; Sumner commented: "it is not astonishing that there is on the seaboard, immediately within this influence, a certain sentiment in favor of annexation. But when you penetrate the interior, beyond the sight of their smoke, at least beyond the influence of their money, it is otherwise."

Not only had American emissaries, backed by warships, sought to annex the eastern half of the island; the American commodore had threatened to bombard the capital of Haiti if that country objected to the proceedings, and the language of President Grant's communications with Congress seemed to reveal an intent to annex the island as a whole. Sumner said that, rather than obey so unjust an order as to shell the Haitian capital, the American commander should have committed civil disobedience: "He ought to have thrown his sword into the sea."

Foreshadowing the doctrine of FDR, Sumner said that America should practice "good neighbourhood" toward the black nations which were beginning to arise in the Caribbean, and would eventually appear in Africa too. The "principles of our republic," according to Sumner required Americans to regard all nations—no matter how small or weak—as equal before the law of nations, just as all individuals—whatever their economic standing or educational attainments—as equals before the domestic law of this land.

What was especially interesting was that in 1870–1871 when Sumner was urging that American warships stay out of Haitian waters he was urging that Federal troops be employed more vigorously in the American South. For him there was no contradiction: both policies were designed to protect the African race in its striving toward self-government. "It is difficult to see," said Sumner, "how we can condemn, with proper, whole-hearted reprobation, our own domestic Ku-Klux, with its fearful outrages, while the President puts himself at the head of a powerful and costly proceeding operating abroad in defiance of International Law and the Constitution of the United States." To the applause of the Senate galleries, Sumner concluded on this contemporary note: If the President had spent one-fourth of the "time, money, zeal, will, personal attention, personal effort, and personal intercession" protecting the rights of Negroes in America that he had spent on "his attempt to obtain half an island in the Caribbean Sea," the KKK would exist in name only.

A third and last example. Eugene Debs began his agitation against war when early in 1914 President Woodrow Wilson sent United States marines into Mexico. So Debs' biographer paraphrases his position. "American citizens who chose to live and invest their money in foreign countries should do so at their own risk, not at the risk of our soldiers' lives."

When the United States went to war with Germany, Debs was sentenced to ten years in the Atlanta penitentiary for a speech in 1916 at Canton, Ohio. Debs made his speech immediately after visiting three socialists imprisoned in the Canton workhouse; indeed, as he spoke he could see the workhouse and pointed to it. Since this speech is less well-known than his great declaration upon sentencing in September 1918, let me quote a few passages from it, perhaps particularly appropriate for this occasion:

> ... I would rather a thousand times be a free soul in jail than a sycophant or coward on the streets. They may put those boys in jail, and some of the rest of us in jail, but they cannot put the Socialist movement in jail. Those prison bars separate their bodies from ours, but their souls are here this afternoon. They are simply paying the penalty that all men have paid in all of the ages of history for standing erect and seeking to pave the way for better conditions for mankind ...

Parenthetically, when a dozen years ago I worked as periodicals librarian at Roosevelt University, I met the reporter who had taken notes on Debs' Canton Speech and turned them over to the Justice Dept., which used them as its principal evidence at Debs' trial. At the time I knew him, the former reporter was a member of the Roosevelt faculty and a Debs admirer.

A more recent precedent for American resistance to the draft for the war in Vietnam is French resistance to the draft for the war in Algeria. Two days ago I received a manuscript history of that movement, entitled "The Refusal Of The Young." At first, according to the manuscript, opponents of the war went into the army with the aim of agitating among the troops. But they discovered "their powerlessness to act, to resist, to oppose once taken inside the military machine." The next stage was to go to jail rather than accept induction, a course chosen by about thirty young men, "mostly active militants from political organizations." But, according to the manuscript, "it was suffocated by silence and had not even the tiniest echo." "The Refusal Of The Young" had a third stage, which the manuscript calls "Insubordination." The Algerian revolt began in November, 1954.

In 1956 and 1957 the first desertions began. The ideas of insubordination, of desertion, seemed to some youths the only issues: they were based on two past experiences, that of the recalled men and that of those imprisoned. The recalled men had taught them the horrors of this war of repression, the entangling complexity of violence, the powerlessness of forces of resistance within the army itself; the fate of those imprisoned, the ineffectiveness of their act, the muteness which made their refusal a ridiculous form of protest. Why go to prison, if this choice remains without echo, if no one supports you? Powerlessness at the heart of the army, powerlessness between the walls of a cell; the idea of a different form of refusal, one that did not deprive one of his liberty, of his political effectiveness, appeared. Insubmission, desertion, these kept open the possibility of fighting actively against the war, of organizing more widely refusal in all its forms.

The movement of insubmission and desertion touched some three thousand youths between 1958 and 1961. It attained its culminating point in 1960: during this time the insubmission and desertion took organized form . . . "Young Resistance," it is under these two words that the young designated themselves and their movement. They refer themselves explicitly to the experience of the years 1940–1944 in the struggle against fascism. They broke the silence concerning tortures, massacres. In 1959 "Young Resistance" published a manifesto. This attempted to explain to the young the choice of insubmission, and above all it exposed to them the material possibilities which permitted them to accomplish acts of desertion and insubmission. A network was organized with neighboring countries: Switzerland, Belgium, Germany, Italy. It was arranged that young men as they came into these countries would be taken in charge, found jobs, provided with identity papers.

Rapidly, the insubmission and desertion converged with another form of opposition to the war. There were 400,000 Algerians in France. Most of them were organized in the FLN. Their activities were harassed by the Police. A certain number of Frenchmen concluded that it was indispensable to give concrete assistance: to hide and to feed those haunted by the police, to hide money, to facilitate contracts. This form of solidarity was, to begin with, undertaken for moral reasons. Then it came to be politically based on anticolonialism. 1960 was marked by the convergence of the refusal of the young and concrete solidarity with the Algerians in their struggle. A revolutionary alliance was formed between anticolonialists and the colonized. In June 1960, a public conference on insubmission was called in Paris. The police arrested a number of students, concerned for assistance to the FLN. The movement became the center for lively debate. The manifesto of the 121 in September 1960 declared respect for, and justified, refusal to bear arms against the people of Algeria.

American intellectuals, too, need to clarify where they stand in relation to the refusal of the young. They must make it known that they support and encourage refusal to be inducted for the war in Vietnam. They should publicize their conviction that young men who are deeply convinced that this war in Vietnam is an unjust war have, in the language of the Declaration of Independence, not only the right but the duty to say: We Won't Go.

Figure 5.4: Staughton Lynd supporting the Fort Hood Three—Dennis Mora, James Johnson, and David Samas—at their press conference on 30 June 1966 announcing their refusal to fight in Vietnam. The photograph is taken from the Fort Hood Three Defense Committee's pamphlet *The Fort Hood Three: The Case of the Three G.I.'s Who Said "No" to the War in Vietnam*.

Left to right: Dave Dellinger, Stokely Carmichael, A. J. Muste, Dennis Mora, James Johnson, David Samas, Lincoln Lynch, and Staughton Lynd. Courtesy of The International Labour and Radical History Pamphlet Collection, Archives & Special Collections, Memorial University Libraries, St. John's, Newfoundland, Canada.

CHAPTER 6

WHAT IS RESISTANCE?

Introduction

In 1967, the Selective Service System became a potent symbol of coercion in an increasingly unpopular war. In the eyes of many radicalized draft-age youths, the call shifted from "protest to resistance" against the war and the draft. The efforts of Staughton and Alice Lynd and the nascent antidraft movement throughout 1966 proved dramatically important in laying the groundwork for 1967, the year in which a mass movement against the draft emerged. For the early draft resisters, it was a difficult and often lonely time, and the support and encouragement offered by the Lynds provided a much-needed boost as governmental, familial, and other social forces pushed for obedience of the law and the Selective Service.

As table 1 demonstrates, draft calls rose during the period of escalation and with them so did prosecutions and convictions of Selective Service violators. Not all violations of the draft laws are attributable to opposition to the war as such; however, the dramatic events of 1967 foisted into the public space the willingness of growing numbers of draft-age Americans who were openly willing to refuse to participate with the draft. With increasing draft calls and the reality of rising combat deaths came a heightened sense of awareness for each of the Vietnam era's 26.8 million men who were vulnerable to the growing reach of the Selective Service System.

The first draftees who entered Vietnam after President Johnson's July 1965 troop surge and raised monthly draft calls began entering Vietnam in 1966. Because President Johnson and Secretary of Defense McNamara refused to activate the reserves and the National Guard, 1967 was the year in which draftees began systematically replacing professional, enlisted soldiers on the battlefield. This was reflected in the growing rate at which draftees were killed in action. By 1969, eighty-eight percent of infantry soldiers were draftees, and throughout the totality of the war, draftees would represent more than fifty percent of all

US soldiers killed in the US Army.[1] During the Vietnam War era, of the 26.8 million men who engaged with the Selective Service, 10.9 million served in the military, out of which 8.7 million enlisted voluntarily and another 2.2 million were drafted. Of this large active-duty pool of soldiers, 2.1 million were sent to Vietnam and 1.6 million of them saw combat. This meant that a far greater pool of young Americans avoided the military through refusing to participate with it or an even larger number who got a deferment.[2]

Table 6.1					
Year	Draft Calls	Prosecutions for Selective Service violations	Convictions	Percentage of draftees killed in combat	US soldiers killed in action
1964	150,808	316	227	—	216
1965	103,328	506	272	16	1,928
1966	343,481	1,015	536	21	6,350
1967	298,559	1,648	952	33	11,363

Sources: "Draft Efficiency, 1953–1967" in George Q. Flynn, *The Draft, 1940–1973* (Lawrence: University Press of Kansas, 1993), 212; "450 Convicted in '66 as Draft Violators," *New York Times*, 6 January 1967, 2; Fred P. Graham, "952 Draft Foes Convicted in 1967," *New York Times*, 13 January 1968, 2; John Prados, *Vietnam: The History of an Unwinnable War, 1945–1975* (Lawrence: University of Kansas Press, 2009), 151–152.

What was the nature of the draft or conscription? Systemically, the Selective Service System and conscription as it existed from 1948 to 1973 was a product of the Cold War and the perceived needs of the United States to project power across the globe to undergird the Western liberal order after the end of World War II. Therefore, under a complex system of deferments, the roughly 26.8 million men of the Vietnam War era were "channeled" into occupations in the United States' "national interests" and "defense effort." This meant that the system privileged children of the well-educated middle-class or of the ruling elite, who were the beneficiaries of the very world order the US protected with its military and economic power. This was spelled out in the infamous July 1965 "Channeling Memorandum" by Selective Service director general Lewis B. Hershey, which was obtained and published first in the SDS national newspaper, *New Left Notes*, on 20 January 1967 and by *Ramparts* in December 1967. The "channeling" memo laid out the way in which the Selective Service System procured manpower for military and nonmilitary roles by singling out students and professionals such as scientists, engineers, educators, and skilled workers as well as ministers and divinity students who would contribute to the expanding military-industrial complex either directly or indirectly. During the Cold War, the entire economy was a function of US national security and the defense complex, and as envisioned by the Selective Service, everyone had a role to play in the functioning of this system. This meant that poor and working-class youth would be channeled into the US armed forces to fight in the expanding conflict in Vietnam.[3] By drafting or inducing American youth to enlist out of fear of being drafted, the armed forces would always have enough manpower to fill the ranks of an active-duty force capable of projecting American power all over the world. Historian Christian Appy estimates that of those who served in Southeast Asia, 25 percent were from poor backgrounds, 55 percent were working class, 20 percent were from the middle class, and a statistically negligible number were from wealthy backgrounds.[4] This meant that while middle-class students could obtain deferments to go to college, poor and working-class Americans were serving and being killed in the jungles of Vietnam. Students who received the 2-S student deferment were increasingly forced to confront the privilege such a status conferred as draft calls mounted and the war escalated. As we have seen, the pressure mounted on campuses across the country in 1966 to renounce their student deferments or indicate "We Won't Go" after graduation in opposition to the war.

On a personal level, the Selective Service System was a coercive force. Under the law, men between the ages of eighteen and twenty-six were compelled to register with their local draft board and were issued a draft card, which they had to keep with them at all times. Even men older than the legal draft age had to continue to carry their draft card on them. Therefore, the act of draft card destruction—through burning one's card, ripping it up, or sending it back to your local draft board—was a symbolic yet subversively illegal act after August 1965. Moreover, simply protesting the draft also carried the overt threat made by General Hershey that protesters would be reclassified 1-A, eligible for service and ready for induction into the armed forces, as had happened in October 1965 when University of Michigan students sat in at the Ann Arbor draft board. Under this framework, opposition to the draft by growing numbers of students and nonstudents and their older supporters was viewed by many commentators in the media and members of the Johnson administration as an attack on the American way of life because of these connections to the national security state and Cold War notions of American exceptionalism.

This process of channeling manpower highlighted the intersection of class and race as major factors in determining who served, and it exposed the gaping chasm of inequity at the heart of the system. At the end of 1965, African Americans represented 14.8 percent of the US Army in Vietnam, but between 1961 and 1965 the death rate of African Americans was 18.3 percent. African Americans comprised 8.9 percent of the Marine Corps forces in Vietnam but

had a death rate of 11.3 percent between 1961 and 1965. What these numbers demonstrated to the African American community in the United States
was that Black people were serving on the front lines in Vietnam and dying in
disproportionately high numbers. The Pentagon attributed this to the "valor"
of the African Americans serving in Vietnam and claimed this demonstrated
that progress was being achieved after the armed services were desegregated in
1948.[5] Between 1965 and 1967, African Americans represented 20 percent of
combat deaths in South Vietnam, a figure higher than the percentage of African
Americans in US society as a whole, at 11 percent, as well as the percentage of
draft-aged men in the US, which was around 12 percent. Due to pressure within
the military and outside from the civil rights and antiwar movements, the military brass would lean less heavily on African Americans on the front lines after
1967, and the total percentage of Black people killed in action would represent
12.5 percent of all US combat deaths by the end of the war. Statistics on other
minority groups are difficult to come by because of the nature of the Defense
Department's own record keeping. Latinos served in large numbers and suffered
heavy casualties. Approximately 48,000 Puerto Ricans served in Vietnam, and
345 died in combat during the length of the war. While Mexican Americans
made up 10 percent of the population of Arizona, Colorado, California, New
Mexico, and Texas, they accounted for 20 percent of all combat deaths from
these states. By one estimate, 20 percent of all Latinos who served in Vietnam
were killed. Native Americans also disproportionately served in the military.
While only 1 percent of the total US population, Indigenous peoples from a
variety of nations comprised 2 percent of Vietnam veterans, which equaled
42,000 people, with 250 combat deaths.[6]

Such unequal service in the military and the coercive nature of the Selective
Service System was precisely the reason why the Student Nonviolent Coordinating
Committee's (SNCC) militant antiwar and antidraft statement in January 1966
was so dangerous: it confronted this system that was disproportionately affecting
the lives of African Americans who fought and died in Vietnam for Vietnamese
freedom and democracy when they could not touch that freedom and democracy at home. Stokely Carmichael summed up the interracial complexity of the
Selective Service System in 1967 as "white people sending black people to make
war on yellow people to defend land they stole from red people."[7] Many young
African Americans involved in the civil rights movement full time who were not
students faced the possibility of being drafted. From 1965 to 1967, Carmichael
was reclassified three times and ultimately given 4-F status. When Bob Moses
(who changed his name in late 1965 to Robert Parris) received his draft notice
in July 1966, he chose to go to Montreal, Quebec, where he lived for two years

before moving to Tanzania. Clayborne Carson, another member of SNCC and later renowned historian of the civil rights and Black power movements, also left the United States for Europe.[8]

As of February 1965, Staughton Lynd was on the cutting edge of advocating for civil disobedience and nonviolent revolution to end the war. Part of this struggle included recognizing that conscientious objection as defined by US law was too narrow to accommodate a new generation of war resisters who would have fought in World War II, for instance, but opposed the war in Vietnam based not just on religious, moral, or political principles, but on the fact that the war in Vietnam was undeclared by the US Congress and also violated international law. This was also the position of David Mitchell, an early nonpacifist noncooperator with the draft who was aided in his opposition by Lynd. Not a student at Yale, but nonetheless put on trial in New Haven where his draft board was located, Mitchell attempted to use his trial to raise awareness about the illegality of the war and the illegitimacy of the draft. For Lynd and Mitchell, this type of opposition went beyond mere individual witness against the war and the draft based on conscience, religious or political pacifism, or civil libertarian grounds, which opposed state-sanctioned coercion of the individual into the military. Instead, they advocated for building a mass political movement against the draft that confronted the question of the war's legality under domestic and international law. Here, Lynd connected such resistance and breaking of the law to the internationalist idea "my country is the world, my countrymen are all mankind" in his writings and speeches. At a 5 October 1965 debate on the draft titled "The Draft or Free Choice?" at Yale's Linsly-Chittenden Hall in front of a capacity audience, Lynd received applause when he invoked the tradition of Thomas Paine, Henry David Thoreau, William Lloyd Garrison, Eugene Debs, and other prominent American dissenters when he stated, "My strongest allegiance is not to the US but to the world as a whole," in connection with the idea that the Nuremberg principles of 1950 conferred a sense of individual responsibility that owed its adherence to international law above national law.[9]

As the war escalated and draft calls increased, it was clear that a majority of those in the crosshairs of the Selective Service System were not absolute pacifists who opposed all wars. In 1967, the issue of selective conscientious objection rose to prominence during the debate over congressional reauthorization of the Selective Service Act, which was set to expire every four years. A diverse set of groups from Clergy and Laymen Concerned about Vietnam (CALCAV) to Women Strike for Peace (WSP) were lobbying Congress to adopt a new provision for selective conscientious objection. Responding to a speech by Reverend William Sloane Coffin in Washington, DC, in February 1967, Staughton Lynd told the *Yale Daily News* that despite novel attempts in the courts, conscientious objector status was still only being given to the "typical Protestant objectors such as the Quakers or the Mennonites." Recognizing the new realities of different types of war resisters, Coffin called for a massive campaign of civil disobedience against the draft: five thousand students to renounce their student deferments, turn in their draft cards, and face the possibility of prosecution by the federal government and for ministers and divinity students to do the same by giving up their 4-D deferment and applying for conscientious objector status even if they were not pacifists.[10] Such calls for civil disobedience were still controversial and demonstrative of the radicalizing effect the war had on people like Coffin who were skeptical of Lynd's radicalism two short years earlier.

In making such bold pronouncements, Lynd, Coffin, and others put themselves well within the sites of federal government prosecution for violating section 12 of the Selective Service Act, which made it illegal for someone who "knowingly counsels, aids, or abets another to refuse or evade registration or service in the armed forces" and therefore became criminally liable for prosecution and a maximum of five years in prison or a $10,000 fine, or both. Not content with simply advocating for a new type of mass resistance, Lynd supported the early resisters who were not pacifists and who refused to cooperate with the Selective Service or the military once they were inducted. He was one of the first civilian supporters of three soldiers at Fort Hood—Private First Class James Johnson, Private Dennis Mora, and Private David Samas—who refused orders to deploy to Vietnam and quickly became known as the Fort Hood Three. David Mitchell and the Fort Hood Three were not pacifists and did not apply for conscientious objector status; instead they argued that their participation would violate both the US Constitution and international law. Lynd supported these early acts of resistance in both words and deeds and by showing up to court dates to physically demonstrate support. This kind of solidarity cannot be overstated, and it is vitally important for the growth of any movement, especially in the period between 1965 and 1967, when the movement consisted of the disparate acts of individuals who stepped into the unknown by breaking the law and with it Cold War orthodoxy and the demands of loyalty and patriotism during wartime.

The question of individual and collective responsibility during an immoral and illegal war, and confronting one's relationship to the Selective Service System and the war in Vietnam, by the end of 1966 was rapidly simmering throughout the country but not yet boiling over, as it did by the end of 1967. Participants in the December 1966 "We Won't Go" conference at the University of Chicago returned to their communities and campuses and set up over twenty-five We

Won't Go groups by March. Importantly, this was accomplished without assistance from the largest radical student group—the Students for a Democratic Society (SDS)—and demonstrated that independent antidraft organizing on campus could forge ahead despite the absence of the SDS's national council leadership.[11] At the urging of numerous individuals and groups throughout 1965 and 1966, including Stokely Carmichael, SDS finally declared their opposition to the draft and called for a mass movement against it in late December 1966 at Berkeley. The resolution called the draft "coercive and anti-democratic" and argued "that a sense of urgency must be developed that will move people to leave the campus and organize a movement of resistance to the draft and the war, with its base in poor, working class, and middle class communities." SDS encouraged "all young men to resist the draft."[12]

The debate about the Selective Service System was aided by the quadrennial, and near automatic, renewal of the Selective Service Act by the Congress. When calls to abolish or reform the draft went unheeded in 1963, President Johnson appointed a committee to investigate the draft. In the lead-up to the vote in June 1967, the National Advisory Commission on Selective Service—headed by Burke Marshall, the former head of the Justice Department's civil rights division—released its report *In Pursuit of Equity: Who Serves When Not All Serve?*[13] Included in the calls to reform the draft were Kingman Brewster at Yale, the *New York Times*, and a plethora of individuals and groups across the United States. Despite the best efforts of these groups, legislators led by Senator Mendel Rivers and Representative Edward Hebert rushed the bill through Congress in June 1967 without any provision for selective conscientious objectors. The new draft law ended marriage and fatherhood deferments for those married after 1965 and provided that graduate student deferments would end in 1968. According to historian Michael Foley, despite the work of the Marshall Commission and the calls for reform, the renewal of the draft law included the same "fundamental inequalities" as before.[14]

The centerpiece of much of the antiwar and antidraft organizing throughout the country was the Spring Mobilization to be held on 15 April 1967. The day of protests exceeded the organizers' expectations and in part was aided by Martin Luther King Jr.'s decision on April 4 to openly declare his opposition to the war at Riverside Church in Harlem and to speak at the rally scheduled at Central Park on April 15. Crowds surpassed three hundred thousand in New York and another fifty thousand in San Francisco. Two weeks after the Spring Mobilization, Muhammad Ali (formerly Cassius Clay) announced his intention to refuse induction into the military based on religious convictions and his status as a minister in the Nation of Islam.[15] Through these organizing and mobilizing efforts, inspirations and connections made on the day of the mobilization, and the bonds cemented afterward all came together to help forge what former Stanford student body president and draft resister David Harris in Palo Alto called "the Resistance." Groups such as the Resistance, the Chicago Area Draft Resisters (CADRE), the Boston Draft Resistance Group, and others focused on the Selective Service System and laid the groundwork for confrontation by the end of 1967.

The work of draft resistance groups, draft counseling groups, antiwar organizations, civil rights organizations, and the jailing of resisters led to a dramatic increase in the number of conscientious objector applications. While it was controversial to advocate for nonpacifists or those not opposed to all wars to apply for conscientious objector status, more and more people and organizations respectable to the media and the liberal establishment entered the fray in the context of the escalating war. In May 1967, Martin Luther King Jr. argued that "every young man who believes this war is abominable and unjust should file as a conscientious objector."[16] This combined work led to the largest wave of CO applications in US history. The ratios for conscientious objector exemptions per 100 inductees into the military jumped precipitously: 6.1/100 in 1966, 8.1/100 in 1967, 8.5/100 in 1968, 13.45/100 in 1969, 42.62/100 in 1970, and 130.72/100 in 1971. As historian John Whiteclay Chambers II points out, by 1971 the Selective Service was exempting more CO applicants than they were inducting into the armed forces.[17] In total, there were 170,000 CO applications approved during the war, while 300,000 CO applications or deferment requests were denied.[18] Within the military itself, there were 17,000 in-service applications for CO status between 1967 and 1973 (829; 1,387; 2,556; 3,196; 4,381; 2,673; and 2,056 respectively). The breakdown of the numbers corresponds to the breakdown in discipline in the military and growing disaffection with the war in Vietnam.[19]

In their own personal way, the Lynds provided much support and guidance in aiding these developments. Nineteen sixty-seven was a year of big changes for the Lynds, as they decided to move from New Haven to Chicago after Staughton received official confirmation in September 1966 that his chances of getting tenure at Yale were close to zero. Rumors began circulating that Lynd was looking northwest toward the Chicago area after he was invited by the History Department at Northern Illinois University in DeKalb in October 1966 to speak about his research. Moreover, in the winter and spring of 1967, Lynd was offered full-time tenure-track employment at two universities—Northern Illinois University and the University of Illinois at Chicago Circle—only to be quashed by the administration of both schools. Northern Illinois was especially attractive because Alfred Young, Lynd's closest colleague in the study of the role of ordinary working people in the American Revolution, was there. Before leaving New Haven, Lynd had obtained the commitments of Chicago State College for a one-year contract and a part-time graduate student seminar in history at Roosevelt University. In July 1967 the Lynds returned to Chicago, leaving New Haven behind them.

The FBI closely followed the couple's possible move from New Haven to Chicago, indicating on 29 May 1967 that the *New Haven Register* wrote that Lynd would be granted a second leave of absence from Yale and that he planned to leave for Chicago in July. Moreover, the FBI's New Haven field office also reported on June 22 that Lynd was expected to sign a one-year teaching contract at the Chicago State College and would teach one graduate studies seminar at Roosevelt University. An alert was sent out to the Chicago field office to monitor Lynd's arrival and for the New Haven field office to note any departure.[20]

On July 17, shortly after the Lynds arrived in Chicago, the Board of Governors of the State Colleges and Universities of the State of Illinois voted 6–1 to quash Lynd's employment at the Chicago State College. In a prepared statement, the Board of Governors did not question his teaching skills,

> But in assessing his ability to make a contribution which would be for the best interests of the college, the board feels that his public activities, which include a visit to North Viet Nam and China without a valid passport, and his statement that "deliberate law breaking thru nonviolent civil disobedi-ence is a valid, and should become a routine, form of democratic dialog," goes beyond mere dissent.[21]

In response to this action, Lynd told the media he was considering filing suit against the Board of Governors for breach of contract, and Local 1600 of the Cook County College Teachers Union vowed to support him. The Illinois chapter of the American Civil Liberties Union agreed and prepared a friend of the court brief.[22] This was now the third Chicago-area university where Lynd's employment was struck down despite the fact he had received the blessing of each history department chair.

While there is no direct evidence linking Lynd's troubles at Yale to the FBI, this was not the case with his difficulties at the Chicago-area universities. On 24 February 1967, with Lynd's name on the list of speakers for the SDS Midwest Regional Conference on the draft and the Vietnam War, an unidentified official from Northern Illinois University visited the FBI field office in Chicago, informing the bureau that Lynd was possibly being recruited and that "[name redacted] is concerned over the activities of Dr. LYND and his possible future involvement in the affairs of Northern Illinois University. He has requested that he be advised if there is any information available which might give him a better insight into the true nature of Dr. LYND and his activities."[23] During the height of the McCarthy period, Hoover created the Responsibilities Program, which distributed open-source intelligence on suspected communists or subversives to trusted officials at public institutions in order to root out and dismiss these individuals from their positions. This was sometimes done surreptitiously and at other times at the behest of officially trusted administrators at these institutions. The program lasted only four years, from 1951 to 1955, and was closed because of embarrassing publicity that the FBI was distributing such information.[24]

As the Lynd cases in Chicago demonstrate, however, the Responsibilities Program continued to operate beyond 1955 and evolved into a more restricted and closely guarded program producing information on suspected subversives. Hoover tasked the New Haven field office to prepare the "blind memorandum" about Lynd, designed to conceal any FBI involvement, and interestingly the special agent in charge at New Haven declined to prepare the memorandum, citing a policy that barred the FBI from doing so. In response, Hoover indicated he would only approve passing information to university officials if Lynd was employed there. The bureau ascertained that Lynd was not employed at Northern Illinois University and indeed was denied a contract by the university administration. Therefore, Hoover took a more cautious approach to the Responsibilities Program than in previous years because he was concerned that such cooperation would be revealed if Lynd decided to sue Northern Illinois University.[25]

As the controversy developed in July and August over the canceling of Lynd's contract at the Chicago State College, members of the Board of Governors of the State Colleges and Universities of the State of Illinois were startled by the prospects of a lawsuit for breaching Lynd's contract and a second expensive lawsuit seeking financial damages in the amount of $264,000. In response, Frederick McKelvey, executive secretary of the Board of Governors, and a redacted second board member visited the FBI field office in Springfield, Illinois, on July 19, explaining they were concerned by the legal troubles they would soon find themselves in. The special agent in charge of the Springfield office relayed to J. Edgar Hoover, in part,

> [Redacted name] explained that technically before LYND was hired by the college in Chicago, the hiring should have been approved by the Board of Governors. However, the President of this college in Chicago failed to secure the approval of the Board and signed LYND to a contract. When the Board finally considered this matter, the Board voted against hiring LYND. They are now, therefore, faced with going through with the contract or facing litigation.

[Redacted name] desired to know whether the Bureau had any information which could be furnished to the Board concerning the background of LYND. They desired this information to aid them in handling him as an employee. As an example, [redacted name] stated that if they knew enough about him they may be able to make a decision if they must honor his contract that they could relegate him to a relatively minor administrative post, thus keeping him out of the classroom.[26]

In response to the request for information on Lynd, Director Hoover responded that the reliability of the two members of the Board of Governors was unknown and that until Lynd was an employee the bureau would not provide the information because the FBI "does not desire to be placed in the position of having furnished information to [redacted name] with the possibility that the Bureau might be drawn into any public controversy arising out of litigation." Nonetheless, Hoover mentioned it was "probable" this information could be handed over to the Board of Governors once Lynd was employed and ordered the New Haven field office to prepare the open-source intelligence report "either for use in this instance or other situations which will probably arise."[27] This time, the New Haven office dutifully prepared an eleven-page report and sent it to FBI headquarters for approval on August 10. Among a long list of media sources highly critical of Lynd, which were commented upon and editorialized by the New Haven special agent, it included a summary and quotations from the *Ottawa Journal* recounting Lynd's speech at Carleton University: "The article reflects that LYND spoke to an audience at Carlton [sic] University. He compared President JOHNSON's actions in Viet Nam to HITLER's actions in Europe and called on Canada for help as a 'Voice of Sanity.'"[28] The agents excised inconvenient facts that were clearly available in the text of Lynd's speech, which they had at their disposal, as we saw in the previous chapter. Such recounting was meant to slander Lynd and aid in his being forced out of yet another teaching position.

Lynd received a significant amount of support after he was so clearly rejected on the basis of his political beliefs and actions. The Chicago Area Council of the American Association of University Professors issued a strong statement in defense of Lynd, accusing the Board of Governors that it "overlooked a fundamental principle of American justice; namely, that a person is presumed to be innocent until he has been proved guilty."[29] On August 23, three circuit court judges for the state of Illinois upheld the rescinding of Lynd's contract and set the stage for an appeal. Intervening on behalf of Lynd, fellow historians Alfred Young and Christopher Lasch created the Committee for Academic Freedom in Illinois to defend Lynd and distributed "The Staughton Lynd Case—A Fact Sheet," a national statement in support of Lynd, and created a legal defense fund.[30] In facing the appeal and financial damages suit, the Board of Governors agreed to reach a settlement on 19 October 1967, which allowed Lynd to teach only history graduate students starting in January 1968 at full-year's pay if he agreed to drop his ongoing litigation. This was a partial victory for Lynd, as he received only a one-year contract that was not renewed. Moreover, Lynd was denied a full-time position at Roosevelt University, where he taught only one graduate student seminar on a part-time basis. When this decision came down, out of principle, he decided to refuse the renewal of his part-time contract for the 1968–1969 academic year.[31] Based on J. Edgar Hoover's own decision-making during this period, and his avowed acceptance of providing information on Lynd only to his employers, we can credibly wonder if the FBI then provided this dossier to administrators at the Chicago State College and Roosevelt University and reinforced the efforts to push Lynd out by September 1968. On a personal and professional level for Lynd, the academic year 1967–1968 "was a very unsatisfactory and humiliating arrangement" and marked the end of an otherwise promising future as an academic historian.[32]

As these events unfolded, Alice Lynd continued work on her collection *We Won't Go: Personal Accounts of War Objectors*. While working on the project, which she began in October 1966 and was published by Beacon Press in September 1968, Alice was pregnant and gave birth to the Lynds' third child, Martha, in February 1967. The introduction to the book is provided in document 9 of this chapter and is demonstrative of what the Lynds eventually came to call "accompaniment" (discussed further in the epilogue). Alice later developed relationships with draft resisters on the basis of what she referred to as the "two experts" idea: the draft counselor as an expert in Selective Service regulations and conscientious objector status and the draft counselee as an expert in his own life and circumstances. For Alice, this was crucial to her success as a draft counselor, and *We Won't Go: Personal Accounts of War Objectors* is a perfect example of how she lets those who already went through the process of refusing to participate with the draft, or refused orders in the military, or left for Canada tell their own stories so that they could help those who were going through the same difficult decisions and discussions with friends and family.

When the Lynds moved to Chicago, Alice continued draft counseling first as a trainer of draft counselors for the Midwest Committee for Draft Counseling, a local affiliate of the Central Committee for Conscientious Objectors (CCCO), and then as coordinator of all draft counseling in the Chicago regional office of the American Friends Service Committee (AFSC). This was a large undertaking, and by this time Alice developed the reputation as one of the preeminent draft counselors in the country. By 1969 the Lynds had to find the appropriate means for juggling life in the movement and having a family. Staughton regards the transition to Chicago as a time when Alice carved out her own space in the antiwar movement and excelled as a draft counselor while he slowly began the process of taking a step back from the spotlight.[33] More on this dynamic in a moment.

While Staughton Lynd's antiwar activism interfered with his ability to be employed at a university in the United States, by 1967 the war continued unabated, and resistance to the draft flourished across the country. The public increasingly became dissatisfied with the war despite strong popular support in 1965. Between August 1966 and April 1967, Gallup polling indicated that 43 percent of Americans approved of Johnson's war policies. Beginning in July 1967, that number fluctuated downward from 33 percent in July, 39 percent in December, 35 percent in February 1968, and finally 26 percent in March 1968. In October 1967, the number of Americans who thought "the U.S. made a mistake sending troops" to Vietnam surpassed the number of Americans who supported the decision. By August 1968, the time of the Democratic National Convention in Chicago, 53 percent thought the war was a mistake.[34] Realities on the ground in Vietnam and increasing casualties broke through the rosy propaganda of the Johnson administration and forced a questioning of the war like never before in US history.

The draft resistance movement accelerated after the 15 April 1967 Spring Mobilization, and plans for a "Stop the Draft Week" commenced for October 16 to 21 across the country. A series of antidraft solidarity statements were released in the fall of 1967 that added growing weight to the movement. The most significant was "A Call to Resist Illegitimate Authority," released by Arthur Waskow and Marcus Raskin, colleagues at the Institute for Policy Studies, with Bob Zevin of Columbia University. Lynd was asked to sign the statement on 31 May 1967, and it was officially released on 28 September 1967. It appeared shortly after in the pages of the *New York Review of Books* and the *New Republic*.[35] Other statements against the draft and in support of draft resisters were made by WSP and CALCAV.

These statements attracted a growing and widening base of support for more radical actions against the war, which would be dramatized during the "Stop the Draft Week" beginning on October 16 and culminated in the March on the Pentagon on 21 October 1967. In cities across the country, with major sites of activity in New York, Washington, DC, Boston, and Oakland, thousands were mobilized to obstruct the draft, culminating in a massive draft-card turn-in on October 20 at the Justice Department in Washington. As part of the week of actions, on October 16, members of the Fort Hood Three Defense Committee submitted a petition of thirty thousand signatures protesting the court-martial of the three Army privates who were in prison at Fort Leavenworth for refusing to go to Vietnam.[36] The tumultuous week ended with the March on the Pentagon, where perhaps thirty thousand demonstrators descended on the Pentagon, creating scenes of confrontation between antiwar activists, US Marshals, and military personnel. Some demonstrators got into the Pentagon, running through the halls before they were tackled and arrested. There were tense moments between demonstrators and the military police, while others called on the soldiers to "Join us!" in an impromptu teach-in.[37] The iconic March on the Pentagon proved a turning point for the antiwar movement.

Lynd was as busy participating in events in Chicago for Stop the Draft Week. On October 16, he spoke at the University of Illinois in front of a crowd of seven hundred announcing he was turning in his own draft card "as an expression of solidarity with the young men of the draft resistance movement" and urged older Americans to do the same. Earlier in the day, nine students sat in at the local draft board in Chicago and were arrested. It was estimated that forty members of CADRE turned in their draft cards that day. Other estimates for October 16 demonstrate the strength of the growing movement: 340 draft cards were turned in in Boston, 300 in San Francisco, 180 in New York, 15 at Cornell University, 10 in Philadelphia, and 5 in Minneapolis.[38] In total, sociologist Tom Wells estimated that 1,200 to 1,500 draft cards were turned in or burned on October 16. Another 992 were collected on the steps of the Justice Department in Washington, DC, on October 20, and finally 200 more were destroyed at the Pentagon on October 21. In total, according to Wells, between 2,392 and 2,692 cards were turned in or burned during Stop the Draft Week.[39]

Violation of the August 1965 draft card law in such an open and public fashion was a new phenomenon in the history of American radicalism. However, what was dubbed "the ultra-resistance" escalated the tactic from individual to mass draft file destruction. Activists from all stripes devised plans throughout the war to subvert the draft through open property destruction in the form of draft-board raids, destroying Selective Service files at their source in local draft boards. The first such case occurred on 25 February 1966, when twenty-year-old Barry Bondhus walked into his Sherburne County draft board in Elk River, Minnesota, and poured two buckets of his family's excrement in six file cases. He was arrested and served eighteen months in prison with a $2,500 fine.[40] Other examples of mass draft file destruction would occur during the war by different groups of activists throughout the country. Ultra-resistance reached national attention when on October 27 Father Philip Berrigan and three others—dubbed the Baltimore Four—entered the Baltimore Customs House, where the local draft board was housed, and poured blood over the 1-A draft records. Philip Berrigan would recruit his brother Father Daniel Berrigan for a larger and more daring action in Catonsville on 17 May 1968, when they obtained a homemade recipe for napalm from a Special Forces manual and poured it on draft files in front of cameras. Before the police arrived, Daniel Berrigan famously said, "We have chosen to be powerless criminals in a time of criminal power. We have chosen to be branded as peace criminals by war criminals." From 1967 to 1971, over 230 people participated in 53 similar draft-board raids, destroyed files at Dow Chemical, and even raided the FBI field office in Media, Pennsylvania, where the first disclosure of the bureau's secret counterintelligence (COINTELPRO) operations were found. In total, it is estimated that one million draft records were destroyed through the efforts of the ultra-resistance.[41]

As these events unfolded, Staughton Lynd received a major victory in his passport case. While the Illinois Board of Governors prejudged Lynd's trip to Hanoi via Prague, Moscow, and Beijing to be unlawful, the US Court of Appeals for the District of Columbia stated in a significant decision that the secretary of state can control the travel of a passport but not a person. "In short," the three judges unanimously declared, "we think the Secretary has authority to control the lawful travel of the passport, even though Congress has not given authority to control the travel of the person."[42] This decision ultimately struck down the final plank in the scaffolding of Cold War travel restrictions: the secretary of state legally could determine countries forbidden to travel to but could not prevent a US citizen from traveling to them if they did not use their passport. The decision went even farther, suggesting US consular services worldwide could provide the service of safely holding a passport while the person traveled to a restricted country. The gravity of the decision, which the Justice Department declined to appeal to the Supreme Court, was not lost on State and Justice Department officials. "This decision effectively destroys the basic premise of travel restrictions which is that the travel or presence of a U.S. citizen in a restricted area is what is prejudicial to our foreign policy not merely whether they used the passport for such travel," wrote an unnamed official from the US passport office to the Senate Internal Security Subcommittee (SISS). Even more, the decision had "further repercussions" because it would stymie "possible criminal prosecutions in the cases of Stokely Carmichael and Ralph Benedek Schoenman." Just eleven days earlier, Carmichael returned from lengthy travels to Africa, Europe, North Vietnam, and Cuba. This time, unlike when Lynd, Hayden, and Aptheker arrived home from Hanoi, a US Marshall holding a search warrant took Carmichael's passport. Schoenman, a US citizen and secretary of the Bertrand Russell International War Crimes Tribunal, had his passport canceled in the fall of 1967 because he also traveled to North Vietnam and Cuba. As the passport office official informed the SISS, "Both of the possible criminal prosecutions in these cases depend in varying degrees on the validity of the Department's action in revoking their passports for violation of area restrictions. If these actions are void under the Lynd decision, and they very well may be, then the basis for criminal prosecution disappears."[43] This is an example of how legal actions taken in the courts by middle-class professionals can produce significant precedents to protect racialized and marginalized groups.

In late December 1967, Lynd was submitted as a candidate for the FBI's recently created Rabble Rouser Index, which was approved by J. Edgar Hoover on 24 January 1968. In the Chicago field office's application to Hoover, they wrote that Lynd "has since February, 1965, violently protested the U.S. role in the Vietnam war in various newspaper articles and speeches and has advocated civil disobedience until U.S. Vietnam war has ended. During 1966 he defied a State Department ban on travel to North Vietnam and Red China."[44] This is a perfect example of how the bureau often inflated the threat of domestic dissent in order to push investigations of individuals who were otherwise participating in lawfully protected dissent. While Lynd advocated civil disobedience and was arrested three times, he was never arrested for, or accused, of being "violent" during the 1960s. He was one of 1,191 people to be included on the Rabble Rouser Index, which on August 3 and 4, 1967, originally singled out those "fomenting racial discord" but was expanded in the fall of 1967 to include "agitators who have demonstrated by their actions and speeches that they have a propensity for fomenting disorder of a racial and/or security nature and (2) have attracted such attention, nationally or locally, as to be of significant interest with regard to the overall civil disturbance picture."[45] Lynd was singled out because of his antiwar activism.

The course of the Vietnam War and antiwar opposition changed in 1968. Beginning 30 January 1968, the National Liberation Front and the North Vietnamese launched their most audacious and largest coordinated attack of the war at the beginning of the Tet New Year. Laying siege on more than one hundred cities, including intense street fighting in the capital, Saigon, the event would become a turning point in the war for Americans watching on television and reading newspapers. Just two months earlier, General William Westmoreland pronounced that the end of the war was soon approaching and it was the United States that was winning. In reassessing the situation after the Tet Offensive, on February 27, General Westmoreland and General Earle Wheeler requested a troop increase of 206,756, which would have brought the total US troop commitment in South Vietnam from 525,000 to 731,756. Upon receiving this shocking request, President Johnson ordered his soon to be sworn-in secretary of defense, Clark Clifford, to conduct a "complete and searching reassessment of the entire U.S. strategy and commitment in South Vietnam."[46]

RABBLE ROUSER INDEX

NAME   STAUGHTON CRAIG LYND   SEX   MALE

ALIASES --   RACE WHITE

DATE & PLACE OF BIRTH   NATIONALITY

November 22, 1929, Philadelphia,   American
Pennsylvania

ORGANIZATION AFFILIATION   --

POSITION IN ORGANIZATION   --

DESCRIPTION
                                               DISTINGUISHING
HEIGHT   WEIGHT   HAIR   EYES   CHARACTERISTICS

5'11"   190 pounds   Brown   Blue   --

FBI #   365 711 F   OTHER IDENT #

RESIDENCE   BUSINESS ADDRESS

7359 Bennett Avenue, Chicago, Illinois   Roosevelt University
                                         430 South Michigan
                                         Avenue, Chicago, Illinois

SUCCINCT RESUME OF ACTIVITIES   LYND, presently an associate
                                history professor at Roosevelt
University, Chicago, has since February, 1965, violently protested U.S. role in Vietnam war in various newspaper articles
and speeches and has advocated civil disobedience until U.S.
Vietnam war has ended. During 1966 he defied a State Department
ban on travel to North Vietnam and Red China.

BUFILE # 100-396916
FIELD OFFICE FILE # 100-26453
SUBMITTING OFFICE CHICAGO

5 - Bureau
2 - Chicago
    1-100-26453
    1-157-2153

Figure 6.1: Staughton Lynd's Rabble Rouser Index card. Notice how the FBI falsely claimed Lynd had "violently protested" against the US war in Vietnam. Source: Lynd's FBI file.

The reality on the ground in Vietnam combined with growing calls to "dump Johnson" in unprecedented maneuvers to unseat a sitting US president. Minnesota Senator Eugene McCarthy accepted the challenge with the help of Allard Lowenstein and won 42 percent of the vote to Johnson's 48 percent in the New Hampshire primary on March 12. Senator Robert Kennedy entered the race four days later. Intervening in these historic political developments, some- one leaked a copy of the Wheeler/Westmoreland troop requests to the *New York Times*, which printed the request on March 10. The leak infuriated Johnson and effectively made the troop request a dead letter. Instead, the president replaced General Westmoreland in a significant shake-up of Vietnam policy, and the replacement led directly to the gathering of the so-called Wise Men at the State Department on the evening of March 25 and morning of March 26.[47]

There were other significant factors being discussed in the Pentagon over the feasibility and capacity of such an enormous buildup of forces in Vietnam. For the Joint Chiefs of Staff, the US military was spread too thin, and to meet the requested 206,756 troops, the reserves would have to be called up. Up until this point, to President Johnson and Robert McNamara, who left the Pentagon in February 1968, such a massive call-up of the reserves was never acceptable. So alienated by the war by the end of 1967, McNamara ordered a thorough study of US involvement in Vietnam, which came to be known as the *Pentagon Papers* when they were leaked by Daniel Ellsberg in 1971. After combing through the top-secret study, Noam Chomsky pointed out in 1973 that Pentagon planners and national security officials were concerned in early 1968 with the possibility of massive "domestic disruption," especially after the 21 October 1967 March on the Pentagon and urban uprisings and rebellions in places like Detroit and elsewhere. This had a direct bearing on whether the Joint Chiefs of Staff could authorize such a troop request because any further deployment of troops had to take into consideration whether "sufficient forces would still be available for civil disorder control."[48] This much was admitted in the so-called A to Z reassessment ordered by President Johnson. A top-secret memorandum prepared for Johnson, edited and approved at the highest levels of the Pentagon on March 1, concluded in part that a new round of escalation would have dramatic domestic consequences:

> We will have to mobilize reserves, increase our budget by billions, and see U.S. casualties climb to 1,300–1,400 per month. Our balance of payments will be worsened considerably, and we will need a larger tax increase— justified as a war tax, or wage and price controls....
>
> It will be difficult to convince critics that we are not simply destroying South Viet Nam in order to "save" it and that we genuinely want peace talks. This growing disaffection accompanied, as it certainly will be, by increased defiance of the draft and growing unrest in the cities because of the belief that we are neglecting domestic problems, runs great risks of provoking a domestic crisis of unprecedented proportions.[49]

Facing these realities, President Johnson shocked the nation when he announced on 31 March 1968 that he was initiating a partial bombing halt of North Vietnam and stopping new troop reinforcements to South Vietnam in order "to move immediately toward peace through negotiations." Finally, in one of the most famous moments in presidential history, Johnson stated, "I shall not seek, and I will not accept, the nomination of my party for another term as your President." In response, Hanoi agreed in May to begin negotiations in Paris, France. In reality, the bombing halt was north of the 20th parallel, leaving a wide area still open to American bombing, and the bombs that would have fallen on the DRV were diverted to South Vietnam, Laos, and Cambodia.[50] Such a major announcement, indeed a major victory for the antiwar movement and for the Vietnamese themselves, led to spontaneous eruptions of joy in the streets of the United States that would come crashing down when Martin Luther King Jr. was gunned down in Memphis, Tennessee, on April 4. The riots that broke out made it seem like the United States was unraveling.

This was also a period of personal upheaval for Staughton Lynd. By late 1967 and into early 1968, Staughton began the process of reevaluating his movement praxis and where he would focus his energies. This was also a period of difficult separation for him. On the eve of the March on the Pentagon, David Dellinger uncharacteristically called Staughton and asked him to join him in Washington. Embroiled with legal proceedings over his job contract and busy in Chicago with Stop the Draft Week, Lynd said no. As we will see in document 6 below, Lynd and Dellinger also disagreed over the Bertrand Russell–sponsored International War Crimes Tribunal (IWCT), which took place in Stockholm, Sweden, in May and Roskilde, Denmark, in November–December 1967. Dellinger assumed that Lynd would participate and nominated him to be a member of the IWCT.[51] Lynd refused to participate in the tribunal, which led to "separation [from] my main colleague in the nonviolent movement." For Lynd and Dellinger, it "was a real parting of the ways" and was extremely difficult.[52]

The burden of Lynd's national and international prominence and a speaking schedule that few in the movement were committed to was beginning to take its toll on his family and personal life. Lynd's recalculations were aided by some movement organizations' turning away from participatory democracy to a hierarchical vanguardism and from nonviolence to the embrace of violent tactics over 1968 and 1969. As the Lynds reflected in their memoir, "the Movement as we found it when we arrived in Chicago was changing rapidly." In what was a "lonely and confusing time," Lynd recalled a moment in his Chicago living room where he decided to step back from the national and international spotlight and focus on community-based organizing that centered on the family and community-based resistance instead of national actions. In his speeches and writings, this evolution is pronounced in how he envisions building a movement that could structurally change the United States.[53]

Nineteen sixty-eight was a year of confrontation across the globe. The Democratic National Convention in Chicago from August 26 to 28, 1968,

produced some of the most dramatic pictures of a police crackdown on demonstrators. Lynd did not participate with the larger contingent of demonstrators
seeking disruption, which included his friends Dave Dellinger, Rennie Davis,
and Tom Hayden. Instead, on August 28, the final day of the DNC, Lynd
decided to organize a nonviolent march to the convention at the International
Amphitheatre, protesting the restrictions on free speech the police had imposed
around the building. Before they could finish their action, Lynd was arrested
with a group of activists from the American Friends Service Committee (AFSC)
for interfering with a police officer and trespassing outside the amphitheater.
The FBI investigated Lynd but "failed to indicate any violation of antiriot
laws," and therefore "Assistant United States Attorney (AUSA), Chicago,
Illinois, declined prosecution in this matter advising it did not appear to be a
prosecutable violation."[54] Nonetheless, the Justice Department, with the help
of the FBI, chose eight individuals to indict on conspiracy charges, who would
be dubbed the Chicago 8.

As Lynd sat in jail, two police cars parked outside the Lynds' house on the
South Side of Chicago. Released from jail, Staughton called Alice to see how she
and the kids were doing. When he was walking toward home, Alice slipped out
the door with Martha in the stroller to meet him. Arriving home and soaking
in a hot bath, Lynd received a call from Saul Alinsky, who had just set up the
Industrial Areas Foundation Training Institute and asked if Staughton would be
one of four inaugural teachers. With no full-time university teaching contract
starting in September, he agreed.[55] As the following readings in this chapter will
demonstrate, this was a period of immense resistance against the war, and Lynd
was at the forefront of imagining and participating in that resistance. It was also
a period of immense difficulty, as the movement he had spent nearly a decade to
help build was turning away from the principles it was founded on.

Document 1

"A CALL FOR NONCOOPERATION," BY STAUGHTON LYND
AND DAVE DELLINGER, FEBRUARY 1967

During the fall of 1966, students at Cornell University organized their own "We Won't Go" group, and on December 14 Bruce Dancis dramatically ripped up his draft card outside Olin Hall in front of two hundred people and the media. Out of these events emerged the idea to call for a mass draft-card burning as part of the 15 April 1967 Spring Mobilization. Writing in his memoir, Dancis recalled that the April draft-card burning "was one of the most poorly organized acts of mass civil disobedience in the history of the antiwar movement." Citing a lack of publicity and difficulties in using the US mail to circulate the callout, Dancis credits several non-draft-age supporters for helping spread the word. One was this solidarity statement cowritten by Dave Dellinger and Staughton Lynd.[56]

The Cornell antidraft statement was published in various places and read,

> The armies of the United States have, through conscription, already oppressed or destroyed the lives and consciences of millions of Americans and Vietnamese. We have argued and demonstrated to stop this destruction. We have not succeeded. Powerful resistance is now demanded.
>
> In Vietnam the war machine is directed against young and old, soldiers and civilians, without distinction. In our own country, the war machine is directed specifically against the young, against blacks more than against whites.
>
> Body and soul, we are oppressed in common. Body and soul, we must resist in common. The undersigned believe that we should begin this mass resistance by publicly destroying our draft cards at the Spring Mobilization.
>
> WE URGE ALL PEOPLE WHO HAVE CONTEMPLATED THE ACT OF DESTROYING THEIR DRAFT CARDS TO CARRY OUT THIS ACT ON APRIL 15, WITH THE UNDERSTANDING THAT THIS PLEDGE BECOMES BINDING ONLY WHEN 500 PEOPLE HAVE MADE IT.
>
> The climate of anti-war opinion is changing. In the last few months student governments, church groups and other organizations have publicly expressed understanding and sympathy with the position of individuals who refuse to fight in Vietnam, who resist the draft.
>
> We are fully aware that our action makes us liable for penalties of up to five years in prison and $10,000 in fines. We believe, however, that the more people who take part in this action, the more difficult it will be for the government to prosecute.[57]

We support members of the We Won't Go group at Cornell University in their call for at least five hundred young men to burn their draft cards at the April 15 Mobilization in New York City.

Personal refusal to fight in Vietnam is the heart of the movement against the war. This is more rather than less true as the war escalates and as the draft law is changed to expose more students to induction.

Moreover, the noncooperator—the draft card-burner, the tax-refuser, the violator of the travel ban—challenges the assumptions of the Cold War as well as its results. When Senator Robert Kennedy proposes a new plan for negotiations, he helps to keep alive the possibility of dissent. But the weakness of all such proposals is that they assume the United States' right to be in Vietnam and to have a voice in what happens there. They take it for granted that America will continue to raise an army, to manufacture napalm, to invest in Latin America, Africa and Asia, and, if need be, to protect those investments.

Noncooperation tries to force the onlooker, perhaps at the same time that he feels contempt and anger, to question the hitherto unquestionable.

A massive draft-card burning will be a dramatic act of noncooperation. And should less than five hundred burn their cards now they will nonetheless give courage to others to burn their cards later. They will also encourage kindred acts of noncooperation, such as the returning of draft cards or the renunciation of 2-S and 4-D deferments. The aim of draft refusal must be, as S.D.S. National Secretary Greg Calvert has said, not protest but resistance. The Cornell group conceives its action as a beginning in the organization of intensified resistance.

All of us grow numb to the reality of napalm and fragmentation bombs, even as their use increases. Our indignation at a lying government fades, even as the lies become more threadbare. We all need to be moved to say "no" by acts: "radical, illegal, unpleasant, sustained."

Document 2

"WHITHER DRAFT RESISTANCE?" SUMMER 1967

Faced with the prospect of decreased activity against the war over the summer of 1967 and seeking to continue the momentum created by the Spring Mobilization, Staughton Lynd proposed solutions to continue building the movement over the summer of 1967. This text was found in Lynd's papers at Kent State University.

Last summer, when the "Fort Hood Three" declared that they would refuse to go to Vietnam, Stokely Carmichael urged them to go to Harlem and tell their story there. This summer, the organization of opposition to the war in the ghetto (white and black) is the frontier of peace activity.

Anti-war activity among young people has been undertaken in two kinds of community: the campus and the ghetto. The month of April 1967 represented a turning-point in both kinds of work.

Crucial for the campus anti-war movement was the fact that the We Won't Go group at the University of Cornell, having committed itself to burn draft cards if 500 persons took part, decided on the eve of the April 15 Mobilization to go ahead even if those participating were only fifty. The immediate consequence of this step in faith was that more than 150 burned their cards the next day. Since then, older persons not personally subject to the draft have circulated perhaps as many as half a dozen statements of support. One, initiated by Paul Goodman, explicitly invites men over thirty-five to "join the conspiracy." Another, initiated by Noam Chomsky, is modeled on the statement made by 121 French intellectuals in support of draft resistance to the war in Algeria.

Equally significant for the developing draft resistance movement off the campus were Martin Luther King's advocacy of a "boycott" of the war by young men of draft age, and Muhammad Ali's personal refusal to be inducted.

The potential impact of Muhammad Ali's action was suggested in a column by Tom Wicker. "What happens," asked Wicker, "when enough citizens simply refuse to obey the positive commands of government and of the national majority?" The *New York Times* columnist went on to answer his own question. If, he said, "100,000 young men flatly refused to serve in the armed forces, regardless of their legal position, regardless of the consequences," the Johnson Administration's *"real power to pursue the Vietnam war or any other policy would be crippled if not destroyed. It would then be faced not with dissent but with civil disobedience on a scale amounting to revolt"* (*New York Times*, May 2, 1967; my italics).

A succeeding column by James Reston made clear how the Administration planned to deal with this imminent threat to its war. Draft deferments for college undergraduates will be continued, Reston declared, because Administration officials estimate *one out of every four* male undergraduates might simply refuse to go (*New York Times*, May 5, 1967).

A little arithmetic makes clear the immense and sobering fact that if there were no student deferments 100,000 men would refuse to go and the war would end. Every student and every teacher should ponder what this means for his life.

How shall we confront the second fact that the Administration, making the same calculation we do, plans to continue undergraduate deferments? A way forward is indicated by another product of the April events, the newsletter of the new Draft Resistance Clearing House created by a number of We Won't Go groups at a meeting after the Mobilization on April 16. "At this time," the first newsletter states, "most draft resistance activities are located on the campus. When summer comes and most students leave the campuses, the Movement will be extremely vulnerable and scattered. We feel that it is necessary to relocate draft resistance activities to the urban areas where students will probably be located, and where organizing can really begin."

Here is the beginning of an answer to our dilemma, not only (so it seems to me) for the summer but for next winter as well. If the Administration plans to continue student deferments then students must reach out to the young men who are drafted for this war: ghetto youth. Programs need to be developed to make contact with these young men both before and after induction. Draft information centers should be started in off-campus areas (but they should be started slowly and carefully, in consultation with those already doing other kinds of community organization and in the context of that broader program). Research should be done as to the race, class, age, and sex composition of local draft boards, and appropriate legal cases and political demands developed. (Why shouldn't draft board members be elected, or at the very least, like jurymen, be chosen randomly from the same neighborhood as the young men whose lives they will dispose of?)

Such a program will require students to leave the campus and thereby expose themselves to the draft, not for the sake of being martyrs, but because long-term commitments to ghetto communities are necessary to organize effectively. A growing number of young men, one dares hope, will say not only, We Won't Go, but also, We *will* go to the place where we can do the kind of work which has the most chance to stop this war.

Document 3

COMMENT IN RESPONSE TO A. J. MUSTE'S LAST SPEECH, SEPTEMBER–OCTOBER 1967

When A. J. Muste, the venerable pacifist leader, passed away on 11 February 1967, the antiwar movement lost a pillar of stability and force for unity. Throughout 1965–1966 and early 1967, Muste was credited with almost single-handedly holding fractious meetings and coalitions together with his calculated interventions.

Here Staughton Lynd pays tribute to the late warrior for peace in the September–October 1967 commemorative edition of *Liberation* magazine. In this comment, Lynd reflects on the international admiration A. J. Muste commanded when Lynd spoke with Vietnamese representatives at the World Council of Peace conference in Geneva, Switzerland, in June 1966.

In June 1966 I attended a meeting of the World Peace Council in Geneva, Switzerland as a last-minute substitute for A. J. At the conference I discussed with the North Vietnamese delegates a trip to Hanoi by a team of women which had been proposed by the Committee for Nonviolent Action (the trip subsequently made by Barbara Deming, Grace Newman, Dianne Bevel and Pat Griffith).

The Vietnamese were interested in one other possible visitor: A. J. They had been deeply moved by his journey to Saigon a few months previously, together with Barbara, Brad Lyttle and others, to protest American policy. They said to me at Geneva: "Tell A. J. Muste he can come whenever he wishes. He has only to wire us. But perhaps he will prefer to wait until the fall, when it is cooler."

Less than a fortnight later Hanoi and Haiphong were bombed. A. J., Dave Dellinger and I met at the press conference where the Fort Hood Three announced their refusal to go to Vietnam. Afterwards we went to a restaurant together and our talk turned to the possibility of an immediate trip to Hanoi to demonstrate our solidarity with the Vietnamese people under the bombs. Had the Vietnamese not said that A. J. might come at any time?

There followed a series of discussions at A. J.'s apartment. (I had never been there before.) It seemed clear that A. J. and Dave should go.

That trip never materialized. After initially accepting the proposed visit by A. J., Dave and an unnamed third person, the Vietnamese changed their minds, apparently because of the decision to evacuate Hanoi. Direct contact was broken until Dave's persistent search from Tokyo to Phnom Penh to Moscow once more opened the door. But after that June meeting, all of us understood that A. J. would go to Hanoi as soon as an occasion offered.

In view of what I have since learned from Dave, regarding A. J.'s attitude toward his own health and remaining strength, I believe we should consider his decision to go to Hanoi a deliberate decision to lay down his life, if need be, to stop the war in Vietnam.

Wherever there is a young man who wakes in the early morning to face yet another day of prison for opposition to this war, or to all wars; wherever a person takes risks on behalf of the vision of a peaceable kingdom; wherever—to use one of A. J.'s favorite images—a man, like Abraham, leaves behind him the city of his nativity and turns his face toward the city of his dreams, A. J. is at his side.

Document 4

"DISSENT AS DUTY," 27 OCTOBER 1967

Dramatic scenes played out during "Stop the Draft Week." Perhaps the most iconic scenes of the entire movement against the Vietnam War played out on October 21 when thirty thousand marched across the Potomac River and descended on the Pentagon. Lynd was not in Washington this time, opting instead to stay in Chicago to aid local efforts there. Nonetheless, Lynd wrote this editorial in the *New York Times* defending the escalating opposition to the draft and the war.

To the Editor:

Many Americans have been profoundly disturbed by the tactics of the antiwar movement during the week of Oct. 16–21. Efforts to shut down the Oakland Induction Center or the Pentagon by sitting in entranceways have dismayed even some long-time pacifists. Perhaps the commonest objection is this one: Who gave a handful of peaceniks the authority to shut down the United States Government or any part thereof?

And what if the shoe were on the other foot? Would those now obstructing recruiters for Dow Chemical and the United States Navy tolerate similar disruption of recruitment for Students for a Democratic Society? When left-wing demonstrators impatiently abandon traditional political methods, do they not create precedents for right-wing direct actionists who, given the present temper of the country, would prove far stronger in any foreseeable confrontation?

I would like to respond to this objection.

Nonviolent Protest

First, it is no small matter that on the whole the antiwar movement has remained non-violent. Right-wing direct actionists prefer guns. Were there hawks or segregationists prepared to practice nonviolent obstructive tactics and go to jail as the result, I do not believe such an expression of concern would destroy the democratic process.

To use the words which caused my appointment at Chicago State College to be delayed three months: "Nonviolent civil disobedience is a valid, and should become a routine, form of democratic dialogue." I affirm this for my opponents as well as for myself.

Second, those who condemn the tactics of Oct. 16–21 should make more clear their solution to the problem created by President Johnson's continued indifference to the United Nations Charter, the United States Constitution, his pre-election promises, and this summer's public opinion polls. We who burn draft cards, refuse induction and block doorways believe that we act in response to an executive branch which is out of control.

Third, I believe there are certain actions so evil that they should be resisted by any means necessary and even if the resister is a minority of one. I confess that burning alive women and children with napalm seems to me such an action. I think history will uphold the judgment of those who sought to clog as best they could the American warmaking process in Vietnam, just as most of us now praise the lawbreaking abolitionists of the 1840's and the European resistance movements of World War II.

Staughton Lynd
Chicago, Oct. 21, 1967

Document 5

"RESISTANCE: FROM MOOD TO STRATEGY," NOVEMBER 1967

Here Lynd discusses possible strategies for the draft resistance movement in *Liberation*. We begin to see the evolution of Lynd's ideas and how he envisioned student and middle-class movements interacting outside of the campus to build a "community draft-resistance strategy." Lynd presented portions of this article under the title "The Vision of the New Radicalism" at the fall retreat of the Methodist Theological Fellowship at the University of Chicago on 3 November 1967.[58]

Since roughly January 1967, the Movement has turned toward what it terms resistance. The new slogans are "from protest to resistance" (title of an article by former S.D.S. national secretary Greg Calvert), "from dissent to resistance" (slogan of the October 21 mobilization in Washington) or just "resist" (S.D.S. button). Resistance is thus far a mood rather than a strategy. Often when a movement is groping toward a new strategy there must be an initial period when individuals take a new kind of action without fully understanding what strategy the action implies. Thus, in the South, the mood exemplified by Rosa Parks' refusal to move to the back of the bus and by the Greensboro sit-inners of 1960 crystallized by late 1961 into the strategy of voter registration in Southwest Georgia and Mississippi.

Similarly, the teach-in with the troops at Washington on October 21–22 profoundly expressed the new mood of direct confrontation with oppressive authority. But it was not yet a strategy. The Washington mobilization, like the Albany, Georgia marches of 1962 or the Birmingham demonstration of May 1963, requires a complementary program of day-to-day activity to keep people at work in the same spirit of militancy between semiannual mass events. In the South the day-to-day activity that tied together mass demonstrations was voter registration. In the North the day-to-day activity that functions as the equivalent of voter registration in the South may be draft resistance.

The activity of draft resistance may express either a mood or a strategy. When young men say "hell no, we won't go," what is uppermost in their minds may be either a personal, conscientious refusal to fight or the hope of producing consequences that will help to stop the war. Naturally, any given man, any particular action, is likely to reflect both of these attitudes in some measure, but as draft resistance moves from a mood toward a strategy the concern to produce consequences will be increasingly important.

This means that the traditional pacifist scenario which leads from dramatic individual witness to the martyrdom of jail will be questioned in terms of its effects. Thus Carl Davidson of S.D.S. inquired last spring whether the onlooker, watching the pacifist dragged off to jail, may find his own will to resistance weakened rather than made stronger. Thus, too, the question has been raised as to whether ways cannot be found such that the draft resister publicly says "No"—for example, at a preliminary court hearing—yet does not permit himself to be jailed and thereby lost to the Movement for the period of his imprisonment. Finally, conceptualization of draft resistance from the standpoint of strategy will mean understanding this act of refusal as a transition to long-term radical activity. In the Movement, saying "No" to the draft at the inception of one's adulthood will become a characteristic rite of initiation—a commencement exercise, so to speak—for the man brave or foolish enough to drop out of preparation for a conventional career and turn his face instead toward the vocation of revolution. And the draft-resistance organizer will seek to create conditions such that as many persons as possible from the groups most exposed to the draft undergo this radicalization in the shortest possible time.

Clearly, draft resistance—thus far the characteristic expression of the new resistance mood—is linked to another widespread concern of the past year: the tendency to visualize radicalism as the work of a lifetime rather than a two-year or three-year "experience," with the attendant need to ask how one can be a radical if he is married and has children, or is involved with a professional career. David Harris, an initiator of The Resistance movement, the members of which returned their draft cards on October 16, explained at a conference this summer that for him going to jail for five years no longer signified compulsory retirement from the Movement, since he expected to work in the Movement all his life. At another summer conference, on "radicals in the professions," teachers, lawyers, city planners, social workers debated whether it is possible to be radical yet make a living as a professional. Three things stand out from this new questioning still very much in process.

First, the problem to be solved is seen more seriously and somberly than was the case only a few years ago. A liberal ideology was implicit in the pattern of dropping out for a few years and then returning to graduate school, catching up and proceeding to a conventional career. America, basically a good society, was understood to have a problem: "the Negro problem." Just as the problem was small compared to the goodness of the society as a whole, so one devoted only a fraction of a lifetime to its solution. Two or three years was felt to be equivalent to the magnitude of the difficulty.

The Problem Is America

Now there is a different vision. The civil-rights movement has become a black-liberation movement. The movement against the war in Vietnam has been understood to be necessarily a movement against all the similar wars which will follow the termination of this one. The Movement as a whole—even though operating in separate white and black parts—has redefined itself as a movement against racist capitalist imperialism at home and abroad. The question is no longer that American society *has* a problem. What we think now is that American society *is* a problem. Accordingly, we demand of ourselves a commitment of all our energies to the solution of this pervasive problem. Little as we yet understand what these words mean, awkwardly as we move toward their expression in decisions about job and family, nevertheless we are now clear that nothing less than all our lives will be enough.

Second, there is new thinking about what it means to be an "organizer" and what constitutes a "project." In the old days an organizer was an unmarried student who lived in a freedom house where, when he was not in jail, he slept on the floor and ate peanut-butter sandwiches. A project was the several students who lived in that freedom house and worked together in the neighborhood. If radicalism is to become a lifetime vocation, these definitions must be expanded. Married couples with children must be able to be part of a project. It follows that members of a project may not all live under one roof. And not all project members will do the same work. What remains of a project? Perhaps the following elements:

1. All members of the project regard the Movement—the task of social change—as their principal work, the axis of their lives, regardless of how each one makes a living.

2. Project members determine together a rough sense of priorities as to what kinds of organizing most need to be done, who should do them, what has to happen to make that possible.

3. Belonging to the project makes it possible for each participant to take greater risks on behalf of their shared task. The teacher risks dismissal with less anxiety because he knows others will help financially should he be temporarily unemployed. The mother joins students in blocking an induction center because she knows that, should she be arrested, others will care for her children.

Third, it follows from these new understandings of radical vocation that Movement activity becomes simultaneously more demanding and less specified. More demanding, because in a Movement turned toward resistance every member *must* be ready to lose a job, go to jail, perhaps to die. Less specified, because a variety of roles become possible. Consider draft resistance. A given draft-resistance project might involve:

- a full-time student organizer, leafleting draft boards and induction centers, visiting men classified I-A, himself refusing induction and extracting from that circumstance maximum legal and public-relations leverage;

- a lawyer specializing in Selective Service law who takes draft cases free of charge;

- housewives who man a draft-counseling center in their spare time:

- high-school students who stimulate discussion among their schoolmates through all available channels;

- a minister who offers his church as a sanctuary for resisters and ceremonially presides at draft-card burnings;

- professors who, besides returning their own draft cards, make their time available to speak on the political philosophy of resistance;

- other full-time organizers who, while mainly concerned with other community issues, see draft resistance to be connected with their activity; and so on.

No longer is it possible for Dick or Jane to excuse himself from the Movement on grounds of temperamental unfitness for a supposed single task. The task has been diversified at the same time that its risk has been escalated.

Resistance Strategy

Come back now to the question of resistance strategy. On the campus, there has been a transition from publication in the student newspaper of a letter saying "We Won't Go" (a somewhat quixotic gesture since the signers characteristically held II-S deferments) to burning and return of draft cards and, at the same time, campaigns for driving the military from the campus. The latter take the form of exposing war-related research, as at the University of Pennsylvania or, now, the University of Chicago, or obstructing the activity of Dow Chemical or United States Navy recruiters, as at the University of Wisconsin and Oberlin College. What is needed is a similarly explicit strategy for draft resistance off the campus.

The community has come to the campus in the form of policemen called in by university authorities. The campus must find means to go to the community. As usual, Berkeley points a direction in its week-long attempt to obstruct the functioning of the Oakland Induction Center. Yet so long as the activists remain students sheltered from the draft the action retains a symbolic character.

A draft-resistance strategy in the community will develop not from abstract speculation but from practical experimentation, much of which is presently afoot in Chicago. Nevertheless I want to conclude by offering a few general observations about the strategy of a resistance movement.

Resistance is negative. It is a movement against something. The rhetoric of a resistance movement—whether in America in 1776, or in France, Italy, China and Vietnam during the 1930's—calls on an entire national community to put aside former differences and unite against a common foe. Student and general, merchant and tenant farmer, join in creating a united front. Communists shelve their ultimate ambitions. S.D.S. and Y.A.F. members find common ground, for example in opposing conscription. Inevitably a resistance movement tends to the restoration of a status quo ante: the British empire as it was governed before the Stamp Act or United States foreign policy in the creative year between the Cuba missile crisis and the Dallas assassination. The gravitation of a resistance movement to a normalcy assumed to have previously existed is suggested by the conclusion of Camus' *The Plague*: the weekend family picnic, the restoration of ordinariness.

This implicit ideology of resistance movements is delusive. Very rarely is the status quo ante recoverable. The causes which led to the crisis have typi-cally changed the entire society so that mere return to the past is not possible. Accordingly, within the resistance coalition some will become frustrated and embittered as the recovery of things past forever eludes them. Others, foreseeing the power vacuum which will ensue from the oppressor's fall, will reach out all too firmly toward a future which may be the vision only of a small minority. There needs to be found a method to work democratically toward the future in the midst of saying "Here I stand," "Don't tread on me," "They shall not pass," "Not with my life you don't." Responsible resistance must be both for and against, positive as well as negative. But this makes extraordinary demands on the resistance fighter, who is constantly in danger, forever hardening his heart to enormities unthinkable in ordinary times, yet is at the same time required to practice the flexibility, the patience, the tolerance and the ability to see things from many standpoints simultaneously which are essential to democracy.

This dilemma is not so abstract as it may seem. It is at the heart of the unre-solved tension within the Movement between violence and nonviolence. It accounts for the universal nostalgia for the first years when people held hands in a circle and sang "We Shall Overcome."

This problem, like the problem of inventing a community draft-resistance strategy, will be resolved in practice. Indeed practice holds out a very specific hope. Is it not the case that the objective circumstances of a resistance movement impose many of the same habits previously adhered to for subjective, idealistic reasons? Decentralization, for instance, once espoused because of the presumed ethical superiority of participatory democracy, is an objective requirement of resistance work. Hence those Communist movements which came to power through decentralized guerrilla warfare prove most resistant to bureaucratization and class inequality after the seizure of power. What can be said of the distinction between leaders and followers can also be said of distinctions between manual and intellectual work, or between the work of men and women. The elemental conditions of resistance struggle break down the barriers between persons. An unintended community, a necessitarian brotherhood, comes into being. Just as the early Christian church discovered itself under the heel of Caesars, so twentieth-century revolutionary socialism finds in repression and the need for resistance an opportunity to clarify its positive vision. Chinese and Cuban revolutionaries seek to forestall the development of Soviet revisionism by harking back to "how it was in the mountains" or "how we did it in the jungle" as an experienced spiritual regulator. The American New Left need not fear that its turn toward resistance must destroy the idealism of the early 1960's.

But maturation in such a way as to become more effective without sacrificing humaneness will not happen spontaneously. To move from a resistance mood to a strategy of resistance we need to create the functional equivalent of a revolutionary vanguard party.

This need is felt both by those involved in national mass action, as at the Pentagon, and by those working at a local level. Coordination, discipline, a mechanism for evolving a common perspective of action, training of replacements for leaders who may be arrested, systematizing the recreation of successful organizing initiatives: these tasks are upon us, are required by what we call "being serious." None of us can yet envision how socialism will come to the United States. But it is clear that fundamental change in our society will not occur unless (a) more and more of us determine to make producing that change the main business of our lives and (b) those who have made that commitment find more effective ways to coordinate their work.

In this, too, experimenting is underway in Chicago. The hundred or so white organizers in the city have divided themselves into eight groups. Care has been taken that each group include staff members from each of the city's principal organizing efforts: the JOIN community union among Appalachian poor whites, the 49th Ward Committee for Independent Political Action among middle-class whites, the Chicago Area Draft Resisters, the new attempts at organizing in white working-class communities. For the time being the groups restrict themselves to discussion, with the aim that a Movement perspective for city-wide action emerge from below.

We move now into a year during which all creative work will be distracted by elections. But throughout the Movement, hopefully, another kind of voting and a different sort of party participation will be in process these next twelve months. Hundreds of graduating college seniors will vote their whole selves, in Thoreau's phrase, by choosing the Movement as a vocation. And on the other side of that decision, in the humdrum, frustrating, lonely world of day-to-day organizing, comrades will draw together to transform their Movement from a mood into a weapon.

Document 6

"THE WAR CRIMES TRIBUNAL: A DISSENT," DECEMBER 1967–JANUARY 1968

The International War Crimes Tribunal (IWCT, or simply the Russell Tribunal) organized by the Bertrand Russell Peace Foundation (BRPF) convened two sessions from May 2 to 10 in Stockholm, Sweden, and from November 20 to December 1, 1967, in Roskilde, Denmark. On 29 November 1966, Lynd was invited to participate by Bertrand Russell along with several leading figures such as Dave Dellinger, Stokely Carmichael, James Baldwin, I. F. Stone, Harrison Salisbury, Donald Duncan, Carl Oglesby, and others.[59] In the following article published in *Liberation*, Lynd reproduces his correspondence with Bertrand Russell and Ralph Schoenman, the IWCT's secretary and personal assistant to Russell, whereby Lynd stakes out his central concern with the Russell Tribunal: that the tribunal would not consider crimes of both sides, but if the tribunal were to change its opinion, allowing crimes from both sides to be submitted as evidence, it would overwhelmingly show that the United States' war crimes in Vietnam far outweighed, incomparably so, those of the National Liberation Front (NLF). A series of letters exchanged between Lynd and Dave Dellinger, appended to the same edition of *Liberation*, marked the beginning of the coming apart between the two friends and activists.

I have found that to question any aspect of the War Crimes Tribunal tends to elicit one of two responses from friends on the Left. One is: Surely you don't mean to suggest that the two sides in Vietnam are equally guilty? The other is: Your questions arise because you are a pacifist and therefore condemn all violence.

Let me begin by responding to these responses. Of course I do not mean to suggest that both sides in Vietnam are equally guilty. If there was ever a war in which one side was clearly the aggressor and the other side aggressed against, if there was ever a war in which the behavior of one side could appropriately be termed "barbarous" and the behavior of the other side restrained and humane, Vietnam, I believe, is that war.

Nor is it true that my concern about the Tribunal is, at least in any simple sense, an expression of pacifism. I do not ask that the Tribunal condemn any use of violence. What I ask is that it inquire into the acts of both sides and use the same criteria in evaluating the acts of one side that it uses in evaluating the acts of the other.

I was asked by Lord Russell to be a member of the Tribunal. The invitation was the more attractive in that three friends—David Dellinger, Carl Oglesby, Stokely Carmichael—had agreed to join it. Nevertheless I declined. I may have been mistaken, but I would like to share the decision-making process that went on in my mind.

The best way to do this is by quoting the correspondence between myself, Lord Russell and Lord Russell's representative Ralph Schoenman.

Correspondence with Lord Russell

Lord Russell's letter of invitation came on November 29, 1966. I answered, with apologies for my delay, on January 13. I did not decline to join the Tribunal but stated the following problem:

> [My] hesitation arises from the fact that, so far as I have been able to ascertain, the Tribunal proposes to investigate the actions of only one side in the war.
>
> I hope I will not be understood to believe that both sides are "equally guilty." I believe nothing of the kind. I am convinced that a systematic inquiry into N.L.F. terror as well as United States use of napalm, toxic chemicals and gases, fragmentation bombs, and torture would prove the more convincingly—especially to public opinion in this country—that the United States has committed overwhelmingly more war crimes than the N.L.F.
>
> But is it the position of the Tribunal that the N.L.F. is completely innocent? That when a little child is killed by American napalm it is clearly a crime, but that if that same child were killed by an N.L.F. terrorist it would be no crime at all?
>
> Such a position seems to me implied [by the remarks of Jean-Paul Sartre, president of the Tribunal]. As I understand him, he says: Everyone must make a political decision as to which side he is on in this war. All the members of the Tribunal have made such a decision, and believe that the N.L.F. is right and that the United States is wrong. Therefore, it would be absurd for them to use the Tribunal to judge between the United States and the N.L.F., for that decision has already been made. Rather, the Tribunal seeks to compare the acts of the United States aggressor with those standards of international behavior to which the United States itself has adhered.
>
> I consider this to be a very dangerous position. I believe it amounts to judging one side (the N.L.F.) by its ends, the other side (the United States) by its means. Precisely this double standard is what I had thought all of us, in this post-Stalin era, wished to avoid.

Lord Russell responded that he considered my letter confused but would not comment in detail since the decision as to my participation in the Tribunal belonged to its Secretariat, not to himself. On February 15 Ralph Schoenman wrote me on behalf of the Secretariat as follows:

> There is no reluctance to examine the nature of the Vietnamese resistance in the South. This resistance has to be placed in its full context, but to constitute the resistance as terror and to examine it in that light runs contrary to the convictions of those who have joined the Tribunal ... They no more regard the National Liberation Front's resistance to the United States as terror than they would have done the resistance of the Jews against the Nazis where it occurred ...
>
> It is not a question of whether one accepts crimes to consist only in actions of those one considers the aggressor. It is the automatic assumption on your part that violence in itself is a crime which is not shared by the Tribunal and many people outside it. The nature of criminality is something which has to be examined with care by this Tribunal, but the question of the distinction between the aggressor and the victim of that aggression remains fundamental.

Reply to Schoenman

I replied to Ralph Schoenman on March 10:

> In my letter to you I intended the word "terror" to be simply descriptive of (a) assassination or execution of officials, (b) the use of explosives in public places in Saigon and elsewhere. For more than a century there has been debate within the Marxist tradition itself regarding the justification of such tactics. Regarding the Tribunal, my concern is simply that this debate take place there as well. I hope you will see that my question is not (as you put it) whether "violence in itself is a crime" but whether certain kinds of violence should be considered crimes no matter who practices them.

Schoenman in turn wrote to me on March 16, closing the correspondence:

> This Tribunal came into existence because of a prima facie case sufficient to induce the conviction that war crimes were occurring and that it was necessary to investigate this fact. We see no reason to investigate the resistance of the National Liberation Front as if it were indistinguishable from the aggressor's role. More than this, the moral impetus, so far from residing in apprehension about the Vietnamese resistance, arises out of intense admiration for a small people struggling against a great imperialist power. It is fatuous to call a Tribunal of this kind into existence and then to retreat ten steps behind the moral and intellectual level necessary to reach that point, and to re-open the possibility that the victim is a criminal. We shall hear evidence concerning the resistance of the Front but we refuse to be drawn into treating it with a mind that pretends to be tabula rasa but is, in fact, tortured by the conditioning it struggles to reject rather unsuccessfully.

Basic Concerns

Fundamentally, I am not questioning what the Tribunal has done but what it has not done. My concern is not to dispute its findings but to ask it to do something more. Nevertheless, I am inclined to think that the mode of procedure of this body which chose to call itself a court is not only morally questionable, but also open to question from the standpoint of effective truth-seeking. I thought and still think that failure to investigate the actions of each party and to give each party the opportunity to rebut the claims of the other stood in the way of the Tribunal's discovering what the historian usually finds, namely, that the truth is somewhat different from the position of any of the parties directly involved.

Consider the controversy concerning the United States' use of fragmentation bombs. This weapon, also known as a "pellet bomb," "cluster bomb unit," and in one of its crude early variants, as a "lazy dog," has been in use since 1965. I believe that Ralph Schoenman, to his credit, was the first to document its existence. At or near the ground the fragmentation bomb explodes into countless small pieces of metal which fly in all directions. Contrary to initial official assurances that our bombs in North Vietnam were directed only against concrete and steel, the United States now concedes that the pellet bomb is an antipersonnel weapon.

The question is: against which personnel are fragmentation bombs directed? The first session of the War Crimes Tribunal concluded that, in general, American bombing of civilian targets such as schools and hospitals was "systematic and deliberate" because "in the vast majority of instances . . . [it was] preceded by reconnaissance flights," and that fragmentation bombs, in particular, were "intended solely to reach the greatest number of persons in the civilian population" because "these pellets can cause no serious damage to buildings or plants or to protected military personnel (for example, civil defense workers behind their sandbags) (*Bulletin of The Bertrand Russell Peace Foundation,* June 1, 1967). In reaching this conclusion the Tribunal relied particularly on the testimony of Dr. Jean-Paul Vigier, a former member of the French General Staff. Vigier stated that fragmentation bombs "are a weapon designed to harm noncombatants and civilian populations" (from notes taken by David Dellinger, LIBERATION, April 1967, p.8; see also Donald Duncan in *Ramparts*, May 1967, pp. 30–31).

The day after Vigier's testimony the United States government rebutted that fragmentation bombs were not used against civilians, but against antiaircraft batteries (*New York Times*, May 6, 1967). The Tribunal professed itself "astonished" at this response (*ibid.*, May 7, 1967). My own view is that quite possibly both the United States government and the Tribunal are right, or at least that neither is deliberately misrepresenting the truth. Let me explain.

Bombing Civilians

All sources concur that fragmentation bombs are typically used in combination with conventional explosives. This is the testimony not only of "Vigier and most other witnesses" at the Tribunal (Dellinger, *op. cit.*, p. 10) and of the Pentagon (*New York Times*, May 6 and July 24, 1967) but also, according to the North Vietnamese government, of captured American pilot Richard Stratton (*Vietnam Courier*, March 13–20, 1967). Both sides also agree that American planes typically make very low bombing runs, to evade missiles at the highest altitudes, and the radar which directs the missiles at intermediate heights (see, in addition to the above-cited sources, *New York Times*, May 22, 1967 and Wilfred Burchett, *Vietnam North*, pp. 24–26). Thus the greatest danger to American planes comes from weapons effective near the ground, not only conventional antiaircraft batteries but also concerted rifle fire. Burchett, a Communist journalist who observed the process from the ground, stresses the effectiveness against American planes of the field of fire thrown up by armed militiamen who practice endlessly for the moment when, implausible Davids against our mechanical Goliaths, they may nevertheless bring one more bomber down. The same point is made by American anti-Communist journalist Frank Harvey on the basis of conversations with United States pilots. Navy pilots told him that "you were safer if you stayed under the SAM envelope (below 3,000 feet) but that when you did that, you opened yourself up to ground fire from automatic weapons." A Marine pilot said:

> It's not just the triple-A and the SAMs that bother you; you can see where that is coming from and you get a chance to take it out. But the small arms fire—everything from rifles to 12.7 mm. automatic weapons—is deadly. You can't see where it's coming from, and the amount of metal they can throw up over a target is so great it's just bound to hit something. The enemy knows that to hit with any accuracy, we've got to come in fairly low and right over the target. So every troop in the area just fires whatever he's got straight up in the air. It makes for quite a barrage and they've been very successful with it. (Frank Harvey, *Air War—Vietnam*, pp. 175, 154).

May it not be that it is these riflemen, teen-age girls or men too old to fight though they may be, against which the fragmentation bombs are directed? And if so, would it not be the case both that (as the Tribunal claims) the fragmentation bomb takes a terrible toll among civilians but also that (in keeping with the assertions of the United States government) some of those who are killed— for the bomb is necessarily indiscriminate—are armed civilians dangerous to American planes?

Targets of Opportunity

Let me add a similar point about the selection of targets. The Tribunal asserts that schools, churches, hospitals are bombed deliberately. The United States government responds that they are not bombed at all. It is evident that the United States government is wrong. But it is not equally clear to me that the Tribunal is altogether right. Schools, churches, hospitals have been bombed on a very large scale but not, conceivably, as the result of a deliberate decision by the United States. This possibility arises from the circumstance that bombing forays over North Vietnam have preselected primary targets and also secondary targets, so-called "targets of opportunity," which are selected on the spot by individual pilots for discharge of their remaining ammunition. America's leading flyer over North Vietnam, Major James Kasler, described to Harvey what happened after the raid on Hanoi's oil dumps in 1966:

> We all had a load of 20 mm. cannon ammo in our M-61s so we went out looking for targets of opportunity. We ran across a convoy of 25 trucks on a mountain road and we were able to destroy 12 of them before we ran out of ammo.

Kasler's commanding officer reproved him for his interest in secondary targets. "He was too valuable. Hit the primary and come home, the general said." Kasler reportedly answered that "you took a big risk crossing all that flak along the Red River and, when you made it, you didn't feel like going home until you'd expended all your ammo. You were up there to do damage. And as long as he had a bullet in his gun or a bomb on his rack, he was going to use it—not bring it back" (*Air War—Vietnam*, pp. 144–145). In the same spirit, Commander Henry Urban Jr., who led the first raid against North Vietnam in August 1965, says: "There are . . . a lot of nice buildings in Haiphong. What their contributions are to the war effort I didn't know, but the desire to bomb a virgin building is terrific" (*New York Times*, Jan. 20, 1968). I suspect this may explain how the schools, churches and hospitals get bombed.

In the hope of removing all misunderstanding, let me make clear that it seems to me altogether possible that the United States *does* use fragmentation bombs primarily to terrorize the civilian population, and *does* deliberately bomb schools, churches and hospitals. Circumstantial evidence—such as the repeated attacks on the geographically isolated leprosarium—certainly exists in abundance. But direct evidence of motivation is very scanty. The most impressive such evidence of which I am aware is the previously cited interview with Stratton in *Vietnam Courier*, which describes raids on Vinh, Nam Dinh and Hanoi with conventional explosives, fragmentation bombs and napalm. According to Stratton, the briefing officers said the purpose of these raids was "that the people themselves must

be made to feel the pressures and realities of war," the targets were clearly populated areas of no military significance, and the raids were timed "so that as many
people would be exposed as possible." What Stratton describes is saturation
bombing like that routinely practiced over Germany and Japan in World War
II. To be sure, his account is a prisoner's interview appearing in a propaganda
organ of the government of North Vietnam; but it is very concrete and detailed.

Drift Toward Stalinism

The essential question, however, is not factual but ethical and political.

My position is that an action defined as a "crime" remains criminal no matter
who commits it. The Nuremberg Tribunal was at fault, as I see it, in that it pos-
ited a framework of universal morality but excluded from its inquiry Hiroshima,
Nagasaki and Dresden. The War Crimes Tribunal should not repeat that error.
In saying this I do not mean to imply that anything the National Liberation
Front has done is remotely equivalent to the mass slaughter of unarmed civilians
by Allied saturation and atomic bombing in World War II. As I attempted to
persuade Lord Russell and Ralph Schoenman, I believe that scrutiny of acts of
violence committed by the N.L.F. would redound to the Front's benefit. But I
consider it imperative that the Tribunal not consider its work ended until it has
conducted that scrutiny, too.

Why? At a time when women and children are being burned alive, when a
small and relatively defenseless people is fighting to exist against a remorseless
enemy, why press such apparently niggling and abstract concerns?

Because not to do so is to drift back toward a Stalinist approach to ethics
which holds all things permitted against the class enemy. That approach has
become widespread on the American Left this fall. S.D.S. leaders argue in *New
Left Notes* that we should move beyond "bourgeois democratic" legalism and
consider ourselves mandated by history to do anything necessary to anyone in
order to destroy American imperialism. S.N.C.C. leaders suggest in the *National
Guardian* that we should regard our opponents as mad dogs and exterminate
them accordingly.

It would seem to follow that if the N.L.F. had access to napalm, it should use
it; or that were it demonstrated beyond doubt that the Front had, on occasion,
tortured and/or executed unarmed prisoners, these acts would be historically
justified. Thus Sartre stated before the first session of the Tribunal: "I refuse to
place on the same plane the action of a group of poor peasants, obliged to make
iron discipline rule in their ranks, and that of an immense army sustained by a
superindustrialized country of two hundred million inhabitants ... During the

Algerian war, I always refused to draw a parallel between the terrorism of the bomb, which was the sole arm at the disposal of the Algerians, and the actions and exactions of a rich army of five hundred thousand men occupying the whole country" (*Liberation*, Jan. 1967, p. 16). The argument is persuasive. The problem is that it can justify anything: a Chinese nuclear strike, forced labor camps, political frame-ups, whatever "iron discipline" may appear to require.

I raise this problem in connection with the Tribunal because it was among the Tribunal's American supporters that I first encountered within the New Left the Old Left attitude to ethics just described. I asked one young man working on arrangements for the Tribunal whether he could imagine anything the Front might do which he would condemn. He answered that anything which helped to drive America from Vietnam would be justified. Another representative of the Tribunal in this country told me that an absolute distinction must be made between the actions of the aggressor and the actions of the aggressor's victim. When he went on to say that, in his opinion, Germany had attacked the Soviet Union in 1941 but France and England had attacked Germany in 1939, I asked whether German treatment of Soviet prisoners in concentration camps should, then, be evaluated by altogether different criteria than German treatment of French and English prisoners in concentration camps. To my astonishment he answered, Yes.

The Vietnamese guerrillas whom I have encountered displayed a more humanistic attitude toward their Vietnamese and even American antagonists. I believe the guerrillas perceive, as their foreign defenders often do not, that every revolutionary movement must seek to win over the human beings who at any given moment face it gun in hand. To this end it is essential—not only for moral reasons, but also for pragmatic political reasons—to be able to understand the enemy as a man playing a role he may yet decide to throw off, to attempt to be sensitive to the enemy's motivation at the same time that one condemns and resists his acts: in a word, to continue to regard him not as a thing but as a man.

Document 7

STATEMENT OF COMPLICITY WITH THE BOSTON FIVE, 8 JANUARY 1968

On Friday, 5 January 1968, the Justice Department announced the indictment of the Boston Five—Benjamin Spock, the Reverend William Sloane Coffin, Michael Ferber, Marcus Raskin, and Mitchell Goodman—for violations of the Selective Service Act. Over the weekend, RESIST, a Boston-area group of supporters of draft resistance who were themselves too old to be drafted, quickly organized solidarity actions. Part of this campaign included the following "Statement of Complicity with the Boston Five." At the Chicago Area Draft Resisters (CADRE) headquarters on the North Side of Chicago, Staughton Lynd, Richard Falk, the Reverend James Bevel, and Sidney Lens signed the statement of complicity and spoke to the press. There were numerous spontaneous actions across the United States in response to the indictment of the Boston Five.[60] Below is Lynd's statement read at the press conference in Chicago.

Complicity Statement in Support of: Benjamin Spock
Michael Ferber
Marcus Raskin
Mitchell Goodman

We stand beside the men who have been indicted for support of draft resistance. If they are sentenced, we too must be sentenced. If they are imprisoned we will take their places and continue to use what means we can to bring this war to an end. We will not stand by silently as our government conducts a criminal war. We will continue to offer support, as we have been doing, to those who refuse to serve in Vietnam, to these indicted men, and all others who refuse to be passive accomplices in war crimes. The war is illegitimate and our actions are legitimate.

Noam Chomsky
Robert McAfee Brown
Dwight McDonald
Frederick Crews
Arthur Waskow
Sidney Peck

Prof. Donald Kalish
Paul Lauter

Issued by National Adult Support organization:
RESIST
763 Massachusetts Ave.
Cambridge, Mass.
National Director—Paul Lauter

Staughton Lynd's Statement, 8 January 1968

There is an old tradition that when a friend is jailed or shot you go to where it happened and take his place. The Wobblies won their free speech fights by filling the jails until it became more burdensome to the authorities to feed them than to let them talk on street corners. In June 1964, when James Chaney, Michael Schwerner, and Andrew Goodman were reported missing, people in SNCC went to Philadelphia, Mississippi, and searched the woods at night. Looking back on the anti-fascist resistance in Germany, Martin Niemoeller believes that the great mistake of the Protestant ministry was that in 1933 it worried about what would happen to the church, and only in 1935 realized that it was responsible for what happened to any one in Germany. Hence Niemoeller's famous saying: When the Jews were deported, I was not a Jew; when the trade unions were smashed, I was not a trade unionist; when the Communists were imprisoned, I was not a Communist; and when they came for me, it was too late.

We are here tonight to say with the IWW that an injury to one is an injury to all. We are here to remember the young Americans of the 1930s who sought out fascism in embattled Spain, and to say again: They shall not pass. We are here tonight to affirm, with the same confidence we used those brave words in the South, that we shall overcome.

Repression is frightening. Many of us may be in jail soon. Some may be killed. But repression is also an opportunity. If we can keep our heads and our cool, repression can make the American anti-imperialist movement stronger not weaker, and bring closer that humane society best briefly described—so far as I am concerned—by the word "socialism."

First, one or two thoughts about the law. There are opposite dangers here. One is to become trapped in legal technicalities.... The opposite danger, surely, is to dismiss the law as nothing more than an expression of "bourgeois democracy" or of an inevitably coercive central state. Legal forms can be used for the defense of democratic values. In the South, and again today, it is possible for us to take the legal initiative, to be plaintiffs as often as defendants. The response to HUAC hearings here in Chicago illustrates what I mean. Relying on the Supreme Court decision in the Dombrowski case, itself the fruit of movement activity, persons subpoenaed by HUAC brought injunctions challenging HUAC's constitutionality and appeared in the hearing chamber only long enough to explain their reasons for withdrawing.

We should be careful to distinguish 1968 from 1938. In those happier days a majority of the people which desired new social legislation found itself frustrated by the so-called nine old men on the Supreme Court. By standing pat the Court stood in the way of the people. But today the tendency of things is toward repression. By standing pat today the courts can protect us. White people in particular have a responsibility to extract every possible ounce of protection from the machinery of the law. This is one of the few services we can still legitimately offer our more harried and embattled black associates.

I should like to recommend a similar middle course concerning jail. The statement of complicity we are signing tonight itself suggests the ambivalence of the draft resistance movement about jail. On the one hand it seems almost to invite prosecution: "If they are sentenced, we too must be sentenced." On the other hand it stresses the work to be done out of jail: "If they are imprisoned we will take their places." What we should keep in mind as we struggle with this ambivalence in ourselves, and in the movement, is that it arises from the objective situation. The draft picks men off one by one. Hence to take a collective stand against the draft it is necessary to contrive occasions of solidarity: thus the signing of pledges, the mass returning of cards, the symbolic blocking of induction centers, all ways in which men seek to collectivize their personal anxieties and turn their individual predicaments into a political force. Our coming together tonight to sign this statement together is just such a transforming action. In taking it we risk jail but we do not court jail. Our action seems to me functionally equivalent to that of the Wobblies who converged on Spokane or the SNCC staff who went together to Philadelphia, Mississippi.

Third, morality. Lately it has become fashionable to contrast "being moral" with "being political." The suggestion is that those old days of singing, and holding hands, and talking about love, are out of date. We should put away those childish things. We should recognize Utopian illusions for what they are. We should decide to become disciplined and effective.

I find this perspective unconvincing. I'm sure the idea of participatory democracy is something more than a product of middle-class affluence because I first encountered it not in SDS but in SNCC. SNCC made decisions by consensus, not because it was morally desirable, but because the decisions were so serious that every one hesitated to tell anyone else where and when to risk his life. Perhaps centralized bureaucratic organization is the bourgeois luxury, and decentralized participatory democracy the organizational style best suited to resistance. Certainly resistance requires decentralization, local initiative, flexibility. Precisely in life-and-death situations the quality of personal relations, the ability of one individual to trust another, becomes critical. In my opinion it would be the reverse of politically effective to conclude that, because the times are urgent, there is no longer time to straighten out personal misunderstandings, to persist in winning through to trust and friendship. Think of Camus, Bonhoeffer, Gramsci, Silone, Buber and perhaps you will agree that the distinctive character of anti-fascist resistance is to strip things back to the elemental, to break through institutional forms and require us to confront one another as men.

Finally, something about militancy. Militancy is better done than talked about. But just this one word. It takes militancy, and manhood, and grace under pressure, to return a draft card; and it takes exactly those same qualities to get out of bed the morning after you returned your card and do your work for the day. I remember when people first talked about full-time draft resistance organizing they thought the best organizer would be the man who had just burned or returned his card. Maybe that expectation was superficial. It's hard to work methodically and patiently when you don't know how much time you have, when the knock on the door will come. It's hard not to put a lot of energy into wondering whether you did the right thing and still more energy into wondering whether you'll be able to deal with the consequences. We've got to learn to work creatively in the medium, not just of episodic confrontations. The point I'm trying to make can be set out another way. Whether or not our five friends go to jail will depend partly on how big tomorrow's demonstrations are. But it may depend even more on which way those thousands of SDS members who will leave the campus in June decide to turn their lives. Will they, will we, take the step into the dark, make the more risky choice, follow the deepest inward leading? I am convinced that this is where the struggle to create a long-term resistance movement is really at. It is the decisions made at this level which will make us or break us.

Remember the old song of the 1930s, "Talking Union?" The one that goes: Now if you don't let Red-baiting break you up. And if you don't let goon squads break you up—and so on? Maybe I can rephrase what I have been trying to say about being cool in the face of repression with the help of that song.

> If we can use the law but not rely on it,
> And if we can risk jail without courting it,

And if we can get more disciplined without getting more mean,
And if we escalate our militancy while settling in for the long haul,
Then, like the old song said, We'll win,
What I mean is take it easy but, take it.

Document 8

"TURNING IN YOUR CARD THEN WHAT?" SPEECH AT BOSTON COMMON AND YALE UNIVERSITY WAR MEMORIAL, 3 APRIL 1968

Staughton Lynd was a featured speaker at the 3 April 1968 national draft-card turn-in organized by various antidraft groups. On this occasion, like other major days of action during the war, Lynd would speak in two places on the same day. Speaking at the Boston Common event organized by the New England Resistance in front of five thousand onlookers, Lynd would join others including Noam Chomsky and Howard Zinn. In total, 235 burned or turned in their draft cards in Boston. Also speaking in front of the Yale War Memorial in New Haven at Beinecke Plaza the same day in front of a smaller crowd of one thousand, twenty-nine people turned in their draft cards. According to Lynd and Michael Ferber, over one thousand resisters turned in or burned their draft cards throughout the United States on April 3.[61]

Lynd's speech below continued to urge those in attendance to think about what comes after such major days of action and proposes ideas on the best way to proceed. There was a sense of optimism in the air during this national day of action, which came on the heels of President Lyndon Johnson's bombshell announcement just three days earlier that he would not seek reelection. This hope would come crashing down the following day when Martin Luther King Jr. was gunned down by an assassin's bullet in Memphis, Tennessee, after he spoke at a sanitation workers' strike. The text of the speech appeared in the April 3–15, 1968, edition of the *Resistance* magazine.

It is a common saying among resisters that "April 3 will be the last mass return of draft cards." Why do we say this? What lies on the other side of that decision?

One thing draft resisters are feeling is that, while draft resistance remains the heart of the anti-war movement, for any particular person draft resistance cannot be a way of life. A person must say "Yes" as well as "No." A man must have a pattern of daily life which sustains him: he cannot live for very long from one confrontation to the next.

Of course, the obvious first answer to the problem, "What do I do after turning in my card?" was, "Organize other people to do the same thing."

And this remains a fundamental and helpful answer in that few draft resistance organizations have even begun to carry their message to the plethora of off-campus communities where it may come to have meaning as draft calls rise.

For instance, it is not necessarily true that the recent Selective Service decisions concerning graduate students mean that resistance organizers should turn their attention back to campus.

The students who sign "We Won't Go" pledges at Vietnam commencements will actually confront induction in the off-campus communities to which they return at the end of the academic year.

Nevertheless, in a sequence of actions beginning with step A, an individual cannot forever evade discovering what B is merely by helping others beside himself to go as far as A.

Clearly, the largest possible return of draft cards on April 3 is essential. Equally clearly, what the Resistance movement does after April 3 is even more important.

This is why conferences on radical vocations, discussions concerning the "new working-class" and "radicalism in the professions," institutions seeking to offer "drop-out counselling," are appearing all over the country.

Whether they leave the campus before or after graduation, young radicals want an alternative to conventional careers; in this sense we are all drop-outs.

The new Selective Service decisions enforce what was already implicit in our situation: the need to learn how to be off-campus life-long radicals.

The act of draft refusal, whether in the form of returning a draft card or in some less obtrusive manner, is a necessary beginning but still only a beginning.

The problem of radical vocation ought to be stated as harshly as those who struggle with it really feel it to be. Flatly then: very few of us have found personal answers, imitable models, in this area.

All too many of us side-step the challenge by some form of teaching, simply passing on to our students the problem we have been unable to solve (and without sufficiently realizing that they may imitate us, become teachers in *their* turn, and leave the hard work to *their* students).

The personal problem of radical vocation is immensely complicated by the fact that the movement has no idea of a strategy for fundamental social change. Had we work to do which seemed to lead rationally toward our goal, the frustrations and anxieties in our lives would be so much easier to manage. But we do not have a strategy. We must be honest about that, too.

I do not have an answer to the question of after April 3. I have one suggestion, which like any suggestion unproven by experience ought to be viewed skeptically. I will make it nevertheless, since I find it viscerally impossible to end on a note of despair, and since the recent decisions about graduate students (like every other form of repression) do seem to me to hold out rational hope that resistance can be broadened and strengthened.

My suggestion is this. The typical draft resistance organization raises funds from adult supporters with which it pays subsistence salaries to full-time draft resistance organizers.

In Chicago, these organizers live in two communal apartments, leaflet the induction center and the office housing most of the city's draft boards, and counsel at the CADRE office.

If the draft resistance operation in Chicago and other cities were radically decentralized, I believe it would spread draft resistance at the same time that it obliged organizers to begin to deal with the problem of radical vocation.

In the model I am proposing, a draft resistance organization would retain a central office at which functions continued to be performed which required a city-wide scale (printing, for example).

But other functions presently performed on a city-wide basis (draft counselling, perhaps high-school organizing, possibly even fund-raising) would be decentralized. After assigning to indispensable city-wide work a few appropriate individuals, all other organizers would divide themselves into small teams to move into neighborhoods.

These neighborhood teams would support themselves by part-time work, local contributions, or otherwise as they decide. If older couples were involved, not merely as speech-makers and money-givers, but as members of a neighborhood team, then a professional's salary might provide the income base for a team which included the professional and his family, and several single young people.

On the other hand, the student types would often choose to do part-time work as a method of exploring radical vocation at the same time that they organized around the draft.

At first it might seem that in leaving the city-wide communal apartment and the routine of meeting after meeting in which all the organization's members were involved, the neighborhood teams were moving away from community, toward a more lonely and calculating style of work.

I think the reverse might occur. That is, that as each neighborhood team struggled to decide what it should do, how it should support itself, whether it should live under one roof or not, and so on, a more genuine experience of community might emerge than when RESIST people mail checks to sustain the city-wide activity of the Resistance.

What we need in the Resistance movement is a turn outward toward new constituencies at the same time that we turn toward each other, helping our brothers and sisters in the agonizing search for radical vocations. Neighborhood draft resistance work may offer a way to begin to do simultaneously these two only apparently contradictory tasks.

Document 9

INTRODUCTION TO *WE WON'T GO: PERSONAL ACCOUNTS OF WAR OBJECTORS*, BY ALICE LYND

Setting out in earnest in October 1966, Alice Lynd began compiling material that would compose the edited collection *We Won't Go: Personal Accounts of War Objectors,* released by Beacon Press in September 1968. Alice attended some of the major antidraft conferences such as the Eastern Conference on Non-Cooperation with Conscription in New York from October 28 to 30 and the We Won't Go conference in Chicago in December. She contacted lawyers involved with draft and military resister cases, attorneys such as Stanley Faulkner, who represented the Fort Hood Three and Private Robert Luftig. She sent letters to resisters she personally knew, asking them to contribute to the book, and placed advertisements in the Students for a Democratic Society publication *New Left Notes* and in *WIN* magazine, asking for submissions. She collected flyers, legal briefs, petitions, antiwar newspaper advertisements, "Dear Draft Board" letters that noncooperators sent to their local boards, public statements, diary entries, and other documents. In the *New Left Notes* advertisement seeking submissions, Lynd wrote,

> The desire to write this book grows out of the sense that those who are now grappling alone or in small groups should know of the existence and experiences of men who have already made this confrontation, with the hope that such sharing may provide help to those who are now sifting out what to do and understanding support for those who may be in need of it.[62]

After seeing the advertisement, the editors at Beacon Press contacted Alice, seeking to publish the book.

The book presented more than twenty-five personal narratives of resisters from a wide variety of political and nonpolitical persuasions. The book had a universal appeal: pacifists and nonpacifists alike, draftees and enlistees, and military personnel could all appreciate the stories in the book. It also included various "We Won't Go" statements from students in 1966 and 1967 as well as statements from three wives and partners of war objectors. The title itself was inclusive of the various types of resisters, using the term "war objector"—instead of "war resister" or "draft resister" or "military resister" or "conscientious objector"—encompassed all the types of resisters that she took great pains to include. She included pacifist noncooperators such as Gene Keyes and Tom Cornell; nonpacifist noncooperators such as David Mitchell and Muhammad Ali; military resisters such as the Fort Hood Three, Robert Luftig, and Gene Fast (who went AWOL from the army); and military selective conscientious objectors such as Dale Noyd.

Alice Lynd, ca 1968. Courtsey of Alice and Staughton Lynd.

In a detailed appendix, Lynd included documents of immediate importance for committed antiwar activists as well as those who feared being
drafted into the military. She selected "Documents Related to War Crimes"
such as the Kellogg-Briand Pact of 1928, the Charter of the United Nations,
Nuremberg principles of 1950, selections from the four Geneva Conventions
of 1949, the Geneva Accords of 1954, and the Army Field Manual FM 27-10
of July 1956. Moreover, she appended the full application for conscientious
objector classification and the full Seeger Supreme Court decision of 8 March
1965, which broadened the definition of conscientious objection to include
belief in a "Supreme Being" if it occupied the same place in the life of the
objector as an orthodox belief in God.

The book went through two printings, selling twenty thousand copies, and Lynd used her royalties to send the book to every major antidraft
group, antiwar organization, and civil liberties office in the country. With
Staughton's trouble finding employment at Chicago universities, by 1970 the
royalties from the book helped to alleviate the Lynds' financial burdens.[63]
Books such as this, distributed widely by Lynd to every major antiwar organization in the United States and in Canada, would have been shared within
movement circles and essential reading for any serious draft counselor and

antiwar activist. Moreover, the American Library Association (ALA) voted *We Won't Go* one the "Best Books for Young Adults" in 1968. "Told with utter sincerity, these are the personal accounts of Vietnam protesters," the ALA wrote in its blurb announcing the book had been selected one of the best for 1968.[64]

Below is a selection from Alice Lynd's introduction to *We Won't Go: Personal Accounts of War Objectors.*

The uneasiness about the war in Vietnam which led students at Yale and elsewhere to begin formulating "We Won't Go" pledges in the fall of 1966 led also to the idea for this book.

Students meeting in our living room to discuss the draft raised questions that were being asked across the country. Concerned to stop the war, they were troubled by their sheltered position in relation to the draft. They knew they could not participate in the war but felt impotent to stop it.

In one discussion, a girl who had a friend in prison asked, what good does it do to let them put you away like that? When I realized that hardly anyone else in the room had ever heard of her friend, I thought, what a waste! This person had experienced so much that might be pertinent to others. Someone should write a book about the unknown men who had tried to answer with their lives the questions about effectiveness and personal sacrifice being asked by many individuals and little groups.

Since that time draft resistance has mushroomed. Draft information and counseling are much more available. More and more young people are responding to the tension between what is and what could be by saying to themselves, *you* are the agent for change. Resistance organizers regard the draft as a single aspect of a larger problem. Ending the war in Vietnam is not in itself a solution; those who refuse to fight in Vietnam will need to continue to struggle for justice and to resist the arbitrary use of power wherever it occurs.

Those who say "We won't go" draw the line at different points. This line is drawn according to values and priorities which claim their first allegiance. There is a question for anyone faced with the draft—what am I willing to die for?

Here is a collection of accounts by men who wrote about what they had to grapple with and what they did as they confronted the dilemmas of conscience which military participation poses. It is not a book of answers but of questions and examples of attempts to deal with them.

The forms of activity described and the rationales for them may soon seem dated. But some of these concepts and experiences are recurrent because they are rooted in eternal conflicts between power and justice, individual conscience and responsibility to common humanity, means and ends.

This collection is not fully representative. Most noticeably absent from the book but existing in substantial numbers are objectors who engaged in combat in Vietnam, deserters in Europe or other countries, draft evaders who have "gone underground," those who have discovered personal solutions, and drop-outs who are not deliberately taking any principled position. Perhaps most important among the missing are those who were badly hurt by what they did, have retreated, and do not want to talk about it. It is hoped that this book can forestall grief by affording a little more opportunity to anticipate what may be involved in following or not following one's commitment. And apologies are due not so much for failing to represent certain elements or leaning too much stress on others, but for presuming to touch men at this point in their lives where past and future hopes and dreams are brought to a focus and tested by a dire and immediate reality.

To those who wonder, "Why would a person do a thing like that?", this book may afford some insight into views very different from their own. They may be perplexed as they see a young man going off and doing something which seems not to fit with the way he grew up, or in defiance of the law, or without regard for the feelings of others or his family responsibilities, or risking his future in ways he cannot foresee. Yet he still *is* that person whom they love and it may well be that some of the things they love in him are prompting him to do what hurts and puzzles them so much. For most men, where they are now is the result of many steps, decisions, and evaluations interacting with experience. Those who have sketched their development can help us to understand how people, like some we know, were able to do what they did.

It is critical that wives and girl friends be involved in their partner's searchings and decisions about the draft. Both members of a couple will have consequences to bear. It is not helpful to a mutual relationship for one member to stand apart and say, in effect, "You do what you have to do and somehow I'll do what I can to live with it." If a life is to be built together the basis for decisions needs to be shared and differences recognized and understood.

Every man who is faced with induction makes a choice as to whether or not he will go when called. If he goes into the armed forces he is choosing not to say "No." If he comes to think that he has made the wrong choice he can still find ways to honor the dictates of conscience, but the consequences under military law are usually far more severe. This book may serve as background for young men to sift out their thoughts and make choices on the basis of their own convictions.

There are some problems which adequate counseling can prevent but others which emerge only through experience and no one can convey to another person what they will mean. It need not be personally undermining or a breach of faith to change one's mind. Under new circumstances, a new decision may be more realistic than maintaining a position which no longer seems relevant or true. In an area fraught with contradictions and counterpressures, it is nevertheless important that one's feelings and intellectual picture be together, that one take only those voluntary steps which one feels ready to take.

Viktor Frankl, a psychiatrist who survived Nazi concentration camps, observed in *Man's Search for Meaning* (Beacon Press, 1963) that it is normal to react abnormally in an abnormal situation. Self-doubt, uncertainty, confusion, aloneness, depression, irritability, sleeplessness, and a variety of ailments are common as confrontations approach. But some men never feel clearer in their lives. A release of energy and conquering of fear come to them when doing what they think is right. Times of inaction or compromise are usually the hardest. It may make some difference to see oneself as a human being facing inhuman demands.

It is easier to give up security in the present if that which one is choosing has a quality of affirmation. There is something about religious beliefs or political convictions or a sense that "this is what has to be done" which gives strength. The example of another person may help. Ammon Hennacy spent seven and a half months in solitary confinement for refusal to register at the time of World War I. Crouching by the door of his cell on sunny mornings, he could see the top of the head of an anarchist who he knew had spent three and a half years in solitary. This man had been in prison since before Ammon was born and had "a fighting spirit that jails could not kill." It gave Ammon courage.

The men who tell their stories here are not heroes with qualities of character above what the rest of us can attain. They are everyday people like you and me. Rather than measure ourselves as less worthy we need to have faith that there is something in humanness or in relatedness which has tremendous untapped resources and that when circumstances require it ordinary people with hang-ups and quirks may be able to act with a dignity of which mankind can be proud.

To the "two and two and fifty" who contributed to this book, thanks.

Alice Lynd
February 1968

Document 10

"ON RESISTANCE," NOVEMBER 1968

Here in an article for *Liberation*, Lynd continues in advocating for a community-based approach to draft resistance that broadens to include focusing on corporations that aid the war effort, and he proposes a kind of "resistance platform" after the presidential election of November 1968, in which Richard Nixon defeated Hubert Humphrey. Lynd presented a portion of the article as a speech on 28 September 1968 as part of the Chicago Peace Council march and rally, and it was recorded and quoted extensively in Lynd's FBI file.[65]

Staughton Lynd at a 28 September 1968 rally in Chicago where portions of this speech appeared as "On Resistance" in the November 1968 edition of *Liberation*. Courtesy of the *Chicago Maroon* and the University of Chicago Photographic Archive, apf7-00301, Hanna Holborn Gray Special Collections Research Center, University of Chicago Library.

After the election—or at latest, after the inauguration—radicals will have to deal with the question of strategy for the next several years.

Draft resisters are rightly preparing for increased draft calls. The announced December quota is almost twice the average for the pre-election summer and fall months, and there is every reason to believe that the quotas for early 1969 will return to the late spring level (forty to fifty thousand per month).

But resistance after the election should be conceived much more broadly than draft resistance. For one thing, there does not appear to be any rational way of predicting whether the Vietnam war will be quickly ended (Oglesby) or quickly accelerated (Hayden) after the election. High draft calls in early 1969 will be necessary in any case because of the artificially deflated quotas of the pre-election months, but how significant the draft will continue to be as a political issue depends on decisions of the governing class about the war which cannot be confidently forecast. The resistance movement should be prepared for either termination or escalation of the war.

Also, if only because of the growing strength of the Right, it will obviously be necessary to begin to resist illegitimate authorities other than the Selective Service System. What we need is a new style of political resistance, combining the direct action of the draft resistance movement with the sophisticated analysis and multi-issue orientation of, say, S.D.S.

For example, persons who have been active primarily in draft resistance might consider a direct action attack upon selected corporations. The fundamental rationale for such action would be: "Here is the real enemy. Here is the power which stands behind both 'corporate liberalism' and George Wallace, using one or another means depending on circumstances. Here, not in City Hall or the precinct station, is the heart of the system." From a tactical point of view, corporate targets should be selected which combine as many of the following characteristics as possible: (a) direct contribution to the war in Vietnam; (b) demonstrable ties to the local political machine or, in those rare cases where such is already the case, to the extreme Right; (c) substantial overseas investments, preferably in the Third World; (d) antiunion and antiminority labor policies. Action against the corporate target which combines all or most of these characteristics will serve to bring together different elements in the Movement. If possible, the action should combine both realizable concrete demands (union recognition, for instance) and a utopian dimension, such as symbolically taking the corporation into the hands of the people.

Actions of this kind might be combined into a resistance platform. A resistance platform would resemble a conventional political platform in that it would make demands in a series of areas of social life. But it would differ from a conventional political platform in that each or nearly each demand would be accompanied by a description of direct action which individuals and small groups could begin to do at once. Here, simply for illustrative purposes, is a possible resistance platform for the city of Chicago:

1. We need a new Mayor. Organization to this end should begin now.

2. Freedom to parade along reasonable routes and to rally at reasonable sites is a right, not a privilege. An injunction should be sought empowering Federal courts to supervise permit-granting city agencies until those agencies grant permits without unreasonable delay and without discrimination between different groups requesting permits. In the meantime citizens must be prepared to assert their right peaceably to assemble in action, with or without permits.

3. All working men and women must have the right to strike, including public employees such as teachers, transit workers, and sanitation workers. Persons from every section of the city Movement should join public employees on their picket lines until this right is established.

4. Stop-and-frisk legislation, enacted in the city and the state, authorizes unreasonable search and seizure in violation of the Fourth Amendment. Citizens should peaceably refuse to cooperate with this humiliating procedure so that it can be tested in the courts.

5. In a free Chicago, policemen would live in the neighborhoods where they work, and work under the supervision of elected citizen control boards with power to suspend or transfer individual policemen. As a first step in this direction, a corps of citizen observers should be organized to oversee the law enforcement process in the streets, in the courts, and at police stations and jails.

6. Students in the public elementary and high schools should be supported in their assertion of such rights as the right to publish and circulate in their schools their own leaflets and newspapers, and the right to appear in schools in a variety of styles of dress and personal appearance.

7. Legislative and administrative restrictions on the political beliefs, associations and actions of college teachers, students and campus visitors should be resisted and abolished.

8. Investigative bodies such as the House Un-American Activities Committee and the Senate Internal Security Committee should be regarded as illegitimate authorities and resisted.

9. The United States is presently pursuing a repressive foreign policy with which a growing number of young men feel obliged to refuse to cooperate. We should support them in their conscientious objection, seeking amnesty for those now in prison or under indictment, and legislative provision for selective conscientious objection and abolition of the draft.

10. A free Chicago requires that economic resources be freely available to those who need them. Direct actions with this goal in view, such as the refusal of site tenants to be urban-renewed from their homes and the refusal to pay rent for indecent, unsafe and unsanitary dwellings, should have our full support.

Resistance platforms should be projected on a regional not a national level. The number of stable local political movements which the Left has built can be counted on the fingers of one hand. There is the Committee for Independent Political Action in Chicago and the American Independence Movement in New Haven, and then . . . what? Under such circumstances to focus energy on building national organizations appears preposterous. One Ocean Hill-Brownsville governing board is worth more than the four Left presidential campaigns put together. It is worth noting also that not one of the stable local movements which the white Left has built is in a working-class neighborhood. For this reason any national organization put together in the foreseeable future would be dominated by the middle-class, whatever the intention of the organizers.

As a national network emerges from local resistance politics, it may not take the form of a political party. It may resemble the old I.W.W. rather than the old Socialist Party. In any case it will only be built if we can grow into that resistance spirit incarnated by the old I.W.W. and the new resistance communities of Baltimore, Catonsville and Milwaukee: if we can practice "job action" (that is, seek revolutionary reforms through direct action in our own work and living situations), and if, by joining one another's picket lines (or other resistance actions), we live out the belief that "an injury to one is an injury to all."

Document 11

"TELLING RIGHT FROM WRONG," DECEMBER 1968

On 4 November 1968, Lynd was arrested for disorderly conduct outside the South Shore High School supporting African American students sitting in for better access to education. According to the *Chicago Tribune*, "Police said Lynd was encouraging students to cause a disturbance and was asked to leave. When Lynd refused to leave, he was arrested and charged with disorderly conduct."[66] Lynd wrote the following letter while in jail before he was released on bail. Lynd's letter was published in the December 1968 edition of *Liberation*.

I am beginning these notes in the neighborhood lock-up. I am here for a few hours, having been arrested for picketing in support of black students who sat in at our neighborhood high school. These few hours help one to begin to imagine the years which confront the Baltimore Four, the Catonsville Nine, the Boston Two and the Milwaukee Fourteen.

Certain questions occur to anyone considering acts which risk or invite imprisonment. So far as possible they should be thought through before arrest. After arrest there is no opportunity to change one's mind.

The Baltimore, Catonsville, Boston and Milwaukee actions pose questions above and beyond those implicit in any civil disobedience. Perhaps especially these:

1. *Is it right to destroy property?*

2. *What is the justification of disruptive resistance? Why not work for reform within the system?*

3. *If people obviously valuable to the Movement have determined to commit an act exposing them to lengthy jail terms, why do they permit themselves to be arrested?*

1. In destroying Selective Service files, our friends, as they have explained, had more than one object in mind.

First, they tried to contribute to stopping the war. If they could have stolen vital parts of every plant producing napalm in the United States, they would have done that. "Some property has no right to exist," they wrote, because of the ends for which that property is used. One of their objectives was *physically* to impede the war process to the extent of their powers. The draft resister who denies his body to the Army does this, too. The Baltimore, Catonsville, Boston and Milwaukee protagonists took a further step. By destroying the records of all men in a given Selective Service jurisdiction, they sought to deny the Army all bodies whatsoever.

Next, the act sought to educate us as to the relative value of property and people. No human being was hurt; Larry Rosebaugh, writing from the Milwaukee County Jail Annex, even expressed awareness of "the struggle such a confrontation as we provoked will cause" those of us still on the outside. Any risk of unforeseen harm to life was avoided. To burn or bomb a seemingly empty building must run the danger of hurting the watchman who fell asleep and failed to leave at the accustomed time, or the boy shooting marbles in the back alley. At Catonsville and Milwaukee the property which could not be permitted to exist was carefully moved to a nonflammable surrounding, and destroyed. In this as in so much else the action followed the precedent of the Boston Tea Party, a "tea party" indeed because no one was hurt. (Nor did the town of Boston ever pay for the tea.)

By justifying the burning of these files as an act, not only against the war but also against all sacrificing of life to things, these brave men and women help us to broaden the resistance movement beyond the issues of the war and the draft. Their statements make it plain that as they saw what they did they might with equal appropriateness have burned the files of the United Fruit Company or the ships of the Grace Line. They are against capitalism as well as war, they see the Vietnam war as part of a foreign policy which seeks to protect private property the world over. As John Woolman indicted the system which used chattel slaves to make profit from the luxuries of sugar and tobacco, so Phil and Dan Berrigan say No to a society which starves Brazilian children and drops napalm on barefoot Guatemalan guerrillas in order to make a buck from coffee and bananas.

In their own resistance communities, it goes without saying, these rebels share material means of support as needed. Like the early Christians they are good practicing communists.

Finally, the outcry of these brave men and women against property is an outcry against worshipping false gods. Think of a child, Paul Goodman wrote in *Growing Up Absurd*, "trying to cope with Property Rights." The child can understand what the grownups have in mind "when it is a case of something being used by somebody else, when Jack tries to take Bobby's shovel out of his hand."

> The puzzlement comes when the shovel is idle and Mamma says, "You musn't use that shovel, it's Bobby's." What impresses the child is no precise idea, but the grownup's tone of conviction. The child "believes," though there is no evidence of his senses. It is the beginning of what Marx called the fetishism of commodities.

Seen in this context, burning Selective Service files merges with other acts of protest against other golden calves: against dead institutions, meaningless routines, outward forms in which the spirit smothers.

Tom Cornell, a draft-card burner, offered in partial explanation of his act the words:

> Throughout the Old Testament there is the recurring theme of idolatry. The early Christians were well aware of it too . . . The state today, the Government of the United States of America, is just as much a pagan god as Caesar was in imperial Rome.

Following a suggestion of Karl Meyer's, Tom Cornell went on to suggest that carrying a draft card was like placing a pinch of incense on the altar before Caesar's image.

> . . . the Congress took a small piece of paper, of no significant value to anyone but a bartender, and said over it, "Hoc est enim Corpus Meum." The sacrament of the state then had to be honored. So the act of burning the draft card was for me an act of purposeful desecration and an act of purification.

And so for Dan Berrigan of the Catonsville group, burning Selective Service files expressed a recognition that "Christians pay conscious, indeed religious, tribute to Caesar and Mars . . . They embrace their society with all their heart, and abandon the cross."

Fighting the System

2. The Four, the Nine, the Two and the Fourteen do not think of themselves as reformers. They are at least resisters; some might proudly take the name "revolutionaries." What is the difference between reform, resistance and revolution? What does it mean to give up working for reform within the system? How can the resister answer the charge that by extreme tactics offensive to many people he actually makes change more difficult?

We can approach this difficult set of problems by distinguishing two kinds of civil disobedience, reformist and resistant. Reformist civil disobedience takes several forms. A man who believes a particular law to be unconstitutional breaks the law in order to create a constitutional test case and make it possible for the judiciary to overrule the legislature. In other words, his civil disobedience is intended to energize the conventional machinery of decision making. Similarly, Dr. King's civil-rights campaigns were designed to put pressure on Northern liberals who would in turn press for the passage of new laws. Such civil disobedience is a kind of lobbying, a form of petition to the powers-that-be.

At the other extreme, revolution, far from energizing the conventional political machinery of petitioning existing powers, seeks to destroy them.

Twilight Zone

Classical democratic theory offers no intermediate steps between reform and revolution. Look again, for instance, at Locke's *Second Treatise Of Government*. According to Locke one either strives for change through existing structures, perhaps prodding them by acts of reformist civil disobedience, or one attempts to overthrow the government.

Resistance, or resistant civil disobedience, explores the twilight zone between reform and revolution. It is a form of social action suited to a pre-revolutionary or pre-Fascist situation. Resistance attacks evils which cannot be remedied by a single administrative decision or a particular new law. Its targets are deep-seated ills such as racism, or this country's imperialist foreign policy. It does not look to others, at some future time and distant place, to stop what is wrong. Without yet seeking to overthrow the government, resisters declare their determination to overthrow a given policy or complex of institutions by refusing to obey them or permit them to function. The resister does not rely on the electoral process or the courts to bring about the change he seeks, but he leaves open the possibility that these conventional institutions can adapt themselves to changes effected by more direct means. From the standpoint of society as a whole, resistance might be seen as an experiment, a probing operation, which determines if revolution is required.

Of course extreme tactics alienate some people. There does not seem to be any ready-made formula or external yardstick for evaluating the appropriateness of a given tactic. No one can know in advance whether his solitary spark will start a prairie fire. Rosa Parks did not know when she refused to go to the back of the bus. The four who sat in at Greensboro on February 1, 1960 had no way of knowing. David Miller and Tom Cornell could not know; nor can our brothers and sisters of Baltimore, Catonsville, Boston and Milwaukee. Perhaps the best that can be said is that if a person believes "deep in his heart" that he must take a certain action; if he has meditated over the act or if the act, suddenly presenting itself, still flowers from a deep root of reflection; above all if it is an action *he* will take, the consequences of which will fall first on his own shoulders—then any other person can only stand aside and let his friend go on. Certainly immediate consequences are no criterion of anything. Dwight Macdonald once described the prophet as a man who touched something even in those who stoned him to death.

3. This brings us to the third question: Why did the protagonists at Baltimore, Catonsville, Boston and Milwaukee stay at the scene and invite arrest? For in fact the act of burning Selective Service files, while undoubtedly extreme in many ways, remained within limits. It was nonviolent, as already observed; paper was destroyed but human beings were not. And in addition a course of action was chosen which will end in prison. Why?

One possible explanation can be discarded at the outset. These law breakers are *not* accepting jail in the legalistic belief that because they broke a law, they should accept society's penalty. That is a reasonable line of argument for the man who thinks that a particular law is wrong but the larger system of law and order is sound. It is reasonable for the man who thinks the Vietnam war infamous but American foreign policy since World War II well-intentioned. It is not a reasonable argument for one who agrees with the Milwaukee 14 that American society as a whole is: "[married] to coercive political methods, exercised within as without its borders." I feel sure that the Baltimore, Catonsville, Boston and Milwaukee resisters would concur with this passage from Howard Zinn's *Disobedience and Democracy:*

> If the social function of protest is to change the unjust conditions of society, then that protest cannot stop with a court decision or a jail sentence. If the protest is morally justified (whether it breaks the law or not) it is morally justified to the very end, even past the point where the court has imposed a penalty . . . How potent an effect can protest have if it stops dead in its tracks as soon as the very government it is criticizing decides against it?

Resisters like the Berrigans and their associates seek not only to disrupt the Selective Service System, but to disrupt the legal system which, when confronted by the Vietnam war, walks by on the other side, and which, as was said in the Baltimore courtroom, imprisons Jesus Christ.

Flowers and Fire

And yet they permitted themselves to be arrested and went to jail. So again: why?

The Milwaukee group used these words in their statement: "To make visible another community of resistance and to better explain our action, we have chosen to act publicly and to accept the consequences." If I may be presumptuous enough to add something to this explanation, I would say that these file burners seek simultaneously to reject the hypocritical *forms* in which Christianity and democracy express themselves in our society, yet to act in a way which preserves the *spirit* of love and mutual respect. Thus they seize keys from the cleaning woman in the draft-board office but, as their first act after imprisonment, send her flowers and candy in apology for having frightened her. And thus, instead of blowing up the draft board anonymously at night, they stole the files, burned them publicly, and waited by the fire, as if to say: "Here we are. You see, it was individual human beings who did this thing. We have signed this action with our names. We are not faceless. Like yourselves, some of us have children, were deeply committed to a vocation. Now you must deal not only with our action but with us." By waiting for arrest they humanized sabotage, turned terror into an encounter.

That is to say: They practiced disruption in a manner which kept the spirit of dialogue alive. During the year in which these acts were undertaken, the larger Movement for change in American society has tended to a different thesis: Once you go over to disruption, there are no limits, anything goes. But the file burners took a step as militant as any without vilifying their antagonists (they do not call draft-board members "pigs"), without harming their antagonists, without denying the right of their antagonists to take nonviolent disruptive actions of their own.

Personally I believe this last point to be critical. If we say that we, because we are moral, may do anything we like, but that our enemies may not, then we invite our enemies to think in the same way. We declare the situation a trial of brute strength. We say that we, if we can get the power, will repress the rights of our antagonists, and so open the door for our antagonists, who have the power to repress us without limit.

This is the argument of Herbert Marcuse, who in *A Critique Of Pure Tolerance* advocates "withdrawal of toleration of speech and assembly from groups and movements which promote aggressive policies, armament, chauvinism, discrimination on the grounds of race and religion, or which oppose the extension of public services, social security, medical care, etc." Indeed Marcuse advocates repression even of our opponents' speech, "new and rigid restrictions on teachings and practices in the educational institutions," and the like. Howard Zinn, too, while maintaining that "all promulgation of ideas by speech or press, whether odious to us or not, should be tolerated without distinction," agrees with Marcuse that "where we go beyond speech to action, universal tolerance is replaced by choosing of sides." Zinn insists that it is in the interest of democracy for us to be permitted to practice even disruptive civil disobedience. But were he in power he would deny the same freedom to those who disagree with him.

EPILOGUE

When the Lynds arrived in Chicago in the summer of 1967, the movement was rapidly changing. The events between 1967 and the early 1970s demonstrated to Staughton and Alice that a new way forward was necessary, both personally and politically, in the struggle to build a new world. One of the foremost lessons to be learned was the centrality of family in order to carry out the goals of sixties radicals: listening, consensus decision-making, participatory democracy, direct action, nonviolence, spontaneity, and experimentation.

By 1967–1968, disagreements over tactics within the movement, which led to tensions between friends and allies, as well as Lynd's blacklisting from the academy, were taking their toll. For Staughton, this "was a very difficult time personally," and in response to these new developments he shifted his focus away from national antiwar activity toward building strong grassroots and regional capacity to contribute to national actions instead of national action influencing local and regional activity. By the late 1960s and into the 1970s, Lynd chose to focus on Chicago and northwest Indiana as he began searching for new directions for the New Left and especially the labor movement. This was an important shift from his days as an intrepid national and international antiwar spokesman. It would amount to the opening of a new chapter in his life.[1]

To understand the end of the 1960s and Lynd's decision-making, there are five elements that undergirded Lynd's thinking during this period. First, by 1968–1969 the radical student / youth wing of the antiwar movement was turning toward confrontation, violence, and street fighting while Lynd chose to maintain his adherence to nonviolence and participatory democracy. The adoption of tactics that lacked a clear strategy led to the New Left adopting the coercive tactics of the Old Left and eventually self-destructing. The heady idealism of the early 1960s had given way to splinter groups, vanguard factions, paranoia, revolutionary rhetoric, outbursts of violence including street fighting and bombings, and a loss of faith in mass actions among some members of the New Left. Intensely depressing for Lynd was the fact that the two groups most associated with the New Left in which he was a participant—SDS and SNCC—disintegrated by 1970.

Figure 7.1: Staughton Lynd speaking at the War Resisters in North America Conference, Steelworkers Hall, Toronto, 24 September 2011. *Left to right:* Lee Zaslofsky (a US Army deserter to Canada during the Vietnam War), Staughton Lynd, Michael Mandel (an international legal expert), and Jeremy Hinzman (a US Army deserter during the war on Iraq). Courtesy of James Swarts.

When Tom Hayden and Rennie Davis visited the Lynds in the lead-up to the 1968 Democratic National Convention and informed them they were planning confrontation and violence if need be, Lynd objected. In response, he organized a nonviolent march to the amphitheater to challenge the crackdown on free speech and was arrested. Unlike his comrade Dave Dellinger, Lynd did not want to find "some compromise or middle-road with people who wanted to engage in violence," and the two parted ways. Lynd's separation from his friend and comrade left Lynd "feel[ing] very much alone in whatever it was that I was trying to represent." This did not mean that he retreated from the movement. Instead, he used every opportunity to convince those moving toward violence to return to the principles that launched the New Left in the first place. Cathy Wilkerson, an SDSer who worked on the organization's newspaper, *New Left Notes,* in Chicago and later member of the Weathermen faction of SDS, recalled an evening in 1969 where Lynd talked the group down from street fighting at an upcoming demonstration. By this time, Wilkerson lived in the Washington, DC, regional SDS house, and a group that had gathered there was planning a confrontation at the demonstration. Lynd was invited to the house, and he engaged in a dialogue with the youthful militants, who were increasingly alienated by the fact their actions to date had not, as they thought, had an impact on the course of the war in Vietnam. Lynd was able to talk the rebels down, and they did not engage in the planned confrontation.[2]

Second, by the summer of 1967 Lynd no longer believed that he was indispensable to the antiwar movement. When SDS backed away from antiwar organizing after their successful April 1965 demonstration in Washington, DC, Lynd felt he needed to keep momentum going over the summer by helping to organize the Assembly of Unrepresented People. Lynd's subsequent trip to Hanoi and advocacy on behalf of draft resisters were crucial. However, after two years and, especially for Lynd, Martin Luther King Jr.'s speeches against the war at Riverside Church in New York City on 4 April 1967 and again eleven days later at the Spring Mobilization in Central Park, Lynd was convinced that he had outlived his role as a leader in the movement.[3]

Third, in December 1966 SNCC asked its white members to leave the organization and organize the white working class in their own communities. This was the time that Black power was in ascendance within the radical civil rights movement, and the decision to expel white people was years in the making. One of the reasons that the Lynds moved to Chicago was to work with Rennie Davis on community organizing in what SDS was calling "an interracial movement of the poor." By the summer of 1967, however, the landscape had shifted dramatically. "I was being told by the most radical people in the Movement of the 1960s to stop giving all your attention to civil rights," Lynd said in an interview. "What we need from you is to organize white workers," and that is what he slowly did after he moved to Chicago.[4]

Fourth, Staughton and Alice's relationship as a married couple was being sacrificed for the needs of the movement, and this had an impact on their family life. Alice was working on her book *We Won't Go* and becoming much more involved as a draft counselor. In 1969, Alice took the position of the coordinator of draft counseling in the Chicago regional office of the American Friends Service Committee. This was quite a large undertaking, and the reality was that Staughton and Alice could not both do full-time work in the antiwar movement with three children.[5] The Lynds would continue discussing opposition to the war in their living room as they did in New Haven, this time hosting weekly meetings with members of the Chicago Area Draft Resisters and other young people.

Finally, with all these activities swirling around, Lynd still found time to be experimental in his research and writing of history. While the doors to the academy were all but shut to Lynd by 1969, he did not give up practicing his craft. On the contrary, Lynd was blacklisted at the very moment he was at the prime of his life as a professional historian. His most influential work, *Intellectual Origins of American Radicalism*, was published in 1968, and by 1969 he turned his attention toward the labor movement of the 1930s. Here, Lynd began engaging in what he called "guerrilla history," or "oral history from the bottom-up," with rank-and-file labor organizers from the 1930s and draft resisters. Lynd elucidated the methodology of guerrilla history in an October 1969 *Liberation* article "Guerrilla History in Gary," wherein he explained that oral histories of rank-and-file workers from the 1930s were often omitted from efforts to reconstruct the struggles of that era and this was producing incomplete and skewed history. "For labor history the memories which 'common men carry around in their heads' are indispensable," Lynd wrote. "They are the primary sources which written records of any kind can only supplement and, when necessary, correct." Crucially for Lynd, this untapped resource, so vital to historians in reconstructing the past, was not just significant for academic historians because those in the contemporary labor movement naturally did history themselves by assessing past decisions, strikes, picket lines, and actions not taken and attempting to learn from these experiences. This too was doing history, Lynd contended, and the historical establishment could no longer ignore the history-making that non-professionals who seldom left paper trails also engaged in.[6]

Lynd took the idea that ordinary people make history and can interpret it themselves to the infamous December 1969 American Historical Association's annual meeting in Washington, DC.[7] In an atmosphere where New Left and radical historians were under attack in the profession, the newly formed Radical Caucus of the American Historical Association nominated Lynd for president of the AHA and submitted their "Resolution on the War and Repression" to be voted on at the business meeting. The Radical Caucus emerged out of a series of meetings beginning at the launching of the New University Conference at the University of Chicago in March 1968, where Lynd gave a keynote speech on the "Responsibility of Radical Intellectuals." At the 1968 AHA, the radicals decided to prepare for confrontation at the 1969 annual meeting and set out in earnest in September 1969 by drafting several resolutions. The insurgent candidacy of Staughton Lynd was the first time in decades that there was a contested presidential election in the normally mild-mannered, gentlemanly gathering—gentlemanly because there were parallel rumblings from the Coordinating Committee on Women in the Historical Profession group seeking better representation for female historians in the profession and protections such as childcare facilities and the end of nepotism. By all accounts, the December meeting was a raucous affair that saw Lynd losing the election to Yale's R. R. Palmer by a vote of 1,040–396 and the "Resolution on the

War and Repression" defeated 493–833. In fact, there was a second group of historians under the auspices of the Conference on Peace Research in History that also proposed a resolution against the Vietnam War, which was voted on first and lost 611–42. At the time there was speculation that if the vote on the two resolutions were switched, the Conference on Peace Research's proposal could have won. Nonetheless, the fact that Lynd got 30 percent of the vote was a wake-up call to the association.[8]

While the war continued and Lynd gave speeches and wrote articles against it, his attention turned toward the question, What are the prospects for the New Left in the United States? For this, Lynd sought to enmesh the question of peace activism within the broader struggles of the day and connect them to the everyday realities of people at a local grassroots level. Admittedly, by the early 1970s such prospects were not good as the major organizations of the New Left self-destructed. In 1971 Staughton joined the New American Movement, an organization of former SDSers and sympathizers of New Left politics trying to build a new socialist movement in the United States. As a historian, Lynd turned his attention toward the labor movement of the 1930s and worked with Alice on doing guerrilla history with labor activists. The Lynds' activities led to a documentary movie about female union organizers titled *Union Maids*; community forums in which an older generation of labor radicals described their struggles to a younger generation; an imaginary basic steel contract setting forth rank-and-file demands; and a collection of oral histories titled *Rank and File: Personal Histories by Working-Class Organizers*. Staughton was unable to get a job as a historian, and so he and Alice, frustrated by the lack of legal counsel who would represent rank-and-file workers, both decided in 1973 to go into law. Staughton went to law school at the University of Chicago (1973–1976), and Alice completed a program for legal assistants at Roosevelt University in 1974. In 1982–1985, Alice went to the University of Pittsburgh School of Law.

When the Lynds moved to Youngstown, Ohio, in 1976, already in their forties, they began life anew during the era of the great steel mill shutdowns and outsourcing of the late 1970s and 1980s. While their focus in the 1970s was on the struggles of workers and the labor movement, and after their retirement in the 1990s on prisoners, the issue of United States interventionism and participation in the peace movement never suffered from lack of attention. In many respects, the end of the 1960s for Staughton and Alice Lynd was a reorientation toward picking up the pieces of the shattered New Left and continuing to lay the foundations for a movement in the United States that combined the best attributes of the movements of the 1930s and the 1960s.

The Nature of US Military Interventionism after 1945

During the Vietnam War, Staughton Lynd was a leading critic of what would come to be called the imperial presidency. Since 1945, the United States has deployed its military forces over 160 times. This number represents nearly half of the more than 330 times the US has used force abroad since 1798, when it fought an undeclared war against France. In all the major military operations utilizing combat forces or bombing missions, no president since 1945 has obtained a constitutionally mandated declaration of war from the Congress.

Writing in January 1990, with the experiences of the 1980s dirty wars in Central America and the overt conflicts in Grenada and Panama, Lynd argued that such presidential war making was "not democratic self-government. It is the reduction of foreign policy to a spectator sport." As he pointed out, one of the consequences of the Vietnam War "is that presidents who start wars in secret, and without the formally expressed support of the people, had better win them fast."[9] This was of course a central element in what Washington's power elite called the "Vietnam syndrome," or the uneasiness of the American public to agree to open-ended military confrontations with the potential of large-scale civilian casualties and harm to US soldiers. The question of the illegality or unconstitutionality of American war making since 1945 is a feature of US foreign policy and not, as Lynd pointed out in the 1960s and beyond, an aberration. Lynd would make this argument in the 1990s after the bombing of Kosovo and in the early 2000s after the invasion of Iraq. When lawsuits challenging the legality of US interventionism would make it to federal courts, judges would rely on the "political question" doctrine to quash such lawsuits. In effect, the courts wash their hands of questions relating to foreign policy and argue it is a question more suitable to the legislative and executive branches of government.

Staughton Lynd played a minor role researching this question of the war-making powers within the US Constitution for a lawsuit challenging official US government aid to the Contras in Nicaragua. The lawsuit focused on protecting US volunteer aid workers who traveled to Nicaragua and was bolstered by the June 1986 International Court of Justice ruling that stated the Reagan administration violated international law by arming, training, and financing the Contras, directly attacking the country, and laying mines in Nicaraguan territorial waters. The federal court dismissed the lawsuit, ruling that this was a "political question." In response, Lynd concluded that "the Founding Fathers took it for granted that international law would apply to the actions of American officials and would be enforced by American courts. If we are to be faithful to the original intent of the framers in this, as in other areas of constitutional jurisprudence, we must conclude that the American president is not above the law—including international law—when he acts in the arena of foreign policy."[10] One of the conclusions from such legal questions during Vietnam and after is that the courts are just as much an enabler of the imperial presidency as are the Congress and the White House.

The major shift since Vietnam has been the initiation by President Nixon in 1973 of the all-volunteer military, which replaced the draft then in operation from 1948 to 1973. The all-volunteer army was not significantly tested until the post–September 11, 2001, conflicts in Afghanistan and Iraq, and as Lynd observed at a war resisters conference in Toronto in September 2011, this has had dramatic consequences for the soldiers fighting in these wars. "To field a military capable of worldwide imperial dominance, the Pentagon finds that it must call forth its volunteers in successive deployments," Lynd observed. Unlike the war in Vietnam, where draftees would face a tour of duty of twelve months, volunteer soldiers during the long, drawn-out conflicts in the war on terror have been sent into battle in deployment after deployment as the military struggled to recruit soldiers.[11]

A major consequence of the all-volunteer armed forces has been the way in which it has significantly freed the hand of US presidents to use military force. Coupled with fighting undeclared wars, the lack of congressional oversight, and courts refusing to rule on the legality of a particular war, the all-volunteer military has contributed to a major escalation in the use of military force. As noted above, since 1945 the US has engaged its forces in over 160 conflicts. However, retired lieutenant general Karl Eikenberry observed, during the period of the draft (1948–1973), there were only nineteen such overt interventions. Remarkably, after the creation of the all-volunteer force that number jumped to over 144 military operations.[12] This has permeated every aspect of American life.

As we will see, the Lynds have crafted a novel criticism of the all-volunteer force and its impact on war resistance and conscientious objection within the military. It is important to point out that in the face of such militarism and interventionism the Lynds have been staunch supporters of those opposing such undeclared wars and its victims. "It might be comforting to suppose that Vietnam was a Great Aberration," Lynd wrote in 1999. However, since 1945 the United States and its major multinational corporations created, in the words of the writers at *Politics* magazine, a "permanent war economy." Just as Lynd had argued in the 1960s, he continued to argue after the Cold War for the necessity of developing alternative lifestyles that would help create "a permanent resistance on behalf of life" in opposition to the permanent war economy.[13]

"My Country Is the World, My Countrymen Are All Mankind"

In the 1960s, Staughton Lynd encouraged young radicals to find inspiration from a homegrown American radical tradition that said, in part, "My country is the world, my countrymen are all mankind." This kind of internationalism led to the breaking down of Cold War stereotypes used to dehumanize the enemies of the US government, whether at home or abroad. An important part of this process was making connections with Vietnamese communists in Czechoslovakia, the Soviet Union, China, and North Vietnam. Later, the Lynds would travel to Nicaragua, Guatemala, Mexico, and Palestine. For the Lynds, opposing US interventionism—whether overt or clandestine military operations or the use of financial, military, or diplomatic aid—meant also affirming the sacredness of life.

During the Reagan administration's dirty wars in Central America, the Lynds used their time off from work in the summer and visited Nicaragua five times between 1985 and 1990. Alice recalled watching television in December 1983 where "a Quaker woman was going to Nicaragua with a group called Witness for Peace. They were going to go into areas of conflict and stand between the warring parties as a deterrent. I thought, wow, that's what nonviolent advocates have talked about for years, but here are people who are going to do it!"[14]

One of those nonviolent advocates, it should be recalled, was Staughton himself both at the Berkeley Teach-In in May 1965 and again at the International Teach-In in Toronto in October 1965, when he encouraged young people to go to "North Vietnam to rebuild hospitals and schools destroyed by American bombing, and to act while they are there as inadvertent hostages."[15] While Witness for Peace was the first group to send American volunteers to stand between the US-backed counterrevolutionaries (the Contras) and Nicaraguan villagers, the Lynds first visited the country through the efforts of the Interreligious Foundation for Community Organization.[16] The Lynds' five trips to Nicaragua had a tremendous impact on their lives as they traveled throughout the country and spoke with and learned from advocates of liberation theology. Once they returned, they sought out any opportunity they could to show slides and to speak about their experiences in Nicaragua. They also made it possible for steel and electrical workers associated with the Workers' Solidarity Club of Youngstown to travel to Nicaragua and Mexico and broaden the reach of solidarity across borders.

It was during the brief movement against the US war against Iraq in January–February 1991 (another undeclared war, but this time with the support of a UN Security Council resolution to expel Saddam Hussein's forces out of Kuwait) that the Lynds were exposed to the rather large Palestinian community in Youngstown, Ohio. Among the leading opponents of the US intervention in the Middle East were Sami Bahour and his son Sam, Palestinians who spoke both English and Arabic. Through this connection, the Lynds traveled twice to Palestine and Israel in the summers of 1991 and 1992 with Sam Bahour and interviewed numerous Palestinians. Out of these interviews came the collection *Homeland: Oral Histories of Palestine and Palestinians*, coedited by Sam Bahour and the Lynds.[17]

Alice and Staughton. Courtsey of Alice and Staughton Lynd

Accompaniment

The Lynds' lives since the early 1970s have represented in many respects the attempt to grapple with the failures of the movements of the 1960s. It pained Staughton that by 1970 both SDS and the Student Nonviolent Coordinating Committee (SNCC) ceased to function and were disbanded despite the significant gains each organization had achieved. It was not until the 1980s during their trips to Nicaragua that Staughton and Alice found a word to describe what they had been doing the majority of their adult lives: *accompaniment*. The term comes from the Salvadoran archbishop Óscar Romero and liberation theology. As the Lynds wrote in their 1996 pamphlet *Liberation Theology for Quakers*, despite the major successes of the movements of the 1960s—the Civil Rights and Voting Rights Acts, contributing to ending the war in Vietnam, and the emergence of the women's movement—"it is sobering that so many who called themselves 'revolutionaries' in the 1960s burned out or dropped out when the movements of that decade failed to produce instantaneous, total transformation." Instead, here and elsewhere, the Lynds called on Quakers and radicals to "be prepared to be long-distance runners."[18]

One of the main problems the Lynds tried to address was a very personal one: they were middle-class professionals and it was impossible for them to pretend to be otherwise. Like the student radicals of the 1960s, it was a question of how they related to poor, racialized, or marginalized people. How could they contribute in a meaningful way to rebuilding the movement that had faltered at the end of the 1960s? In *Liberation Theology for Quakers*, the Lynds offered five lessons from their lives that stand as a good definition of what accompaniment meant in practice.

First, drawn from Alice's experience as a draft counselor, there must be the creation of a "society of equals" wherein the middle-class protagonist works toward fostering a space of equality with the rank-and-file worker, draftee, soldier, or prisoner. In other words, it should not be presumed that the middle-class organizer has all the answers.

Second, the professional must be able to provide some kind of skill that would be useful to marginalized people in their day-to-day lives. For the Lynds, this was provided through draft counseling, oral history, and later lawyering.

Third, the necessity of living outside of areas populated by fellow radicals and getting to know people who do not necessarily agree with your worldview. This may mean staying in the same place for a long time.

Fourth, the importance of building community. One of the ways in which such community has been fostered by the Lynds is in creating or joining organizations such as the We Won't Go movement or the Youngstown Workers' Solidarity Club.

Finally, as Quakers writing a pamphlet for fellow Quakers, the Lynds called on fellow Friends "to trust their weight to the idea that the Kingdom of God is available here and now."[19] Of course, the idea of accompaniment does not lend itself easily to theorization and is better suited to the practice of doing it. In his conversation with the Yugoslav anarchist Andrej Grubacic, Staughton offered a concise definition: "The key is to acquire a skill useful to poor and working persons. Armed with such a skill, just behave as a moderately decent human being and 'accompaniment' will be a piece of cake. People will need you, and over time, as you offer a useful service trust and friendship will emerge of themselves."[20]

Guerrilla History as Accompaniment

Staughton credits Alice's work as a draft counselor during the Vietnam War in setting the template for the Lynds' form of accompaniment. Specifically, it was Alice's idea of the "two experts" that has informed how the Lynds would relate to workers, prisoners, peasants in Nicaragua, Palestinians, and soldiers in the latter years of their lives. Alice's book *We Won't Go: Personal Accounts of War Objectors* was both guerrilla history and accompaniment. It was through assembling these personal stories, statements, interviews, and articles that Alice created a larger platform for individuals to share their stories so others could help make up their minds about their participation in the war. This process would be duplicated by Staughton and Michael Ferber in their book, *The Resistance*. Guerrilla history was not just using the craft of oral history or personal narratives; it was also using Alice's concept of the two experts and in the case of war resistance having the additional goal of challenging US foreign policy.

It was during the Lynds' participation in the Central American solidarity movement in the early 1990s that they met, through Roxanne Dunbar-Ortiz, S. Brian Willson. Willson was a Vietnam veteran who began his opposition to the dirty war in Nicaragua first by traveling there in January 1986 and then in September 1986 joining a hunger strike on the steps of the Capitol in Washington, DC, launched by two other Vietnam veterans. As part of a national campaign of nonviolent opposition to the Reagan administration's war in Nicaragua, and again with Vietnam veterans, Willson launched what he called "Nuremberg Actions" on 1 September 1987. The Nuremberg Actions targeted the railway lines where weapons shipments bound for Central America traveled via the Concord Naval Weapons Station outside Oakland, California. By creating a human blockade over the train tracks, the veterans upheld international law and condemned United States support for repressive governments in Central America. Tragically, the very first day of the action Willson was run over by the train when the conductor accelerated, attempting to break the human blockade. Willson lost both his legs, and he became an overnight folk hero in the United States and a hero to the Nicaraguan people. For those who have read the Lynds' work, Willson has left a large impact on their lives as well.

The Lynds accompanied Willson first by simply traveling to his home and slowly developing a friendship. During their visits, the Lynds began recording Willson as he explained his life, his experiences in Vietnam, and his most recent opposition to US foreign policy in Central America. Slowly Staughton crafted a narrative using other materials such as Willson's own statements, interviews, and writings. According to Willson, it was Staughton who "encouraged and provoked me to share my story and to express my passions and anguish and who so faithfully advised me in writing this autobiography."[21] This was guerrilla history in action and presents a model for doing history that can be somewhat difficult for academic historians to accept. But it is a perfect illustration of guerrilla history as accompaniment.

Lynd sent the first manuscript to Willson, and after a series of revisions and additions the process would repeat itself until *On Third World Legs* was published in 1992. In the introduction, Staughton argued that after the 1960s "the center of gravity of nonviolence" spread throughout the world to places like Poland, South Africa, and Central America. "With Brian Willson, we can again begin to hope for a mass movement of nonviolent resistance and transformation within the North American colossus."

For Lynd, Willson's nonviolence differed from that of the 1950s and 1960s because it was initiated by a working-class veteran: "Willson's historical significance goes beyond his role in reviving the practice of nonviolence in the United States, and the fact is that he does so as a person of working-class background. The awesome additional fact is that, finding his way on the basis of his own first-hand experience in the Vietnam War, this working-class practitioner of nonviolence seeks to confront United States imperialism."[22]

Historians against the War

In the lead-up to the attack and occupation of Iraq, as the drums of war were pounding louder, Historians against the War (HAW) was formed at the annual meeting of the American Historical Association (AHA) in Chicago, held from January 2 to 5, 2003. From its inception, Lynd was a founding member of the HAW steering committee and an active participant. One of the major contributions he made was the constant encouragement for fellow historians and academics to include veterans from the wars in Afghanistan and Iraq on their panels or in teach-ins.

Speaking at the HAW roundtable "Imperial Crisis and Domestic Dissent" at the January 2004 AHA annual meeting in Washington, DC, Lynd criticized the indefinite detention of terrorism suspects at Guantánamo Bay and discussed whether the Bush doctrine of preemptive war was new to the American experience. When it came to solutions, Lynd urged the historians in attendance that "we can seek out and encourage veterans who may wish to share their experience. We should try to make contact with returning veterans and their families, listen to what they want to say, and if they are willing, include them in teach-ins that we organize. In this way we can combine the teach-ins against war in Vietnam that took place in 1965 and 1966 with the later Winter Soldier forums in which returning vets told their stories."[23] Within HAW, Lynd later helped form the Oral History Working Group, which created a guide on doing oral history with veterans, organized conferences where veterans spoke, and then produced pamphlets of these oral histories.

In his capacity as a lawyer and a member of HAW, Staughton wrote three amicus curiae briefs on behalf of soldiers who refused to participate in the war on Iraq. First Staff Sergeant Camilo Mejía and then Sergeant Kevin Benderman both served tours of duty in Iraq before they renounced war and applied for conscientious objector status. Instead of receiving CO status, they were court-martialed and sent to prison. The third soldier, Lieutenant Ehren Watada, was the highest-ranking soldier to refuse to fight in Iraq. Watada did not apply for CO status and argued instead that while he would have fought in Afghanistan, the war on Iraq was a crime against peace or a war of aggression lacking both a congressional declaration of war and a UN Security Council resolution. After a lengthy three-year legal battle, Watada was eventually discharged from the military in 2009 on a technicality. Lynd was a jurist at the Citizen's Hearing on the Legality of US Actions in Iraq: The Case of Lt. Ehren Watada, held in Tacoma, Washington, January 20–21, 2007. At this hearing, it was the testimony of the veterans of the Iraq War that had the most impact on Lynd.[24]

One of HAW's most significant accomplishments came in the successful ratification by the American Historical Association of the "Resolution on Iraq" in 2007. Always cognizant of the failure of the Radical Historians' Caucus to pass their resolution opposing the Vietnam War in December 1969, HAW renewed the push for the AHA to condemn illegal war and its consequences on the historical profession. Reflecting on the differences between the 1969 resolution and the successful 2007 resolution, Staughton Lynd wrote, "Back then we asked historians not only to oppose the Vietnam war but to protest harassment of the Black Panthers and to call for freeing political prisoners. This resolution focuses on government practices that obstruct the practice of history. It asks the American Historical Association only to encourage its members, as individuals, in finding ways to end the war in Iraq."[25] Indeed for Lynd, the passage of the Resolution on Iraq helped to sweeten whatever bitter taste lingered over the fabled 1969 fight within the AHA.

War Resisters in an All-Volunteer Army

Whether it was the first Gulf War in 1991 or the subsequent wars during the global war on terror, one of the most important contributions to the antiwar movement by Staughton and Alice Lynd has been answering the question of how soldiers can resist war when they volunteered to serve. The reality, as the Lynds have reflected in various pamphlets, books, and speeches since the adoption of the all-volunteer force, is that there will be few conscientious objectors in an all-volunteer force. Military regulations do allow soldiers, just as in the Vietnam experience, to apply for CO status. However, as the cases of Camilo Mejía and Kevin Benderman demonstrate, it is very difficult once in the military to attain CO status, and more often than not soldiers are harassed for or dissuaded from applying. Therefore, using their experiences from the Vietnam War resistance movement, the Lynds have attempted to provide their expertise in defending soldiers once they refuse orders to fight.

When the Gulf War broke out in January 1991, the Lynds demonstrated against the war every lunchtime in downtown Youngstown with members of the Workers' Solidarity Club. They also attended peace meetings in churches that consistently attracted sixty to seventy people. While it was not clear during the early days of the war just how short the conflict would be, the Lynds decided to organize a series of workshops on conscientious objection and military regulations. They devised six two-hour workshops that were held at the Saint Columba Cathedral. They gathered material on the latest military regulations and prepared information in case the draft would be reinstituted. The first meeting on February 21 had twenty people in attendance, including "mothers concerned about their children, a junior high school guidance counselor, a Vietnam veteran and various other people who have contact with young men."[26] When the war ended one week later, they continued the workshops but changed the topics to include the Holocaust, Palestine and Israel, Lebanon, and other hot-button issues.[27]

Staughton Lynd later reflected that if the war had continued, the number of "people opposed to what was happening would have increased rapidly." This was certainly the Lynds' experience, as they did not expect the sustained high turnout at peace meetings or the seven busloads of peace activists who traveled from Youngstown to Washington, DC, for the massive January 26 antiwar demonstration. Comparing the Vietnam experience to the first Gulf War, the Lynds' recollections were strengthened by Carl Mirra's observation that the first major antiwar demonstration in Washington on 19 January 1991 attracted twenty-five thousand people, whereas the second demonstration one week later on January 26 had one hundred thousand in the nation's capital and another hundred thousand in San Francisco. Such numbers dwarfed the first major demonstration against the Vietnam War, which, as Mirra points out, was roughly twenty thousand people on 17 April 1965.[28] Moreover, Mirra, himself a Marine who obtained conscientious objector status during the first Gulf War, estimates that between 1 August 1990 and 31 July 1991, there were 1,500 to 2,500 CO applications within the military in addition to 8,000 soldiers who went absent without leave (AWOL) between October 1990 and March 1991. If the low estimate of 1,500 applications during the Gulf War is correct, this is nearly double that of 1967 (two years after the Johnson administration escalated the war).[29] When the Lynds' decided in 1995 to coedit an updated version of Staughton's 1965 *Nonviolence in America: A Documentary History*, they included three statements from soldiers who refused to participate in the Gulf War.[30]

It was not until the war on Iraq in 2003 that the all-volunteer force was tested and stretched to a near breaking point. Staughton Lynd found that the major difference between the volunteer army of the war on Iraq and the conscript army of the war on Vietnam was that in the former, the experience of combat, coupled with a period of rest and relaxation, led to soldiers confronting their conscience and then applying for CO status, going AWOL/deserting, or both.

While the rate of desertion during the Iraq conflict was nowhere near that of the Vietnam War, the US Army reported that between 2001 and 2014 there were 36,195 soldiers who deserted their posts. These numbers do not include the other two branches of the military or the number of soldiers who had gone AWOL. Investigative journalist Wil S. Hylton reported that per his research, there were easily fifty thousand soldiers from all branches of the US military who deserted during the war on terror. In 2006, the number of soldiers deserting were on the rise, with stories published stating that in the three years after the invasion of Iraq, more than eight thousand soldiers deserted the US Army. In 2007, the *New York Times* reported, on the basis of the Pentagon's own data, that growing numbers of soldiers were going AWOL during their two weeks of rest and relaxation before redeployment, and some of these became deserters.[31]

Moreover, it has been estimated that from 2004 to 2008 between two hundred and three hundred US soldiers fled to Canada. According to statistics from the Canadian government, forty-four of these soldiers officially applied for refugee status, arguing that the war on Iraq was illegal and that they would not receive a fair trial in the United States for refusing to deploy.[32] In 2008 US Army specialist André Shepherd deserted his base in Germany, citing the war's illegality and the fact that the Apache helicopters he serviced while in Iraq were responsible for war crimes. He also officially applied for refugee status.[33] The nature of the volunteer force, the heavy reliance on activating the National Guard and the Reserves (which was not done during the Vietnam War), plus low recruitment numbers caused some to speculate that the US Armed Forces were entering a period of crisis by 2006. The military quickly responded by cracking down on deserters who left the military, but especially those who publicly opposed the war. After the financial crisis of 2008, the Pentagon reported that it no longer had the recruiting problems it faced earlier in the global war on terror, and the desertion rate dropped precipitously as it appeared the wars in Iraq and Afghanistan were winding down.

The number of soldiers who applied for conscientious objector status is much more difficult to obtain, but the numbers that do exist suggest that the Lynds' assumption there would be very few conscientious objectors in an all-volunteer force rings true. The US Government Accountability Office (GAO) reported that between 2002 and 2006 there were 425 applications for CO status across all three branches of the military. The Center on Conscience and War (CCW) released a report challenging the GAO's numbers as "absurdly low." Pointing out the GAO's flawed methodology, the CCW states that the report counts only those applicants who made it all the way up the chain of command to the Pentagon for the final decision (the last step in a nearly eighteen-month process). As a member of the GI Rights Hotline, the CCW regularly took calls from soldiers asking about CO status. On the basis of their own internal numbers, the CCW argued that of the fifty-six applicants reported by the GAO for 2006 the CCW would have "spoken to the majority" of them. "Of course," the CCW writes about the GAO's findings, "we know that such a conclusion would be false." Moreover, attesting to the difficulties of obtaining CO status, of the reported 425 applications, only 53 percent were finally approved.[34]

What does all this mean? While each case is unique to the individual war resister, Staughton Lynd helped to summarize the predicament soldiers face who become resisters once inside the US military. Using his experience helping Mejía and Benderman, Lynd wrote a friend-of-the-court brief for Lieutenant Watada's Article 32 pretrial hearing on 17 August 2006. In the brief, Lynd stated that soldiers who oppose the wars they fight nonetheless seldom refuse to fight while on the battlefield out of loyalty to their fellow soldiers, or because there isn't sufficient time or space for them to process these kinds of thoughts. It is usually during time off, outside the battle zone during their period of rest and relaxation, that their ideas crystalize into action and opposition. This is when soldiers, if they get the right help, begin to think about CO status. Sometimes, as in the case of Mejía, soldiers will go AWOL because they face redeployment to a war they have come to oppose.

Soldiers in this situation have no good options under current US military regulations. First, the *Manual for Courts-Martial* has adopted the position that "an order requiring the performance of a military duty or act may be inferred to be lawful, and it is disobeyed at the peril of the subordinate. This inference does not apply to a patently illegal order, such as one that directs the commission of a crime." Moreover, it is the authority of a military judge to determine "the lawfulness of an order."[35] Such orders include refusing deployment or redeployment or refusing to carry out an order in the field. Therefore, if a soldier refuses to commit what they believe to be a war crime in the heat of the moment, this could carry harsh penalties. If the soldier carries out the order, the possible war crime would have been committed, and it would be too late. Finally, if the soldier believes the war they are being told to fight in is a war of aggression or a crime against peace, as defined by the Nuremberg principles, both civilian and military courts (as in the case of David Mitchell, the Fort Hood Three, and Lieutenant Watada) argue that the question of the war's legality is a "political question" and therefore irrelevant.

Second, soldiers who believe that war crimes or crimes against humanity are being committed or the war they're being told to fight in is itself illegal—lacking congressional approval or a UN Security Council resolution—face three options: refuse orders and face court-martial and imprisonment, go AWOL and desert, or apply for conscientious objector status.

Finally, for soldiers hoping to apply for conscientious objector status, US military regulations define CO status as "a firm, fixed, and sincere objection to participation in war in any form or the bearing of arms, by reason of religious training and/or belief."

Therefore, under these precarious circumstances, Lynd argued in his friend-of-the-court brief for a change in the definition of conscientious objector status to include those who oppose particular wars but not all wars. Moreover—and this is central to Lynd's opposition to US interventionism since the end of World War II—US domestic and military law must incorporate the Nuremberg principles so that "a potential or actual soldier should be entitled to refuse orders not only because they require 'war crimes' or 'crimes against humanity,' but also because they demand obedience to a 'crime against peace': aggressive war."[36]

During public talks Lynd gave during this period, he went further than his friend-of-the-court brief. Speaking about the "circumscribed" definition of conscientious objection under US regulations, he argued that the Nuremberg principles of 1950 do not require the beliefs of an absolute pacifist to refuse illegal orders. In other words, "A soldier can and must be able to say No to orders in a particular war that he perceives to be war crimes and that deeply offend his conscience" *because* the Nuremberg principles expressly reject the defense of superior orders, affirm the doctrine that international law is superior to domestic laws, and affirm that war of aggression is a crime even if committed by the United States. This was a radical redefinition of conscientious objection under past and current American conscientious objector regulations.

The first recognition in international law of the principle of selective conscientious objection followed not the Nuremberg principles but the International Covenant on Civil and Political Rights. In 1978, the General Assembly of the United Nations passed a resolution recognizing the right of persons in the South African military or police forces to refuse to enforce apartheid.[37]

While Lynd himself was a conscientious objector during the Korean War and a passionate adherent to nonviolence, conscientious objection as it exists according to him

> is a legal system written to accommodate the tender consciences of members of certain small Christian sects that came into being during the Radical Reformation: Hutterites, Quakers, Amish, Mennonites, Brethren, and the like. And let's be honest, Conscientious Objection thus defined exists because the powers that be know that it will never be the world view of more than a handful of persons....
> ... The system can tolerate traditional Conscientious Objectors. For those who remember Herbert Marcuse's concept of "repressive tolerance," this is an example: precisely by making room for such atypical refuseniks, the system as a whole can continue undisturbed.[38]

Both Staughton and Alice Lynd have noted that in an all-volunteer military it would be more likely that there would be selective conscientious objectors: those like Mitchell, the Fort Hood Three, and Lieutenant Watada who were not absolute conscientious objectors but opposed to the particular war they were being asked to fight. More often than not these particular war objectors would base their reasons on domestic and international law that the courts of the United States have refused to adjudicate.

Moral Injury and the Rejection of War

Facing the consequences of such a legal system, in the summer of 2015 Alice Lynd published a ninety-eight-page pamphlet from Historians against the War titled *Moral Injury and Conscientious Objection: Saying No to Military Service. In the pamphlet*, Alice, with the assistance of Staughton, had created a masterful guide for soldiers, their families, and peace activists wishing to explore the relevant international laws and conscientious objector regulations that might aid their opposition to war. Comparing this pamphlet with her 1968 book *We Won't Go*, Alice wrote,

> It is our hope that this article, like *We Won't Go*, may help men and women to reflect on what they may want to do about participation in war, or to explain to their families why they may make what would otherwise be

incomprehensible decisions. We also hope that those of us who have never served in the military will take more seriously the burdens placed on those who have. It is up to all of us to find ways other than war to solve international and ethnic conflicts.[39]

The Lynds expanded the scope of this pamphlet and published it as a book in 2017 titled *Moral Injury and Nonviolent Resistance: Breaking the Cycle of Violence in the Military and Behind Bars*. Covering many of these same themes addressed here, the Lynds found a unique way of discussing the scourge of post-1945 militarism that has infected the American body politic. When the Lynds contacted the various "ordinary people" highlighted in the book, seeking their permission to quote them, they set out a definition of *moral injury*:

> People may experience moral injury after they did, or saw, or failed to prevent something that deeply offends their sense of right and wrong. They may not know what it is that makes them feel that way, but the sense of mankind as to what is and is not morally permissible has been expressed in international law and other declarations of fundamental human rights.[40]

Alice was introduced to the concept of moral injury from Quaker and military counselor Lynn Newsom of Fayetteville, North Carolina, who had been counseling soldiers from Fort Bragg on many of the same questions the Lynds were addressing. Looking back on their lives and experiences with members of the armed forces and veterans who have come to oppose war, the Lynds found many examples of soldiers experiencing moral injury with or without expressly using the term. For Alice and Staughton, it was clear there were certain redlines that ordinary people refused to cross, whether they were based on conscience, the law, or both.

In the book, the Lynds address the contradictions between the role of international law in limiting both the use of force and the tactics employed in warfare, and the way in which states "put their own interests ahead of the rights of others." For the Lynds, the significance of moral injury is inseparable from the legality of the war and the commission of war crimes in particular. For them, "As long as we live in a violent society, more people will become victims and some of the victimizers will suffer moral injury. There is no solution to physical and moral injury as long as people are willing to fight wars."

However, the sad reality as documented in this collection and through their lifetime of activism is that "for the foreseeable future individuals and small groups of service men and women who are confronted with orders perceived to be unlawful and immoral may have to step forward in the knowledge that they may be punished if they say No but with faith in the possibility of a better future."[41] The Lynds ask "whether anything other than rejection of warfare and taking action in affirmation of life can truly bring about healing."[42] Ultimately, *Moral Injury and Nonviolent Resistance* is a crowning achievement on a lifetime of service to the United States and the world in opposing war and militarism.

APPENDIX A

SELECTIVE SERVICE SYSTEM
DRAFT CLASSIFICATIONS

1-A	available for duty
1-A-O	CO, available for noncombat
1-O	CO, available for civilian alternative service
1-S	high school student
1-Y	physically and mentally qualified only in war
2-A	deferred for civilian occupation
2-C	deferred for agricultural occupation
2-S	deferred as college student
1-D	member of Reserve or ROTC
3-A	father or has dependents
4-B	deferred official by law
4-D	minister or divinity student
4-F	physically, mentally, or morally disqualified
4-A	veteran or sole surviving son
5-A	over age of liability
1-C	member of armed forces

FINAL DECLARATION OF THE GENEVA CONFERENCE ON THE PROBLEM OF RESTORING PEACE IN INDO-CHINA, 21 JULY 1954

FINAL DECLARATION, dated the 21st July, 1954, of the Geneva Conference on the problem of restoring peace in Indo-China, in which the representatives of Cambodia, the Democratic Republic of Viet-Nam, France, Laos, the People's Republic of China, the State of Viet-Nam, the Union of Soviet Socialist Republics, the United Kingdom, and the United States of America took part.

1. The Conference takes note of the agreements ending hostilities in Cambodia, Laos and Viet-Nam and organizing international control and the supervision of the execution of the provisions of these agreements.

2. The Conference expresses satisfaction at the ending of hostilities in Cambodia, Laos and Viet-Nam; the Conference expresses its conviction that the execution of the provisions set out in the present declaration and in the agreements on the cessation of hostilities will permit Cambodia, Laos and Viet-Nam henceforth to play their part, in full independence and sovereignty, in the peaceful community of nations.

3. The Conference takes note of the declarations made by the Governments of Cambodia and of Laos of their intention to adopt measures permitting all citizens to take their place in the national community, in particular by participating in the next general elections, which, in conformity with the constitution of each of these countries, shall take place in the course of the year 1955, by secret ballot and in conditions of respect for fundamental freedoms.

4. The Conference takes note of the clauses in the agreement on the cessation of hostilities in Viet-Nam prohibiting the introduction into Viet-Nam of foreign troops and military personnel as well as of all kinds of arms and munitions. The Conference also takes note of the declarations made by

the Governments of Cambodia and Laos of their resolution not to request foreign aid, whether in war material, in personnel or in instructors except for the purpose of the effective defence of their territory and, in the case of Laos, to the extent defined by the agreements on the cessation of hostilities in Laos.

5. The Conference takes note of the clauses in the agreement on the cessation of hostilities in Viet-Nam to the effect that no military base under the control of a foreign State may be established in the regrouping zones of the two parties, the latter having the obligation to see that the zones allotted to them shall not constitute part of any military alliance and shall not be utilized for the resumption of hostilities or in the service of an aggressive policy. The Conference also takes note of the declarations of the Governments of Cambodia and Laos to the effect that they will not join in any agreement with other States if this agreement includes the obligation to participate in a military alliance not in conformity with the principles of the Charter of the United Nations or, in the case of Laos, with the principles of the agreement on the cessation of hostilities in Laos or, so long as their security is not threatened, the obligation to establish bases on Cambodian or Laotian territory for the military forces of foreign Powers.

6. The Conference recognizes that the essential purpose of the agreement relating to Viet-Nam is to settle military questions with a view to ending hostilities and that the military demarcation line is provisional and should not in any way be interpreted as constituting a political or territorial boundary. The Conference expresses its conviction that the execution of the provisions set out in the present declaration and in the agreement on the cessation of hostilities creates the necessary basis for the achievement in the near future of a political settlement in Viet-Nam.

7. The Conference declares that, so far as Viet-Nam is concerned. the settlement of political problems, effected on the basis of respect for the principles of independence, unity and territorial integrity, shall permit the Viet-Namese people to enjoy the fundamental freedoms, guaranteed by democratic institutions established as a result of free general elections by secret ballot. In order to ensure that sufficient progress in the restoration of peace has been made, and that all the necessary conditions obtain for free expression of the national will, general elections shall be held in July 1956, under the supervision of an international commission composed of representatives of the Member States of the International Supervisory

Commission, referred to in the agreement on the cessation of hostilities. Consultations will be held on this subject between the competent representative authorities of the two zones from 20 July 1955 onwards.

8. The provisions of the agreements on the cessation of hostilities intended to ensure the protection of individuals and of property must be most strictly applied and must, in particular, allow everyone in Viet-Nam to decide freely in which zone he wishes to live.

9. The competent representative authorities of the Northern and Southern zones of Viet-Nam, as well as the authorities of Laos and Cambodia, must not permit any individual or collective reprisals against persons who have collaborated in any way with one of the parties during the war, or against members of such persons' families.

10. The Conference takes note of the declaration of the Government of the French Republic to the effect that it is ready to withdraw its troops from the territory of Cambodia, Intros and Viet-Nam, at the request of the governments concerned and within periods which shall be fixed by agreement between the parties except in the cases where, by agreement between the two parties, a certain number of French troops shall remain at specified points and for a specified time.

11. The Conference takes note of the declaration of the French Government to the effect that for the settlement of all the problems connected with the re-establishment and consolidation of peace in Cambodia, Laos and Viet-Nam, the French Government will proceed from the principle of respect for the independence and sovereignty, unity and territorial integrity of Cambodia, Laos and Viet-Nam.

12. In their relations with Cambodia, Laos and Viet-Nam, each member of the Geneva Conference undertakes to respect the sovereignty, the independence, the unity and the territorial integrity of the above-mentioned states, and to refrain from any interference in their internal affairs.

13. The members of the Conference agree to consult one another on any question which may be referred to them by the International Supervisory Commission, in order to study such measures as may prove necessary to ensure that the agreements on the cessation of hostilities in Cambodia, Laos and Viet-Nam are respected.

THE FIVE-POINT PROGRAM OF THE NATIONAL LIBERATION FRONT OF SOUTH VIETNAM

Facing the present situation of utmost gravity, the South Vietnam National Front for Liberation deems it necessary to reaffirm once again its ironlike and unswerving stand to carry through the war of resistance against the American imperialists:

1. The US imperialists are the saboteurs of the Geneva Accords, the most brazen warmonger and aggressor and the sworn enemy of the Vietnamese people.

2. The heroic South Vietnamese people are resolved to drive out the US imperialists in order to liberate South Vietnam and achieve an independent, democratic, peaceful, and neutral South Vietnam, with a view to national reunification.

3. The valiant South Vietnamese people and the South Vietnam Liberation Army are resolved to carry out fully their sacred duty to drive out the US imperialists so as to liberate South Vietnam and defend North Vietnam.

4. The South Vietnamese people express their profound gratitude for the wholehearted support of the people of the world who cherish peace and justice and declare their readiness to receive all assistance, including weapons and all other war material, from their friends on five continents.

5. To unite the whole people, to arm the whole people, to continue to march forward heroically, and to resolve to fight and defeat the US aggressors and the Vietnamese traitors.

THE DEMOCRATIC REPUBLIC OF VIETNAM'S FOUR POINTS, 8 APRIL 1965

1. Recognition of the basic national rights of the Vietnamese people: peace, independence, sovereignty, unity and territorial integrity. According to the Geneva Agreements, the U.S. government must withdraw from South Vietnam all U.S. troops, military personnel, and weapons of all kinds, dismantle all U.S. military bases there, cancel its 'military alliance' with South Vietnam. It must end its policy of intervention and aggression in South Vietnam. According to the Geneva Agreements, the U.S. government must stop its acts of war against North Vietnam, completely cease all encroachments on the territory and sovereignty of the Democratic Republic of Vietnam.

2. Pending the peaceful reunification of Vietnam, while Vietnam is still temporarily divided into two zones the *military* provision of the 1954 Geneva Agreements on Vietnam must be strictly respected: the two zones must refrain from joining any military alliance with foreign countries, there must be no foreign military bases, troops and military personnel in their respective territory.

3. The internal affairs of South Vietnam must be settled by the South Vietnamese people themselves, in accordance with the programme of the South Vietnam National Front for Liberation, without any foreign interference.

4. The peaceful reunification of Vietnam is to be settled by the Vietnamese people in both zones, without any foreign interference.

This stand unquestionably enjoys the approval and support of all peace and justice loving governments and people in the world.

The Government of the Democratic Republic of Vietnam is of the view that the above-expounded sand is the basis for the soundest political settlement of the

Vietnam problem. If this basis is recognized, favorable conditions will be created for the peaceful settlement of the Vietnam problem and it will be possible to consider the reconvening of an international conference along the pattern of the 1954 Geneva Conference on Vietnam.

REPUBLIC OF [SOUTH] VIET NAM'S
FOUR POINTS, 22 JUNE 1965

1. Since the present war in Viet Nam was provoked by Communist aggression and subversion, first of all, it is important that subversive and military activities undertaken, directed and supported by outside forces against the independence and liberty of the people of South Viet Nam must cease. The principle of non-interference in the internal affairs of the two parts—principles declared in the Geneva Accords of 1954 as well as by international morality—must be respected. Consequently, the Hanoi Communist regime must dissolve all the puppet organizations it has formed in South Viet Nam under the names of "Front for the Liberation of the South," "Liberation Radio" and the "People's Revolutionary Party." Also it must withdraw from South Viet Nam troops, political and military cadres it had illegally introduced into South Viet Nam.

2. South Viet Nam must be left alone, to choose and shape for itself its own destiny in accordance with established democratic processes without any intervention of whatever form and whatever source. Obviously these could be realized only when the aggression initiated by the Hanoi regime is ended and its intimidation campaign against the South Vietnamese people decisively suppressed.

3. Only when aggression has ceased, and only then, it will be possible for the Government of the Republic of Viet Nam and for nations which provide it with assistance, to withhold defensive military measures on the territory of South Viet Nam and outside its borders. Such measures are presently necessary for defending the territory of South Viet Nam against Communist aggression. Besides, the Government of the Republic of Viet Nam is ready to ask these friendly countries to withdraw their military forces from South Viet Nam. However, it shall reserve its right to take all measures to restore order and law on the entire territory of South Viet

Nam and to assure security for the people of South Viet Nam as well as the right to call again for foreign assistance in case of renewed aggression or renewed threat of aggression.

4. Finally, the independence and liberty of the Vietnamese people must be effectively guaranteed.

THE UNITED STATES' FOURTEEN POINTS, 27 DECEMBER 1965

1. The Geneva Agreements of 1954 and 1962 are an adequate basis for peace in Southeast Asia;

2. We would welcome a conference on Southeast Asia or on any part thereof;

3. We would welcome "negotiations without pre-conditions" as the 17 nations put it;

4. We would welcome unconditional discussions as President Johnson put it;

5. A cessation of hostilities could be the first order of business at a conference or could be the subject of preliminary discussions;

6. Hanoi's four points could be discussed along with other points which others might wish to propose;

7. We want no U.S. bases in Southeast Asia;

8. We do not desire to retain U.S. troops in South Viet-Nam after peace is assured;

9. We support free elections in South Viet-Nam to give the South Vietnamese a government of their own choice;

10. The question of reunification of Viet-Nam should be determined by the Vietnamese through their own free decision;

11. The countries of Southeast Asia can be non-aligned or neutral if that be their option;

12. We would much prefer to use our resources for the economic reconstruction of Southeast Asia than in war. If there is peace, North Viet-Nam could participate in a regional effort to which we would be prepared to contribute at least one billion dollars;

13. The President has said "The Viet Cong would not have difficulty being represented and having their views represented if for a moment Hanoi decided she wanted to cease aggression. I don't think that would be an insurmountable problem."

14. We have said publicly and privately that we could stop the bombing of North Viet-Nam as a step toward peace although there has not been the slightest hint or suggestion from the other side as to what they would do if the bombing stopped.

ACKNOWLEDGMENTS

I would like to thank Staughton and Alice Lynd for generously offering their time for interviews, engaging in a detailed and rich email correspondence, and offering comments during the writing of the book. The Lynds' cooperation gave me an in-depth insight into their thinking and motivation during this tumultuous period in their lives.

The team at Haymarket books deserves a heap of gratitude as well. Anthony Arnove, Bill Roberts, and Eric Kerl immediately understood the significance of this project and provided the resources and know-how to get this book into your hands or screens. I would also like to thank Michael Trudeau, whose detailed and diligent copyediting and fact-checking helped produce the best book possible.

Without the help of Marcus Rediker and David McNally, this book would not have reached the Haymarket team.

I would also like to thank Carl Mirra, who provided invaluable moral support during the two-year period the book was being written. Mirra's biography of Lynd, *The Admirable Radical: Staughton Lynd and Cold War Dissent, 1945–1970*, should be read in conjunction with this book and was an important resource in helping to contextualize Lynd's life.

Jim O'Brien, Van Gosse, Marc Becker, and Andor Skotnes all provided important context for the founding of Historians against the War and Lynd's participation as a founding member of its steering committee.

While the Lynds immediately provided their permission to use their work for this project, I would like to especially thank the following people for providing the further necessary permission or help in obtaining permission: Patch Dellinger, Aron DiBacco, Barbara Webster, Chris Marino, Claire Desroches, Simone Bent, Troy Garity, Rowland Scherman, Patrick Warner, James Swarts, Kathleen Feeney, Christine Colburn, Melica Bloom, Lisa Marine, Caroline White, and Michael Cheng.

Finally, thank you to Ambre and Zoey for all your love and support during the making of this book. To the rest of my family in Canada, France, and the United States, thank you for the ongoing support and love.

NOTES

Foreword

1   Christian Appy, *American Reckoning: The Vietnam War and Our National Identity* (New York: Viking, 2015), 82.

2   See Alice Lynd, *We Won't Go: Personal Accounts of War Objectors* (Boston: Beacon Press, 1968), 95–107. David Mitchell died from Parkinson's disease on 1 July 2021.

3   See notes on the making of *We Won't Go*, Swarthmore Peace Collection, (A) box 10, 8; (B) box 1; and (C) box 8, letter from Alice Lynd to William G. Smith, 30 July 1969.

4   See Alice Lynd and Staughton Lynd, *Moral Injury and Nonviolent Resistance: Breaking the Cycle of Violence in the Military and Behind Bars* (Oakland, CA: PM Press, 2017). See also, by a journalist who spent more than thirty years covering the US military, embedding himself with the troops, David Wood, *What Have We Done: The Moral Injury of Our Longest Wars* (New York: Little, Brown, 2016), especially p. 186.

5   Jonathan Shay, *Achilles in Vietnam: Combat Trauma and the Undoing of Character* (New York: Scribner, 1994) and *Odysseus in America: Combat Trauma and the Trials of Homecoming* (New York: Scribner, 2002).

6   Shay, *Achilles in Vietnam*, pt. 1, chap. 1.

7   Shay, *Achilles in Vietnam*, 21.

8   Shay, *Achilles in Vietnam*, 9.

9   See Tod Ensign, "Who Serves?" in Mary Susannah Robbins, *Peace Not Terror: Leaders of the Antiwar Movement Speak Out against U.S. Foreign Policy Post 9/11* (Lanham, MD: Lexington Books, 2008), 109–30.

10 Camilo E. Mejía, "Healing Moral Injury: A Lifelong Journey," *Fellowship* 76 (Winter 2011): 25–27.

11 *New York Times,* 16 August 2016, A1.

12 See Alice Lynd and Staughton Lynd, eds., *Rank and File: Personal Histories by Working-Class Organizers*, expanded ed. (Chicago: Haymarket Books, 2011), 105–10 (John Sargent) and 356–65 (Ed Mann); see citations to George Skatzes in Staughton Lynd, *Lucasville: The Untold Story of a Prison Uprising*, 2nd ed. (Oakland: PM Press, 2011).

Introduction

1   During a Senate Foreign Relations Committee (SFRC) investigation of the Gulf of Tonkin incident in late 1967 and early 1968, it was revealed that the USS *Maddox* was in the Gulf aiding South Vietnamese offensive raids on two North Vietnamese islands as part of the Johnson administration's covert OPLAN 34-Alpha missions. This threw into question the "unprovoked attack" narrative and the whole rationale for US retaliatory

strikes. The subsequent release of the *Pentagon Papers* by Daniel Ellsberg in June 1971 provided more details on the role of the USS *Maddox* in the Gulf of Tonkin, beginning on July 31. In February 1964, President Johnson approved OPLAN 34-Alpha, which called for escalated and directed covert operations north of the seventeenth parallel and cross-border operations in Laos directed against the Ho Chi Minh Trail. The covert program increased surveillance of the North via air and sea (expanding naval intelligence operations known as DESOTO begun in 1962) as well as increased commando raids focusing on sabotaging DRV infrastructure. See the original *Pentagon Papers* released by the National Archives: *Report of the Office of the Secretary of Defense Vietnam Task Force*, pt. 4, C.2.a. (Evolution of the War, Direct Action: The Johnson Commitments, 1964–1968, Military Pressures against NVN, February–June 1964") and C.2.b. ("July–October 1964"). The first major scholarly account of the incident is Edwin Moïse's *Tonkin Gulf and the Escalation of the Vietnam War* (Chapel Hill: University of North Carolina Press, 1996). Moïse, after conducting extensive archival research and interviews with participants, concludes the alleged attack of August 4 did not occur and that nonetheless President Johnson acted believing it did and launched retaliatory strikes against North Vietnam.

In 2004 and 2005, a large trove of US government declassified documents concerning the incident were released by the National Security Archive, including an article by former National Security Administration (NSA) analyst and historian Robert J. Hanyok that concluded, on the basis of reviewing National Security Agency Signals Intelligence (SIGINT), that (1) "*no attack* happened that night. Through a compound of analytic errors and an unwillingness to consider contrary evidence, American SIGINT elements in the region and at NSA HQs reported Hanoi's plans to attack the two ships of the Desoto patrol" and (2) "SIGNIT information was presented in such a manner as to preclude responsible decisionmakers in the Johnson administration from having the complete and objective narrative of events of 4 August 1964" (Robert J. Hanyok, "Skunks, Bogies, Silent Hounds, and the Flying Fish: The Gulf of Tonkin Mystery, 2–4 August 1964," *Cryptologic Quarterly*, 2001, p. 3.) For the complete declassified documents, see John Prados, ed., *The Gulf of Tonkin Incident, 40 Years Later: Flawed Intelligence and the Decision for War in Vietnam*, National Security Archive Electronic Briefing Book No. 132, 4 August 2004 (updated 1 December 2005), available at https://nsarchive2.gwu.edu//NSAEBB/NSAEBB132/index.htm.

2   Bob Moses quoted in Howard Zinn, *Vietnam: The Logic of Withdrawal* (Boston: Beacon Press, 1967), 27. There is no contemporaneous account of Bob Moses's statement at the informal memorial service; however, it is corroborated by both Staughton Lynd and Howard Zinn. Lynd first paraphrased Moses's statement in a widely circulated August 1964 essay, "SNCC: The Beginning of Ideology," and then again in a book review essay, "Intruders in the Dust: To Plant the Seeds of Liberation in a Violent Land, They Marched—and Fell," *Sunday New York Herald-Tribune*, Book Week section, 16 May 1965. Lynd would also cite Moses in the introduction to his edited collection *Nonviolence in America: A Documentary History* (Indianapolis: Bobbs-Merrill, 1966), xliv. Zinn was the first to quote Moses directly. Moses would later speak at the first March on Washington on 17 April 1965 and the University at California Berkeley Teach-In, 21–22 May 1965, and he participated in the Assembly of Unrepresented People in Washington, DC, 6–9 August 1965, where he would be arrested alongside Staughton Lynd and Dave Dellinger. Moses's participation connected the struggle for civil rights for African Americans and the war in Vietnam.

3   "Leader of New Left Is a Quaker Teacher at Yale," *New York Times*, 28 December 1965, 10.

4   Staughton Lynd and Andrej Grubacic, *Wobblies and Zapatistas: Conversations on Anarchism, Marxism and Radical History* (Oakland: PM Press, 2008), 200.

5   "Lynd Denounced Policy of U.S. in Hanoi Speech," *New York Times*, 12 January 1966, 6; Kingman Brewster, "Statement to the NEWS," *Yale Daily News*, 19 January 1966; and, "FBIS 133, Lynd Speech, Hanoi VNA International Service in English," 11 January 1966, box 138, folder 12, Kingman Brewster Papers, Sterling Memorial Library Manuscripts and Archives, Yale University. I am grateful to Carl Mirra for providing me with the readout of Lynd's speech from Radio Hanoi that ended up in the hands of Kingman Brewster.

6   "Academic youth and scholars in focus of the Trotskyist and Communist Press in the U.S.A.," CIA file, 12 October 1965, MSS 395, box 4, folder 8; Subject: Staughton (Craig) LYND, 24 May 1967, CIA file, MSS 395, box 4, folder 9; and, "Biography of Staughton Lynd," CIA file, n.d., MSS 395, box 4, folder 10.

7   J. Edgar Hoover to SAC [Special Agent in Charge], New Haven, 27 August 1965, "Staughton Lynd," Federal Bureau of Investigation file no. 100-HQ-396916. Lynd was originally placed on the Reserve Index in the summer of 1962 as an academic and someone associated with communists. The Security Index identified Lynd as someone to be arrested and detained in the event of a national emergency. The first record in Lynd's FBI file is dated 2 December 1952 and spanned two decades. For more on the origins of the Security Index, see United States Senate, Senate Select Committee to Study Governmental Operations with Respect to Intelligence Activities, 1975–76 (Church Committee), Final Report, book III, *Supplementary Detailed Staff Reports on Intelligence Activities and the Rights of Americans*, 420–421.

8   "The Anti-Vietnam Agitation and the Teach-In Movement: The Problem of Communist Infiltration," a Staff Study Prepared for the Subcommittee to Investigate the Administration of the Internal Security Act and Other Internal Security Laws, Committee on the Judiciary, United States Senate, 89th Congress, 1st Session, 13 October 1965 (Washington, DC: US Government Printing Office, 1965), 75–76.

9   Staughton Lynd took part in heated debates about these two movement-building issues: exclusion of communists and Trotskyists from the antiwar coalition and coalition politics within the Democratic Party. In a series of exchanges, explored in chapter 2, "We Are Not at War with the People of Vietnam," this debate began in earnest in response to Bayard Rustin's essay "From Protest to Politics: The Future of the Civil Rights Movement," *Commentary* 39, no. 2 (February 1965): 25–31. Lynd made his views clear about these two key issues, first with Tom Hayden in "Reply: 'The New Radicalism: Sect or Action Movement?' By Herbert J. Gans," *Studies on the Left* 5, no. 3 (Summer 1965): 132–36, and then with "Coalition Politics or Nonviolent Revolution?" *Liberation* (June–July 1965): 18–21.

10   Arthur Schlesinger Jr., "A Middle Way Out of Vietnam," *New York Times Magazine*, 18 September 1966, 117.

11   John Whiteclay Chambers II, "Conscientious Objection and the American State from Colonial Times to the Present," in Charles C. Moskos and John Whiteclay Chambers II, eds., *The New Conscientious Objection: From Sacred to Secular Resistance* (New York: Oxford University Press, 1993), 41.

12   Robert Pickus, "Political Integrity and Its Critics," *Liberation* (June–July 1965): 36–40, 46. Lynd's response to Bayard Rustin engendered a number of critical responses in particular. See for instance, David McReynolds, "Transition: Personal and Political Notes," *Liberation* (August 1965): 5–11.

13   Quoted from Staughton Lynd, "Socialism, the Forbidden Word," *Studies on the Left* 3, no. 3 (Summer, 1963): 20.

14   Staughton Lynd, address at Morris Brown College Honors Day, 12 December 1963, ser. 2, box 6, folder 20, Staughton and Alice Lynd Collection, Kent State Special Collections and Archives, Kent State University.

15   Staughton Lynd, "The Responsibility of Radical Intellectuals," address to the New University Conference, University of Chicago, 22 March 1968, ser. 2, box 6, folder 20, Staughton and Alice Lynd Collection, Kent State Special Collections and Archives, Kent State University.

16   Lynd, "The Responsibility of Radical Intellectuals."

17   In 1995 and 2018 Staughton and Alice Lynd coedited the second and third editions of *Nonviolence in America*. Moreover, in 2009 Cambridge University Press republished Lynd's two classics: *Class Conflict, Slavery and the United States Constitution: Ten Essays* and *Intellectual Origins of American Radicalism*.

18   Lynd, "The Responsibility of Radical Intellectuals."

19   Lynd addressed these questions in various essays and articles during the period. See for instance, "Socialism, the Forbidden Word," *Studies on the Left* 3, no. 3 (Summer, 1963): 14–20; "The New Radicals and 'Participatory Democracy,'" *Dissent* 7, no. 3 (Summer 1965): 324–333; and, "The New Left," *The Annals of the American Academy of Political and Social Studies*, vol. 382, "Protest in the Sixties" (March 1969): 64–72.

20   John Corry, "'We Must Say Yes to Our Souls'—Staughton Lynd: Spokesman for the New Left," *New York Times Magazine*, 23 January 1966, 12.

21   In an interview I conducted with Staughton Lynd on 26 August 2009, he explicitly told me that being a Quaker was not his primary motivation for opposing the war in Vietnam. The Lynds discuss the influence of Quakerism on their lives in Alice Lynd and Staughton Lynd, *Stepping Stones: Memoir of a Life Together* (Lanham: Lexington Books, 2009); and Alice Lynd and Staughton Lynd, *Liberation Theology for Quakers*, Pendle Hill Pamphlet no. 326, April 1996, reproduced in Staughton Lynd, *Living inside Our Hope: A Steadfast Radical's Thoughts on Rebuilding the Movement* (Ithaca: Cornell University Press, 1997), 55–60. For Lynd's November 1967 comments, see Staughton Lynd, "The Vision of the New Radicalism," presented at the fall retreat of the Methodist Theological Fellowship at the University of Chicago, 3 November 1967, ser. 2, box 6, folder 20, Staughton and Alice Lynd Papers, Kent State Special Collections and Archives, Kent State University.

22   Ken Burns and Lynn Novick, *The Vietnam War*, PBS, 2017. As Maurice Isserman, historian of the Old and New Left and the 1960s, highlights, Burns and Novick's portrayal of the antiwar movement is "at best, inconsistent, at worst, intellectually lazy." Maurice Isserman, "Give Peace a Chance," *Dissent* 64, no.4 (Fall 2017): 6–11. See also Michael S. Foley, "There Is No Single Lie in War (Films): Ken Burns, Lynn Novick, and The Vietnam War," *The Sixties: A Journal of History, Politics and Culture* 11, no. 1 (2018): 93–104. Melvin Small estimates that six million Americans actively participated in the antiwar movement and another twenty-five million sympathized with it. *Antiwarriors: The Vietnam War and the Battle for America's Hearts and Minds* (Wilmington, DE: SR Books, 2002), 3.

Chapter 1: Declarations of Conscience

1   President Lyndon Johnson, address to the nation, 4 August 1964, available at https://millercenter.org/the-presidency/presidential-speeches/august-4–1964-report-gulf-tonkin-incident.

2   There were some twenty Yale students and recent graduates who participated in the Freedom Summer in Mississippi as volunteers. Philip A. McCombs, "Summer Project: Yale in Mississippi," *Yale Daily News*, 14 September 1964, 19. Not long into the beginning of his first semester at Yale, Lynd addressed the community at the law school

auditorium about his experiences in the South and of the civil rights movement. See
Philip A. McCombs, "Professor Staughton Lynd: A Plan for Freedom," *Yale Daily News*,
29 September 1964, 8.

3   William Sloane Coffin, Jr. *Once to Every Man: A Memoir* (New York: Atheneum, 1977),
       209.

4   Staughton Lynd's Speech to the *National Guardian* Dinner, 24 November 1964, ser. 2,
       box 6, folder 20, Kent State University Special Collections and Archives, Kent, Ohio.
       The reference refers to the murder of Kitty Genovese on 13 March 1964 while thirty-
       eight people watched and did not call the police. See Martin Gansberg, "37 Who Saw
       Murder Didn't Call the Police," *New York Times*, 27 March 1964, 1. Recent research has
       cast doubt on the so-called bystander effect in the Genovese case, citing at least three
       interventions by witnesses to the murder. See Saul M. Kassin, "The Killing of Kitty
       Genovese: What Else Does This Case Tell Us?" *Perspectives on Psychological Science* 12, no.
       3 (2017): 374–81.

5   For Lynd's trip to Selma and reading about the Pleiku attacks, see Alice Lynd and
       Staughton Lynd, *Stepping Stones*, 77. Lynd's participation in the discussions in Selma
       is recorded in "WATS Reports Sunday February 7, 1965," Mississippi Freedom
       Democratic Party Lauderdale County—Wide Area Telephone Service (WATS) Reports,
       February 1965, p. 1, Mississippi Freedom Democratic Party, Lauderdale County,
       Mississippi, records, 1964–1966; Wisconsin Historical Society Library Microforms
       Room, micro 55, reel 3, seg. 66, Wisconsin Historical Society, Madison. For more on
       US retaliation after Pleiku, see John Prados, *The Blood Road:* The Ho Chi Minh Trail and
       the Vietnam War (New York: John Wiley & Sons, 1999), 91–98. See also "Evolution of
       the War. ROLLING THUNDER Program Begins: January–June 1965, Part IV. C. 3.,"
       in Report of the Office of the Secretary of Defense Vietnam Task Force [the *Pentagon
       Papers*], 1–2, 23–31. Available from the National Archives Records Administration,
       https://www.archives.gov/research/pentagon-papers.

6   Boris M. Baczynskj, "Professors Condemn US Vietnam Policy: Critics Urge Withdrawal
       of Troops," *Yale Daily News*, 12 February 1965.

7   SAC [Special Agent in Charge], New Haven, to J. Edgar Hoover, 16 February 1965,
       Staughton Lynd FBI file.

8   "Aggression from the North: The Record of North Viet-Nam's Campaign to Conquer
       South Viet-Nam," Department of State Publication 7839, released February 1965
       (Washington, DC: US Government Printing Office, 1965), 29; and, "Legal Basis for
       United States Actions against North Vietnam," Department of State Memorandum, 8
       March 1965, folder 8, box 48, Douglas Pike Collection, unit 03, Legal and Legislative,
       the Vietnam Center and Archive, Texas Tech University, available at http://www.
       vietnam.ttu.edu/virtualarchive/items.php?item=2184808024.

9   "Legal Basis for United States Actions"; and, E. W. Kenworthy, "Rusk Says Peace of
       World Is Issue in Vietnam War," *New York Times*, 19 February 1966, 1.

10   The Geneva Accords of 1954 and the "Cessation of Hostilities" agreement are available
       online from the Yale Law School's Lillian Goldman Law Library's "The Avalon Project:
       Documents in Law, History and Diplomacy." See "Indochina—Final Declaration of the
       Geneva Conference on the Problem of Restoring Peace in Indo-China, July 21, 1954,"
       available at https://avalon.law.yale.edu/20th_century/inch005.asp; and, "Indochina—
       Agreement on the Cessation of Hostilities in Viet-Nam, July 20, 1954," available at
       https://avalon.law.yale.edu/20th_century/inch001.asp.

11   These details are discussed at length in Fredrik Logevall's *Embers of War*, pts. V and VII.
       See also John Prados, *Vietnam: The History of an Unwinnable War, 1945–1975* (Lawrence:

University Press of Kansas, 2009), 26–61; Robert D. Schulzinger, *A Time for War*, chap. 4; Marilyn B. Young, *The Vietnam Wars*, chaps. 3 and 4. For an excellent account from the Vietnamese perspective, see Pierre Asselin, *Hanoi's Road to the Vietnam War*.

12   The Lynds' letter to the IRS, dated 9 April 1965, quoted in Edward Jasek, "Yale Prof Rejects Added Tax Payment," *New Haven Register,* 15 April 1965. For more on the Yale antiwar rally, see "Lynd Tells Marchers He Won't Pay Taxes," *Yale Daily News*, 15 April 1965; and, John Rothchild, "Lynd's Tax Protest: 'I Feel This War Is Evil,'" *Yale Daily News*, 16 April 1965.

13   Bayard Rustin, A. J. Muste, Norman Thomas, et al., "Statement on the Student March on Washington," 16 April 1965, micro 44, reel 2, seg. 31b, WIHVM4340-A, Lucile Montgomery Papers, 1963–1967, Historical Society Library Microforms Room, Wisconsin Historical Society, Madison. William Sloane Coffin Jr. argued that despite his reservations, the speakers, including Staughton Lynd, were "excellent." Coffin, *Once to Every Man: A Memoir* (New York: Atheneum, 1977), 211–12. For Muste distancing himself from the April 16 statement, he wrote to Staughton Lynd and included a letter to I. F. Stone. A. J. Muste to Staughton Lynd, 20 April 1965; and, A. J. Muste to I. F. Stone, 20 April 1965, ser. 2, box 6, folder 14, Staughton and Alice Lynd Collection, Kent State University Special Collections and Archives, Kent, Ohio.

14   Staughton Lynd interview with the editor, 26 August 2009. For SDS's decision-making in this period, see Kirkpatrick Sale, *SDS* (New York: Random House, 1973), 138–42, 169–99.

15   SAC Los Angeles to J. Edgar Hoover, 4 June 1965; SAC San Francisco to J. Edgar Hoover, 8 June 1965; SAC San Francisco, Memorandum to Department of Justice, 8 June 1965; SAC Washington, DC, to J. Edgar Hoover, 16 June 1965; SAC Washington, DC, to J. Edgar Hoover, 17 June 1965; Los Angeles Field Office to J. Edgar Hoover, 20 June 1965; Informative Note, Domestic Intelligence Division, 1 July 1965; Los Angeles Field Office, Memorandum to Department of Justice, 1 July 1965; and, New Haven Field Office, Intelligence Report, 10 August 1965. All contained in Staughton Lynd's FBI file.

16   The origins of the declaration are presented in *The Committee for Nonviolent Action Bulletin*, 25 January 1965, 1–4, and *WRL News*, January–February 1965, 1.

17   Staughton Lynd and Alice Lynd, eds., *Nonviolence in America*, 269–70.

18   *Yale Daily News* featured extensive coverage, editorial comment, and letters to the editor about the rallies and protests at Yale and in New Haven in its 11, 12, 15, 16 and 18 February 1965 editions of the paper.

19   Lyndon Johnson, "Peace without Conquest," 7 April 1965. Available at https://millercenter.org/the-presidency/presidential-speeches/april-7-1965-address-johns-hopkins-university.

20   For full coverage of the March on Washington, see the *National Guardian*, 24 April 1965.

21   Tom Wells, *The War Within: America's Battle over Vietnam* (New York: Henry Holt, 1996), 23–26.

22   Statement of Robert A. Scalapino, *San Francisco Chronicle*, 21 May 1965, reproduced in "The Anti-Vietnam Agitation and the Teach-In Movement: The Problem of Communist Infiltration," *A Staff Study Prepared for the Subcommittee to Investigate the Administration of the Internal Security Act and Other Internal Security Laws, Committee on the Judiciary*, United States Senate, 89th Congress, 1st Session, 13 October 1965 (Washington, DC: US Government Printing Office, 1965), 25. There is a further exchange between Lynd and Scalapino concerning the nature of the Vietnam War and of the use of terrorism by the National Liberation Front of South Vietnam. Robert Scalapino to Staughton Lynd, 27

May 1965; Staughton Lynd to Robert Scalapino, 3 June 1965; and Robert Scalapino to Staughton Lynd, 23 June 1965, ser. 2, box 6, folder 10, Staughton and Alice Lynd Collection, Kent State University Special Collections and Archives, Kent, Ohio.

Chapter 2: We Are Not at War
with the People of Vietnam

1   "National Antiwar Activity," *Vietnam Day Committee News* 1, no. 1 (June 22–30, 1965): 2.

2   The CNVA's callout for its conference at the White House was printed in the *Committee for Nonviolent Action Bulletin* 5, no. 4 (9 July 1965).

3   Alice Lynd and Staughton Lynd, *Stepping Stones*, 79.

4   The Speak-Out at the Pentagon is given wide coverage in the Committee for Nonviolent Action's *Bulletin* 5, no. 4 (9 July 1965) and the War Resisters League's newsletter, *WRL News*, no. 132 (July–August 1965): 1–2.

5   Paul Goodman, "The Ballad of the Pentagon," in *Collected Poems* (New York: Random House, 1975), 180–181.

6   A. J. Muste to Lucy Montgomery, 28 June 1965, micro 44, reel 2, seg. 31b, WIHVM4340-A, Lucile Montgomery Papers, 1963–1967, Historical Society Library Microforms Room, Wisconsin Historical Society, Madison.

7   Walter Tillow et al., "An idea for a project based in Wash., D. C. this summer," in *Staff Newsletter*, 17 July 1965. Lynd helped to circulate the proposal.

8   Lyndon B. Johnson, "The President's News Conference," 28 July 1965. Available at https://millercenter.org/the-presidency/presidential-speeches/july-28-1965-press-conference.

9   John Prados, *Vietnam*, 151–52.

10 "Protests on Principle and Some Practical Options," *Life*, 20 August 1965, 30–31.

11 Douglas Robinson, "Induction Center Picketed by 400," *New York Times*, 30 July 1965, 2. House Resolution 10306 passed in the House of Representatives on 10 August 1965 (*Congressional Record*, 19871–19872) and S. 2381 passed in the Senate on 13 August 1965 (*Congressional Record*, 20433–20434). The president signed the bill into law (Public Law 89–152) on 30 August 1965.

12 Document 29: "Stop the Troop Train!" collected 13 August 1965 at the University of California at Berkeley, in G. Louis Heath, ed., *Mutiny Does Not Happen Lightly: The Literature of the American Resistance to the Vietnam War* (Metuchen, NJ: Scarecrow Press, 1976), 121.

13 John R. Murphy and Robert J. Hayes, "'Traitor' Cry Greets Speakers," *Philadelphia Inquirer*, 16 October 1965, 1; and "Hell's Angels Attack March—Officer Hurt," *Oakland Sunday Tribune*, 17 October 1965, 1.

14 For an extensive discussion of the October 1965 events, see Tom Wells, *The War Within*, 51–58.

15 "Vietnam Protesters Plan Drive to Avoid the Draft," *New York Times*, 18 October 1965, 9.

16 Robert B. Semple Jr., "Johnson Decries Draft Protests: Presses Inquiry," *New York Times*, 19 October 1965, 1.

17 Quoted in the *Congressional Record*, 18 October 1965 (Washington, DC: United States Government Printing Office, 1965), 26292–93.

18 Dodd quoted in William Chapman, "Students to Continue Anti-Draft Crusade," *Washington Post*, 21 October 1965, A9.

19 "19 November 1966, Communists and Demonstrations," in *The Gallup Poll: Public Opinion 1935–1971, Vol. III, 1959–1971* (New York: Random House, 1972), 1971.

20   "A Priest Tells How Our Bombers Razed His Church and Killed His People," *I. F. Stone's Weekly*, 1 November 1965, 3.

21   For more on Norman Morrison's self-immolation, see Anne Morrison Welsh, *Held in the Light: Norman Morrison's Sacrifice for Peace and His Family's Journey of Healing* (Maryknoll, NY: Orbis Books, 2008); Sallie B. King, "They Who Burned Themselves for Peace: Quaker and Buddhist Self-Immolators during the Vietnam War," *Buddhist-Christian Studies* 20 (2000): 127–50; Nicholas Patler, "Norman's Triumph: The Transcendent Language of Self-Immolation," *Quaker History* 104, no. 2 (2015): 18–39. For the effects on Robert S. McNamara, see Robert S. McNamara with Brian VanDeMark, *In Retrospect: the Tragedy and Lessons of Vietnam* (New York: Times Books, 1995), 216–17; Deborah Shapley, *Promise and Power: the Life and Times of Robert McNamara* (Boston: Little, Brown, 1993), 353–55; and Paul Hendrickson, *The Living and the Dead: Robert McNamara and Five Lives of a Lost War* (New York: Alfred A. Knopf, 1996), 187–240. For more on Staughton Lynd and the Vietnamese response to Norman Morrison, see chapter 3.

22   Alice Lynd and Staughton Lynd, *Stepping Stones*, 85; and Alice Lynd, "Accompanying War Objectors," in Staughton Lynd, *Accompanying: Pathways to Social Change* (Oakland: PM Press, 2012), 72.

23   Reproduced with permission from Bruce Hartford, Civil Rights Movement Archive, www.crmvet.org.

24   Bayard Rustin, "From Protest to Politics: The Future of the Civil Rights Movement," *Commentary* 39, no. 2 (February 1965): 29.

25   Bayard Rustin et al., "Statement on the Student March on Washington," 16 April 1965.

26   In response to Lynd's article, see David McReynolds's lengthy response, "Transition: Personal and Political Notes," *Liberation* (5–10 August 1965): 39. Tom Kahn, longtime confidant of Rustin, circulated a letter that garnered the signatures of Norman Thomas, Michael Harrington, Irving Howe, and many others that was published in *Liberation*, October 1965, p. 29. Lynd was given space in the same edition to respond. Rustin chose to respond to Lynd in "The New Radicalism: Round III," *Partisan Review* 32, no. 4 (Fall 1965): 526–42.

27   For *Viet-Report*'s distribution, see John Corry, "Yale Professor Is Visiting Hanoi," *New York Times*, 28 December 1965, 1.

28   "Toward Vietnam Talks," *New York Times*, 25 August 1965, 38.

29   "4,000 at Teach-In Laud U.S. Pacifist," *Globe and Mail*, 11 October 1965, 13; "Audience of 1,000,000 for Teach-In Session," *Globe and Mail*, 11 October 1965, 13; and "Million Hear of U of T Teach-In," *Varsity*, 12 October 1965, 1.

30   Selections from the teach-in were later published in the book *Revolution and Response: Selections from the Toronto International Teach-In* (Toronto: McClelland & Steward, 1966).

31   "The Vietnam Protest," *New York Review of Books*, 25 November 1965. The authors and credentials as presented: Irving Howe, *Editor of Dissent*; Michael Harrington, Chairman of Board, League for Industrial Democracy; Bayard Rustin, A. Philip Randolph Institute; Lewis Coser, Executive Committee, PAX; Penn Kemble, Chairman, New York Students for a Democratic Society.

32   See the full-page spread: "March on Washington for Peace in Vietnam: A Call to Mobilize the Conscience of America," *New York Times*, 23 November 1965, 28–29.

33   John D. Morris, "March in Capital Selects Slogans," *New York Times*, 24 November 1965, 14.

Chapter 3: To Hanoi and Back

1   Herbert Aptheker describes the origins of the trip and his invitation to Lynd in his book *Mission to Hanoi* (New York: International Publishers, 1966), 12. He also relayed these details, plus new information, in an interview with James Clinton, in which he disclosed that Lynd first asked Bob Moses, who declined the invitation. See Herbert Aptheker interview with James W. Clinton, *The Loyal Opposition: Americans in North Vietnam, 1965–1972* (Boulder: University Press of Colorado, 1995), 13–14. Staughton Lynd clarified that he first asked Bob Moses, who then conferred with SNCC about the trip. By then, SNCC was already facing accusations of communist infiltration and manipulation. Moreover, Moses told Lynd that SNCC was in the process of writing a statement against the draft and Julian Bond was running for election in the Georgia legislature. For these reasons, Moses had to refuse to go with Lynd and Aptheker. See Alice Lynd and Staughton Lynd, *Stepping Stones*, 80. Lynd also clarified these details in an interview with the editor, 26 August 2009, and in an email to editor, 24 April 2020.

2   Dennis T. Jaffe, "Socialist Symposium Airs Divergent Views," *Yale Daily News*, 3 May 1965, 1, 5.

3   There is an excellent and growing body of scholarship on Vietnamese "people's diplomacy" during the Vietnam War. In particular, see Harish C. Mehta, *People's Diplomacy of Vietnam: Soft Power in the Resistance War* (Newcastle upon Tyne: Cambridge Scholars, 2019); Jessica M. Frazier, *Women's Antiwar Diplomacy during the Vietnam War Era* (Chapel Hill: University of North Carolina Press, 2017); Lien-Hang T. Nguyen, "Revolutionary Circuits: Toward Internationalizing America in the World," *Diplomatic History* 39, no. 3 (June 2015): 411–22; Judy Tzu-Chun Wu, *Radicals on the Road: Internationalism, Orientalism, and Feminism during the Vietnam Era* (Cornell University Press, 2013); and Mary Hershberger, *Traveling to Vietnam: American Peace Activists and the War* (Syracuse University Press, 1998).

4   Report, Lynd FBI file, 17 February 1966.

5   On 14 December 1965, Fay Aptheker's coworker at the Consolidated Tours company "secured the flight information from Fay Aptheker without her knowledge or consent." Brand Alvey to John H. Davitt, 8 February 1966, Staughton Lynd's Department of Justice (DoJ) file 146-1-19-117, sec. 1, 8-14-63 to 2-8-66, RG 60 General Records of the Department of Justice, National Archives and Records Administration II (NARA II), College Park, Maryland.

6   J. Walter Yeagley to Robert F. Kennedy, 17 February 1966, Staughton Lynd's DoJ file 146-1-19-117, sec. 1, 8-14-63 to 2-8-66, RG 60 General Records of the Department of Justice, NARA II, College Park, Maryland.

7   Abba P. Schwartz to Staughton Lynd, 2 February 1966, Lynd's DoJ file 146-1-19-117, sec. 2, 2-9-66 to 4-12-66, RG 60 General Records of the Department of Justice, NARA II, College Park, Maryland.

8   I could find no single memorandum summarizing the failure to indict Lynd. This information is pulled together from two FBI memorandums: F. J. Baumgardner to W. C. Sullivan, 15 March 1966; and F. J. Baumgardner to W. C. Sullivan, 21 March 1966, Lynd FBI file. These materials from the Department of Justice: J. Walter Yeagley to Bob Wilson, 3 June 1966; J. Walter Yeagley to Robert L. Funk, 28 April 1966; and J. Walter Yeagley to Abraham A. Ribicoff, 9 June 1966, Staughton Lynd's DoJ file 146-1-19-117, sec. 1, 8-14-63 to 2-8-66, RG 60 General Records of the Department of Justice, NARA II, College Park, Maryland.

9   "Lynd Denounced Policy of U.S. in Hanoi Speech," *New York Times*, 12 January 1966, 6; Kingman Brewster, "Statement to the NEWS," *Yale Daily News*, 19 January 1966;

Staughton Lynd in an email to editor clarified that North Vietnam released a text of Lynd's speech without his permission. Staughton Lynd email to editor, 21 April 2020. Carl Mirra discusses the Yale history department denying Lynd tenure in great detail and concludes, "Lynd was denied appointment at five Illinois colleges in 1967–1968 and at anywhere from three to five colleges in Indiana in 1970–71. As Alfred F. Young puts it, 'Lynd was blacklisted'" (Mirra, *The Admirable Radical: Staughton Lynd and Cold War Dissent, 1945–1970* [Kent: Kent State University Press, 2010], 139).

10   English-language scholars have begun using an array of Vietnamese archival sources. See for instance: Pierre Asselin, *Vietnam's American War: A History* (Cambridge: Cambridge University Press, 2018); Lien-Hang T. Nguyen, *Hanoi's War: An International History of the War for Peace in Vietnam* (Chapel Hill: University of North Carolina Press, 2016); Pierre Asselin, "'We Don't Want a Munich': Hanoi's Diplomatic Strategy, 1965–1968," *Diplomatic History* 36, no. 3 (June 2012): 547–81; Pierre Asselin, *A Bitter Peace: Washington, Hanoi, and the Making of the Paris Agreement* (Chapel Hill: University of North Carolina Press, 2002); Robert S. McNamara, James G. Blight, and Robert K. Brigham, *Argument without End: In Search of Answers to the Vietnam Tragedy* (New York: Public Affairs, 1999); Robert K. Brigham, *Guerrilla Diplomacy: the NLF's Foreign Relations and the Vietnam War* (Ithaca, NY: Cornell University Press, 1998). To be sure, there are many other excellent works that have used Vietnamese archival sources; these are the significant contributions dealing with Vietnamese diplomacy.

11   Quoted in Staughton Lynd and Tom Hayden, *The Other Side* (New York: New American Library, 1966), 111.

12   Arthur Schlesinger Jr., "A Middle Way out of Vietnam," *New York Times Sunday Magazine*, 18 September 1966, 117.

13   James Hershberg, *Marigold: The Lost Chance for Peace in Vietnam* (Washington, DC: Woodrow Wilson Center Press / Stanford: Stanford University Press, 2012); Lloyd C. Gardner and Ted Gittinger, *The Search for Peace in Vietnam, 1964–1968* (College Station: Texas A&M University Press, 2004); George C. Herring, "Fighting Without Allies: The International Dimensions of America's Failure in Vietnam," in Marc Jason Gilbert, ed., *Why the North Won the Vietnam War* (New York: Palgrave, 2002), 77–96; McNamara, Blight, and Brigham, *Argument without End*; George C. Herring, *LBJ and Vietnam: A Different Kind of War* (Austin: University of Texas Press, 1994); George C. Herring, *The Secret Diplomacy of the Vietnam War: The Negotiating Volumes of the Pentagon Papers* (Austin: University of Texas Press, 1983); Wallace J. Thies, *When Governments Collide: Coercion and Diplomacy in the Vietnam Conflict, 1964–1968* (Berkeley: University of California Press, 1979); and David Kraslow and Stuart Loory, *The Secret Search for Peace in Vietnam* (New York: Random House, 1968).

14   Robert McNamara was speaking at a meeting of the president's principal foreign policy advisers discussing the merits of a second bombing pause and launching the first "Peace Offensive." Notes of Meeting, 18 December 1965, Meeting Notes file, box 1, folder December 18, 1965—12:35 p.m. Meeting with Foreign Policy Advisors on Bombing Pause, Lyndon Baines Johnson Presidential Library (LBJPL).

15   Dean Rusk, "The Heart of the Matter in Viet-Nam," 27 December 1965, Foreign Relations of the United States (FRUS), 1964–1968, Volume III, Vietnam, June–December 1965, Document 247. For an excellent discussion of the Fourteen Points between US and Vietnamese policy-makers in 1997, see Robert S. McNamara, James G. Blight, and Robert K. Brigham, *Argument without End: In Search of Answers to the Vietnam Tragedy* (New York: Public Affairs, 1999), 232–239.

16   These points were made in a twenty-nine-page memorandum written by William P. Bundy, Assistant Secretary of State for Far Eastern Affairs, summarizing negotiations

up until that point. Bundy writes, "Every negotiating action must be considered in relation to its effect on the morale of the government and people in South Vietnam." Moreover, the Ky government in South Vietnam publicly and privately explained to the US government that any recognition of the NLF "would not only weaken morale but open the government to charges of neutralism that could well lead to its overthrow. This sensitivity would apply almost equally to any US recognition of the NLF as an independent party, or to any belief that the US was dealing in any way with the NLF." William P. Bundy, "Memorandum: Negotiating and International Actions Concerning Vietnam," 24 July 1965, National Security file, country file, Vietnam, box 192, LBJPL.

17   Documents relating to the XYZ Channel are available in "Report of the Office of the Secretary of Defense Vietnam Task Force [the Pentagon Papers]," pt. 6-C-1, Settlement of the Conflict, History of Contacts, Negotiations, 1965–1966: (4) XYZ (US Contacts with Mai Van Bo in Paris), 19 May 1965–6 May 1966, 69–107.

18   John Prados, *Vietnam*, 135, 146, 151–52.

19   Robert S. McNamara to Lyndon Johnson, 30 November 1965, Document 112, *Foreign Relations of the United States, 1964–1968, Volume III, Vietnam, June–December 1965*, 591–592.

20   Eric Sevareid, "The Final Troubled Hours of Adlai Stevenson," *Look*, 30 November 1965, 81–86.

21   U Thant quoted in Thomas J. Hamilton, "Thant Asks Vietnam Talks Leading to a U.S. Pullout," *New York Times*, 25 February 1965, 1. The affair, beginning on August 6, 1964, during the height of the Gulf of Tonkin controversy, is described in Bernard J. Firestone, "Failed Mediation: U Thant, the Johnson Administration, and the Vietnam War," *Diplomatic History* 37; no. 5 (2013): 1060–1089. See also U Thant, *View From the UN* (Garden City: Doubleday & Company, Inc., 1977), Chapter V.

22   "Statement Concerning 1964 Peace Overtures," in: "Report of the Office of the Secretary of Defense Vietnam Task Force [the *Pentagon Papers*]," pt. 6-B, Settlement of the Conflict, Negotiations, 1965–1967: Announced Position Statements, 24–26.

23   Staughton Lynd and Tom Hayden, *The Other Side* (New York: The New American Library, Inc., 1966), 110.

24   John Corry, "Yale Professor is Visiting Hanoi," *New York Times*, 28 December 1965, 1.

25   Luke Stewart, "The Unauthorized Diplomat: Staughton Lynd, Vietnam War Diplomacy, and a Missed 'Missed Opportunity' in the Peace Offensive, December 1965-January 1966," *Rising Asia Journal 2, no. 1* (January 2022): 60–121.

26   "Johnson Prodded on Peace By Lynd," *New York Times*, 25 January 1966, 4; and "Lynd Urges Talks with Viet 'Front,'" *Washington Post*, 25 January 1966, 7.

27   Jack Valenti to Lyndon Johnson, 25 January 1966, *FRUS, 1964–1968, Volume IV, Vietnam, 1966*, Document 42.

28   Staughton Lynd and Tom Hayden, *The Other Side* (New York: New American Library, 1966), 129. The full unofficial and official transcript are reprinted on pages 126–34.

29   Paul Montgomery, "Vietnam Debated by Intellectuals," *New York Times*, 16 January 1966, 5. An abridged transcript of the debate is available: "A Talk-In on Vietnam," *New York Times Sunday Magazine*, 6 February 1966, 12, 72, 74–76. The Fifth Avenue Peace Parade Committee event at the Manhattan Center was organized by A. J. Muste with Lynd, Aptheker, and Hayden while they were still in Hanoi via Western Union telegram. Staughton Lynd, Herbert Aptheker, and Tom Hayden to A. J. Muste, 1 January 1966; and, Lynd to Muste, 6 January 1966, A. J. Muste Papers, box 45, micro reel 89:25, Swarthmore College Peace Collection, Swarthmore, Pennsylvania.

30 "Lynd to Report on Trip Monday at Woolsey Hall," *Yale Daily News*, 11 January 1966; and Strobe Talbott, "Lynd Reports from Hanoi; Encourages Hope for Peace," *Yale Daily News*, 19 January 1966.

31 Report, Lynd FBI file, 25 January 1966.

32 J. Edgar Hoover to SAC, Washington Field Office, 16 March 1966; and J. Edgard Hoover to J. Walter Yeagley, 28 March 1966, Lynd FBI file.

33 "Lynd's Passport Cancelled by U.S.," *New York Times*, 6 February 1965, 7.

Chapter 4: What Would Victory Be?

1 A sortie is one airplane, and the numbers listed here are only those planes that dropped bombs. The numbers for South Vietnam in 1965 come only from the US Air Force, while the rest of the figures for both South and North Vietnam include statistics from the Air Force, Navy, and Marine Corps. See John Prados, *Vietnam*, 154–55; John Schlight, *The War in South Vietnam: The Years of the Offensive, 1965–1968* (Washington, DC: Air Force History and Museum Program, 1999); Richard P. Hallion, *Rolling Thunder, 1965–1968: Johnson's Air War over Vietnam* (Oxford: Osprey Publishing, 2018); John T. Correll, "The Vietnam War Almanac," *Air Force Magazine*, September 2004, 51; Mark Clodfelter, *The Limits of Air Power: The American Bombing of North Vietnam* (New York: Free Press, 1989), 129.

2 The origin of the enclave strategy at the time was credited to retired lieutenant general James Gavin's *Harper's Monthly* article in February 1966. However, the idea was first proposed by Hans Morgenthau Jr. in the summer of 1965. See Louis B. Zimmer, *The Vietnam War Debate: Hans J. Morgenthau and the Attempt to Halt the Drift into Disaster* (Plymouth, UK: Lexington Books, 2011), 248 and especially chapter 6 for a full discussion. For senators who supported the enclave strategy as well as George Kennan, see E. W. Kenworthy, "Senate Panel Will Conduct Broad Inquiry on Vietnam," *New York Times*, 4 February 1966, 1; and, "The Dispute," *New York Times*, 13 February 1966, 165.

3 "How the American Left Can Change the System: Text of Address at 26 March Demonstration of Protest against the War," ser. 2, box 6, folder 42, Staughton Lynd Papers, Special Collections, Kent State, Ohio.

4 "Statement by the Student Nonviolent Coordinating Committee on the War in Vietnam," 6 January 1966. For a detailed discussion on the release of the statement and the fallout, see Clayborne Carson, *In Struggle: SNCC and the Black Awakening of the 1960s* (Cambridge, MA: Harvard University Press, 1981), chap. 12. SNCC's opposition to the draft and the Vietnam War will be discussed in chapter 6 of this collection.

5 Mitchell K. Hall, *Because of Their Faith: CALCAV and Religious Opposition to the Vietnam War* (New York: Columbia University Press, 1990), 20–25.

6 Donald Duncan, "The Whole Thing Was a Lie!" *Ramparts*, February 1966, 12–24. See also: Luke Stewart, "'I Quit!': The Vietnam War and the Early Antiwar Activism of Master Sergeant Donald Duncan," *Revue française d'études américaines* 2, no. 147 (2016): 100–116.

7 Files dated from 9 December 1965 to 16 March 1966, Donald Duncan, FBI file no. 100-56090 (San Francisco) and no. 100-74878 (Los Angeles).

8 "Transcript of a speech given by Professor Staughton Lynd, Yale University, at Carleton University, Ottawa, Canada," Lynd FBI file.

9 Veterans for Peace in Vietnam, paid advertisement, *Chicago Daily Defender*, 22 March 1966, 9.

10 Felix Belair Jr., "Senators Challenge Rusk on Vietnam Policy Legality," *New York Times*, 29 January 1966, 1; and E. W. Kenworthy, "Morse Is Seeking Shift on Vietnam," *New York Times*, 30 January 1966, 1.

11   E. W. Kenworthy, "Senate Panel Will Conduct Broad Inquiry on Vietnam," *New York Times*, 4 February 1966, 1. For a full transcript of the hearings, see Hearings before the Committee on Foreign Relations, United States Senate, 89th Congress, Second Session on S. 2793 to Amend further the Foreign Assistance Act of 1961, as Amended, January 28; February 4, 8, 10, 17, and 18, 1966 (Washington, DC: United States Government Printing Office, 1966).

12   Johnson even resorted to calling Frank Stanton, president of CBS, to convince him not to cover the hearings. Instead of airing George Kennan's testimony, CBS played reruns of *I Love Lucy*. Johnson also had J. Edgar Hoover place members of the Senate Foreign Relations Committee under surveillance to see if they were influenced by Russian diplomats in Washington. For President Johnson's reaction to the Fulbright hearings, see Randall Bennett Woods, *J. William Fulbright, Vietnam, and the Search for a Cold War Foreign Policy* (Cambridge, UK: Cambridge University Press, 1998), 115–20; and Melvin Small, *Johnson, Nixon, and the Doves* (New Brunswick, NJ: Rutgers University Press, 1988), 78–80.

13   "The Declaration of Honolulu," 8 February 1966, doc. 55, *Public Papers of the Presidents of the United States, Lyndon B. Johnson, Containing the Public Messages, Speeches, and Statements of the President, 1966, Book I—January 1 to June 30, 1966* (Washington, DC: United States Government Printing Office, 1967), 153–55.

14   DRV Aide-Mémoire, 19 February 1966, quoted in Byroade to Rusk, 21 February 1966, in *Pentagon Papers*, 146.

15   Tom Wicker, "Key Senators Ask That U.S. Continue Pause in Bombing," *New York Times*, 25 January 1966, 1.

16   E. W. Kenworthy, "Kennedy Bids U.S. Offer Vietcong a Role in Saigon," *New York Times*, 20 February 1966, 1; and E. W. Kenworthy, "Fulbright Backs Kennedy on Role for the Vietcong," *New York Times*, 21 February 1966, 1.

17   Carl Mirra, *Admirable Radical*, 136.

18   Charles DeBenedetti and Charles Chatfield, *An American Ordeal: The Antiwar Movement of the Vietnam Era* (Syracuse: Syracuse University Press, 1990), 149–150.

19   Press Release No. 227, Yale University News Bureau, Kingman Brewster Statement, 19 January 1966, Lynd FBI file. Brewster's statement appears in Lynd's FBI file as it was shared by an unnamed U.S. citizen who complained to Kingman Brewster about Lynd and William Sloane Coffin being "un-American," "traitors," and "dangerous Reds."

20   "Easter Monday Rally, Trafalgar Square 3 p.m.," *Sanity: Voice of CND*, April 1966, 12.

21   F. J. Baumgardner to W. C. Sullivan, 24 March 1966; F. J. Baumgardner to W. C. Sullivan, 5 April 1966; Memorandum for the Record, 21 April 1966; Legat, London, to J. Edgar Hoover, 25 May 1966, Lynd FBI file.

Chapter 5: Treason?

1   The first report on Staughton Lynd highlights: "Basis for this investigation is an allegation made on April 19 and April, 30, 1952 by Boston Confidential Informant T-1, of unknown reliability, a recent graduate of Harvard College, that STAUGHTON CRAIG LYND during his years of attendance at Harvard College was a member of the Harvard Chapter of the American Youth for Democracy; was a member of the John Reed Society of Harvard and was believed by T-1 to have been a member of the Communist Party." Intelligence Report, 2 December 1952, Staughton Lynd FBI file no. 100-HQ-396916.

2   Lynd talks about his first memories of a possible US intervention in Vietnam in *The Other Side* (New York: The New American Library, 1966), 2. The reasons for Lynd's

undesirable discharge are outlined in the FBI report, 31 January 1955, Staughton Lynd FBI file. Lynd's journey in the US Army is retold in Carl Mirra, *Admirable Radical*, 22–29.

3   Ellen W. Schrecker, *Many Are the Crimes: McCarthyism in America* (New York: Little, Brown and Company, 1998), 203.

4   Individual / Lynd, Staughton, 1961–1970, RG 233 Records of the US House of Representatives, Un-American Activities Committee (H.U.A.C.), Files and Reference section, Individual Name files, box 205, 9E3/2/16/5; and Staughton Lynd Name file, RG 46 Records of the US Senate Internal Security Subcommittee (S.I.S.S.), Name files, ser. 1, box 64, 8E12a/8/2/4 and ser. 2, box 64, 8E2a/5/2/4. Both records at National Archives and Records Administration I, Washington, DC.

5   *Congressional Record—Senate*, 20 January 1966, 720–21.

6   Mirra, *Admirable Radical*, 115. Staughton Lynd CIA file, Staughton and Alice Lynd Collection, State Historical Society of Wisconsin Archives, MSS 345, box 4, folders 8–10, Madison.

7   Kingman Brewster to Staughton Lynd, 2 June 1965; and Staughton Lynd to Kingman Brewster, 4 June 1965, box 24, folder 1, M91-219, Staughton Lynd Papers, Wisconsin Historical Society, Division of Library, Archives, and Museum Collections, Madison.

8   David L. Schalk, *War and the Ivory Tower: Algeria and Vietnam* (Oxford, UK: Oxford University Press, 1991), 18. Legal scholar Robert Strassfeld also makes this point in relation to Dr. Howard Levy, an army doctor who refused to train Green Beret medical aidmen for counterinsurgency operations. Strassfeld argued: "Nuremberg carried with it connotations of Nazis and Nazi atrocities and in so doing set too high a threshold. Certainly few Americans could accept an analogy likening U.S. behavior to the Nazis. Indeed, Americans would find it hard to believe that we could be capable of atrocities of any sort." Robert N. Strassfeld, "The Vietnam War on Trial: The Court-Martial of Dr. Howard Levy," *Wisconsin Law Review* 839 (1994): 923. For a discussion of the concept of aggression and its use by US officials, see Christian G. Appy, *American Reckoning: The Vietnam War and Our National Identity* (New York: Viking, 2015), chap. 2, "Aggression."

9   Mirra, *Admirable Radical*, chap. 6, "Blacklisted."

10   John Morton Blum to George May and Henry Chauncey Jr., 15 April 1966, Kingman Brewster, President of Yale University Records, RU 11, ser. I, box 138, folder 12. See also John Morton Blum, *A Life with History* (University of Kansas Press, 2004), 183–84; and Mirra, *Admirable Radical*, 131–32.

11   William Sloane Coffin to Kingman Brewster, 5 May 1966; and Kingman Brewster to William Sloane Coffin, 9 May 1966, Kingman Brewster, President of Yale University Records, RU 11, ser. I, box 139, folder 7.

12   Independent Group of Yale Alumni to Kingman Brewster, 15 June 1966, as quoted in Geoffrey Kabaservice, *The Guardians: Kingman Brewster, His Circle, and the Rise of the Liberal Establishment* (New York: Henry Holt, 2004), 257.

13   Special agent in charge (SAC), New York, US Government Memorandum, to FBI director J. Edgar Hoover, 28 October 1966, Lynd FBI file.

14   Legat, Ottawa, to J. Edgar Hoover, 4 March 1966 and 18 March 1966, Lynd FBI file.

15   Ellen W. Schrecker, *No Ivory Tower: McCarthyism and the Universities* (Oxford, UK: Oxford University Press, 1986), 257–58.

16   Victor H. Asche interview with Averell Harriman, "Harriman, Bush Support LBJ in Vietnam," *Yale Daily News*, 8 April 1966.

17   John Morton Blum, *A Life with History*, 183–85; and Mirra, *Admirable Radical*, 141–45. Staughton Lynd discussed these events in a speech in Chicago in September 1967 and published as "Academic Freedom: Your Story and Mine," *Columbia University Forum* 10,

no. 3 (Fall 1967): 23–28. Finally, Lynd discusses and reflects on these events in his own memoir after receiving some closure about the affair after the publication of Blum's memoir and Mirra's biography, in his own memoir. See Alice and Staughton Lynd, *Stepping Stones*, 82–84.

18 John Darnton, "Pullout Is Urged by Lee, Brewster," *New York Times*, 10 October 1969, 17.

19 Edmund Morgan, "To Atone for Songmy [My Lai]," *New York Times*, 27 November 1969, 28.

20 Staughton Lynd, "The Two Yales," 28 April 2005, reproduced in Andrej Grubacic, ed., *From Here to There: The Staughton Lynd Reader* (Oakland: PM Press, 2010), 141.

21 "Lynd to Visit Montreal 'To Prove I Can Travel,'" *New Haven Register*, 9 February 1966; and "Immigration Department Sees No Bar to Lynd Visit Here," *Montreal Gazette*, 10 February 1966. At the request of the FBI's legal attaché in Ottawa, the SAC at the New Haven field office sent information on Lynd to the legal attaché in Ottawa. This information would have been shared with the Royal Canadian Mounted Police, at the time the Canadian equivalent of both the FBI and the CIA. Intelligence sharing between Canadian and American authorities, formally begun during World War II, was widespread. SAC, New Haven to Legat, Ottawa, 16 February 1966, Lynd FBI file.

22 "Ostracized Professor Cites Canada's Role," *Montreal Star*, 19 February 1966; and, "Prof. Hits 'Nazi' U.S.," *Toronto Telegram*, 19 February 1966. French-language newspapers had the following headlines: "L'action américaine au Viet-nam: crime de guerre! [American Intervention in Vietnam: A War Crime!]," *Dimanche-matin*, 20 February 1966; "Un professeur américain condamne la politique de Washington au Vietnam [An American Professor Condemns Washington's Vietnam Policy]," *Le Devoir*, 21 February 1966. These newspaper articles were sent from the US embassy in Ottawa to the FBI in Washington and distributed to the New Haven field office. Legat, Ottawa, to J. Edgar Hoover, 22 March 1966, Lynd FBI file.

23 Doug MacRae, "Racial Bias behind LBJ War Policies," *Ottawa Citizen,* 3 March 1966.

24 Catherine Janitch, "LBJ Compared to Hitler," *Ottawa Journal*, 3 March 1966. Both the articles were sent to FBI headquarters in Washington and the New Haven field office. It is interesting to note that the FBI received these articles before they received the newspaper articles covering Lynd's speech in Montreal. The Montreal articles would not be forwarded until 22 March 1966 as quoted above. Legat, Ottawa, to J. Edgar Hoover, 4 March 1966, Lynd FBI file.

25 William F. Buckley Jr., "The Prof's Trip," *Providence Journal,* 19 January 1966.

26 "Lynd Refuses to Pay Tax in Protest of US Actions," *Yale Daily News*, 11 April 1966.

27 Melvin Small, *Antiwarriors: The Vietnam War and the Battle for America's Hearts and Minds* (Wilmington, DE: SR Books, 2002), 33–34; "Hershey to Tighten Draft," *Yale Daily News*, 19 January 1966; David Detweiler interview with Gen. Lewis Hershey, "Hershey Prepared for Higher Quotas," *Yale Daily News*, 2 March 1966; and "U.S. Gives Students Some Hints on Earning Both B.A. and 2-S," *New York Times*, 18 March 1966, 1.

28 "Testing for the Draft," *New York Times*, 14 May 1966, 23; and Staughton Lynd, "Student Protest against the Draft," *New York Times*, 20 May 1966, 46.

29 "Lynd to Speak Here on North Vietnam," *Long-Islander*, 9 June 1966, 5.

30 For an excellent discussion of the summertime events, see Staughton Lynd and Michael Ferber, *The Resistance* (Boston: Beacon Press, 1971), 47–58.

31 Lynd and Ferber, *The Resistance*, 118–19.

32 Quoted in Lynd and Ferber, *The Resistance*, 59.

33 For other examples of "We Won't Go" statements, see Alice Lynd, ed., *We Won't Go: Personal Accounts of War Objectors* (Boston: Beacon Press, 1968), 203–205.

34 "We Refuse Induction," *Yale Daily News,* 23 November 1966, 2.

35 "Ad Hoc Group to Consider Draft Protest," *Yale Daily News,* 22 November 1966, 1.

36 "Scores of U.S. Pilots Paraded, Hanoi Says," *Washington Post,* 7 July 1966, A1; "Captured U.S. Pilots in Forced Hanoi March," *Los Angeles Times,* 7 July 1966, 25; "Hanoi Says Pilots Are Paraded in City," *New York Times,* 7 July 1966, 5; and Tom Lambert, "U.S. Accuses Reds of Geneva Violation by Parading Fliers," *Los Angeles Times,* 8 July 1966, 1.

37 Max Frankel, "Hanoi Alarms U.S. on Fate of Fliers," *New York Times,* 13 July 1966, 1.

38 Tom Gushurst, introduction, We Won't Go Conference, 4 December 1966, in Alice Niles Lynd and Staughton Lynd Papers (DG 099), box 1, We Won't Go, Chicago, 4 December 1966, Swarthmore College Peace Collection.

Chapter 6: What Is Resistance?

1 John Whiteclay Chambers, "Conscientious Objectors and the American State from Colonial Times to the Present," 39.

2 Figure 1: Vietnam Generation, Laurence M. Baskir and William A. Strauss, *Chance and Circumstance: The Draft, the War and the Vietnam Generation* (New York: Vintage, 1978), 5.

3 Peter Henig, "On the Manpower Channelers," *New Left Notes,* 20 January 1967, 1, 4; and "Channeling," *Ramparts,* December 1967, 34–35.

4 Christian Appy, *Working Class War: American Combat Soldiers and Vietnam* (Chapel Hill: University of North Carolina Press, 1993), 27–29.

5 Jack Raymond, "Negro Death Rate in Vietnam Exceeds Whites," *New York Times,* 10 March 1966, 4.

6 Appy, *Working Class War,* 19, 21–22; Kyle Longley, *Grunts: The American Combat Soldier in Vietnam* (Armonk, NY: M. E. Sharpe, 2008), 28–35; and Tom Holm, *Strong Hearts, Wounded Souls: Native American Veterans of the Vietnam War* (Austin: University of Texas Press, 1996), 10–11.

7 Stokely Carmichael quoted in Tom Wells, *The War Within: America's Battle over Vietnam* (Berkeley: University of California Press, 1994), 124.

8 Peniel Joseph, *Stokely: A Life* (New York: Basic Civitas, 2014), 155–57, 183–84; Eric Burner, *And Gently He Shall Lead Them: Robert Parris Moses and Civil Rights in Mississippi* (New York: New York University Press, 1994), 218–20; and Clayborne Carson, *Martin's Dream: My Journey and the Legacy of Martin Luther King Jr.* (New York: Palgrave MacMillan, 2013), chap. 5, "Voluntary Exile."

9 "Panelists Split in Heated Debate over Issue of Cold War Draft," *Yale Daily News,* 5 October 1965.

10 "Coffin: Protest War, Return Draft Cards," *Yale Daily News,* 23 February 1967.

11 Wells, *The War Within,* 124–29.

12 Quoted in Lynd and Ferber, *The Resistance,* 60–61. See also Michael Foley, *Confronting the War Machine: Draft Resistance during the Vietnam War* (Chapel Hill: University of North Carolina Press, 2003), 57–58.

13 Report of the National Advisory Commission on Selective Service, *In Pursuit of Equity: Who Serves When Not All Serve?* (Washington, DC: United States Government Printing Office, 1967).

14 Foley, *Confronting the War Machine,* 59–66.

15 Small, *Antiwarriors,* 60–64.

16 Martin Luther King, Jr., quoted in James Finn, ed., *A Conflict of Loyalties: The Case for Selective Conscientious Objection* (New York: Pegasus, 1968), viii.

17 John Whiteclay Chambers II, "Conscientious Objection and the American State from Colonial Times to the Present," in Charles C. Moskos and John Whiteclay Chambers II, eds., *The New Conscientious Objection: From Sacred to Secular Resistance* (New York: Oxford University Press, 1993), 42.

18 Marilyn Young, John Fitzgerald, and A. Tom Grunfeld, *The Vietnam War: A History in Documents* (Oxford, UK: Oxford University Press, 2002), 117.

19 David Cortright, *Soldiers in Revolt: GI Resistance during the Vietnam War* (Chicago: Haymarket Books, 2005), 15–17.

20 SAC New Haven to J. Edgar Hoover, 29 May 1967; and SAC New Haven to J. Edgar Hoover, 22 June 1967.

21 Casey Banas, "College Unit Rejects Viet Foe," *Chicago Tribune*, 18 July 1967, 10.

22 "Seek to Hire Lynd," *Chicago Tribune*, 29 July 1967, B16; and "Lynd Says He'll Sue on College Rejection," *Chicago Tribune*, 1 August 1967, B6.

23 SAC Chicago to J. Edgar Hoover, 24 February 1967, Lynd FBI file.

24 For more on the Responsibilities Program, see Ellen W. Schrecker, *Many Are the Crimes: McCarthyism in America* (New York: Little, Brown, 1998), 212–13; Seth Rosenfeld, *Subversives: The FBI's War on Student Radicals, and Reagan's Rise to Power* (New York: Farrar, Straus and Giroux, 2012), chap. 2, "The Responsibilities Program," and Betty Medsger, *The Burglary: The Discovery of J. Edgar Hoover's Secret FBI* (New York: Alfred A. Knopf, 2014), 357–58.

25 J. Edgar Hoover to SAC New Haven, 9 March 1967; and SAC New Haven to J. Edgar Hoover, 12 April 1967, Lynd FBI file. The policy is dated 30 March 1967, "Contacts with Educational Institutions." As Betty Medsger points out, the Responsibilities Program, like COINTELPRO, the FBI's counterintelligence program, "continued to operate after the director 'closed' it—removed its name—a gesture he thought would make it more difficult for this secret program to be discovered." Medsger, *The Burglary*, 357–58.

26 SAC Springfield to J. Edgar Hoover, 19 July 1967, Lynd FBI file.

27 J. Edgar Hoover to SAC Springfield, 28 July 1967, Lynd FBI file.

28 SAC New Haven to J. Edgar Hoover, 10 August 1967, with attached eleven-page open-source intelligence report, "Staughton Craig Lynd," Lynd FBI file.

29 Casey Banas, "Professors Demand Lynd Be Given Post," *Chicago Tribune*, 10 August 1967, 3.

30 Alfred Young and Christopher Lasch, "Staughton Lynd," *New York Review of Books*, 28 September 1967; "The Staughton Lynd Case—A Fact Sheet," prepared by the Committee for Academic Freedom in Illinois, 29 August 1967; and "A National Statement on the Staughton Lynd Case," October 1967, both in box 14, folder 3, MSS 395, Staughton Lynd Papers, Wisconsin Historical Society, Division of Library, Archives, and Museum Collections, Madison.

31 "O.K. Lynd for College Post: State Seeks Withdrawal of Lawsuit," *Chicago Tribune*, 20 October 1967, 1; and "Roosevelt U.'s Chief Firm on Not Hiring Lynd," *Chicago Tribune*, 7 May 1968, 10.

32 Staughton Lynd interview with the editor, 13 August 2020.

33 Alice and Staughton Lynd interviews with the editor, 13 August 2020 and 28 September 2020. See also Alice Lynd and Staughton Lynd, *Stepping Stones*, 84–90; and Alice Lynd, "Accompanying War Objectors," in Staughton Lynd, *Accompanying: Pathways to Social Change* (Oakland: PM Press, 2012), 71–74.

34 The Gallup poll provided journalist Harrison Salisbury this statistical analysis based on several questions. The first question, "Do you approve or disapprove of the way President Johnson is handling the situation in Vietnam?" conducted from December

1965 to March 1968. The second question, "In view of the developments since we entered the fighting in Vietnam, do you think the U.S. made a mistake sending troops to fight?" from August 1965 to May 1971. Jim Shriver to Linda Amster, 18 January 1977, box 400, folder 14, Harrison Salisbury Collection, Rare Book and Manuscript Library, Butler Library, Columbia University, New York.

35 Bob Zevin to Staughton Lynd, 31 May 1967, box 6, folder "Staughton Correspondence 1967–1969," Staughton and Alice Lynd Collection, DG 99, Swarthmore College Peace Collection, Swarthmore, Pennsylvania.

36 "War Protesters Rally in U.S.," *Washington Post,* 17 October 1967, A8.

37 See Staughton Lynd, "The Visions of the New Radicalism," 3 November 1967, box 6, folder 20, Kent State; and Staughton Lynd, *Accompanying: Pathways to Social Change* (Oakland: PM Press, 2012), 71.

38 Collegiate Press Service, "Disobedience Across U.S.," *Daily Illini,* 17 October 1967.

39 Wells, *The War Within,* 192–94, 201.

40 "Youth, 20, Arrested after Draft Protest," *Minneapolis Star,* 25 February 1966, 1; and "Man Gets 18 Months, $2,500 in Draft Incident," *Minneapolis Star,* 17 January 1967, 1.

41 Charles A. Meconis, *With Clumsy Grace: The American Catholic Left, 1961–1975* (New York: Seabury Press, 1979), 151; Lynd and Ferber, *The Resistance,* chap. 13, "The Ultra Resistance"; Marian Mollin, "Communities of Resistance: Women and the Catholic Left of the Late 1960s," *Oral History Review* 31, no. 2 (Summer–Autumn, 2004): 29–51; and Shawn Francis Peters, *The Catonsville Nine: A Story of Faith and Resistance in the Vietnam Era* (Oxford, UK: Oxford University Press, 2012).

42 Lynd v. Rusk, 389 F.2d 940 (Court of Appeals, Dist. of Columbia Circuit 1967) at 984.

43 "Staughton C. Lynd," undated, unsigned, Staughton Lynd Name file, RG 46 Records of the U.S. Senate Internal Security Subcommittee, Name files, ser. 2, box 64, 8E2a/5/2/4, National Archives and Records Administration I, Washington, DC. See also Peniel Joseph, *Stokely: A Life* (New York: Basic Civitas, 2014), 229. Ralph Schoenman's passport was likewise revoked for traveling to North Vietnam and Cuba.

44 Staughton Craig Lynd, Rabble Rouser Index, 27 December 1967, Lynd FBI file.

45 SAC letter, 67–70, 28 November 1967, Rabble Rouser FBI file no. 157-HQ-7782.

46 *Pentagon Papers* (Senator Gravel Edition): *The Defense Department History of United States Decisionmaking on Vietnam,* vol. 4 (Boston: Beacon Press, 1971), 546–61.

47 John Prados, *Vietnam,* 248.

48 Noam Chomsky, *For Reasons of State* (New York: Pantheon Books, 1973), 25.

49 Memorandum for the President, "Subject: Alternative Strategies in SVN," 3rd draft, 1 March 1968, annex 2, Alternative Courses of Military Action, 12–13, as quoted in "United States–Vietnam Relations, 1945–1967," Vietnam Task Force, Office of the Secretary of Defense,

pt. 4, C.6.c., *Evolution of the War: U.S. Ground Strategy and Force Deployments; 1965–1967,* vol. 3, program 6, p. 37.

50 "President Lyndon B. Johnson's Address to the Nation Announcing Steps to Limit the War in Vietnam and Reporting His Decision Not to Seek Reelection," 31 March 1968, in *Public Papers of the Presidents of the United States: Lyndon B. Johnson, 1968–69,* vol. 1 (Washington, DC: Government Printing Office, 1970), 469–76. For further discussion on Lyndon Johnson's decision to refuse the troop reinforcement request, see John Prados, *Vietnam,* 247–49, and Tom Wells, *The War Within,* 248–62. For more on the diversion of bombs after March 1968, see Marilyn Young, "Bombing Civilians from the Twentieth to the Twenty-First Centuries," in Yuki Tanaka and Marilyn Young, eds., *Bombing Civilians: A Twentieth-Century History* (New York: New Press, 2009), 165.

51   David Dellinger to Ralph Schoenman, telegram, 18 March 1967, box 10.2, document
     no. 170517, Bertrand Russell Archives II, McMaster University, Hamilton, Ontario,
     Canada.

52   Staughton Lynd interview with the editor, 13 August 2020.

53   Alice and Staughton Lynd, *Stepping Stones*, 88–89.

54   SAC Chicago to J. Edgar Hoover, 29 August 1968; and SAC Chicago to J. Edgar Hoover,
     29 October 1968, Lynd FBI file.

55   Alice and Staughton Lynd, *Stepping Stones*, 96–97; and Alice and Staughton Lynd
     interviews with the editor, 13 August 2020 and 28 September 2020.

56   Bruce Dancis, *Resister: A Story of Protest and Prison during the Vietnam War* (Ithaca: Cornell
     University Press, 2014), 88–91.

57   For example, the call was published in *Cornell Daily Sun*, 7 March 1967, and *New Left
     Notes*, 27 March 1967, 9. It was also publicized in *Draft Action News* 1, no. 1 (6 April
     1967): 1; and "Roundup #2 of Nationwide Mobilization Activity," *Spring Mobilization
     Committee,* 3 April 1967, 3–4.

58   Staughton Lynd, "The Vision of the New Radicalism," presented at the fall retreat of
     the Methodist Theological Fellowship at the University of Chicago, 3 November 1967,
     ser. 2, box 6, folder 20, Staughton and Alice Lynd Papers, Kent State Special Collections
     and Archives, Kent State University.

59   The correspondence between Lynd and the IWCT begins with Russell's letter to Lynd
     on 29 November 1966. Thereafter, there are five separate letters: Lynd to Russell,
     13 January 1967; Russell to Lynd, 30 January 1967; Ralph Schoenman to Lynd, 15
     February 1967; Lynd to Schoenman, 10 March 1967; and Schoenman to Lynd, 16
     March 1967. All letters are found in box 10.3, ser. 372, IWCT "Refusals," Bertrand
     Russell Archives II, McMaster University, Hamilton, Ontario.

60   Karen Gellen, "Reports on Support Actions," *New Left Notes*, 15 January 1968, 1, 4.

61   Tom Linden, "29 Turn In Cards at Resistance Rally," *Yale Daily News*, 4 April 1968;
     Lynd and Ferber, *The Resistance* (Boston: Beacon Press, 1971), 222; and Foley, *Confronting
     the War Machine*, 262.

62   "A Book on Draft Resistance," *New Left Notes*, 3 February 1967, 2.

63   Alice Lynd to Beacon Press, "Organizations" and "Additional Draft Resistance Groups,"
     undated, Alice Niles Lynd and Staughton Lynd Papers, DG 099, box 10, folder "Alice:
     book We Won't Go—list of people & orgs to send courtesy copies to," Swarthmore
     College Peace Collection, Swarthmore Pennsylvania.

64   "Best Books for Young Adults, 1968," American Library Association Pamphlet, in Alice
     Niles Lynd and Staughton Lynd Papers, DG 099, box 10, folder "Alice: book We Won't
     Go—publicity," Swarthmore College Peace Collection, Swarthmore, Pennsylvania.

65   FBI report, 5 February 1970.

66   "Cops Control Sit-Ins at City High Schools," *Chicago Tribune*, 5 November 1968, 2.

Epilogue

1   How Staughton Lynd navigated the end of the 1960s can be chartered through a series
     of articles he published. During 1968 and 1969, Lynd intervened numerous times
     trying to forestall the splintering of the New Left. In these interventions, Lynd made
     proposals that address many of the arduous debates that undergirded the emergence of
     different strands of activism within the Students for a Democratic Society (SDS) and
     the antiwar movement. See, for instance, "Factionalism," *New Left Notes*, 5 February
     1969, 2, 5; "The Movement: A New Beginning," *Liberation*, May 1969, 6–20; "On

'Anti-Communism,'" *Liberation*, June 1969, 2–3; "Radicals and White Racism: Toward an Interracial Movement of the Poor," *Liberation*, July 1969, 26–30; and "A Program for Post-Campus Radicals," *Liberation*, August–September 1969, 44–45. Lynd's shift toward the labor movement, labor history, and finding a new strategy for the left can be found in a series of articles: "Guerrilla History in Gary," *Liberation*, October 1969, 17–20; Ernest Mandel's America," *Liberation*, December 1969, 32–35; "Prospects for a New Left," *Liberation*, January 1971, 13–28; "Organizing the New Politics: A Proposal," *Ramparts*, December 1971, 14–15, 51; "A Phase Two Strategy for the Left," *Ramparts*, February 1972, 46–48; Staughton and Alice Lynd, "Conversations with Steelmill Rebels," *Ramparts*, December 1972, 21–24, 53; and Lynd with Gar Alperovitz, *Strategy and Program: Two Essays Toward a New American Socialism* (Boston: Beacon Press, 1973).

2   Alice and Staughton Lynd interviews with the editor, 13 August 2020 and 28 September 2020. The Lynds alerted me to this event as told by Cathy Wilkerson on 3 August 2019 at "Accompanying the Future: A Gathering in Youngstown, Ohio." Wilkerson clarified that the event in Washington was likely the counter-inaugural demonstration when Richard Nixon assumed the presidency on 20 January 1969. Wilkerson email to the editor, 20 November 2020.

3   Alice and Staughton Lynd interviews with the editor, 13 August and 28 September 2020.

4   Staughton Lynd interview with the editor, 28 September 2020.

5   Alice and Staughton Lynd interview with the editor, 28 September 2020.

6   Staughton Lynd, "Guerrilla History in Gary," *Liberation,* October 1969, 17–20. Lynd was also engaged in guerrilla history with draft resisters during 1969–1970 with Michael Ferber, draft resister with the Boston Draft Resistance Group and member of the Boston Five. Lynd and Ferber cowrote *The Resistance*, published by Beacon Press in 1971, which was one of the first histories of the draft resistance movement during the Vietnam War.

7   Martin Weil, "'Radicals' Plan to Run Lynd for President of Historians," *Washington Post*, 22 December 1969, A6.

8   There were other resolutions submitted by the Radical Caucus, including a code of ethics for historians, reforms of the AHA executive council, and a fund for historians who faced institutional backlash and repression. All these were reprinted in the *Newsletter of the Radical Historians' Caucus*, no. 2 (Spring 1970). For more on the origins of the Radical Caucus, see Martin Duberman, *Howard Zinn: A Life on the Left* (New York: New Press, 2012), 155–65; Carl Mirra, *Admirable Radical*, chap. 7, "Guerrilla Historians Combat the American Historical Association"; Jim O'Brien, "'Be Realistic, Demand the Impossible': Staughton Lynd, Jesse Lemisch, and a Committed History," *Radical History Review*, no. 82 (Winter 2002): 65–90; and Jesse Lemisch, "Radicals, Marxists, and Gentlemen: A Memoir of Twenty Years Ago," *Radical Historians Newsletter*, no. 59 (November 1989), 2, 7–8. For the Resolutions of the Temporary Co-Ordinating Committee on Women in the Historical Profession, see the *Newsletter of the Radical Historians' Caucus*, no. 2 (Spring 1970), 13–14. For more on the success of the CCWHP, see Eileen Boris and Nupur Chaudhuri, eds., *Voices of Women Historians: The Personal, The Professional, The Political* (Bloomington: Indiana University Press, 1999). For an excellent overview of the radical confrontation in academia during the 1960s, including a discussion of the 1969 AHA, see Ellen Schrecker, *The Lost Soul of Higher Education: Corporatization, the Assault on Academic Freedom, and the End of the American University* (New York: New Press, 2010), chap. 3, "Part of the Struggle': Faculties Confront the 1960s."

9   Staughton Lynd, "Making War: The Sport of Presidents," *Washington Post*, 28 January 1990, L1, L3. Lynd was reviewing Richard J. Barnet's *The Rocket's Red Glare: When America Goes to War—the Presidents and the People*.

10   Staughton Lynd, "Constitutional Encounters," *Ohio Lawyer* 1, no. 5 (September–October 1987): 17.

11   Staughton Lynd, remarks at the "Looking Back, Moving Forward: War Resisters in North America" conference, 24 September 2011. Recording in the editor's possession.

12   Karl W. Eikenberry, "Reassessing the All-Volunteer Force," *Washington Quarterly* 36, no. 1 (2003): 10. There have been other prominent criticisms of the all-volunteer force. See, for example, Arthur M. Schlesinger Jr., *The Imperial Presidency* (Boston: Houghton Mifflin, 2004), 199; and Andrew J. Bacevich, *Breach of Trust: How Americans Failed Their Soldiers and Their Country* (New York: Metropolitan Books, 2013), 124–25.

13   Staughton Lynd, "Déja Vu All Over Again," in Mary Susannah Robbins, ed., *Against the Vietnam War: Writings by Activists* (Syracuse: Syracuse University Press, 1999), 304–305.

14   Alice Lynd and Staughton Lynd, *Liberation Theory for Quakers*, Pendle Hill Pamphlet no. 326, April 1996, reproduced in Staughton Lynd, *Living inside Our Hope: A Steadfast Radical's Thoughts on Rebuilding the Movement* (Ithaca: Cornell University Press, 1997), 55.

15   See chapter 1, document 6, and chapter 2, document 5.

16   Alice Lynd and Staughton Lynd, *Liberation Theory for Quakers*, 55–60.

17   Staughton Lynd, Sam Bahour, and Alice Lynd, *Homeland: Oral Histories of Palestine and Palestinians* (New York: Olive Branch, 1994). See also Staughton Lynd and Alice Lynd, "Coming to Understand the Palestinian Struggle," *In These Times*, September–October 1991, 16–17.

18   Alice Lynd and Staughton Lynd, "Liberation Theory for Quakers," 63–64. Staughton added much to this discussion in his book *Accompanying: Pathways to Social Change* (Oakland: PM Press, 2012).

19   Alice Lynd and Staughton Lynd, "Liberation Theory for Quakers," 63–64.

20   Staughton Lynd and Andrej Grubacic, *Wobblies and Zapatistas: Conversations on Anarchism, Marxism and Radical History* (Oakland: PM Press, 2008), 58–59.

21   S. Brian Willson, On Third World Legs: An Autobiography (Chicago: Charles H. Kerr, 1992). Willson's short book has long been out of print. However, he has reproduced it on his website, available at www.brianwillson.com/on-third-world-legs/.

22   Staughton Lynd, "Oral History from Below," *Oral History Review* 21, no. 1 (Spring 1993): 6–7; Staughton Lynd, introduction, in S. Brian Willson, *On Third World Legs* (Chicago: Charles H. Kerr, 1992); and Alice and Staughton Lynd telephone interview with the editor, 28 September 2020.

23   Staughton Lynd, remarks at HAW Roundtable on "Imperial Crisis and Domestic Dissent," American Historical Association, Washington, DC, January 2004, available at, https://www.historiansagainstwar.org/aha04/lynd.html.

24   *Report of the Citizen's Hearing on the Legality of U.S. Actions in Iraq: The Case of Lt. Ehren Watada, Tacoma, Washington, January 20–21, 2007*. The report was published on the now defunct website www.wartribunal.org and is in the editor's possession, also available at https://web.archive.org/web/20070211083917/http://www.wartribunal.org. For the influence of the veteran's testimony on Lynd, see Lynd and Grubacic, *Wobblies and Zapatistas*, 111.

25   Staughton Lynd quoted in HAW press release, "American Historical Association Denounces the War in Iraq," 13 March 2007, available at https://www.historiansagainstwar.org/aha07/13march07.html. The full resolution can be read at https://www.historiansagainstwar.org/aha07/aha2007.html.

26   Mark Niquette, "Local Workshop Informs Men about Their Options," *Vindicator*, 22 February 1991, A5.

27   Alice Lynd and Staughton Lynd, "Liberation Theory for Quakers," 60–61. Alice Lynd and Staughton Lynd, *Stepping Stones*, 133.

28 Staughton Lynd, "Déja Vu," 304; Alice and Staughton Lynd interview with the editor, 28 September 2020; and Carl Mirra, "Mutation of the Vietnam Syndrome," 268–69.

29 The Defense Department officially maintained that during the same period, there were only 473 CO applications. Mirra challenges these statistics and comes to the 1,500–2,500 number after examining other independent sources. Carl Mirra, "Mutation of the Vietnam Syndrome," 270–71.

30 Staughton Lynd and Alice Lynd, eds., Nonviolence in America, 477–84.

31 Statistics on desertion during the war on terror have been gathered from these sources: Bill Nichols, "8,000 Desert during Iraq War," USA Today, 7 Jul 2006; Paul von Zielbauer, "Army, Intent on Sending a Message, Cracks Down on Deserters," New York Times, 9 April 2007; Sig Christenson, "US Army Desertion Rate at Lowest since Vietnam," Agence France Presse, November 7, 2011; Tasneem Raja, "Was Bergdahl a Deserter? This Is What Happens When a Soldier Disappears," Mother Jones, 4 June 2014; Travis Lupick, "Marked for Deportation, Iraq War Resisters Fight to Stay in Canada," Al Jazeera America, 29 November 2014; Wil S. Hylton, "American Deserter: Why AWOL U.S. Soldiers Are Most at Risk in Canada," New York Magazine, 25 February 2015; and Tamara Khandaker, "These American Deserters from the Iraq War May Finally Get Refuge in Canada," Vice News, 17 August 2016.

32 Sarah Hipworth and Luke Stewart, eds., Let Them Stay: U.S. War Resisters in Canada, 2004–2016 (Toronto: Iguana Books, 2016). The number of US soldiers seeking refugee status in Canada was made available to the editor through an Access to Information request to the Canadian Department of Citizenship and Immigration, ATI no. A-2013–16501.

33 An online archive documenting André Shepherd's statements, refugee claim, and support in Germany is available by the German-affiliated War Resisters League organization Connection e.V.: https://en.connection-ev.org/index.php.

34 United States Government Accountability Office, "Military Personnel: Number of Formally Reported Applications for Conscientious Objectors Is Small Relative to the Total Size of the Armed Forces," September 2007, report no. GAO-07-1196; Center on Conscience and War, "Analysis of the GAO Report on Conscientious Objectors," 7 August 2007, available at https://centeronconscience.org/analysis-of-the-2007-gao-report-on-conscientious-objectors; and "Military CO Report Fails Congressional Mandate," The Reporter, Winter 2007, 1, 4.

35 Manual for Courts-Martial, pt. 4, para. 14, art. 90, "Assaulting or Willfully Disobeying Superior Commissioned Officer," C(2)(a)(i and iii).

36 Staughton Lynd, amicus curiae brief, Lt. Ehren Watada Article 32 Hearing, 17 August 2006. Copy in the editor's possession provided by Staughton Lynd.

37 UN General Assembly Resolution 33/165, "Status of persons refusing service in military or police forces used to enforce apartheid," 20 December 1978.

38 Staughton Lynd, "Someday They'll Have a War and Nobody Will Come," a talk delivered at the First Annual War Resisters League Dave Dellinger Memorial Lecture, Judson Memorial Church, New York City, 19 October 2006, copy in the editor's possession. See also Lynd's updated version of this talk presented to the Peace History Society's Biennial Meeting, 30 October 2009, reprinted in From Here to There, 265–78.

39 Alice Lynd with Staughton Lynd, "Moral Injury and Conscientious Objection: Saying No to Military Service," HAW, Conflicts in Context pamphlet, Summer 2015, 6.

40 Alice Lynd and Staughton Lynd, Moral Injury and Nonviolent Resistance: Breaking the Cycle of Violence in the Military and Behind Bars (Oakland: PM Press, 2017), 161.

41 Alice Lynd and Staughton Lynd, Moral Injury and Nonviolent Resistance, 7–8.

42 Alice Lynd and Staughton Lynd, Moral Injury and Nonviolent Resistance, 33.

INDEX